JOHN'S APOLOGETIC CHRISTOLOGY
LEGITIMATION AND DEVELOPMENT IN JOHANNINE CHRISTOLOGY

The Gospel according to John presents Jesus in a unique way as compared with other New Testament writings. Scholars have long puzzled and pondered over why this should be. In this book, James McGrath offers a convincing explanation of how and why the author of the Fourth Gospel arrived at a christological portrait of Jesus that is so different from that of other New Testament authors, and yet at the same time clearly has its roots in earlier tradition. McGrath suggests that as the author of this Gospel sought to defend his beliefs about Jesus against the objections brought by opponents, he developed and drew out further implications from the beliefs he inherited. The book studies this process using insights from the field of sociology which helps to bring methodological clarity to the important issue of the development of Johannine Christology.

James F. McGrath has been Lecturer in New Testament Studies at Emanuel University, Oradea and the University of Oradea, Romania for the past three years. He has published articles in *New Testament Studies*, *Irish Biblical Studies*, *Irish Theological Quarterly*, *Religion and Theology* and *Koinonia Journal*.

SOCIETY FOR NEW TESTAMENT STUDIES

MONOGRAPH SERIES

General Editor: Richard Bauckham

111

JOHN'S APOLOGETIC CHRISTOLOGY

John's Apologetic Christology

Legitimation and development in Johannine Christology

JAMES F. McGRATH

CAMBRIDGE
UNIVERSITY PRESS

PUBLISHED BY THE PRESS SYNDICATE OF THE UNIVERSITY OF CAMBRIDGE
The Pitt Building, Trumpington Street, Cambridge, United Kingdom

CAMBRIDGE UNIVERSITY PRESS
The Edinburgh Building, Cambridge CB2 2RU, UK
40 West 20th Street, New York, NY 10011–4211, USA
10 Stamford Road, Oakleigh, Melbourne 3166, Australia
Ruiz de Alarcón 13, 28014 Madrid, Spain
Dock House, The Waterfront, Cape Town 8001, South Africa

http://www.cambridge.org

First published

Printed in the United Kingdom at the University Press, Cambridge

Typeface 10/12pt Times Roman   *System* 3B2   [CE]

A catalogue record for this book is available from the British Library

Library of Congress cataloguing in publication data

McGrath, James F. (James Frank), 1972–
   John's apologetic christology: legitimation and development in
Johannine christology / James F. McGrath.
     p.   cm. – (Society for New Testament Studies monograph series ; 111)
Includes bibliographical references and index.
ISBN 0 521 80348 9
1. Jesus Christ – History of doctrines – Early church, ca. 30–600.
2. Jesus Christ – Person and offices – Biblical teaching.
3. Bible N.T. John – Theology. I. Title
II. Monograph series (Society for New Testament Studies) ; 111.

BT198 M34 2001
226.5′06–dc21   00–054663

ISBN 0 521 80348 9 hardback

CONTENTS

PREFACE

Having studied John's Gospel over several years, I was glad when a recent visit to the US included an invitation to teach a freshman class on the subject. I had had surprisingly little opportunity to do so since completing the research presented in this book. My usual theme – that of John's apologetic portrait of Jesus – was, however, met by a perplexed look from one student. Raising her hand, she asked, 'What makes you think John is being apologetic?'

It took me a few moments to realize that the 'technical' meaning of the term 'apologetic' is unfamiliar to many in our day and age. I should perhaps therefore explain that the title of this book, *John's Apologetic Christology*, does not use the term in its modern sense, as if John were 'apologizing' for his beliefs concerning Jesus. Rather, the argument of the present work is that John's *defence* (the other meaning of 'apologetic') of certain christological beliefs led to their development and the unique configuration of christological motifs known as Johannine Christology. It would be a pity indeed if a merely verbal confusion were to obscure this book's main theme from the outset!

The book is a revised version of my 1998 University of Durham Ph.D. dissertation. While a Ph.D. thesis is by definition the work of a single individual, I doubt whether any student has ever successfully completed such a course of study without the support of many people, the endless list of 'without whoms'. Here I have attempted to thank in particular some of the key friends, encouragers and supporters who have made the completion of this work possible, representatives of a much larger number of individuals who provided advice, support and encouragement at many points throughout this project.

In relation to the academic side of this work, I wish to thank above all Prof. James Dunn for his supervision, providing helpful guidance and insightful criticisms throughout my period of research; Prof. Larry Hurtado, Dr Stephen Barton, Dr Paul N. Anderson, Prof. Richard Bauckham and Mr Jerry Truex, for their helpful comments, constructive criticisms and advice; the members of the Durham New Testament Seminar from 1995 to 1998 and of the JOHN-LITR and IOUDAIOS-L discussion groups for feedback and countless useful pieces of information; and Ray Porter and Eryl Rowlands for teaching me about the Gospel of John and helping me to fall in love with it. All faults with the book of course remain my own.

For financial assistance, I wish to thank in particular the Miss Elizabeth Drummond's Trust, the Mylne Trust, the Gilchrist Educational Trust and the De Bury Scholarship for their help with the cost of undertaking and completing this course of study. Many others are to be thanked for their help in times of crisis, with the cost of books and/or attending conferences, and for various other forms of financial support, among them especially the Dean's Fund, Ted and Mary Baines, the Romanian Missionary Society, Trinity Tabernacle of Gravesend, the Listeners Trust, the New Durlston Trust and the Butterworth and Bayley Charity.

Lastly, but most of all rather than least, my wife Elena, for providing encouragement and support from before the beginning of this project until its completion.

Part 1

INTRODUCTION

1

INTRODUCTION: THE DEVELOPMENT OF JOHANNINE CHRISTOLOGY

In recent times an area which has attracted a great deal of scholarly attention is the development of Christian doctrine, and in particular Christology. *That* Christology – whether in New Testament times or in the subsequent centuries – has undergone changes and developments of some sort, appears to be beyond question.[1] However, the question of *how* and/or *why* doctrine develops has not been answered with any similar degree of consensus. This lack of consensus is perhaps nowhere more clearly visible than in the case of the Fourth Gospel. In the numerous recent attempts to trace the history of the 'Johannine community', appeals have been made by different scholars to the influence of diverse individuals, groups, cultures and ideas, each trying to explain thereby the link between the earliest traditions about Jesus and the distinctive portrait of him found in the Fourth Gospel. In the present work we will not be attempting to write a history of the Christian community or communities within which the Gospel took shape. We shall nonetheless seek insights from the realm of sociology in order to provide an explanatory mechanism for understanding the process of christological development evidenced in the final product we know as the Gospel according to John. This Gospel appears not only to have deep roots in early Jewish Christianity, but also to have been written by and/or for Christians who were in continuing dialogue with non-Christian Judaism. How this Gospel and the beliefs it expresses can have sprung from Jewish roots, and yet at the same time have become an issue of conflict between Christians and non-Christian Jews, is the perplexing riddle which the present work hopes to help solve.[2] But before we can attempt to do this, we must

---

[1] Cf. James D. G. Dunn, *Christology in the Making. An Inquiry into the Origins of the Doctrine of the Incarnation*, London: SCM, 1989, p.xii, who calls the fact of development in the New Testament period an 'unassailable observation'.

[2] To argue here the case that the primary dialogue partners of the author of the

review representatives of the major previous treatments of and approaches to this issue, and the methods used therein.

Previous approaches

In contemporary scholarship a number of different approaches have been taken to the question of *why* Christology developed and, more specifically, why the Fourth Gospel presents a Christology that is so distinctive. Although all attempts to categorize the views of others risk oversimplification, it is nonetheless necessary to distinguish between and categorize different approaches if we are to evaluate them briefly and effectively. We may thus for convenience group the different perspectives we shall be examining here into the following categories:

(1) *History of Religions approaches*: These generally argue that the Gospel of John is different from earlier writings primarily because of an influx of Gentiles and/or Samaritans into the church. These new converts brought with them their own backgrounds and worldviews, which led to the character of the church's Christology taking on a different form, one which more closely resembles Gentile or Samaritan beliefs than those of earlier Jewish Christians.[3]

(2) *Organic development*: These approaches consider that the Gospel of John simply draws out the logical implications of what was already implicit in earlier beliefs. This is not to say that there is no development, but simply that the development does not represent a departure from the

---

Fourth Gospel are non-Christian Jews would excessively lengthen the introduction to this book. The key evidence is surveyed, albeit briefly, in the first part of chapter 2. It is felt that the arguments and evidences surveyed throughout the present work will adequately sustain this initial hypothesis.

[3] So e.g. Michael Goulder, 'The Two Roots of the Christian Myth', in John Hick (ed.), *The Myth of God Incarnate*, London: SCM, 1977, pp. 64–86; Raymond E. Brown, *The Community of the Beloved Disciple*, London: Geoffrey Chapman, 1979, pp. 34–58; Maurice Casey, *From Jewish Prophet to Gentile God. The Origins and Development of New Testament Christology. The Edward Cadbury Lectures at the University of Birmingham, 1985–86*, Cambridge: James Clarke and Co., 1991. Brown's name sits uncomfortably among these other examples; even though the stimulus to development he proposed is similar to that proposed by others in the 'History of Religions' category, Brown nonetheless sought to do justice to the continuity between earlier and later stages (cf., e.g., Raymond E. Brown, *An Introduction to New Testament Christology*, London: Geoffrey Chapman, 1994, pp. 109, 140, 150).

original content and character of early Jewish-Christian Christology. It is rather the drawing out of the implications which naturally follow from these earlier beliefs, implications which, in a sense, someone was bound to draw out sooner or later.[4]

(3) *Individual creativity*: These approaches suggest that the distinctive Johannine developments are the product of a particular individual, presumably a Christian leader of some description, who reinterpreted earlier christological traditions in light of his own distinctive viewpoint, imagination and personality. The distinctive Johannine Christology thus represents above all else the unique insight of a particular individual.[5]

(4) *Sociological approaches*: These regard the distinctive Johannine Christology as the product of a particular social setting. Some upholders of this type of perspective emphasize that development takes place as earlier traditions are applied to new contexts and issues.[6] The approach that we shall be adopting in the present study falls into this final category, although without excluding certain important insights offered by other approaches.

---

[4] So e.g. C. F. D. Moule, *The Origin of Christology*, Cambridge: Cambridge University Press, 1977, pp. 2–4; I. Howard Marshall, 'The Development of Christology in the Early Church', *Tyndale Bulletin* 18 (1967), 77–93; R. T. France, *Matthew – Evangelist and Teacher*, Carlisle: Paternoster, 1989, pp. 316–17; 'Development in New Testament Christology', in William R. Farmer (ed.), *Crisis in Christology. Essays in Quest of Resolution*, Livonia, MN: Dove, 1995, pp. 63–82.

[5] So e.g. John A. T. Robinson, *The Priority of John*, London: SCM, 1985, pp. 296–300; Martin Hengel, *The Johannine Question*, London: SCM/ Philadelphia: Trinity, 1989, pp. 104–5, 134.

[6] So e.g. Wayne A. Meeks, 'The Divine Agent and His Counterfeit in Philo and the Fourth Gospel', in Elizabeth Schüssler Fiorenza (ed.), *Aspects of Religious Propaganda in Judaism and Early Christianity*, Notre Dame, University of Notre Dame Press, 1976, pp. 43–67; 'The Man from Heaven in Johannine Sectarianism', in John Ashton (ed.), *The Interpretation of John*, Philadelphia: Fortress/ London: SPCK, 1986, pp. 141–73; Jerome H. Neyrey, *Christ is Community: The Christologies of the New Testament*, Wilmington, DE: Michael Glazier, 1985; *An Ideology of Revolt. John's Christology in Social-Science Perspective*, Philadelphia: Fortress, 1988; James F. McGrath, 'Change in Christology: New Testament Models and the Contemporary Task', *ITQ* 63/1 (1998), 42, 49; also Robert Kysar, 'Pursuing the Paradoxes of Johannine Thought: Conceptual Tensions in John 6. A Redaction-Critical Proposal', in Dennis E. Groh and Robert Jewett (eds.), *The Living Text: Essays in Honor of Ernest W. Saunders*, Lanham, MD: University Press of America, 1985, pp. 190, 200, 203; Martinus C. de Boer, *Johannine Perspectives on the Death of Jesus*, Kampen: Kok Pharos, 1996, pp. 112–17, 311, who take a similar approach to the one adopted here but without the explicit use of sociological models.

These categories are simply heuristic, and it would be quite possible to distinguish the views of various scholars along other lines. There is also potential for overlap, as some scholars seek to utilize more than one of the approaches just mentioned. For our purposes, however, this categorization will be adequate as representing the principal types of explanation offered concerning the stimuli to the development of Johannine Christology, and so we may now turn to an evaluation of the work and results of key recent advocates of each.

History of Religions approaches

The earliest proponents of the History of Religions approach argued that Christology underwent a major transformation when it moved from the world of Palestinian Judaism (which was believed to be a purer form of Judaism) to that of the Hellenistic Judaism of the Diaspora, which was subject to the influences of paganism. Such a view has been rendered untenable by the realization that the traditional distinction between 'Judaism' and 'Hellenism' does not accurately represent the situation in the period we are studying. As the work of Martin Hengel in particular has clearly demonstrated, all Judaism during this period was 'Hellenistic Judaism', inasmuch as there was no Judaism which was not part of the Hellenistic world and influenced in some way by its thought and culture.[7]

The realization that all Judaism, including that found in Palestine and even that of the Pharisees, was influenced by Hellenism in some way or other has been accompanied by an awareness of the diversity which existed in Judaism in and around New Testament times. This diversity is such that Jacob Neusner has even felt it necessary to speak of 'Judaisms' in the plural.[8] Of course, the traditional proponents of History of Religions models of develop-

---

[7] Martin Hengel, *Judaism and Hellenism. Studies in their Encounter in Palestine during the Early Hellenistic Period*, London: SCM, 1974; *The 'Hellenization' of Judaea in the First Century after Christ*, London: SCM, 1989. See also Bartlett, John R., *Jews in the Hellenistic World. Josephus, Aristeas, The Sibylline Oracles, Eupolemus* (CCWJCW, 1), Cambridge: Cambridge University Press, 1985, pp. 7–8; James D. G. Dunn, *The Partings of the Ways Between Judaism and Christianity and their Significance for the Character of Christianity*, London: SCM, 1991, pp. 9–10; John M. G. Barclay, *Jews in the Mediterranean Diaspora. From Alexander to Trajan (323 BCE–117 CE)*, Edinburgh: T&T Clark, 1996, pp. 83–91.

[8] Jacob Neusner, *Judaic Law from Jesus to the Mishnah. A Systematic Reply to Professor E. P. Sanders*, Atlanta: Scholars, 1993, pp. 1–2. See also Dunn, *Partings*, pp. 18, 285 n.1, and the objections of Barclay, *Jews*, pp. 400–1.

ment were aware of this diversity, which they attributed to the differences between the 'purer' Judaism of Palestine and the Judaism of the Diaspora, which had been influenced by Hellenism. But it is precisely this type of distinction that has been proved untenable. The view that the rabbis or Pharisees were the upholders of an orthodox form of Judaism, which was defended from Hellenistic influence in their synagogues, can no longer be maintained. There was simply no generally recognized orthodox Judaism in this period. Nor was there any non-Hellenized Judaism: even the Pharisees show signs of having been influenced by Hellenism.[9] The conclusion which Hengel has reached must be emphasized: given that Palestinian Judaism can be accurately described as Hellenistic Judaism, having been subject to the influence of Greek culture for more than three hundred years, the term 'Hellenistic' no longer makes any meaningful distinction within the history of religions as applied to earliest Christianity.[10] Many works which in earlier times were assumed, because of the evidences of Hellenistic influence upon them, to derive from the Diaspora, may in fact have originated in Palestine.[11]

Yet while this makes certain older views untenable, it may still be possible for scholars who wish to argue for a History of Religions model of development to find ways of expressing that there were genuine differences between Jews on the one hand and other inhabitants of the Hellenistic world on the other, without this implying a return to the old, outmoded 'Judaism vs. Hellenism' schema. A possible way forward is hinted at in a recent article by Jonathan Goldstein. He draws a parallel between the situation of Jews in Greek or Roman-ruled Palestine and that of Indian Muslims in British-ruled India. While the members of the Aligargh movement in colonial India would never have considered converting to Christianity, nonetheless the movement's members actively sought to become 'gentlemen in the English mould' in all other respects. Thus in the same way that their Islamic faith was not felt to exclude many forms of 'Anglicizing', so also the Torah was not considered by many Jews to exclude the acceptance of various aspects of Hellenistic culture.[12] The Jews had a different

---

[9] Hengel, *'Hellenization'*, pp. 51–2.
[10] Ibid., p.53.
[11] Ibid., pp. 22–8.
[12] Jonathan A. Goldstein, 'Jewish Acceptance and Rejection of Hellenism', in E. P. Sanders, A. I. Baumgarten and Alan Mendelson (eds.), *Jewish and Christian Self-*

religion from that of most of their neighbours, and also had a different culture. Both of these inseparable aspects of Jewish life were influenced by Hellenism, but that does not imply that Jewish religion and culture became identical with that of other peoples in the Hellenistic era, any more than Greek influence led Roman culture, for example, to cease to be distinguishable from that of the Greeks. To return to the analogy which Goldstein draws with India under British rule, Indian culture was clearly influenced by British culture, but few if any would question that it was and is still possible to continue to speak meaningfully of 'Indian culture' and 'British culture'. The edges will have been somewhat blurry, and there will have been individual Indians who so wholly adopted British ways that they might appear to have been 'more British than the British themselves'. But on the whole, it would appear that the distinction between different cultures and religious traditions, and thus between 'Jewish' and 'non-Jewish', remains valid, provided it is used carefully and with the important qualifications which have just been discussed.[13]

Having clarified this point, we may define more clearly what a valid History of Religions model might look like. A contemporary form of this type of approach could focus on what important differences existed between Jews and other races and religions of the Hellenistic world, and in particular on the important difference between the monotheistic Jews and their generally polytheistic neighbours.[14] The basic argument of History of Religions models of christological development tends to follow something along

---

Definition. Volume 2: Aspects of Judaism in the Greco-Roman Period, London: SCM, 1981, p.66.
[13] For a helpful approach which avoids defining a religion in monolithic terms cf. J. Z. Smith, 'Fences and Neighbours: Some Contours of Early Judaism', in William Scott Green (ed.), *Approaches to Ancient Judaism. Volume II* (BJS, 9), Chico, CA: Scholars, 1980, pp. 1–25. For the issue of religious and cultural adaptation see further Barclay, *Jews*, pp. 87–91.
[14] Even the definition of monotheism is not without its difficulties. See the useful discussion in Loren T. Stuckenbruck, *Angel Veneration and Christology: A Study in Early Judaism and in the Christology of the Apocalypse of John* (WUNT 2, 70), Tübingen: Mohr-Siebeck, 1995, pp. 15–21; also Larry W. Hurtado, *One God, One Lord. Early Christian Devotion and Ancient Jewish Monotheism*, London: SCM, 1988, pp. 17–39; 'What Do We Mean by "First-Century Jewish Monotheism"?', in Eugene M. Lovering, Jr. (ed.), *SBL 1993 Seminar Papers*, Atlanta: Scholars, 1993, pp. 348–68; Paul A. Rainbow, 'Jewish Monotheism as the Matrix for New Testament Christology: A Review Article', *NovT* 33/1 (1991), 78–91; Dunn, *Partings*, pp. 19–21. See also Hengel, *Judaism and Hellenism*, p.264; Barclay, *Jews*, pp. 99–100, 312–13. See further our discussion in n.70 and n.71 below and in ch.3.

these lines: in contrast with Jews, Gentiles accepted and worshipped more than one god; Jesus was regarded as divine and worshipped; therefore, the concept of Jesus' divinity is a product of Gentile influence on Christianity rather than a natural growth out of the (very Jewish) message of Jesus.[15] To argue this way, in light of our discussion above, is not incoherent, although we shall see reasons below for ultimately rejecting this solution to the problem of the development of Johannine Christology.

Gentile influence on Johannine Christology[16]

We may now consider the views of those who maintain that John's distinctive Christology took its present form under the influence of Gentiles who had joined the community. The most recent exponent of this view is Maurice Casey, whose perspective is representative of this approach to the problem of christological development. Casey's basic argument is that those Christians who came to view Jesus as divine did so under the influence of Gentile thought, to which they were susceptible because the Judaism of which they were a part had already gone some way towards assimilating to Gentile ways.[17] Casey is aware of the problem of Jewish diversity, and compares the issue in relation to New Testament times to the issue in modern times of 'Who is a Jew?'[18] Yet he stresses that in order to reach some sort of conclusion, a concept of orthodoxy is necessary, and this he finds in the Torah-observant Judaism of the Pharisees and Essenes.[19] Casey also suggests eight features as distinctively Jewish, so that if someone has all eight he is clearly Jewish, and if none he is clearly a Gentile. These are ethnicity, Scripture, monotheism, circumcision, Sabbath observance, dietary laws, purity laws and major festivals. Among these ethnicity is at times an overriding factor, so that someone may be perceived as Jewish even if the other factors are lacking, or conversely as a Gentile even though all the other factors are present.[20]

---

[15] So e.g. Casey, *Jewish Prophet*, pp. 23–38. See also Reginald H. Fuller, *The Foundations of New Testament Christology*, New York: Scribners, 1965, pp. 232–3, who nonetheless seeks to emphasize the underlying continuity in spite of these influences.

[16] What follows repeats many of the arguments found in the present author's 'Johannine Christianity – Jewish Christianity?', *Koinonia Journal* 8/1 (1996), 1–20.

[17] Casey, *Jewish Prophet*, pp. 33–4.

[18] Ibid., pp. 11–12.   [19] Ibid., pp. 17–20.

[20] Ibid., p.14. See also Barclay, *Jews*, pp. 402–13.

Casey's work is helpful inasmuch as it sets out clearly the presuppositions and methodology that are used by many who argue along these lines. Yet it will probably already be obvious from our discussion in the previous section that Casey's argument is open to severe criticism at a number of key points. To begin with, Casey is working with a concept of orthodoxy that is anachronistic and therefore inappropriate for the period in question. The Pharisees did not have the authority to define what was and was not legitimately considered Judaism in New Testament times. During this period there were simply no universally recognized leaders in a position to define Judaism in this way.[21] It is true that the Pharisees considered their interpretation of Judaism to be the correct one and the most faithful to Israel's Scriptures and traditions, but this is also true of the Qumran community, and was presumably equally true of all of the other Jewish parties. The situation in Israel/ Judaism during this period has been compared to the situation in a multi-party state such as the US or Great Britain. In such a situation, there are a number of groups, each of whom would like to be in a position of authority and enforce its understanding of the way life in the nation should be lived. Nonetheless, no one party represents the whole population, so that even the party in power cannot legitimately claim to be 'the only truly American/British party'.[22]

It will be helpful to contrast Casey's view with that of Neusner, who emphasizes that the features usually used to define a social entity (such as a common country, language or culture) were not shared by all Jews. He thus considers that, from a purely secular perspective, the portrait of the Jews as a unified entity 'Israel' is 'a pious fantasy'.[23] It may of course be possible to find common

[21] Cf. David E. Aune, 'Orthodoxy in First Century Judaism? A Response to N. J. McEleney', *JSJ* 7/1 (1976), 1–10; Lester L. Grabbe, 'Orthodoxy in First Century Judaism. What Are the Issues?', *JSJ* 8/2 (1977), 149–53; Luke Timothy Johnson, 'The New Testament's Anti-Jewish Slander and the Conventions of Ancient Polemic', *JBL* 108 (1989), 426–8; Bengt Holmberg, *Sociology and the New Testament. An Appraisal*, Minneapolis: Fortress, 1990, p.91; E. P. Sanders, *Judaism: Practice and Belief 63 BCE–66 CE*, London: SCM/ Philadelphia: Trinity, 1992, pp. 388–404; Philip S. Alexander, ' "The Partings of the Ways" from the Perspective of Rabbinic Judaism', in James D. G. Dunn (ed.), *Jews and Christians. The Partings of the Ways A. D. 70 to 135* (WUNT 2, 66), Tübingen: Mohr-Siebeck, 1992, pp. 3, 21; Barclay, *Jews*, p.85.

[22] Cf. Alan F. Segal, *Rebecca's Children. Judaism and Christianity in the Roman World*, Cambridge, MA: Harvard University Press, 1986, p.59. See also Grabbe, 'Orthodoxy', 151–2.

[23] Neusner, *Judaic Law*, p.2; see further his discussion on pp. 50, 62.

denominators, just as Dunn has attempted to do by speaking of 'four pillars of ancient Judaism'.[24] These he defines as monotheism, election of Israel, covenant (focused in Torah) and the Temple. Yet the difficulty is that, precisely as a set of lowest common denominators, these points appear not to have been the central emphases or distinguishing features in the various Jewish groups of this period.[25] We cannot, on the basis of the texts available to us from this period, say that there was universal agreement on precisely what monotheism meant in practice, on the place of the Gentiles, on how the Torah was to be interpreted and applied, or on the validity of the present Temple.[26] It thus becomes impossible to speak of a Jewish 'orthodoxy' in this period, and thus the question 'Who *was* a Jew?' becomes as difficult to answer as its modern analogue, 'Who *is* a Jew?'

This point leads us to another key element of Casey's argument. In his view, it is precisely because the Johannine Christians had lost their Jewish self-identity that they were able to develop a Christology in which Jesus was considered divine.[27] He regards the

---

[24] Dunn, *Partings*, pp. 18–36. Neusner expresses his essential agreement with Dunn's assessment in *Judaic Law*, pp. 52–3. See also Neil J. McEleney, 'Orthodoxy in Judaism of the First Christian Century: Replies to David E. Aune and Lester L. Grabbe', *JSJ* 9/1 (1978), 84–7.

[25] Neusner, *Judaic Law*, p.53. See also Barclay, *Jews*, p.402.

[26] Cf. Aune, 'Orthodoxy', 6–7; Johnson, 'Anti-Jewish Slander', 426–8. There was also wide diversity of practice concerning the observance of purity laws (cf. James D. G. Dunn, *Jesus, Paul and the Law. Studies in Mark and Galatians*, London: SPCK, 1990, pp. 140–7). Thus the explanation concerning water pots for purification (John 2.6; Casey, *Jewish Prophet*, pp. 28–9) need not imply more than that there was at least one 'God-fearer' or non-observant Jew present among John's intended readership. That many Jews observed purity laws even in the Diaspora is clear enough (cf. E. P. Sanders, *Jewish Law from Jesus to the Mishnah. Five Studies*, London: SCM/ Philadelphia: Trinity, 1990, pp. 258–71; *Judaism: Practice and Belief*, pp. 223–4), but nonetheless there were clearly also some who felt that such observance was unnecessary, particularly when there was no occasion for regular contact with the Temple (cf. Philo, *Mig.* 89–93). Likewise, the explanation of terms like 'rabbi' need not imply anything more than the presence of Jews whose first and perhaps only language was Greek. On the epigraphic evidence, which suggests that most Greek-speaking Diaspora Jews used a translation such as (νομο)διδάσκαλος rather than the transliterated 'rabbi', see E. Lohse, 'ῥαββι', *TDNT* VI, pp. 961–5; Shaye J. D. Cohen, 'Epigraphical Rabbis', *JQR* n.s. 72 (1981), 1–17. See also J. Louis Martyn, 'A Gentile Mission That Replaced an Earlier Jewish Mission?', in R. Alan Culpepper and C. Clifton Black (eds.), *Exploring the Gospel of John. In Honor of D. Moody Smith*, Louisville: Westminster John Knox, 1996, pp. 126–7; Richard Bauckham, 'For Whom Were Gospels Written?', in R. Bauckham (ed.), *The Gospels for All Christians. Rethinking the Gospel Audiences*, Edinburgh: T&T Clark, 1998, p.24.

[27] Casey, *Jewish Prophet*, p.27.

Johannine references to 'the Jews' as decisive evidence for this. Casey's conclusion here is questionable on a number of grounds. We may begin with the explicit evidence of 3 John 7. The Johannine epistles may with reasonable certainty be attributed to a member or members of the same early Christian community as that in which the Fourth Gospel was produced, since they show clear affinities in their theology and language.[28] In this text, those who are not part of the author's group are called ἐθνικῶν, 'Gentiles', which clearly suggests that the group of which the author is a part does not have a Gentile self-identity.[29] This is further indicated in the Gospel itself by the fact that the Johannine Christians evaluate positively the title 'Israel(ite)' (John 1.47–9), and that the author can even state that 'salvation is of the Jews' (4.22). However, we also find in the Fourth Gospel that the Johannine Christians defined their identity over against a group whom they called 'the Jews'. This fact does appear to create difficulty for the view that the Johannine Christians had a Jewish self-identity. Thus, if our understanding of John as a Christian-Jewish work is to be maintained, it will be necessary to find an alternative explanation of this Johannine phenomenon.

The key to understanding the Johannine references to 'the Jews' is an awareness of the background against which the Fourth Gospel was written. In ancient Mediterranean cultures, the collective identity was primary, and it was completely normal to engage in what today might be considered unhelpful 'stereotyping'.[30] Even today, statements such as 'the English are very reserved' are made, even by people who are aware that there are exceptions to this generalization. In the case of the Fourth Gospel, the Johannine Christians had been part of a Jewish community that refused to believe in Jesus, and which took a hostile attitude towards the teaching and beliefs promulgated by these Christians.[31] It was

[28] On this see further Raymond E. Brown, *The Epistles of John* (Anchor Bible, 30), New York: Doubleday and Co, 1982, pp. 20–30; Judith Lieu, *The Theology of the Johannine Epistles*, Cambridge: Cambridge University Press, 1991, pp. 16–17.

[29] Cf. Maurice Casey, *Is John's Gospel True?*, London: Routledge, 1996, pp. 115–16.

[30] Cf. Bruce J. Malina, *The New Testament World. Insights from Cultural Anthropology*, Atlanta: John Knox, 1981, pp. 53–60. See further Sean Freyne, 'Vilifying the Other and Defining the Self: Matthew's and John's Anti-Jewish Polemic in Focus', in Jacob Neusner and Ernest S. Frerichs (eds.), *'To See Ourselves as Others See Us'. Christians, Jews, 'Others' in Late Antiquity*, Chico: Scholars, 1985, pp. 117–143; Johnson, 'Anti-Jewish Slander'; McGrath, 'Johannine Christianity', 13–4.

[31] Cf. the evidence amassed in the first part of ch.2 below.

'natural', in this cultural context, for a group that had had such experiences to think of 'the Jews' as typically 'those who have hardened their hearts and refused to believe in their own Messiah'.[32] However, in thinking this way the author is still aware that there were Jews who believed openly in Jesus, as well as secret sympathizers within the Jewish community.

It must also be kept in mind that not long prior to John writing, a number of Christians had been expelled from the synagogue against their will. The background to this occurrence is usually thought to be the attempt by certain rabbis in the post-70 period to define more clearly, and in line with their own particular views and emphases, what it meant to be a Jew.[33] These Christians had been 'defined out' by the leaders of their community. Some would even argue that the majority of Jews in the community from which they were expelled refused to regard these Christians as genuine or faithful Jews, perhaps even going so far as to claim that title exclusively for themselves. The author of the Fourth Gospel cedes the term, but in other ways claims that Christians are the true Israelites and those who have truly remained faithful to the heritage of Israel's traditions and Scriptures.[34]

---

[32] This is not to condone the many fiery statements made by the author of the Gospel, but simply to demonstrate that it appears less striking against the context of its cultural setting than it does to us today, after so many years of Christian anti-Semitism. See further Johnson, 'Anti-Jewish Slander'; John Painter, *The Quest for the Messiah. The History, Literature and Theology of the Johannine Community*, Edinburgh: T&T Clark, 1993, pp. 29–31; Casey, *Is John's Gospel True?*, p.225.

[33] See Klaus Wengst, *Bedrängte Gemeinde und verherrlichter Christus. Der historische Ort des Johannesevangeliums als Schlüssel zu einer Interpretation*, Neukirchen-Vluyn: Neukirchener Verlag, 1981, pp. 48–73; Dunn, *Partings*, pp. 222, 238–9; Frédéric Manns, *L'Evangile de Jean à la lumière du Judaisme* (SBFA, 33), Jerusalem: Franciscan, 1991, pp. 469–509. We are not suggesting that the Jewish community of which these Christians had been a part will have been directly affected by the council of Jamnia, but simply that the aforementioned Jewish community was part of a wider mood current in the post-70 period. See also Kysar, 'Pursuing the Paradoxes', pp. 191–2 n.6; John Ashton, *Understanding the Fourth Gospel*, Oxford: Clarendon, 1991, pp. 151–9. In light of our earlier discussion, we should perhaps also stress that this was an attempt, not to *defend* Jewish orthodoxy, but to *define* it. In the earlier period, differing definitions co-existed, whereas in the post-war period the Pharisaic-Rabbinic school of thought slowly began to predominate, and in those areas where it had sufficient power to do so, sought to enforce its own views, and to exclude proponents of certain other views which threatened its own. See also the discussion and illuminating modern illustration offered in de Boer, *Johannine Perspectives*, p.57.

[34] See further the helpful discussion in Dunn, *Partings*, pp. 156–60. See also Painter, *Quest*, pp. 57–8; D. Moody Smith, *The Theology of the Gospel of John*, Cambridge: Cambridge University Press, 1995, pp. 89–90; McGrath, 'Johannine Christianity', 11–14. Casey, *Is John's Gospel True?*, pp. 124–7 argues against Dunn and others who seek to show that there was a tendency to distinguish between

One of Casey's major points is that the Johannine Christians have defined their identity over against 'the Jews', and are thus no longer 'Jews' themselves. We have just seen that this is not a necessary conclusion to draw on the basis of the available evidence. Once again a crucial factor is that Casey is working with a definition of Judaism which appears to be too narrow for the period in question. In later times, when an 'orthodox' form of Judaism began to take shape, many other groups and beliefs were defined out along with Johannine Christianity, among these some that Casey recognizes as clearly Jewish. For instance, Philo's talk of the Logos as a 'second god' would have been excluded as heresy in this later period in much the same way as were Christian beliefs of the sort found in the Fourth Gospel.[35] Were Casey to allow the same looser definition of monotheism for John as he does for Philo, the former might also be included within the broad spectrum of first-century Judaism. Perhaps it is only because of his knowledge with the benefit of hindsight that Christianity eventually became a separate religion that it is possible for Casey to maintain the view that he does. Thus one cannot help but wonder whether, if Philo's teaching had been more widely propagated and, after such views were excluded by the rabbis, had produced a separate religion called 'Philonism', Casey would not have regarded Philo's teaching concerning this 'second god' as a break with Jewish orthodoxy.[36]

Once it has been accepted that there was no one clear orthodox Judaism in this time, the fact that the Johannine Christians may have held a spiritualizing interpretation of the Temple or of the Jewish feasts, regarding them as fulfiled in Christ, need not prevent us from considering them to have been Jewish Christians. On the contrary, the very fact that they felt the feasts and Temple to be so important that they needed to show in some way their fidelity to these institutions could well suggest just the opposite, that these

'Israel' and 'Jews'. Even if the evidence does not support the case, this does not preclude the possibility that John made such a distinction. This is nonetheless somewhat beside the point, as John can use 'Jews' as well as 'Israel' in a positive sense (John 4.22). Cf. the helpful and balanced discussion in Graham Harvey, *The True Israel. Uses of the Names Jew, Hebrew and Israel in Ancient Jewish and Early Christian Literature*, Leiden: Brill, 1996, pp. 91–2, 249–50.

[35] Cf. Alan F. Segal, *Two Powers in Heaven. Early Rabbinic Reports about Christianity and Gnosticism* (SJLA, 25), Leiden: Brill, 1977, pp. 179–80.

[36] McGrath, 'Johannine Christianity', 6. See further Hurtado, 'First-Century Jewish Monotheism', on this issue. He raises a number of important criticisms of Casey on pp. 350–1. On Johannine Christology and monotheism see below, ch.3.

were indeed Christian Jews.[37] Thus, in contrast to Casey's conclusions, Dunn argues that the prominence of the theme of conflict between Jesus and 'the Jews' in John strongly suggests that the Fourth Gospel stems from a predominantly Jewish setting.[38] Dunn rightly points out that the conflict between the Johannine Christians and 'the Jews' ought to be read, not as a conflict between two distinct religions, but between two Jewish groups, each attempting to claim that it represents the true continuation of Israel's ancient heritage and beliefs. The language of denunciation of 'the Jews' in John, and the references to them as 'children of darkness/the devil', is the language of Jewish sectarianism, as may be seen from much of the Qumran literature, even though the key term 'the Jews' is not found there.[39] It is used, however, by the later Jewish Christians who authored the Pseudo-Clementines, and is not all that different from the denunciations of 'Israel' found in the writings attributed to the (clearly Israelite) prophets in the Jewish Scriptures.[40] Of course, we know in hindsight that the Pharisaic rabbis held on to the title 'Judaism', and that Christianity did become a separate religion; this is not in doubt. However, it is important not to

[37] Cp. Philo's attitude to those who, in interpreting the Torah figuratively, rejected its literal meaning: Philo disagrees with them, but does not regard them as no longer being Jews; see his *Mig.*, 89ff. Casey gives 'half a point' to the Fourth Gospel in relation to monotheism and other distinguishing features on his scale (Casey, *Jewish Prophet*, p.29; *Is John's Gospel True?*, p.114). In our view, this undermines his whole project: if differing views on monotheism, Scripture, etc. can be more or less 'Jewish', then the whole issue of Jewishness becomes much less black and white than even Casey's 8–point scale. This in turns opens up the possibility that John, while probably not getting a full 8 points, will get far more than the 1.5 given by Casey, or alternatively that many authors that are currently classed as Jewish by Casey will need to be recategorized. On the probable observance of Torah by the Johannine Christians see further Severino Pancaro, *The Law in the Fourth Gospel. The Torah and the Gospel, Moses and Jesus, Judaism and Christianity according to John* (NovTSup, 42), Leiden: Brill, 1975, p.530; J. Louis Martyn, 'Glimpses into the History of the Johannine Community', in M. de Jonge (ed.), *L'Evangile de Jean. Sources, rédaction, théologie* (BETL, 44), Leuven: Leuven University Press, 1977, pp. 158–9; Rodney Whitacre, *Johannine Polemic. The Role of Tradition and Theology* (SBLDS, 67), Chico, CA: Scholars, 1982, pp. 64–8; Lloyd Gaston, 'Lobsters in the Fourth Gospel', in Jacob Neusner (ed.), *Approaches to Ancient Judaism. New Series. Volume IV*, Atlanta: Scholars, 1993, pp. 115–23; McGrath, 'Johannine Christianity', 7–10.

[38] James D. G. Dunn, 'Let John Be John: A Gospel for Its Time', in Peter Stuhlmacher (ed.), *The Gospel and the Gospels*, Grand Rapids: Eerdmans, 1991, p.303.

[39] Cf. Johnson, 'Anti-Jewish Slander', on polemical language in early Judaism and Christianity.

[40] Cf. Ps-Clem., *Recognitions* 1.50; 5.11; also McGrath, 'Johannine Christianity', 13.

anachronistically read the final outcome of a development back into its earlier stages.[41]

It would thus seem unwise to follow Casey in regarding the Johannine Christians as 'syncretistic' Jews who essentially apostatized from Judaism to produce Gentile Christianity. The notion of a Judaism that had not been influenced in any way by its neighbours in the wider Hellenistic world is no longer tenable. Although one can sympathize with his desire to find a clear definition of orthodoxy to work with, it has been adequately demonstrated that no such definition can accurately be applied to Judaism in the period in question. Another shortcoming of Casey's thesis is his failure to distinguish with sufficient clarity between the self-understanding of the Johannine Christians and the way others regarded them.[42] He also overemphasizes the sense of alienation from Judaism expressed by the Christians who were responsible for producing the Fourth Gospel, failing to do justice to the complementary fact that it is precisely a group of Jewish origin that feels this way. The paradox of John's Gospel's relationship to Judaism is dealt with much better by Meeks in his famous statement, 'To put the matter sharply, with some risk of misunderstanding, the Fourth Gospel is most anti-Jewish just at the points it is most Jewish.'[43] Were the conflict over Christology reflected in the Gospel also a conflict about openness to Gentile influence, we should expect to find some hint of this in the accusations raised by the Jewish authorities in the course of the Gospel, and yet we do not.[44] Thus,

[41] Cf. James D. G. Dunn, 'Some Clarifications on Issues of Method: A Reply to Holliday and Segal', *Semeia* 30 (1984), 100. On important differences between pagan and Christian forms of anti-Judaism even in the second century, which create difficulties for those who would argue that the latter was simply a sub-category of the former, see Miriam S. Taylor, *Anti-Judaism and Early Christian Identity. A Critique of Scholarly Consensus*, Leiden: Brill, 1995, pp. 116–21.

[42] Cf. again Hurtado, 'First-Century Jewish Monotheism', pp. 354–5, who notes the difficulty of defining first-century Jewish monotheism, and adopts the approach of accepting that 'first century Jewish monotheism' is that which first-century Jewish authors who consider themselves monotheists believe.

[43] Wayne A. Meeks, '"Am I A Jew?" – Johannine Christianity and Judaism', in Jacob Neusner (ed.), *Christianity, Judaism and Other Greco-Roman Cults. Studies for Morton Smith at Sixty. Part One: New Testament*, Leiden: Brill, 1975, p.172.

[44] Cf. McGrath, 'Johannine Christianity', 10. This is admittedly an argument from silence, but it is nonetheless perhaps a valid one, inasmuch as other New Testament documents which clearly express openness to Gentiles also feel the need to defend this fact. See also the recent studies by J. L. Martyn, 'Mission' and Peder Borgen, 'The Gospel of John and Hellenism. Some Observations', both in R. Alan Culpepper and C. Clifton Black (eds.), *Exploring the Gospel of John. In Honor of D. Moody Smith*, Louisville: Westminster John Knox, 1996.

in light of the evidence we have surveyed, it seems justified to reject the claim that Johannine Christianity should be regarded as a Gentile phenomenon rather than a Jewish one. This in turn suggests that Gentile influence cannot provide the key to explaining and understanding the development of Johannine Christology.

Samaritan influence on Johannine Christology

Another suggestion that has been offered as to a possible catalyst for the development of John's high Christology is an influx of Samaritan converts into the community. This suggestion is found particularly in the work of Raymond Brown, although other scholars have also suggested links between either the Gospel of John in particular, or higher Christology in general, and Samaritanism.[45] Brown's hypothesis is among the most convincing of those positing links with Samaritanism, since it allows for the essentially Jewish setting which the work of Martyn and others has shown to be most likely, while also taking seriously the necessity to explain the development of the Christology which brought the Johannine Christians into conflict with the synagogue. Brown does not attempt to argue that the Johannine Christians lost their sense of Jewish identity (especially in view of passages such as John 4.22), but simply that Samaritan converts influenced the development of Johannine thought to a sufficient extent that other Jews took notice of the presence of what they regarded as distinctively Samaritan ideas.[46] Brown's suggestion has the merit of placing Johannine Christianity within a Jewish context, while allowing for a development in this group's christological thinking. The catalyst for this development, an influx of Samaritan converts, would have represented an influx of people holding views that were disliked by the Jewish leaders and would thus have created tensions between them and the Johannine Christians.[47]

[45] Brown, *Community*, pp. 36ff.; John Bowman, *The Samaritan Problem. Studies in the Relationships of Samaritanism, Judaism, and Early Christianity*, Pittsburgh: Pickwick, 1975, ch.3; George Wesley Buchanan, 'The Samaritan Origin of the Gospel of John', in Jacob Neusner (ed.), *Religions in Antiquity. Essays in Memory of Erwin Ramsell Goodenough*, Leiden: Brill, 1968, pp. 149–75; Goulder, 'Two Roots', p.67; P. J. Hartin, 'A Community in Crisis. The Christology of the Johannine Community as the Point at Issue', *Neotestamentica* 19 (1985), 40–1. See too the discussion in Ashton, *Understanding*, pp. 294–9; de Boer, *Johannine Perspectives*, pp. 67, 117.

[46] John 8.48; Brown, *Community*, p.37.

[47] Brown, *Community*, p.39.

One difficulty with Brown's proposal is our lack of knowledge of Samaritanism in the first century. As Meeks notes, even the earliest sources available give us direct access only to roughly the fourth century CE, when a revival of sorts among the Samaritans led to the production of a number of important writings.[48] Thus the use of Samaritan texts to illuminate the New Testament must follow the same cautions that apply to the use of rabbinic texts: they are certainly not wholly irrelevant, but cannot be used directly to provide information about what their particular group believed in earlier times. A relationship will exist between Samaritanism in the first and fourth centuries, as there exists a relationship between Christianity in the first and fourth centuries, but there may have been just as much development in Samaritanism during this period as there obviously was in Christianity between, say, the time of Paul and the Council of Nicaea. Thus any conclusions about Samaritanism prior to the fourth century CE must unfortunately remain tentative.[49]

When Samaritan beliefs and traditions are compared with Jewish/rabbinic texts of a similar date, the distinctiveness of Samaritanism is somewhat lessened. There was evidently borrowing and interaction between Judaism and Samaritanism even after the two had gone their separate ways.[50] Most studies of motifs in Jewish and Samaritan sources find similar beliefs and traditions in both.[51] Brown refers in particular to Meeks' description of the place of Moses in Samaritanism, but is only able to speak of 'strains' in Johannine theology similar to ideas found in Samaritan writings. Meeks himself writes (in the passage referred to by Brown) that Johannine thought was at least partly shaped by hostile interaction between Christians and a *Jewish* community

[48] Wayne A. Meeks, *The Prophet-King. Moses Traditions and the Johannine Christology* (NovTSup, 14), Leiden: Brill, 1967, p.219.

[49] Ibid., p.219. See also Margaret Pamment, 'Is There Convincing Evidence of Samaritan Influence on the Fourth Gospel?', *ZNW* 73 (1982), 221; Ashton, *Understanding*, p. 298; Graham Stanton, 'Samaritan Incarnational Christology?' in Michael Goulder (ed.), *Incarnation and Myth: The Debate Continued*, London: SCM, 1979, p.243.

[50] So Meeks, *Prophet-King*, pp. 216–17, with references to several major experts on Samaritanism. See too Pamment, 'Is There Convincing Evidence', 229–30.

[51] So e.g. Wayne A. Meeks, 'Moses as God and King', in Jacob Neusner (ed.), *Religions in Antiquity: Essays in Memory of E. R. Goodenough*, Leiden: Brill, 1968, pp. 354–71; *Prophet-King*; Jarl E. Fossum, *The Name of God and the Angel of the Lord. Samaritan and Jewish Concepts of Intermediation and the Origin of Gnosticism* (WUNT 2, 36), Tübingen: Mohr-Siebeck, 1985. See also Painter, *Quest*, pp. 122–5; Stanton, 'Samaritan Incarnational Christology?', pp. 243–4.

which attached great importance to Moses, and that the Johannine church had attracted members from among these Jews, as well as from among the Samaritans who held similar beliefs.[52] In his related study of 'Moses as God and King', Meeks concludes that the ideas he is studying concerning Moses' ascension and enthronement were of great importance and influence not only in Samaritanism, but also within certain circles in both Palestinian and Diaspora Judaism.[53] Given our lack of direct knowledge of first-century Samaritanism on the one hand, and the similarity of what we do know about Samaritanism with Jewish thought on the other, appeals to an influx of Samaritan converts do not appear able to provide a convincing explanation of, or catalyst for, the development of Johannine Christology. An influx of Samaritan converts, if one occurred, may not have added anything that could not also be found in contemporary streams of Judaism. In short, the Samaritan hypothesis seems unable to provide a convincing explanation of the development of Johannine Christology.[54]

'Heterodox' Jewish influence on Johannine Christology

A slightly different approach along the same lines is found in the work of Cullmann and Ashton.[55] These scholars have proposed that John be situated within a form of 'heterodox' Judaism, a Judaism which has come under the influence of Gentile modes of thought.[56] Although Cullmann takes the view that there were from the beginning either two types of teaching given by Jesus or two interpretations of his teaching,[57] we have nonetheless felt it appropriate to place his approach in the History of Religions category. This is because he posits the influence of a different worldview, albeit a different Jewish one, in order to explain the distinctive development of Johannine Christology, and in his view the differences between this Judaism and 'mainstream' Judaism are still to be explained in terms of Gentile influence. The key difference

---

[52] Brown, *Community*, p.37; Meeks, *Prophet-King*, pp. 318–19.

[53] Meeks, 'Moses as God and King', p.364.

[54] For further criticisms and discussion cf. Pamment, 'Is There Convincing Evidence'.

[55] Oscar Cullmann, *The Johannine Circle. Its place in Judaism, among the disciples of Jesus and in early Christianity*, London: SCM, 1976, esp. pp. 49–53; Ashton, *Understanding*, pp. 294–301.

[56] Cullmann, *Johannine Circle*, pp. 32–3, 39–41.

[57] Ibid., pp. 93–4.

between the view of Cullmann and his followers and that of Casey is that the former would regard this 'syncretistic' Judaism and the Christianity it produced as still Jewish in a way that the latter would not.

This approach meets with many of the same difficulties that confront the other approaches we have considered. The concept of 'heterodoxy' is anachronistic, since (as we have seen) there was no such thing as an 'orthodox' Judaism in the first century.[58] This view also fails to explain how the Johannine Christians apparently managed to remain part of their local synagogue for so long before they were expelled. However, if the approaches in this last category are related to conflicts between groups who were attempting to put forward different definitions of 'orthodoxy', that is, different definitions of what is and is not Judaism, then a modified version of this approach may indeed be plausible. While we have already seen that all forms of first-century Judaism may correctly be designated 'Hellenistic Judaism', so that the explanatory power of the reference to Hellenism is severely diminished, it is nonetheless possible to speak of different streams of thought and different parties/sects within Second Temple Judaism. While appeals to Hellenistic influence will not solve our problem, the study of inner-Jewish sectarian conflict, particularly in the post-70 period, may have light to shed on our topic, provided it is coupled with appropriate socio-historical perspectives, and we shall thus return to this possibility in our section on sociological approaches later in the present chapter.

Summary

We have found unsatisfactory the attempt to explain the development of Johannine Christology in terms of the adoption of ideas from non-Jewish sources. The Gospel of John gives clear evidence of conflict with another group which is designated 'the Jews', but this most likely reflects a debate about the definition of Judaism which took place between certain Christians and the Jewish majority among whom they lived. There is simply insufficient evidence for an influx of Gentiles into the Christian community of which the Fourth Evangelist was a part, and on the contrary much evidence which indicates that this author and his readers continued to regard themselves as faithful to the beliefs, traditions and Scriptures of

[58] So rightly Brown, *Community*, p.36 n.52 and p.178.

Israel.[59] The evidence from Samaritan sources is too late to be of help to us, and at any rate shares many emphases and beliefs that are also found in various streams of Jewish thought. The development of Johannine Christology is thus not best explained in terms of the influence of ideas and worldviews other than the Jewish one in which Christianity first appeared. Of course, we are not suggesting that Christianity has never been influenced by thought-worlds other than those found in its initial Jewish context. What is being emphasized here is simply that the *Fourth Gospel* seems to be too firmly rooted in Jewish thought, and concerned with Jewish issues, for an appeal to non-Jewish influences to provide a convincing solution to the question of why Johannine Christology developed as it did. Relating the development of Johannine Christology to the different views which existed within contemporary Judaism may provide a more fruitful avenue of approach, but an explanation in terms of the groups or parties which held these different views and of the conflict between them will require the use of relevant social-scientific categories and models. We shall turn our attention to such approaches later in the present chapter.

Organic development

As we turn to consider this second category, it should be stressed that the designation of this type of approach as 'organic' development is not intended to imply that the earliest Christians, in seeking to express their beliefs, were not influenced by the language and concepts available to them in the society of which they were a part. Such a claim would border on the ridiculous. No one wishes to claim that the concepts used by the first Christians to express their Christology did not already have a prior history of meaning which was then inherited by the Christians who made use of these terms. Rather, what is being asserted by proponents of organic models of development is that the later stages of Christology do not make assertions about Jesus which were not already implied by the claims and impact of Jesus himself. This is not to suggest that all of the

---

[59] The 'Greeks' of John 12.20, while probably Gentiles (cf. Raymond E. Brown, *The Gospel According to John (I–XII)* (Anchor Bible, 29), New York: Doubleday, 1966, p.466), were nonetheless clearly proselytes or Gentiles interested in Judaism, since they came to Jerusalem for the feast. See further Barnabas Lindars, *The Gospel of John*, Grand Rapids: Eerdmans/ London: Marshall, Morgan and Scott, 1972, p.427; Martyn, 'Mission', p.128.

later terms and concepts actually derive from Jesus himself, but simply that these later expressions of Christians' understanding of Jesus represent a valid, legitimate expression of who Jesus was.[60] Thus Moule argues that Jesus was such a one as to be appropriately called 'Lord' and even in some sense 'God'. The point for him is not whether these designations were first used early or late, but rather that they represent genuine insights into who Jesus actually was and not an evolution away from that starting point.[61] In a similar vein Dunn concludes his study of the development of Christology by asserting that, although the evidence does not suggest that Jesus understood himself as 'the incarnate Son of God', this way of viewing him was 'an appropriate reflection on and elaboration of Jesus' own sense of sonship and eschatological mission'.[62] Some scholars in this category, while recognizing that the Christology of John is significantly different from that of earlier writings, would nonetheless go so far as to say that, were Jesus to read the Gospel of John, he would be pleased with its presentation of who he is and what he did.[63]

The major advantage that this type of explanation has over the History of Religions explanations surveyed in the previous section is that it does justice to the links between the distinctive Johannine motifs and images and earlier christological formulations. While John uses them in different ways, the presence in both John and earlier literature of designations such as 'Son of Man', and of the use of imagery connected with Wisdom, suggests that what we find in John is a more developed form of what earlier Christians said and believed. However, the organic model is at a disadvantage when it comes to explaining why it is that such significant developments occurred. In the case of Brown, we have a scholar who considers on the one hand that christological development is

[60] Moule, *Origin*, p.5.

[61] Ibid., p.4. So also R. T. France, 'The Worship of Jesus: A Neglected Factor in Christological Debate?', in Harold H. Rowdon (ed.), *Christ the Lord. Studies in Christology Presented to Donald Guthrie*, Leicester: IVP, 1982, p.24; 'Development', p.77; Martin Hengel, *Studies in Early Christology*, Edinburgh: T&T Clark, 1995, pp. 369–70.

[62] Dunn, *Christology*, p.254. See also Ben Witherington III, *The Christology of Jesus*, Minneapolis: Fortress, 1990, pp. 275–7 (who cites Raymond E. Brown, 'Did Jesus Know He Was God?', *BTB* 15 (1985), 77–8). Brown, *Introduction*, pp. 102, 109 emphasizes the close relation between earlier and later Christology, despite his belief (cf. *Community*, pp. 35–40, and our discussion immediately above) that an influx of Samaritans acted as a catalyst to the development.

[63] So e.g. Witherington, *Christology*, pp. 276–7.

essentially organic, an unfolding of the significance of what the earliest Christians believed, yet who on the other hand finds it necessary to appeal to an external catalyst for the developments he sees reflected in the high Christology of the Gospel of John. While Brown is heavily indebted to the work of Martyn and largely accepts his conclusions, it is on precisely this point that he criticizes him: in Martyn's work, no explanation is offered as to *why* Christian Jews developed a Christology which resulted in their being expelled from the synagogue. Brown discerns the need for an explanatory cause or catalyst for these developments.[64]

In other words, earlier Jewish Christians were able to remain a part of the synagogue for decades, whereas the Christians whose experiences are reflected in the Fourth Gospel were expelled precisely because of their christological beliefs. If an explanation in terms of the development of earlier motifs and imagery is going to appear plausible, it will have to offer an explanation of why the Johannine Christians should develop a Christology which would lead to their unwilling expulsion from the synagogue. To simply assert that development inevitably occurs seems inadequate in this context.[65]

Before proceeding, we must consider another recent approach to the question that is probably best included under the heading of organic approaches. This is the suggestion that the earliest Christians began to include Christ in their worship as a result of their religious experience, and this factor of the worship of Jesus – which was present in Christianity from the beginning and which represents a modification of earlier Jewish practice, but one which is nonetheless derived from Judaism and Jewish Christianity – led to the development of 'high' Christology, which is to be found not only in John but much earlier.[66]

[64] Brown, *Community*, p.174. A similar point is made by John Ashton, *Studying John. Approaches to the Fourth Gospel*, Oxford: Clarendon, 1994, p.73.

[65] Cf. Anthony T. Hanson, *The Prophetic Gospel. A Study of John and the Old Testament*, Edinburgh: T&T Clark, 1991, p.322. See also Hengel, *Johannine Question*, pp. 104–5.

[66] Cf. especially Hurtado, *One God*, p.99. The Fourth Gospel has not received much direct attention from advocates of this approach: Richard Bauckham's two key articles on this subject, 'The Worship of Jesus in Apocalyptic Christianity', *NTS* 27 (1980–1), 322–41, and 'The Worship of Jesus', in David N. Freedman (ed.), *The Anchor Bible Dictionary, Vol.III H–J*, New York: Doubleday and Co., 1992, pp. 812–19, do not mention John's Gospel; Hurtado, *One God*, mentions verses from it in passing; see also France, 'Worship', p.34. However, this view, if it is to be convincing, must be applicable to John, and the Johannine emphasis on the Paraclete

One key difficulty with such an approach is that it appears to play down the differences between, for example, the Synoptics and John. Another problem is the lack of agreement on the definition and character of Jewish worship. Even a conservative scholar such as R. T. France would agree that the term 'worship', when used in relation to the Synoptic Jesus, does not denote an attitude or act of devotion appropriate only for God.[67] And as Dunn has rightly pointed out in response to Hurtado, in the earliest period we do not have hymns *to* Christ so much as hymns *about* Christ.[68] This is not to say that Paul and other early Christians did not attribute very exalted status and functions to Jesus, but rather that Jewish Christians may have been able to offer 'worship' of some sort to Jesus without feeling that they were departing from their Jewish roots.[69] To offer praise to a ruler or to prostrate oneself before him (the latter being the root meaning of the word προσκύνεω, 'worship') does not appear to have been contrary to all Jewish sensibilities (cf. 1 Chr. 29.20, 23–5!), and cultic worship in the full sense – involving sacrifice and the like – was not, to our knowledge, offered to Jesus by early Christians.[70] It is the latter that appears to

guiding the Christians into new and deeper understandings makes it logical to approach John from this perspective.

[67] France, 'Worship', pp. 26–7. Cf. also Bauckham, 'Apocalyptic Christianity', 324, and contrast Bauckham's *ABD* article, p.813, the arguments of which should be considered in light of the evidence provided in n.68, n.70 and n.71 below.

[68] Dunn, *Partings*, pp. 204–5; *The Theology of Paul the Apostle*, Grand Rapids: Eerdmans/ Edinburgh: T&T Clark, 1998, pp. 257–60; cf. also Hurtado, *One God*, pp. 102–3; Hengel, *Studies in Early Christology*, p.284. Yet see also Bauckham's *ABD* article, p.815, where he speaks of hymns which 'praise God for his saving acts in the history of Jesus'. He points to Eph. 5.19 as evidence that early Christians did sing hymns *to* Christ, but it is striking that the letter's author catches himself and adds the qualifying statement of 5.20, which follows the more usual pattern. At any rate, we have at least one hymn to/concerning the Davidic king in the Psalms, which Jews did not feel conflicted with monotheism: Ps. 45, where the Davidic king is perhaps even called 'God'. See also the 'praise' offered to the king in 2 Chr. 23.12.

[69] Cf. Larry J. Kreitzer, *Jesus and God in Paul's Eschatology* (JSNTS, 19), Sheffield Academic Press, 1987, pp. 160–1; see also Loren T. Stuckenbruck, 'An Angelic Refusal of Worship: The Tradition and Its Function in the Apocalypse of John', in Eugene Lovelace (ed.), *SBL 1994 Seminar Papers*, Atlanta: Scholars, 1994, pp. 679–96.

[70] See our discussion of this point in greater detail in ch.3 below. Cf. further Moule, *Origin*, pp. 41, 175–6, France, 'Worship', pp. 26–7; A. E. Harvey, *Jesus and the Constraints of History. The Bampton Lectures, 1980*, London: Duckworth, 1982, p.172. Note also D. Steenburg, 'The Worship of Adam and Christ as the Image of God', *JSNT* 39 (1990), 95–8, who discusses Jewish traditions concerning the worship of Adam. He suggests that such ideas provided legitimation for the worship of Jesus by Christians (ibid., 98–101). This is important for our present discussion, since Adam is clearly a figure distinct from God, who is nonetheless to be

have been reserved by Jews exclusively for the one true God (cf. 1 Chr. 29.21).[71]

Another question which must be raised is whether the accounts of heavenly worship – such as we find in Revelation, for example – are more likely to be the *stimulus* for the worship of Christ and for high Christology, or to *reflect* beliefs and practices which were already present in the Christian community. While this is not the place to discuss the nature of religious experience, one point which does seem to be corroborated by research in this field is that religious experiences – and more importantly, literary depictions of religious experiences – to a large extent reflect the beliefs and social setting of the one having or describing the experience.[72] This is not to say that religious experience does not contribute anything that is genuinely innovative to religion.[73] The problem is that we are

worshipped as 'the image of God'. In the case of angels, some did apparently find prostration before angels worrying, perhaps because in the case of angels (who were frequently designated as 'gods') there was a greater danger of confusion and of moves in a polytheistic direction. See further Stuckenbruck, 'Angelic Refusal'; also Bauckham, 'Apocalyptic Christianity'. Philo also objected to the custom of prostrating oneself before kings (*Leg. Gai.* 116; cf. Moule, *Origin*, p.175), here too there being some room for confusion in view of the tendency to regard rulers as divine (the same issue is to the fore in LXX Esther 13.12–14). Nonetheless I know of no evidence of any attempt on the part of the rabbinic authorities to attempt to prohibit or limit the practice. In connection with human figures, Philo clearly appears to be the exception rather than the rule (cf. Moule, *Origin*, p.175). A further problem is the fact that prostration/worship before Christians is apparently evaluated positively in Rev. 3.9, and a similar point applies to sharing the throne in Rev. 3.21. See further Jeyaseelan Joseph Kanagaraj, *'Mysticism' in the Gospel of John: An Inquiry into its Background* (JSNTS, 158), Sheffield: Sheffield Academic Press, 1998, pp. 145–7; also Ezekiel the Tragedian, *Exagoge* 79–80. Unfortunately a full treatment of these difficulties lies beyond the scope of the present work.

[71] On this definition of 'cult' see Rudolf Bultmann, *Theology of the New Testament. Vol. 1*, New York: Charles Scribner's Sons, 1951, p.121; also David E. Aune, *The Cultic Setting of Realized Eschatology in Early Christianity* (NovTSup, 28), Leiden: Brill, 1972, pp. 9–11. This is the type of worship which Jews clearly reserved for God alone (as in 1 Chr. 29.21 – they offered sacrifices to Yahweh and to him alone. I am grateful to Prof. Larry Hurtado for drawing this point to my attention). There may of course have been exceptions, but at least as far as we can tell from the existing evidence from this period, the majority of those who classed themselves as Jews seem to have understood the first commandment to exclude the worship of other gods. Cf. further Barclay, *Jews*, pp. 429–32, and also ch.3 below.

[72] Cf. Dunn, *Jesus, Paul and the Law*, pp. 95–7; Aune, *Cultic Setting*, p. 9; *Prophecy in Early Christianity and the Ancient Mediterranean World*, Grand Rapids: Eerdmans, 1983, pp. 20, 111, 275; Bauckham, 'Apocalyptic Christianity', 331; Hurtado, *One God*, pp. 118–19; Rainbow, 'Jewish Monotheism', 86–7.

[73] See further the discussion in Larry W. Hurtado, 'Christ-Devotion in the First Two Centuries: Reflections and a Proposal', *Toronto Journal of Theology* 12/1 (1996), 25–6.

dealing with a dialectical, two-way process, with belief influencing experience and experience influencing belief. There is thus a need for great caution in assessing the extent of the influence in either direction in any given case. In the New Testament, we have already noted that the clearest evidence of the worship of Christ alongside God is found in Revelation (cf. esp. 5.8, 13). In John, there is only one mention of the 'worship' of Jesus, and it is presumably worship in the broad sense of 'bowing down before', since it provokes no controversy and is not objected to by 'the Jews'. It is thus possible that the worship of Christ found in Revelation represents a further stage of development beyond (and perhaps building upon) the developments which produced the Christology of the Fourth Gospel.[74]

As will become clear later on, we are not denying the importance of either religious experience or the exalted divine functions and status attributed to Jesus by the earliest Christians as a factor in the development of Christology. The question that remains, however, is why later authors should have felt the need to theorize about such beliefs and practices, when earlier ones felt able to offer their praise to Christ, and to attribute divine functions to Christ, untheoretically. If function automatically implies something about nature and essence,[75] then why should it have taken so long for 'ontological' implications to be explicitly drawn? We shall be suggesting below that it is *conflict* over ideas that provides the missing element in this approach. It may be the fact that some Jews eventually did come to object to ideas of this sort which necessitated that Christians reflect on their beliefs and practices and seek to defend them, which as we shall see below would also have involved developments being made.

Thus, we agree that there is much truth in the position and insights of Hurtado and others who take a similar approach, but on its own it does not appear to solve the problem of why Johannine Christology developed along the path that it did. Hurtado himself recognizes this, suggesting that 'opposition to the new movement'

[74] Revelation is usually dated in the 90s CE, the same period in which many believe the Fourth Gospel to have been written. The difficulty here is that, in order to determine the relationship between the Christologies of John and Revelation, we would need to be able to date not only the written works, but also the *ideas* contained therein. Further study of the question of whether there is any influence between the Revelation and the Fourth Gospel, and if so in what direction and to what extent, is certainly required, but unfortunately cannot be undertaken here.

[75] So e.g. France, 'Worship', pp. 33–5; cf. also his 'Development', pp. 76–7.

was also an important stimulus for the Christian 'mutation'.[76] It is this stimulus which we will be exploring further in this study, and which we shall be arguing provides the crucial key to understanding the development of Johannine Christology.[77]

Individual creativity

Scholars in this category do not necessarily deny the continuity between Johannine Christology and earlier Christology. Nor do they necessarily either affirm or deny that the Christology of the Fourth Gospel shows evidence of the influence of non-Jewish modes of thought. What they do stress, however, is that the key reason for the differences between John and other New Testament authors is the unique perspective of the individual who composed the material now found in the Gospel. It is this individual's creativity, imagination and/or distinctive viewpoint that have shaped the earlier traditions which he inherited into their present, distinctive form.[78]

Clearly on one level, to attempt to deny the truthfulness of this position would be to deny that the Fourth Gospel had a human author. To accept that an individual human being wrote the Gospel carries with it the corollary that that individual's character has shaped the way he expressed certain ideas, and influenced his choice of certain words and language over others. However, it is questionable whether such an approach can function as a total explanation of the unique emphases of the Fourth Gospel. The author did not write in isolation, but was part of a Christian community, and it seems likely that the thought-world and experiences of this community will have affected and shaped not only the development of the traditions this author utilized, but also the literary work which he finally produced.[79] The wider context in

---

[76] Hurtado, *One God*, pp. 122–3.

[77] The worship of Christ obviously did play an important role in the development of Christology in later times, on which see Maurice Wiles, *The Making of Christian Doctrine. A Study in the Principles of Early Christian Doctrinal Development*, Cambridge: Cambridge University Press, 1967, pp. 62–93. See further also our discussion of monotheism and worship in ch.3 below.

[78] Cf. Robinson, *Priority*, pp. 298–9; Hengel, *Johannine Question*, pp. 103–5. Francis J. Moloney, *The Johannine Son of Man*, Rome: LAS, 1978, pp. 255–6 is a particularly clear example of the compatibility of this view with other perspectives.

[79] So rightly Cullmann, *Johannine Circle*, p.40. The balance is also maintained well by Moloney, *Johannine Son of Man*, pp. 255–6; see also Painter, *Quest*, pp. 415, 421–2.

which our author wrote is also likely to have been an important factor, as the Gospel of John shows clear signs of having been written in a context of conflict between Christians and non-Christian Jews.[80] Clearly the individual author's contribution is not to be neglected, but what we are seeking to understand are the factors which led that individual to write in the way that he did, i.e. the factors which motivated him to creatively shape the tradition he inherited, and the new context and issues which inspired or stimulated him to adapt and apply these traditions as he did. Thus, while not excluding the importance of the author's own unique contribution, most works of literature were written by a single individual author, and this on its own does not fully answer the question of why Johannine Christology developed along the lines that it did, compared with the seemingly more conservative use of tradition by other early Christian authors, such as Matthew and Luke. We are looking for another level of explanation. At any rate, the important points emphasized by advocates of this approach are not necessarily excluded by advocates of others, as we shall see in the next section.

Sociological approaches

In recent times there has been much focus in Johannine scholarship on the community that produced the Gospel, and the ways in which its changing experience shaped the character of the Johannine tradition. An influential figure in sparking off the contemporary interest in the history of the Johannine community as a key to understanding the Gospel is J. L. Martyn. He asks whether one may discern in the Fourth Gospel the voice of a Christian theologian who is seeking to respond to contemporary events and issues which are relevant to the Christian community of which he is a part. Martyn answers this question in the affirmative, and thus emphasizes that in the Fourth Gospel we find both tradition and 'a new and unique interpretation of that tradition'.[81] Martyn is suggesting that attention to the context in which John wrote, and the needs of the church for which he wrote, can illuminate the question of why the Evangelist wrote as he did. Martyn does not, however, explicitly set forth a sociological model to illuminate this

---

[80] See the evidence presented in the first part of ch.2 below.

[81] J. Louis Martyn, *History and Theology in the Fourth Gospel*, Nashville: Abingdon, 1979, pp. 18–19.

process more clearly. We shall thus need to examine those scholars who do make explicit use of sociological categories and tools, in order to evaluate the possibilities of this sort of approach to the Gospel and its potential to illuminate the development of Johannine Christology.[82] We saw that one of Brown's criticisms of Martyn's work is that he fails to account for the appearance of John's 'high' Christology. We shall need to consider whether there is a sociological approach which can in fact do just that.

A number of scholars have recently issued cautionary remarks in connection with the topic of research into 'the communities behind the Gospels', arguing that Gospels, unlike letters, were foundation documents which would not have been aimed exclusively at the specific contemporary needs of a small group of Christians. As Talbert points out, the problems reflected in the Gospel material may represent not only current issues in the community, but also past issues and issues which are perceived as potential but not actual threats.[83] Some scholars have also warned that the isolated communities which some recent scholarly literature assumes lay behind the Gospels may in fact have been in contact with Christians in many other parts of the Greco-Roman world.[84] These important cautionary remarks need to be taken seriously; however, they do not appear to invalidate the attempt to learn something about the Christian group or groups that produced a particular Gospel. Even today, where mobility and contact between different parts of the world is far greater than in the first century, there can still nonetheless be differences between the issues confronting churches, for example, in New York and in London, or in Bucharest and in Barcelona. Even in the same town or city, problems and issues may arise in one church that do not arise in another. Thus regardless of whether issues reflected in the Gospel were past, present or anticipated future problems, where these issues differ from those found in other Gospels, we may still be justified to conclude that we are

[82] This will also help to narrow down our focus in this section, as it is obviously the case that reconstructions such as Brown's, which we examined in our discussion of History of Religions approaches, are also broadly sociological, inasmuch as they are interested in the history of the Johannine community or church.

[83] Charles H. Talbert, *Reading John. A Literary and Theological Commentary on the Fourth Gospel and the Johannine Epistles*, London: SPCK, 1992, pp. 62–3.

[84] See especially Bauckham, 'For Whom were Gospels Written?', pp. 9–48, and Stephen Barton, 'Can We Identify the Gospel Audiences?', 189–93, both in R. Bauckham (ed.), *The Gospels for all Christians. Rethinking the Gospel Audiences*, Edinburgh: T&T Clark, 1998.

dealing with two different streams of Christian thought and experience. There is no reason to exclude *a priori* the possibility that these different streams of tradition may reflect the different needs of different churches or types of churches.[85]

In the present work we have attempted to avoid the terminology of 'Johannine community'. However, when such language is used by the present author in connection with his own views, it is simply a recognized shorthand for the church community or communities of which the author of the Fourth Gospel was a part and whose experiences are reflected to some extent in the Gospel. It does not presume acceptance of a particular reconstruction of the community's history, as our evaluation of a number of such reconstructions will probably have already made clear. Nor when we speak of the 'Johannine Christians' are we assuming that this was a sectarian group, nor even necessarily that it was only one church in one part of the Greco-Roman world. The term 'Johannine community' as used by the present author should be understood in its broadest possible sense, as the Christian community or communities whose experience influenced the formation of the Fourth Gospel, which are also understood to represent the intended initial audience of the Fourth Gospel, without prejudging the question of its geographical location and relations with other Christian communities. Much of the evidence that we shall survey may well suggest that the author of the Fourth Gospel was taking up traditions that belonged to the whole Church and that he believed that what he wrote was relevant for the whole Church.

We may now turn our attention to the methodology of sociological approaches to the New Testament. Stephen Barton points out that, whereas traditional historical-critical approaches to the New Testament are diachronic, attempting to trace the development of Christian thought and practice over a period of time, sociological approaches are synchronic, inasmuch as they study the function of beliefs and practices at one particular time.[86] If this is

---

[85] On Gospel audiences see further the following articles in Richard Bauckham (ed.), *The Gospels for All Christians*: Richard A. Burridge, 'About People, by People, for People: Gospel Genre and Audiences', pp. 143–4; Barton, 'Gospel Audiences', p.194; also Loveday Alexander, 'Ancient Book Production and the Circulation of the Gospels', pp. 91, 96–7, 104, for the way that works intended for a small circle of friends nonetheless ended up circulating more widely.

[86] Stephen C. Barton, 'Historical Criticism and Social-Scientific Study in New Testament Study', in Joel B. Green (ed.), *Hearing the New Testament. Strategies for Interpretation*, Carlisle: Paternoster/ Grand Rapids: Eerdmans, 1995, p.69.

correct, then the possibility of a sociological explanation of the development of Johannine Christology might appear to be excluded *a priori*. This is in fact the conclusion reached by Neyrey, an influential advocate of sociological approaches. He considers that the origin of John's high Christology will continue to remain inaccessible to us, regardless of how persistent scholars may be in putting such questions to the text.[87] Neyrey is clearly of the view that the sociological approach and methodology which he utilizes in his study of the Fourth Gospel will not answer the question of how and why Johannine Christology developed along the lines that it did.

Yet other scholars advocating a social scientific approach to the New Testament have stressed the need for, and possibility of, a sociological explanation of certain New Testament phenomena, suggesting the possibility of a diachronic sociological approach.[88] In this sort of approach the concern is still with a particular period of time and with social factors in that specific period. However, it also takes into consideration the fact that the use to which tradition is put in certain contexts may function as an explanation concerning its development. We may thus say that it is possible to utilize a synchronic method or approach in order to illuminate a larger diachronic process. In other words, an examination of social factors in a specific period may be able to help explain why that period produced certain developments. This will become clearer as our discussion progresses.

We must now consider a number of criticisms that have been raised in relation to previous attempts at such sociological explanation. For example, it has recently been pointed out by Milbank that sociology deals with what is common to all in a particular social context, and this would appear to leave the unique (and for us most interesting) parts of John beyond the pale of what a sociological approach can explain.[89] Yet there is a fallacy here. To assert that a particular author wrote a particular work in response to certain factors in his social context is a valid explanation of the overall content of that work, even though the details of his work and the

---

[87] Neyrey, *Ideology*, p.96.

[88] Cf. e.g. Philip J. Richter, 'Recent Sociological Approaches to the Study of the New Testament', *Religion* 14 (1984), 78 (also quoted in Holmberg, *Sociology*, pp. 4–5).

[89] John Milbank, *Theology and Social Theory. Beyond Secular Reason*, Oxford: Basil Blackwell, 1990, pp. 117–18.

way he expresses himself will be the result of his own individual character and personality, with the corollary that someone else in the same context would have addressed the same subject matter in a different way. Therefore, once we allow for the creativity of an individual or community as an important factor in the shape of a text, we may still seek a sociological explanation of why they wrote and of the general direction that their work took.[90]

Holmberg warns of the danger of circular reasoning in applying sociology to the New Testament. Discussing Meeks' article, 'The Man from Heaven in Johannine Sectarianism', he concludes that Meeks in fact uses a circular argument, beginning by reconstructing a specific social situation from a religious/theological text, and then proceeding to use this social setting to interpret the text. In his view, only the reverse procedure is legitimate, namely to begin with sociological data that is independent of the text and then to proceed inductively to determine whether and to what extent this sociological data 'fits' the text. [91]

Holmberg is clearly right to advocate the explicit use by New Testament scholars of already-existing sociological models, which may then be used to illuminate a text inasmuch as they seem applicable to it. However, his criticism of circular reasoning appears to be somewhat less valid. This is because, in attempting to interpret a text historically, scholars often have no choice but to seek to find clues as to the historical circumstances which gave rise to the text within the text itself, and from these to seek to reconstruct a plausible background for the text, attempting to find points of contact with what is known of the history of that time period from other texts or sources, on which basis it is hoped that other aspects of the text will also be capable of being better understood or explained. The goal of this process is to find a plausible reading of the text, which also does justice to, and relates the text to, what may be known of the period from other sources. Although there is a certain 'circularity' to this process, scholars will nonetheless need to continue using such approaches, while being

---

[90] Cf. Kysar, 'Pursuing the Paradoxes', p.204; James F. McGrath, 'Going up and coming down in Johannine legitimation', *Neotestamentica* 31/1 (1997), 107–18. See also D. Moody Smith, *Johannine Christianity. Essays on its Setting, Sources, and Theology*, Columbia: University of South Carolina Press, 1984, pp. 181–4; Marianne Meye Thompson, *The Humanity of Jesus in the Fourth Gospel*, Philadelphia: Fortress, 1988, p.123; and also our discussion earlier in this chapter.

[91] Holmberg, *Sociology*, p.127; Meeks, 'Man from Heaven'.

aware of the dangers and pitfalls which such attempts at historical reconstruction and sociological analysis encounter.[92]

A more significant criticism, and one that appears to have greater validity, comes again from Milbank. He notes, and criticizes, those recent sociological attempts to 'explain' a text which suggest that a sociological setting somehow existed prior to any religious beliefs, and that those religious beliefs were then 'built on top of' this pre-religious social setting in order to justify or explain it.[93] Explanations along these lines clearly do not correspond to reality, as those who are confronted with a change of social circumstances are also already part of some religious tradition or other.[94] Sociological explanations need to relate social and religious factors in a more holistic way, recognizing that the influence is dialectical rather than unidirectional. However, Meeks seems to be aware of this. In his aforementioned article he writes, 'I do not mean to say that the symbolic universe suggested by the Johannine literature is only the reflex or projection of the group's social situation. On the contrary, the Johannine dialogues suggest quite clearly that the order of development must have been dialectical . . . It is a case of continual, harmonic reinforcement between social experience and ideology.'[95] A sociological approach which is aware that there can be no ultimate distinction between 'society' and 'religion' as independent and unrelated spheres, and thus deals with what we might call 'socio-religious' phenomena, does not appear to be subject to the criticisms raised by Milbank.

Yet Meeks does not appear to answer the question raised in one of his later articles on Johannine Christology: 'What drove the Johannine Christians to make just these connections, in the face of the social pain that it obviously cost them?'[96] However,

---

[92] So rightly de Boer, *Johannine Perspectives*, p.45. See also the cautionary remarks voiced by Meeks and Elliott in Dale B. Martin, 'Social-Scientific Criticism', in Steven L. McKenzie and Stephen R. Haynes (eds.), *To Each Its Own Meaning. An Introduction to Biblical Criticisms and their Application*, Louisville: Westminster John Knox/ London: Geoffrey Chapman, 1993, p.108. See too Philip F. Esler, *The First Christians in their Social Worlds. Social-scientific approaches to New Testament interpretation*, London and New York: Routledge, 1994, pp. 12–13.

[93] Milbank, *Theology and Social Theory*, pp. 114, 117.

[94] Peter Berger, *The Sacred Canopy. Elements of a Sociological Theory of Religion*, New York: Doubleday, 1967, p.47; Esler, *First Christians*, p.10.

[95] Meeks, 'Man from Heaven', p.164.

[96] Wayne A. Meeks, 'Equal to God', in Robert T. Fortna and Beverly R. Gaventa (eds.), *The Conversation Continues. Studies in Paul and John in Honor of J. Louis Martyn*, Nashville: Abingdon, 1990, p.318.

he hints that here too social factors will be an important part of any explanation. Can the dialectic between ideology and social setting explain the earlier stages of the development of Johannine Christology as well? Holmberg thinks that it can, and that while social factors do not explain the origins of beliefs, they can explain the new uses to which beliefs and traditions are put, and the way that they are developed in the process. Holmberg considers it likely that the same beliefs were put to various different uses as early Christians formulated and maintained their social and symbolic worlds. He designates this the 'multifunctionality' of beliefs, and relates it to 'the dialectical use these central beliefs were put to. Probably many meanings evolved only when the social situation called for a new interpretation or deeper understanding of the faith that had already been transmitted and received.'[97]

The approach to be taken in this study

What is being hinted at by a number of the authors we have mentioned thus far is that the interplay between social factors and religious beliefs in the dialectical manner we have indicated can explain why religious beliefs develop and take on new forms. This suggestion needs to be taken seriously, since it appears to provide a way out of the longstanding stalemate between the History of Religions and organic models of development we have surveyed: an explanation which does not posit merely the influence of other ideologies on Christian doctrine, nor a simple, self-explanatory growth from seed to flower, but an interaction between belief and environment which calls forth apologetic responses, which involve and result in development in the very doctrines which are being defended.[98] In other words, a sociological approach is able to treat

[97] Holmberg, *Sociology*, p.138.
[98] Cf. McGrath, 'Change in Christology', 41–2. This is also hinted at in Hurtado, *One God*, pp. 122–3. It is somewhat ironic that Neyrey, *Christ is Community*, pp. 270–1 takes this view, and yet fails to find in it the key to an explanation of the development of Johannine Christology. See also Thomas M. Dowell, 'Jews and Christians in Conflict: Why the Fourth Gospel Changed the Synoptic Tradition', *Louvain Studies* 15 (1990), 19–37; 'Why John Rewrote the Synoptics', in Adelbert Denaux (ed.), *John and the Synoptics* (BETL, 101), Leuven: Leuven University Press, 1992, pp. 453–7 for a further move in this general direction, although presupposing direct use and redaction of the Synoptics by John. De Boer, *Johannine Perspectives*, only reached me after this book was essentially complete. It likewise represents a move in the direction of the approach adopted here; it is nonetheless felt that the

more fully developed doctrines precisely as developments of what was already there in the tradition, while also indicating an external stimulus that can be appealed to as an explanation of why development occurs. This is an intriguing suggestion, but in order to provide a plausible alternative approach to the Christology of the Fourth Gospel this suggestion will have to be validated by a sociological model.

The relevant model is to be found in the work of Berger and Luckmann in the area of the sociology of knowledge.[99] Berger and Luckmann begin their work by describing how a worldview is a social construction, a human creation that nevertheless, once it is in place, confronts the individual as something objective. The second chapter of their book discusses *legitimation*, which can be described as 'worldview maintenance', as this term refers to the ways in which worldviews are defended or reinforced in response to challenges from alternative understandings of the world, whether from other societies or from 'heretics' within the society itself. A deviant definition of reality challenges the legitimacy of a worldview, and legitimation is the procedure of maintaining and defending the plausibility of that worldview.[100]

To quote from the section of Berger and Luckmann's book most relevant for our current purposes,

> Historically, the problem of heresy has often been the first impetus for the systematic theoretical conceptualization of symbolic universes . . . As in all theorizing, new theoretical implications within the tradition itself appear in the course of this process, and the tradition itself is pushed beyond its original form in new conceptualizations . . . In other words, the symbolic universe is not only legitimated but

present work's explicit use of the model of legitimation, and our decision to trace the development of themes, motifs and ideas rather than that of the literary history of the Gospel, will allow for more secure conclusions.

[99] Peter Berger and Thomas Luckmann, *The Social Construction of Reality. A Treatise in the Sociology of Knowledge*, London: Allen Lane/Penguin, 1967; see also Berger, *Sacred Canopy*.

[100] The work of Berger and Luckmann has already been taken up by Esler for use in the study of Luke-Acts. On the use of models to explain data cf. Holmberg, *Sociology*, pp. 101–2; Philip F. Esler, *Community and Gospel in Luke-Acts* (SNTSMS, 57), Cambridge: Cambridge University Press, 1987, p.50. Esler's work testifies to the ability of such a model to provide an explanation of the specific emphases of a text.

also modified by the conceptual machineries to ward off the challenge of heretical groups within a society.[101]

Just as 'heretical' groups may stimulate legitimation within the parent group, so also the attacks and legitimating arguments of the parent may cause the new group to engage in legitimation of its own.

We may here present in outline form the model which Berger and Luckmann have formulated. Once we have done so, we may test its applicability by using it to consider another period of christological development in the Church's history. The legitimation model essentially proposes that conflict over ideas provokes the need for legitimation, and the process of legitimation causes those ideas to develop and be worked out in greater detail and intricacy. This may be outlined as follows:

Stage 1: Initial diversity

Berger and Luckmann refer to contact with external and/or internal groups that hold a different set of beliefs than the group being studied.[102] Both situations presuppose that a group is being confronted with an alternative worldview. In the case of external contact, the differences may be due to the development of cultures in geographical and linguistic isolation from one another for great lengths of time prior to the contact. In the case of internal contact the diversity will most likely be due to certain ambiguities in the tradition or worldview which is shared by both sub-groups, such as ambiguous aspects of the teaching of the community's founder or of the community's authoritative scriptures, which may then be interpreted in different ways by different individuals or groups within the society. The latter would obviously be applicable to the diversity of first-century Judaism, a diversity of which early Christianity was a part.

---

[101] Berger and Luckmann, *Social Construction*, p.125. The term 'heresy' here implies an alternative view of reality which arises from within a group and threatens the stability of its particular worldview.

[102] Berger and Luckmann, *Social Construction*, pp. 122–6. Wiles, *Making of Christian Doctrine*, p.19 also refers to the same two types of encounter, the challenge from within and from without.

Stage 2: Contact and conflict

However the two different worldviews, or interpretations of the same worldview, arose, once they come into contact with one another, the objective, 'taken for grantedness' of both sides' ideologies will be challenged. This will provoke a reaction of some sort from both sides, most likely in some form of conflict.

The contact between these different groups can come about in numerous different ways. In cases of external conflict, two main factors are migration of people groups and conquest by other nations. In cases of internal conflict, someone proposes a different interpretation of his or her own traditional worldview, which meets with acceptance from some within the community but rejection by others. In the case of post-70 Judaism in which John was written, the situation seems to have been one in which different parties and/ or 'sects', each with their own understanding of Judaism, had existed in tension with one another for quite a long time. Intense conflict arose when one of the various parties began to play a leading role in some local Jewish communities, and sought to exclude other interpretations of Judaism which were felt to threaten their own interpretation and their authority.

Stage 3: Legitimation

The aforementioned contact and conflict will necessitate some type of attempt at legitimation by both groups; i.e., the attempt will be made by each side to demonstrate the validity of their own view of reality over against that of their opponents. In the case of internal conflict, both sides will frequently seek to prove from their shared scriptures and traditions that they are the true preservers of their worldview and heritage. Watson sets out in three points his view of how a sect legitimates its split from its parent: (a) denunciation of the opponents, (b) antithesis (between us and them, believers and unbelievers, saved and unsaved), and (c) reinterpretation of the religious traditions of the parent community so that they apply exclusively to the sect.[103] These three aspects of legitimation seem to be equally valid in the conflict stage, prior to there being any kind of definitive 'split' between the two groups, although certain

---

[103] Francis Watson, *Paul, Judaism and the Gentiles. A Sociological Approach* (SNTSMS, 56), Cambridge: Cambridge University Press, 1986, p.40.

features (in particular antithesis) may be more marked in the wake of such a split or expulsion.

Whatever ideology or doctrine may be at the centre of the conflict, each group will need to engage in legitimation/apologetic for its view.[104] This legitimation will involve the drawing of analogies, the use of proof texts (and the finding of new proof texts, or the relating of authoritative texts to issues/situations to which they had not previously been applied), and other similar means of formulating supporting arguments. Such attempts to defend one's own view will also inevitably involve the thinking through more fully of the implications of beliefs already held, and will often cause earlier beliefs to be understood in new ways. To draw an analogy, just as when a building is reinforced substantial additions and changes are made to the structure under the guise of the defence or maintenance of the original building, so also attempts to reinforce or defend beliefs will result in additions to and developments of that belief.[105] Thus the end result will be a more fully developed ideology or doctrine, the existence of which could not necessarily have been foreseen prior to the conflict.[106] In the case of John's Gospel, we have the attempt of Jewish Christianity (or one strand thereof) to defend and define itself over against one or more other forms of Judaism. In fact, we appear to be dealing with a case of mutual interaction, as two groups defend and define their beliefs

[104] Esler, *Community and Gospel*, pp. 205–19 distinguishes more sharply than the present writer between *apologetic* (a defence of belief aimed at those outside the community with the intention of converting them) and *legitimation* (a defence of belief designed to reinforce the faith of those who already believe). The present author has not done so for several reasons. For instance, many works serve (and are intended to serve) both purposes. It also appears to be true that works of apologetic in Esler's sense are still read more often by those within the community than those outside, and thus in practice do more to legitimate the worldview of believers than to convert unbelievers. The arguments used in both types of work are in most instances the same or very similar, so that it often is difficult to discern the purpose of a document so precisely unless an explicit statement of purpose is made (that found in John 20.31 may be taken either way, depending partly on which reading is accepted as original). At any rate, both processes spur doctrinal development, as Wiles notes (*Making of Christian Doctrine*, p.19).

[105] Cf. McGrath, 'Change in Christology', 42 where we have used the same analogy.

[106] It is worth mentioning that, since 'legitimation' is a dynamic process, our use of the term will reflect this. In the specific case of John's Gospel, we see that legitimation *leads* to the development of Johannine beliefs, and yet the *outcome* of that development is itself a legitimation of earlier beliefs. 'Legitimation' can thus refer to the process of defending/developing, and to the defence/development produced by this process.

and identity over against one another. While there may have been a number of dialogue partners in view and a number of issues to which the author wished to respond, nevertheless the principal interlocutor appears to be the parent Jewish community, and it is the interaction with this group that will be the focus of the present study.

Before examining the Fourth Gospel in more detail from this perspective, we may illustrate this model through a consideration of the way in which this process can be seen to be at work in another period of the Church's history. A logical period to turn to is the period of doctrinal development in the first few centuries of the post-New Testament period, those which led to the formulation of the creeds, as this is actually an example to which Berger and Luckmann appeal in order to illustrate the legitimation process.

> For instance, the precise Christological formulations of the early church councils were necessitated not by the tradition itself but by the heretical challenges to it. As these formulations were elaborated, the tradition was maintained and expanded at the same time. Thus there emerged, among other innovations, a theoretical conception of the Trinity that was not only unnecessary but actually non-existent in the early Christian community.[107]

This same basic thesis has been put forward by Maurice Wiles as an explanation of doctrinal development in this period, albeit without the explicit use of sociological categories or models.[108]

Examples of conflict leading to doctrinal development abound. However, since our concern is primarily with Christology, we may turn to an example from this field to illustrate our model. We can see in the Logos concept in Judaism, and then in early Christianity which inherited it, an essential ambiguity. The Logos (or Wisdom) is presented as being none other than God himself in his interaction with the world, and yet also as separate from and subordinate to God.[109] Discussions of the subject were postponed by Irenaeus, who appealed to Scripture in order to argue that no human being could claim to understand the origins and 'generation' of the Logos (*Adv.Haer*.2.28.6). Others, however, were not satisfied with this approach, and two tendencies or emphases arose, one seeking to

---

[107] Berger and Luckmann, *Social Construction*, p.125.
[108] Wiles, *Making of Christian Doctrine*, p.19.
[109] Cf. Dunn, *Christology*, pp. 168–212, 215–47.

preserve monotheism by accentuating the subordination of the Logos, the other seeking to preserve both monotheism and the divinity of the Logos by emphasizing that the Logos is in fact none other than God. These two streams came into conflict, a conflict that came to a head in particular during the Arian controversy. This controversy has been aptly described as 'the search for the Christian doctrine of God', since there was as yet no definitive answer to the questions which had been raised, and both sides could and did appeal to tradition and Scripture in support of their views.[110] The Arians pointed to the language of Wisdom having been 'created', and of Jesus as the 'firstborn', whereas the Nicenes pointed to the fact that the Word was God, and that Christ was said to be 'before all things'. The most important point for our purposes is that both sides developed Christologies which went beyond anything that had previously existed, and that this was due largely to the fact that ambiguities in the Church's christological tradition led to conflict, which in turn instigated and necessitated doctrinal development.[111]

It thus appears that doctrinal formulations are frequently an attempt to define an aspect of one's beliefs in relation to the formulations or views of others. Apologetic and conflict may thus be said to provide one of the major stimuli to such development. And in this process of development, the possible directions are limited and determined by such factors as Scripture, tradition, worship and practice.[112] Thus, if we know something of the starting point and finishing point of a period in the Church's doctrinal development, as well as that during the period in question debates were taking place in connection with certain doctrines, the latter may legitimately be appealed to as the stimulus of the former, allowing one to understand why doctrine developed in the direction it did during that period of the Church's history.

We may briefly consider another example of the applicability of this model, taken from the period prior to the rise of Christianity, namely the Maccabean conflict and the developments surrounding it. There are a number of important documents stemming from this period, albeit from only one side of the conflict. Segal suggests that

---

[110] R. P. C. Hanson, *The Search for the Christian Doctrine of God: the Arian Controversy 318–381*, Edinburgh: T&T Clark, 1988.

[111] A much more detailed treatment of this subject may be found in Wiles, *Making of Christian Doctrine*, pp. 30–6 and *passim*.

[112] Ibid., p.162.

the parties involved in the conflict of this period were similar to the Orthodox and Reform Judaisms of today. One sought to make concessions to modernity in order to be relevant, by neglecting concern with what were considered not to be core elements of Judaism. The other felt that any concessions that involved neglecting commandments were a violation and denial of the covenant. Both viewpoints presumably appealed to Scripture in their defence, and both were emphasizing something that was there in the Scriptures. These two viewpoints came into conflict, perhaps also in connection with conflict over political authority. As the reform group came into power and sought to enforce its views, those who opposed their views rebelled. The elements neglected by the reformers were predominantly the laws in relation to circumcision, food and purity, and it is very likely because of this conflict that we find in Judaism, in the wake of this conflict, that these issues begin to feature as the key symbols of Jewish identity and faithfulness to the covenant. Ideology and religious belief and practice appear also in this instance to have been shaped and developed by conflict.[113]

We have now seen clear historical examples of the phenomenon which Berger and Luckmann describe in their work, and there can be little doubt that their overall thesis is applicable to the development of Christology in the early church. It will nonetheless be useful to present evidence supporting our contention that the model is equally applicable to the Gospel of John. To begin with, we may note that there is now a growing consensus that the Gospel of John reflects a conflict between certain Christians and the synagogue. There also seems to be sufficient evidence within the Gospel for us to be reasonably certain what was at stake in this conflict: Christology. Again and again, the question of belief in Jesus is raised, and frequently in the context of conflict: does being Moses' disciple prevent or encourage one to become Jesus' disciple? How dare the Johannine Christians claim divine prerogatives for Jesus? Such issues lie at the heart of the Gospel and of the conflict which gave rise to it. We shall consider the evidence for such a conflict more fully in the next chapter.[114]

Most scholars are moving towards a consensus on the broader

---

[113] Segal, *Rebecca's Children*, pp. 31–4. See also Hengel, *Judaism and Hellenism*, pp. 305–9.
[114] Dunn, *Partings*, pp. 222–3 points out the pre-eminence of these two issues, and they will form the focus of parts 2 and 3 of this book.

setting of this conflict, and relate it in some way to the attempt by certain post-70 rabbis to give a new impetus and programme to Judaism.[115] During this period, Judaism was seeking to find ways of coping with the destruction of the Temple and of nationalistic hopes, and many groups within pre-70 Judaism, in particular those whose identity was largely tied to the Temple, ceased to exist as distinct parties. The remaining groups each had different views and emphases on major issues, and in areas where the Pharisaic rabbis began to come into greater power, they set about promoting their understanding of Judaism, and excluding others who they felt threatened their authority and their ideology. It is in this context that the Johannine Christians most likely came into conflict with the leaders of their synagogue.[116] This is not, of course, to return to the idea of 'orthodoxy' which we have already seen is no longer tenable in reference to this period. Rather, we are speaking about a particular group, which has sufficient authority to do so in a particular area or community, attempting to exclude others who do not agree with their position, and to define and enforce their own position as normative. This is thus a continuation of the Jewish sectarian controversies that existed even in the pre-70 period.[117]

[115] Martyn's attempt to relate the Gospel of John directly to the council of Jamnia and more specifically to the *Birkat ha-Minim* has met with much criticism. This study does not presuppose any direct link with the actual council at Jamnia, but only that the Johannine Christians had been part of a Jewish community where Pharisaic rabbis had a sufficient degree of authority and power to exclude opponents from the local synagogue. For further on this issue see Wengst, *Bedrängte Gemeinde*, pp. 37–73; Wayne A. Meeks, 'Breaking Away: Three New Testament Pictures of Christianity's Separation from the Jewish Communities', in Jacob Neusner and Ernest S. Frerichs (eds.), *'To See Ourselves as Others See Us'. Christians, Jews, 'Others' in Late Antiquity*, Chico, CA: Scholars, 1985, pp. 94–104 (although Meeks too quickly discounts the references to 'the Pharisees' as traditional; in fact, John occasionally adds a reference to the Pharisees where such a reference is lacking in parallel passages in the other Gospels); Manns, *L'Evangile*, pp. 488–509; de Boer, *Johannine Perspectives*, p.69. For challenges to Martyn's reading of the evidence concerning the *Birkat ha-Minim* see especially Reuven Kimelman, 'Birkat Ha-Minim and the Lack of Evidence for an Anti-Christian Jewish Prayer in Late Antiquity', in E. P. Sanders, A. I. Baumgarten and Alan Mendelson (eds.), *Jewish and Christian Self-Definition. Volume Two. Aspects of Judaism in the Graeco-Roman Period*, London: SCM, 1981, pp. 226–44; Steven T. Katz, 'Issues in the Separation of Judaism and Christianity After 70 CE: A Reconsideration', *JBL* 103/1 (1984), 43–76; Robinson, *Priority*, pp. 72–81; Esler, *Community and Gospel*, p.55; Mark W. G. Stibbe, *John as Storyteller. Narrative Criticism and the Fourth Gospel* (SNTSMS, 73), Cambridge: Cambridge University Press, 1992, pp. 56–61.

[116] Cf. Painter, *Quest*, pp. 24, 29–30.

[117] Cf. Dunn, *Partings*, p.222; D. M. Smith, *Theology*, p.171. See also J. Andrew Overman, *Matthew's Gospel and Formative Judaism. The Social World of the Matthean Community*, Minneapolis: Fortress, 1990, pp. 38–43.

The relationship of the Johannine Christians to the first two stages in our model is much easier to determine than its relationship to the third stage. This is because in any attempt to reconstruct the process of development in the group's Christology in detail, theories and hypotheses will need to be advanced and discussed concerning the stages in the composition of the Gospel, and the relationship of the fully developed Johannine Christology to the Christology evidenced in earlier documents, as well as in earlier strata of the Gospel, where such can be delineated. It would be unwise in a study of this sort to tie our conclusions too closely to any particular source theory. A better methodology would appear to be an examination of the sorts of christological *motifs and imagery* which appear to have been the general inheritance of early Christianity. This is not to imply that the Gospel of John had direct, literary knowledge of the Pauline epistles or of the Synoptic Gospels, but simply that certain traditions about Jesus and christological imagery such as are preserved in these documents were known also to John. That this was the case does not appear to be in any way controversial, and we shall in each instance make a case for John's knowledge of the earlier tradition(s) in question.[118]

In attempting to relate the Fourth Gospel to this stage of our model, we have certain fixed factors that prevent us from wandering into unchecked speculation. First, we have the final form of the Gospel, which not only shows the result of the development,[119] but also apologetic arguments which may provide some clues as to the course of the controversy and the issues which were at stake. Texts frequently contain 'fossils' of earlier stages in the history of a group and its beliefs. We also have much evidence throughout the rest of the New Testament concerning earlier stages of Christology, which are important inasmuch as many of the motifs found therein

[118] See further the seminal study in this field, C. H. Dodd, *Historical Tradition in the Fourth Gospel*, Cambridge: Cambridge University Press, 1963, *passim*. It seems safest to assume for the purpose of this study that John did not make direct use of any other New Testament document. Those who are convinced that John made direct use of one or more of the written Synoptic Gospels will find it much easier to accept our arguments about John's dependence on certain earlier traditions. However, even if John did not know these works in their written form, he still shows an awareness of Synoptic type traditions, and thus our argument can stand independently of this other, rather controversial issue. On the relationship between John and Paul cf. Rudolf Bultmann, *Theology of the New Testament. Vol. II*, London: SCM, 1955, pp. 6–10.

[119] It would be unwise to refer to the Gospel as the *end* result, since development continued even after the Gospel was written.

appear in a more developed form in the Fourth Gospel.[120] Functions attributed to Jesus in earlier literature are often backed up and justified by a theoretical (in some instances one could perhaps almost say 'ontological') foundation when they appear in John. Whether or not earlier Christology can be related to the Johannine Christology by means of the model we have proposed can only be determined through careful exegesis, and this will be our concern throughout the rest of this study. For now, it is sufficient to point out that, even though we shall at times be moving from text to background and back again, we do have certain firm data in which our exploration is rooted.

Before proceeding, we may engage in some final 'legitimation' of the model we have chosen. In addition to its advantages in doing justice to the best aspects of other models of development, it also avoids the tendency in previous Johannine scholarship to regard the Johannine Christology as *either* the cause *or* the result of the Johannine Christians' expulsion from the synagogue. Once again, we are confronted with a situation where an either/or dichotomy will not do justice to the complexity of the situation.[121] The Johannine Christians already held christological beliefs when they first came into conflict with the leaders of their Jewish community; this conflict in turn provoked developments in their Christology, which provoked further conflict, and so on. It is obviously not new to suggest a link between Johannine Christology and conflict with the Jews, but the complexities of the process of this development merit further study, and an adequate model for tracing this development has long been required. The application of Berger and Luckmann's model to the subject at hand appears therefore to have the potential to clarify a number of methodological questions, and to fill in some of the gaps in our understanding of the process(es) which led to the formation of John's Christology.

Summary and aims

In this first chapter we have reviewed previous scholarship on Johannine christological development, and presented the model of legitimation and development that we shall be using to study John's Christology. The remainder of this study will be devoted to the

---

[120] Cf. our discussion of this point in some detail in the second half of ch.2 below.
[121] So rightly Painter, *Quest*, pp. 62–6, 70–1.

application of this sociological model to John's Gospel, through exegesis of specific texts in the light of the model of legitimation. A discussion of the entire Gospel in detail is impossible within the limited space of this study, and therefore an attempt has been made to choose for discussion texts which depict or reflect conflict between Jesus or the Johannine Christians on the one hand and 'the Jews' on the other, and which also contain important christological affirmations. A brief justification is provided at the start of each chapter for the inclusion of the text under discussion.

In the chapter which follows we shall present and consider the evidence in John that the Gospel has been influenced by conflict between Christians and non-Christian Jews, and also the points of similarity and difference between the motifs which are found in John and those found in earlier Christian writings. In part 2 (chapters 3–8) we shall seek to apply the model of legitimation to the question of the relationship between Jesus and God, and in part 3 (chapters 9–13), we shall consider the debate over the relationship between Jesus and Moses and their respective revelations. Throughout parts 2 and 3 we shall be seeking to determine in what ways the conflicts and debates in these areas stimulated the development of certain christological traditions and ideas, as the Evangelist made creative use of them in his defence of Christian beliefs. Chapter 14 will approach several other related issues in the same way. Chapter 15 will attempt to determine whether and to what extent the various developments that resulted from this process were integrated by the Evangelist into a unified and coherent portrait of Christ. Finally, the conclusion will seek to summarize our findings and draw together their implications and significance.

In order to demonstrate that we are correct in our initial hypothesis that John's distinctive christological developments are part of his work of legitimation, we shall need to establish several points in relation to the passages considered. First, we must show that there are indications that John is engaging in legitimation. In most of the passages we shall be examining there will be clear and explicit signs of this, such as the narrative following the form of objections being raised by 'the Jews' which the Johannine Jesus then directly addresses. In others, however, the indications are less explicit, such as the presence of polemical language and connections with themes that are used by John in his legitimation elsewhere in the Gospel. Second, we must show that the focus of the debate is on issues that are *pre*-Johannine. If the focus in the debates with 'the Jews' is on distinctively Johannine formulations, then we obviously cannot explain the emergence of those distinctive christo-logical ideas in terms of a phenomenon connected with the attempt to respond to objections raised to those very beliefs. If, on the other hand, we can demonstrate that the beliefs being disputed are *pre*-Johannine, then a case can be made that the distinctively Johannine elements are part of an attempt to respond to the objections raised to these earlier beliefs. Third, having shown that the beliefs which are the focus of controversy are essentially the same as beliefs current in earlier times, we must also present a case for the elements of the Johannine presentation of Christ under consideration being developments out of earlier beliefs, and we shall attempt to show that these distinctively Johannine developments are best under-stood as an attempt to respond to objections to Christian christo-logical beliefs in the ways we have outlined in the present chapter.[122]

Thus in outline form our aim is to:

(1)   provide evidence that the evangelist is engaging in legiti-mation.

(2)   provide evidence that the debate centres on beliefs which were part of the wider heritage of early Christianity, i.e. beliefs that are early Christian rather than distinctively Johannine.

(3)   show that the Evangelist's portrait of Christ in these contexts represents a development out of and based on earlier Christian beliefs (including, but not limited to, those included under point (2)).[123]

(4)   make a strong case that, in view of the evidence for controversy and legitimation, and the connections with earlier beliefs, the Evangelist is, in the passage in question,

[122]   It should be noted that, in view of the fact that we are focusing specifically on John's development of *christological* traditions, and that we are not assuming a direct knowledge by John of any other specific document, we will not, for the most part, be focusing on specific details which are different between, for example, John's account of an event and an apparently parallel narrative in the Synoptics. Rather, our focus will be on John's development of motifs and imagery. Obviously those who feel more certain about John's direct literary dependence on other New Testament writings will feel able to engage in socio-*redaction* criticism of John's Gospel to a fuller extent than we will be attempting to do in this study.

[123]   In which contexts frequent reference will be made back to the evidence which has been presented in ch.2.

attempting to defend certain beliefs, by engaging in legitimation in the ways we have outlined earlier. We shall argue that the combined evidence suggests that legitimation provides the key stimulus for, and thus the best explanation of, the course of development followed by Johannine Christology.

2

A CONFLICT SETTING AND A DISTINCTIVE CHRISTOLOGY: SETTING THE STAGE

The conflict setting

In recent scholarship it has become widely accepted that behind the Fourth Gospel lies a debate between a group of Christian Jews and the leaders of their local synagogue, the main focus of which was Christology. Some scholars have detected other conflicts, for instance with Docetists, Gnostics or followers of John the Baptist. However, this work will focus on the conflict between the Johannine Christians and their parent Jewish community, as the latter appears to be the main dialogue partner in view in the Fourth Gospel. It will be useful, before discussing our topic further, to survey some of the evidence for such a conflict.

We may take as our starting point the clearest evidence, namely the hostility and objections expressed by characters in the Fourth Gospel who function as opponents of Jesus. In John 5.16, reference is made to 'the Jews' persecuting Jesus, and in 5.18 we are told that they tried to kill him. The reason that is given for this antagonism is christological: he was 'making himself equal with God'. In John 6 we also find the group described as 'the Jews' 'grumbling' (verse 41) in response to Jesus' claim to have 'come down from heaven', and 'arguing among themselves' (verse 52) in response to Jesus' words about eating his flesh. Even his disciples found this teaching difficult, and many subsequently no longer followed him (6.60–1, 66). In 8.59 we are told of an attempt by 'the Jews' to stone Jesus, which is once again in response to a christological claim made by the Johannine Jesus, namely his application of the divine 'I am' to himself.[1] Similarly, in 10.31 we are told of another attempt by 'the

---

[1] That the divine name is in view in the absolute use of 'I am' in John is widely accepted. Cf. e.g. Hugo Odeberg, *The Fourth Gospel Interpreted in its Relation to Contemporaneous Religious Currents in Palestine and the Hellenistic-Oriental World*, Uppsala/Chicago: Argonaut, 1929, pp. 308–10; C. H. Dodd, *The Interpretation of*

Jews' to stone Jesus; here the reason which is given is a charge of blasphemy, the focus of which is once again christological: the charge is made that Jesus, a mere man, claims to be God. In 11.53 and 12.10–11 we are told of a plot on the part of the chief priests and the Sanhedrin to kill Jesus (see also 7.25).

Further evidence of conflict, and of the issues that were central to it, are to be found on the lips of the Johannine 'Jews'. The Pharisees disparage those who believe in Jesus, pointing out that none of the rulers or Pharisees has believed in him, but only 'this mob that knows nothing of the law' (7.48), who have been deceived (7.47), since the/a prophet does not come from Galilee (7.52). The Pharisees also challenge him because he bears witness to himself, and such testimony they consider invalid (8.13). We also hear of some among 'the crowd' saying that Jesus deceives the people (7.12) or that he is demon-possessed (7.20). 'The Jews' make a similar assertion in 8.48, 52, regarding Jesus as a demon-possessed Samaritan. That Christology is to the fore here as well is clear from the fact that they ask whether Jesus is greater than Abraham, and ask him, 'Who do you make yourself out to be?' (8.53). A similar emphasis is expressed in 10.20.

The Pharisees/'the Jews' are also presented as deciding to expel from the synagogue anyone who regards Jesus as the Messiah (9.22), because they regard Jesus as a sinner who does not keep the Sabbath (9.16). They class themselves as Moses' disciples rather than Jesus', because they know that God spoke to Moses, but do not know where Jesus is from (9.28–9). Here the issue of whether Jesus is a righteous man who is worthy to be listened to, or a sinner and a deceiver, is raised, as is that of how Jesus' teaching relates to Moses'. References to expulsion from the synagogue also appear in 12.42 and 16.2.

There are also other indications of a conflict setting, found either expressed in the words of the narrator or placed on the lips of the

the Fourth Gospel, Cambridge: Cambridge University Press, 1953, pp. 93–6; George R. Beasley-Murray, *John* (WBC, 36), Dallas: Word, 1987, p. 139; Francis J. Moloney, 'Johannine Theology', in Raymond E. Brown, Joseph A. Fitzmyer and Roland E. Murphy (eds.), *New Jerome Biblical Commentary*, London: Geoffrey Chapman, 1989, p. 1423; Pheme Perkins, 'The Gospel According to John', in Raymond E. Brown, Joseph A. Fitzmyer and Roland E. Murphy (eds.), *New Jerome Biblical Commentary*, London: Geoffrey Chapman, 1989, p. 948; Claudia J. Setzer, *Jewish Responses to Early Christians. History and Polemics, 30–150 C.E.*, Minneapolis: Fortress, 1994, pp. 84–5; D. A. Carson, *The Gospel According to John*, Leicester: IVP/ Grand Rapids: Eerdmans, 1991, p. 358. See also our discussion in ch.5 below and the works cited there.

Johannine Jesus. 'The Jews' are called children of the devil (8.44) and liars (8.55). Jesus warns his disciples that they will meet with persecution of various sorts (15.18–21, 25; 16.2–3). We may also note that everywhere Jesus goes, people are divided because of him (6.66–9; 7.12, 43; 9.16; 10.19–21; cf. also 1.5, 10–13). Language suggesting conflict also appears in the prologue, which sets the overall mood of the Gospel: there one finds light/darkness dualism (1.5), and reference to God's own creation and special nation not receiving the Logos (1.10–11). Opposition to Jewish claims concerning their special election or privileges may be in view in 1.13, 17–18. Imagery contrasting light and darkness, above and below, pervades the entire Gospel from beginning to end. The language of explicit or implicit polemic clearly abounds throughout the whole of the Fourth Gospel.[2]

In even the briefest of examinations of these passages, it becomes clear not only that a conflict is presupposed between Christians and the (leaders of the) synagogue, but also that the conflict focused primarily on the christological claims which were being made by Christians in relation to Jesus. This evidence suggests that Berger and Luckmann's model of legitimation, which we have discussed in chapter 1, has the potential to illuminate our understanding of the origins and development of Johannine Christology. However, before we attempt to use this sociological model to study the Fourth Gospel, it will be useful to set forth briefly here the main issues that appear to have been to the fore in the conflict.

(1)   Jesus and God

A key issue in John's Gospel is the question of the relationship of Jesus to God, and whether the exalted claims made for him are legitimate or not (5.18; 8.58–9; 10.32). What exactly is at issue will be clarified in the course of our treatment of this aspect of the conflict (part 2 below).

(2)   Jesus and Moses/Torah

We also find in John a debate about the relationship of Jesus to Moses, and the qualifications Jesus had to reveal things that Moses

---

[2] Further discussion of the Johannine polemical passages can be found in Whitacre, *Johannine Polemic*, pp. 5–119.

could not or did not reveal (1.17–18; 3.10–13; 5.37–40, 45–7; 6.32; 9.28–9). The accusation that Jesus is a 'sinner', who does not keep the Sabbath, also appears (5.16; 9.16). This last point is subsumed under this heading because it is ultimately about whether Jesus obeys Torah, and whether his teaching is in accordance with Torah.

(3) Jesus and other figures

The question of his relationship to Jacob (1.51; 4.12–13) and to Abraham (8.33–40, 53–8) is raised, as is his relationship to the Temple (2.19–21; 4.21–4) and other Jewish institutions and feasts (e.g., 2.6–11; 5.8–17; 7.37–8; 8.12). His relationship to John the Baptist is also an issue (1.6–8, 15, 20–34; 3.25–36; 10.40–2).

(4) The Messiahship of Jesus

The question of whether Jesus is the Messiah, i.e. of whether any christological understanding of Jesus is valid at all, is present in several places (1.41–2; 4.25–6, 29; 7.26–7, 31, 41–2; 9.22; 10.24). The idea of a crucified Messiah was also problematic to the Jews of John's time (12.34), as it presumably was even earlier.

It is possible that these issues were to the fore at different times in the community's history. However, in the present study we will not be attempting to separate redactional layers in the Fourth Gospel in any detail, although in the course of our study we shall note any evidence that may indicate whether these issues were the focus of controversy at the same time or successively. For the time being, however, it is sufficient to have set forth some of the evidence concerning the issues which were to the fore in the Johannine conflict situation, before moving on to seek to demonstrate that the distinctive Johannine development of the Christian tradition is the result of John's legitimation of the beliefs which he and his community held dear.

The distinctive features of Johannine Christology

It is also important, before proceeding further, to consider some of the major elements of the Gospel's Christology which are distinctively Johannine, and to mention aspects of similarity and difference between John's portrait of Jesus and that preserved in earlier Christian sources. We may then refer back to this section in our

discussion of the factors that appear to have provoked or stimulated the Johannine developments. Our focus in this work, as we
have already explained in the previous chapter, will be on the
question of whether the distinctive aspects of John's Christology
can be explained in terms of legitimation, i.e. the development by
the Evangelist of earlier traditions as part of an attempt to defend
his and his community's beliefs. It will therefore be important to
have in mind from the outset what some of the key distinctive
elements are in Johannine Christology, as well as some idea of how
they compare with earlier traditions and documents. Further
discussion of a number of the points made and texts referred to will
be provided later on in the book.

One further point needs to be made in the present context. Since
the present study focuses on John's development of earlier Christology, it is inevitable that some assumptions will be expressed
about the Christologies evidenced in earlier authors' works.
However, even if our provisional conclusions about earlier Christology prove unconvincing, this should only affect the *degree* of
development which John made. That is to say, our arguments
about *why* John developed earlier Christology can stand independently of the question of *how much* John developed earlier Christology. The remainder of this study will be devoted to an attempt to
explore the reasons why John made the developments that he did.
In the present chapter, we shall provide the groundwork for the rest
of our study, by noting the important distinctive features of the
Fourth Gospel's Christology and their character as a development
out of earlier Christology.

Jesus and Wisdom/Logos/Spirit

We may treat together the closely related themes of Wisdom, Word
and Spirit, because, as a number of scholars note, in early Judaism
these were essentially synonymous ways of speaking of God's
interaction with the world and with humankind.[3] The Fourth

---

[3] This point is made by Dunn, *Christology*, p. 266; Gottfried Schimanowski,
*Weisheit und Messias. Die jüdischen Voraussetzungen der urchristlichen Präexistenz-
christologie* (WUNT 2, 17), Tübingen: Mohr-Siebeck, 1985, pp. 75–7; Manns,
L'Evangile, p. 23; Martin Scott, *Sophia and the Johannine Jesus* (JSNTS, 71),
Sheffield: Sheffield Academic Press, 1992, p. 94; Charles H. Talbert, '"And the Word
Became Flesh": When?', in Abraham J. Malherbe and Wayne A. Meeks (eds.), *The
Future of Christology. Essays in Honor of Leander E. Keck*, Minneapolis: Fortress,
1993, pp. 45–6. The identity of Word and Wisdom is very likely ancient (cf. George

Evangelist was not the first Christian writer to present Jesus as speaking with the voice of Wisdom: compare Matthew's adaptation of the Q tradition in Matthew 11.19, 25–30; 23.34–9.[4] However, Matthew's portrait is not to be equated with that of John's in the way that Suggs suggests, when he writes that 'it would not greatly overstate the case to say that *for Matthew* Wisdom has "become flesh and dwelled among us" (John 1.14)'.[5] As Stanton points out, these features still play only a relatively minor role in Matthew, the presentation of Jesus as speaking with the voice of Wisdom occurring in only two or three passages in the whole Gospel.[6] France, who takes a similar view to Suggs, equally fails to do justice to the differences between Matthew and John. In discussing (and rejecting) Dunn's reading of these passages, he concedes that Matthew does not use the same sort of exalted language that Paul does, but asks 'how could he in a gospel?'[7] Yet it is precisely John's presentation of the earthly life of Jesus through the lens of the type of exalted Wisdom language that Paul uses, which immediately *distinguishes* John's *Gospel* from that of Matthew. It therefore seems necessary at the very least to further nuance Suggs' conclusion that Matthew presents Jesus as 'Sophia incarnate'.[8] In contrast

R. Beasley-Murray, 'The Mission of the Logos-Son', in F. Van Segbroeck, C. M. Tuckett, G. Van Belle and J. Verheyden (eds.), *The Four Gospels 1992. Festschrift Frans Neirynck. Volume 3* (BETL, 100), Leuven: Leuven University Press, 1992, p. 1866); see also Craig A. Evans, *Word and Glory. On the Exegetical and Theological Background of John's Prologue* (JSNTS, 89), Sheffield: Sheffield Academic Press, 1993, pp. 84–92 on the Wisdom background of John's prologue. On this point in relation to the second-century apologists cf. Robert M. Grant, *Gods and the One God*, Philadelphia: Westminster, 1986, p. 109. See also Hermas, *Sim.* 5.5–6; 9.1; Justin, 1 *Apol.* 33; Tertullian, *Adv. Prax.* 26–7; *Orat.* 1; *Adv. Marc.* 3.6; Tatian, *Oratio ad Graecos* 7.1; Theophilus, *Ad Autolycum* 2.10 (on these last two see also J. N. Sanders, *The Fourth Gospel in the Early Church. Its Origin and Influence on Christian Theology up to Irenaeus*, Cambridge: Cambridge University Press, 1943, pp. 26, 36). See too Irenaeus, *Adv. Haer.* 4.20, where Wisdom is identified with the Spirit while the Word is identified with the Son.

[4] On this aspect of Matthean Christology cf. Dunn, *Christology*, pp. 197–206. See also Brown, *Introduction*, p. 210.

[5] M. Jack Suggs, *Wisdom, Christology and Law in Matthew's Gospel*, Cambridge, MA: Harvard University Press, 1970, p. 57, empahsis added.

[6] Graham N. Stanton, 'The Origin and Purpose of Matthew's Gospel. Matthean Scholarship from 1945 to 1980', *ANRW* 2.25.3, Berlin: Walter de Gruyter, 1985, p. 1925. See also the fuller discussion in Marshall D. Johnson, 'Reflections on a Wisdom Approach to Matthew's Christology', *CBQ* 36 (1974), 44–64.

[7] France, *Matthew–Evangelist and Teacher*, p. 306 n.66.

[8] Suggs, *Wisdom*, p. 58. We have opted against using the categories of 'inspiration' and 'incarnation' to distinguish between pre-Johannine and Johannine Christology. Although there may be some truth in these categories, such terminology is at best anachronistic, and does not do justice to the blurriness of the line between the

with John, we do not find in Matthew a presentation of Jesus speaking as one who was conscious of having pre-existed and descended from heaven. The lack of any explicit reference to pre-existence is even more significant when one considers that Matthew shows evidence of having drawn on the portrait of the Son of Man in the Similitudes of Enoch.[9] As Brown writes, 'the most significant difference between John and the Synoptics . . . [is] . . . that the Johannine Jesus is clearly conscious of having pre-existed with God before the world began (17.5) and of having come into this world from that world of previous existence in order to say and do what he heard and saw when he was with God'.[10] Matthew has made a significant step in relation to Christian reflection on Christ and Wisdom, but John has taken one or more steps further, which distinguish his portrait from Matthew and other New Testament writers, in particular in the points we will now discuss.[11]

John's Wisdom or Logos Christology is expressed most fully in the prologue.[12] Although the Johannine prologue is often regarded as the fullest and loftiest expression of the Johannine 'high' Christology, the prologue actually has a great deal in common with earlier Christian use of Jewish Wisdom imagery, in particular with the hymnic passage found in Colossians 1.15–20, but also with other passages such as Hebrews 1.3. Thus Kysar describes John's use of Logos as 'a Johannine expression of a common theme of New Testament Christology'.[13] The distinctiveness of the Johan-

two (on which see further James D. G. Dunn, 'Incarnation', in David N. Freedman (ed.), *The Anchor Bible Dictionary Vol.III H–J*, New York: Doubleday, 1992, pp. 398–9).

[9] See our discussion of Son of Man immediately below.

[10] Brown, *Introduction*, p. 205. See also James D. G. Dunn, *Unity and Diversity in the New Testament. An Inquiry into the Character of Earliest Christianity*, London: SCM, 1990, p. 228.

[11] So also Dunn, 'Let John be John', pp. 321–2. On Wisdom Christology in Paul see now Dunn, *Theology of Paul*, pp. 267–81, 292–3.

[12] Lars Hartman, 'Johannine Jesus-Belief and Monotheism', in L. Hartman and B. Olsson (eds.), *Aspects of the Johannine Literature* (CB, 18), Uppsala, 1987, pp. 96–7.

[13] Robert Kysar, 'Christology and Controversy: The Contributions of the Prologue of the Gospel of John to New Testament Christology and their Historical Setting', *CTM* 5 (1978), 348. So also David L. Mealand, 'The Christology of the Fourth Gospel', *SJT* 31 (1978), 462–3; Peter T. O'Brien, *Colossians, Philemon*, Dallas: Word, 1982, p. 40; Richard R. Creech, 'Christology and Conflict: A Comparative Study of Two Central Themes in the Johannine Literature and the Apocalypse', PhD dissertation, Baylor University, 1984, p. 216; Dunn, 'Let John be John', pp. 315, 321; Carson, *John*, pp. 135–6; Ben Witherington III, *John's Wisdom. A Commentary on the Fourth Gospel*, Louisville: Westminster John Knox, 1995,

nine portrait is that this language is placed at the very start of the Gospel, indicating that the pre-existent state of the Logos is the lens through which the rest of the Gospel and the entire life of Jesus are to be viewed.[14] We may also note John's use of other imagery which, while connected with the Wisdom or Logos of God in Jewish tradition, is not used elsewhere in the New Testament, such as 'tabernacling', light and glory. At the very least, John has made an explicit identification between Jesus and God's Wisdom/Word to an extent that no earlier writer did.[15]

Likewise, we see that in all of the Gospels, Jesus is presented as one in whom God's Spirit dwelt. That John has taken a step beyond Matthew and the other Synoptics is indicated by the distinctive emphasis found in John 1.32: the Spirit did not just descend on or come to dwell in Jesus, but *remained* on him. The Fourth Evangelist regards the Spirit and Jesus not just as closely and dynamically related (as is clearly true even in the work of earlier writers), but as inseparable.[16]

p. 56. See too Brown, *Gospel*, pp. cxxiv–cxxv; Marinus de Jonge, 'Monotheism and Christology', in John Barclay and John Sweet (eds.), *Early Christian Thought in its Jewish Context*, Cambridge: Cambridge University Press, 1996, p. 235.

[14] C. K. Barrett, *The Gospel According to St. John. An Introduction with Commentary and Notes on the Greek Text*, London: SPCK (second edition), 1978, p. 156; Dunn, *Unity and Diversity*, pp. 227–8; 'Let John Be John', p. 313; 'Christology (NT)', in David N. Freedman (ed.), *The Anchor Bible Dictionary Vol.I, A–C*, New York: Doubleday, 1992, p. 987; Beasley-Murray, 'Mission', p. 1866; William R. G. Loader, *The Christology of the Fourth Gospel. Structure and Issues* (BET, 23), Frankfurt am Main: Peter Lang, 1992, p. 21. Thus although the designation Logos is never used again after 1.14, it nonetheless remains true that the prologue encapsulates the (or at least a) 'chief emphasis' of Johannine Christology (Dunn, 'Christology (NT)', p. 988). See further Michael E. Willett, *Wisdom Christology in the Fourth Gospel*, San Francisco: Mellen Research University Press, 1992.

[15] Cf. further Dunn, *Christology*, pp. 242–4. On Wisdom language in Hebrews see Mary Rose D'Angelo, *Moses in the Letter to the Hebrews* (SBLDS, 42), Missoula: Scholars, 1979, pp. 174, 177, although she does not appear to entirely do justice to the differences between the Christologies of John and Hebrews.

[16] On earlier moves in this direction which prepared the way for John's own distinctive contribution see Dunn, *Christology*, pp. 136–49, and also the criticisms of Dunn in Max M. B. Turner, 'The Spirit of Christ and "Divine" Christology', in Joel B. Green and Max Turner (eds.), *Jesus of Nazareth: Lord and Christ. Essays on the Historical Jesus and New Testament Christology*, Carlisle: Paternoster/ Grand Rapids: Eerdmans, 1994, pp. 413–36. To determine the exact *degree* to which John went beyond earlier writers would necessitate a detailed treatment of all earlier writers (as well as a clear determination of who was earlier, and how much earlier!) which cannot be undertaken in this context. On the possibility that 1.32 is a parallel description of the incarnation, see Reginald T. Fuller, 'The Incarnation in Historical Perspective', in W. Taylor Stevenson (ed.), *Theology and Culture. Essays in Honor of A. T. Mollegen and C. L. Stanley* (Anglican Theological Review Supplementary Series, 7), November 1976, pp. 61–6; Hartin, 'Community', 45; Piet Schoonenberg,

Jesus the Son of Man

The use of the designation ὁ υἱὸς τοῦ ἀνθρώπου in reference to Jesus is commonplace in the Synoptic Gospels; in John, however, it takes on new features, most notably the idea of pre-existence. The references in 3.13 and 6.62 to the Son of Man having come down from heaven are quite unlike anything else in the New Testament. Here too the Fourth Evangelist appears to be taking up an aspect of traditional Christian language, and developing it in a distinctive way.[17] Given the parallel and roughly contemporary developments which are attested in the Similitudes of Enoch and IV Ezra, it is quite likely that John is here inspired by, or making use of, a growing tendency to use the language of pre-existence in connection with the figure of the 'Son of Man'.[18]

John's distinctiveness can be seen more clearly when we compare his work with that of Matthew, who also seems to show knowledge of the Similitudes of Enoch, inasmuch as he presents Jesus as the Son of Man in his role of judgment 'sitting on his throne of

'A sapiential reading of John's Prologue: some reflection on views of Reginald Fuller and James Dunn', *Theology Digest* 33/4 (1986), 405, 416; Francis Watson, 'Is John's Christology Adoptionist?', in L. D. Hurst and N. T. Wright (eds.), *The Glory of Christ in the New Testament. Studies in Christology in Memory of G. B. Caird*, Oxford: Clarendon, 1987, pp. 113–24; Talbert, *Reading John*, pp. 74–7; 'And the Word Became Flesh'; James F. McGrath, 'Prologue as Legitimation: Christological Controversy and the Interpretation of John 1:1–18', *IBS* 19 (1997), 117–18; 'Johannine Christianity', 4–5. See also Brown, *Community*, pp. 152–3; Michael Theobald, 'Gott, Logos und Pneuma. "Trinitarische" Rede von Gott im Johannesevangelium', in Hans-Josef Klauck (ed.), *Monotheismus und Christologie. Zur Gottesfrage im Hellenistischen Judentum und im Urchristentum*, Freiberg: Herder, 1992, pp. 67–8. It is quite possible that in John, as in the early apologists, a clear distinction between God's Word and God's Spirit has not yet been made. See further n.3 above.

[17] Cf. Stephen S. Smalley, 'The Johannine Son of Man Sayings', *NTS* 15 (1968–9), 297–8; Dunn, *Christology*, p. 90; *Unity and Diversity*, pp. 221–3. See also John Painter, 'The Enigmatic Johannine Son of Man', in F. Van Segbroeck, C. M. Tuckett, G. Van Belle and J. Verheyden (eds.), *The Four Gospels 1992. Festschrift Frans Neirynck. Volume 3* (BETL, 100), Leuven: Leuven University Press, 1992, pp. 1870–2.

[18] Cf. 1 Enoch 48.2–3, 6; IV Ezra 12.32; 13.52; also Painter, 'Enigmatic', p. 1872. A direct knowledge of the Similitudes of Enoch is not impossible; Dunn (*Christology*, p. 78) notes John 5.27 and 1 En. 69.27 as a possible point of contact. This is not to suggest that 'the Son of Man' was a title, but simply that the Danielic 'human-like figure' was given a messianic interpretation in this period, as even Geza Vermes, *Jesus the Jew. A Historian's Reading of the Gospels*, London: Fontana/Collins, 1973, p. 175 and Douglas R. A. Hare, *The Son of Man Tradition*, Minneapolis: Fortress, 1990, pp. 11–12 recognize.

glory'.[19] Yet the focus in Matthew is on this eschatological role of the Son of Man as judge, and while Matthew may have been aware of the idea of pre-existence found in the Similitudes, he gives no clear indication that he intends the reader to interpret his own use of the designation in that way.[20] Nonetheless, pre-existence language is applied to Jesus in passages like Colossians 1.15–17, although not in connection with the designation 'Son of Man'.[21] At any rate, whether John was familiar with the application of pre-existence language to the Son of Man from Christian or Jewish circles, he appears to be the first person to have depicted the Son of Man on earth as being openly and consciously aware of having pre-existed in heaven. On this point John's distinctiveness seems indisputable. The evidence unfortunately does not provide us with an unambiguous answer to the question of to what extent John may have had a different understanding of pre-existence *itself*, and not merely of its *implications*, as over against earlier Jewish and Christian authors.

John also runs together the crucifixion and ascension/exaltation/glorification of the Son of Man, bringing the two ideas together under a single term, 'lifting up' (ὑψουν). In earlier literature, Jesus is thought of as having been crucified and as having been exalted to heaven, but the two are not combined in the way they are by John.[22] Nonetheless, the fact that there is a threefold passion prediction connected with the Son of Man in both Mark and John, taken together with John's use of the traditional language 'the Son of Man must', suggests that John's usage is a development out of the earlier, Synoptic-type tradition.[23]

---

[19] Cp. Matt. 19.28 and 25.31–2 with 1 Enoch 45.3; 55.4; 61.8; 62.5; 69.27. See also Dunn, *Christology*, pp. 77–8; A. J. B. Higgins, *Jesus and the Son of Man*, London: Lutterworth, 1964, pp. 107, 117. Higgins (p. 106) also notes the connection between Matt. 16.28 and 1 En. 62.5–7 inasmuch as both speak of the *kingdom* of the Son of Man.

[20] Dunn, *Christology*, p. 89.

[21] This passage and others like it have been the focus of much recent discussion. Cf. e.g. N. T. Wright, *The Climax of the Covenant. Christ and the Law in Pauline Theology*, Edinburgh: T&T Clark, 1991, pp. 114–18; Dunn, *Christology*, pp. 187–93; *Theology of Paul*, pp. 267–77.

[22] Cf. Smalley, 'Johannine Son of Man', 298.

[23] Mark 8.31; 9.12–31; 10.33–4; John 3.13–15; 8.28–9; 12.32–4. Cf. Rudolf Schnackenburg, *The Gospel According to St. John. Volume I*, London: Burns and Oates, 1968, p. 535; Moloney, *Johannine Son of Man*, pp. 215, 218; Pierre Létourneau, 'Le Quatrième Evangile et les Prédictions de la Passion dans les Evangiles Synoptiques', in Adelbert Denaux (ed.), *John and the Synoptics* (BETL, 101), Leuven: Leuven University Press, 1992, pp. 579–80. See further also Jane Schaberg, 'Daniel 7, 12 and the New Testament Passion-Resurrection Predictions', *NTS* 31 (1985), 217; Moloney, 'Johannine Theology', p. 1423; Rudolf Schnackenburg,

Before proceeding, mention may also be made here of the motif of Jesus as 'not of this world' and 'from above', which has been drawn to the attention of Johannine scholars in particular by the works of Meeks and Neyrey.[24] While this is clearly a Johannine distinctive (frequently understood to be projecting the community's sensation of a division between 'us and them', between a faithful minority and a hostile wider world, upon the Gospel's portrait of Jesus), it nonetheless reflects a type of dualism which is also present in other Jewish and Christian sources.[25] The Pauline doctrine of two ages, the heavenly/earthly contrasts in Hebrews, and even the Matthean logion about two roads/ways, offer an indication that John is once again unique not so much in the individual elements which make up his Christology, as in his emphasis on and development of motifs and imagery which are not entirely absent from earlier Christian writings.[26]

Jesus the prophet (like Moses)

Here too John makes use of a motif and imagery that is not uniquely his, and yet which he uses in his own distinctive way. Dale

---

'Synoptische und Johanneische Christologie. Ein Vergleich', in F. van Segbroeck, C. M. Tuckett, G. van Belle and J. Verheyden (eds.), *The Four Gospels 1992. Festschrift Frans Neirynck. Volume 3* (BETL, 100), Leuven: Leuven University Press, 1992, pp. 1744–5.

[24] Meeks, 'Man from Heaven'; Neyrey, *Ideology*.

[25] On the very striking and significant Qumran parallels cf. James H. Charlesworth, 'A Critical Comparison of the Dualism in 1 QS 3:13–4:26 and the "Dualism" Contained in the Gospel of John', pp. 89–103 and James L. Price, 'Light from Qumran on Some Aspects of Johannine Theology', pp. 18–25, both in James H. Charlesworth (ed.), *John and the Dead Sea Scrolls*, London: Geoffrey Chapman, 1972; also D. A. Fennema, 'Jesus and God According to John. An Analysis of the Fourth Gospel's Father/Son Christology', PhD dissertation, Duke University, 1979, pp. 59–67.

[26] Cf. Larry J. Kreitzer, 'Eschatology', in Gerald F. Hawthorne, Ralph P. Martin and Daniel G. Reid (eds.), *Dictionary of Paul and His Letters*, Leicester: IVP, 1993, pp. 254–5, 259–60 on the 'vertical' and 'horizontal' aspects of Pauline dualism and eschatology. See also J. F. Maile, 'Heaven, Heavenlies, Paradise', in Gerald F. Hawthorne, Ralph P. Martin and Daniel G. Reid (eds.), *Dictionary of Paul and His Letters*, Leicester: IVP, 1993, pp. 381–3. In Hebrews see e.g. Heb. 8.5; 9.23; 11.16; 12.22. On Matthew see especially Matt. 7.14; see also *Didache* 1–6. There are also allusions to a doctrine of two ages in Matthew: cf. e.g. 12.32; 24.14. This is of course a present/future dualism rather than a 'vertical' above/below dualism, but these two different emphases are at times found side by side in Jewish literature. On Johannine dualism see further the summary and discussion of recent scholarship in Robert Kysar, 'The Fourth Gospel. A Report on Recent Research', *ANRW* 2.25.3, Berlin: Walter de Gruyter, 1985, pp. 2451–2; Ashton, *Understanding*, pp. 205–37.

Allison has recently undertaken a fairly comprehensive survey of the Moses typology in the Gospel of Matthew. He notes, however, many examples of the influence of a Moses typology in Luke-Acts, John and many other writings of the New Testament and later Christian literature.[27] Already in Paul we find the covenants established through Jesus and Moses being compared and contrasted, and this theme also has a major part to play in the epistle to the Hebrews.[28] It is thus not true to regard this as a distinctively Johannine emphasis.[29] Nonetheless, in John the belief that Jesus is the 'prophet (like Moses)' is perhaps made more explicit than elsewhere in the New Testament.[30] There is also a focus on Jesus' signs, and on the acceptance or rejection of him by others, motifs that tie in with the portrait of Moses in the Jewish Scriptures.[31]

---

[27] Dale C. Allison, *The New Moses. A Matthean Typology*, Minneapolis, Fortress/Edinburgh: T&T Clark, 1993, pp. 99–100 on Luke-Acts; on Jewish traditions of Mosaic typology in relation to the Messiah see pp. 85–90.

[28] See e.g. 1 Cor. 10.2; 2 Cor. 3.7–11; Heb. 3.3–6; 7.12–14. The whole of Hebrews compares the old covenant with the new. On the Moses-Christ typology in Hebrews see especially D'Angelo, *Moses*.

[29] Cf. also Casey, *Jewish Prophet*, p. 68, who accepts that Jesus described himself as a prophet. On the portrait of Jesus as prophet in the various New Testament documents see Franz Schnider, *Jesus der Prophet*, Universitätsverlag Freiberg Schweiz/ Göttingen: Vandenhoeck & Ruprecht, 1973 (he deals with the theme of prophet like Moses in the Synoptic Gospels on pp. 89–101); Karl Hermann Schelkle, 'Jesus – Lehrer und Prophet', in Paul Hoffmann, N. Brox and W. Pesch (eds.), *Orientierung an Jesus. Zur Theologie der Synoptiker. Für Josef Schmid*, Freiberg: Herder, 1973, pp. 300–8.

[30] See e.g. John 1.21, 25, 45; 5.46; 6.14; 7.40, 52. See further Marie-Emile Boismard, *Le Prologue de Saint Jean*, Paris: Cerf, 1953, pp. 165–6; W. D. Davies, *The Setting of the Sermon on the Mount*, Cambridge: Cambridge University Press, 1964, p. 410; Schnider, *Jesus der Prophet*, pp. 191–230; Schnackenburg, 'Synoptische und Johanneische Christologie', pp. 1738–9; Marianne Meye Thompson, 'John, Gospel of', in Joel B. Green, Scot McKnight, I. Howard Marshall (eds.), *Dictionary of Jesus and the Gospels*, Leicester: IVP, 1992, p. 378; Brown, *Introduction*, pp. 210–13; D. M. Smith, *Theology*, pp. 125–6. It may be true to emphasize, as many commentators do, that for John Jesus is *more than* a prophet, but this does not appear to have moved John to regard the designation 'prophet' as one that is inappropriate for Jesus.

[31] Jesus is still presented as a teacher and 'rabbi' in John. See D. M. Smith, *Johannine Christianity*, pp. 177–8. Yet in contrast with the Synoptics, the 'teaching' which the Johannine Jesus does give is almost exclusively christological. On Moses typology in John see further Ashton, *Understanding*, pp. 277–8, 470–6; John W. Pryor, *John: Evangelist of the Covenant People*, Downers Grove, IL: IVP, 1992, pp. 117–24; D. M. Smith, *Theology*, pp. 108, 126. See also Boismard, *Prologue*, pp. 165–75. On the links between this topic and that which follows (agency), see further Meeks, *Prophet-King*, pp. 301–2; Evans, *Word and Glory*, pp. 135–44; Paul N. Anderson, *The Christology of the Fourth Gospel: Its Unity and Disunity in the Light of John 6* (WUNT 2, 78), Tübingen: Mohr-Siebeck, 1996, p. 175.

Jesus God's Son and agent

In pre-Johannine Christian documents, Jesus is frequently referred to as God's Son, and presented as his chief, ultimate and final/ eschatological agent or envoy. These two motifs may be treated together, since they are linked in both the Synoptic tradition and in John.[32] The key idea behind agency in the ancient world, and early Judaism in particular, is that the one sent is like the one who sent him. Statements to this effect are found outside the New Testament in Philo and the rabbinic literature, and also in non-Jewish sources.[33] They also occur in the New Testament, important examples from the Synoptics being Mark 9.37 and parallels; Matthew 15.24 and Luke 4.43. In John, many more examples of this language are to be found, but they still bear a close resemblance to their Synoptic counterparts (see esp. John 5.23; 6.38; 12.44–5; 13.20; 14.9; 15.23; also 3.34; 7.16; 8.26, 28–9, 42; 14.24).

Not only is the agent *sent* (a point to which we shall return below), but he also bears the authority of the sender and may act with the full authority of the sender. It is for this reason that Jesus can be presented as carrying out what were traditionally divine prerogatives, such as pronouncing sins forgiven (cf. Mark 2.5–10 and parallels; Luke 7.47–9 – the miracle in the former instance is given as a demonstration that God has indeed delegated his power and authority to Jesus). In John, the portrait is very similar to that of the Synoptics in many ways, but the things which Jesus is held to

[32] As e.g. in Mark 12.6; Matt. 11.27; cf. also 10.40; John 5.16–26; 6.44 and 10.36 (see also our discussions of sonship and agency in chs. 4 and 6 below). On the son as the father's agent *par excellence* in the ancient world cf. A. E. Harvey, *Constraints*, p. 161. See further Witherington, *John's Wisdom*, p. 141; also Schnackenburg, 'Synoptische und Johanneische Christologie', pp. 1738–43; Beasley-Murray, 'Mission', p. 1861; Ashton, *Studying John*, pp. 71–89. Jesus is also presented as God's agent in Paul, on which see Donald A. Hagner, 'Paul's Christology and Jewish Monotheism', in Marguerite Shuster and Richard A. Muller (eds.), *Perspectives on Christology: Essays in Honor of Paul K. Jewett*, Grand Rapids: Zondervan, 1991, pp. 20–5. On agency in relation to Christology in general cf. George Wesley Buchanan, 'Apostolic Christology', in K. H. Richards (ed.), *Society of Biblical Literature Seminar Papers 1986*, Atlanta: Scholars, 1986, pp. 172–82.

[33] See for example Philo, *Dec.* 119; *Ber.* 5.5; *Qidd.* 41b, 43a; *Hag.* 10b; *Naz.* 12b; *Baba Qamma* 113b; *Sifre* on Numbers 12.9; *y. Hag.* 76d. See further Meeks, *Prophet-King*, pp. 301–2; Harvey, *Constraints*, pp. 161–2; Peder Borgen, 'God's Agent in the Fourth Gospel', in John Ashton (ed.), *The Interpretation of John*, Philadelphia: Fortress/ London: SPCK, 1986, pp. 67–78; 'John and Hellenism', pp. 101–2, 120 n.22; Beasley-Murray, 'Mission', p. 1857; Margaret M. Mitchell, 'New Testament Envoys in the Context of Greco-Roman Diplomatic and Epistolary Conventions: The Example of Timothy and Titus', *JBL* 111/4 (1992), 644–61.

do as God's Son/agent are intensified. In John, Jesus is said to work on the Sabbath as God does, to judge and to give life to the dead, even eternal life. Although Jesus raises the dead in the Synoptics, and is expected as the eschatological judge, here these points are made much more strongly and emphatically, and the eschatological aspects are moved forward into the life of the earthly Jesus, so that already in the present his ministry brings about judgment and the reception of the gift of eternal life.[34] John's portrait of Jesus as God's agent is central to his Christology, and it is built on ideas that can be traced back much earlier.[35]

One key feature in connection with this motif, which we have already noted briefly but need to discuss further, is the idea of God *sending* his Son, a motif found in both the Synoptics and John, as well as in other New Testament documents.[36] In pre-Johannine

[34] On forgiveness of sins cp. John 20.23; see also 5.14; Mark 2.5–9 and pars.; Luke 7.48. On raising the dead cf. Mark 5.35–43; cp. John 11.11, where the euphemism 'sleep' (albeit a different, synonymous Greek word) is also used for death, in reference to someone Jesus is about to raise from the dead. For further discussion of Jesus as God's agent in John, see Meeks, *Prophet-King*, pp. 301–5; 'Divine Agent', pp. 54–60; J.-A. Bühner, *Der Gesandte und sein Weg im viertem Evangelium: Die kultur- und religionsgeschichtlichen Grundlagen der johanneischen Sendungschristologie sowie ihre traditionsgeschichtliche Entwicklung*, Tübingen: Mohr-Siebeck, 1977, pp. 59–72; Borgen, 'God's Agent'; Buchanan, 'Apostolic Christology', pp. 181–2; A. E. Harvey. 'Christ as Agent', in L. D. Hurst and N. T. Wright (eds.), *The Glory of Christ in the New Testament*, Oxford: Clarendon, 1987, pp. 239–50; Thompson, 'John', pp. 377–9; Pierre Létourneau, *Jésus, Fils de L'Homme et Fils de Dieu: Jean 2, 23–3, 36 et la double christologie johannique*, Montreal: Bellarmin/ Paris: Cerf, 1993, pp. 233–55. The difference in emphasis in the realm of eschatology is closely tied to the distinctives of Johannine Christology, but unfortunately space will not permit a discussion of this here.

[35] Cf. Anderson, *Christology*, p. 176; A. E. Harvey, 'Christ as Agent', p. 241. Kanagaraj, *'Mysticism'*, pp. 255–63 is right to draw attention to the limitations of agency as a *total* explanation of Johannine Christology. Nonetheless, many of the points which he makes apply to earthly agents, but not to heavenly agents/ personified divine attributes (cf. Fennema, 'Jesus and God', pp. 294–6). See further also A. E. Harvey, *Constraints*, pp. 162–3; E. P. Sanders, *Jesus and Judaism*, London: SCM, 1985, p. 240; John A. T. Robinson, 'The Last Tabu? The Self-Consciousness of Jesus', *Twelve More New Testament Studies*, London: SCM, 1984, pp. 155–70; Dunn, *Christology*, pp. 25–6; Witherington, *John's Wisdom*, p. 141.

[36] On John and the Synoptics cf. Schnackenburg, 'Synoptische und Johanneische Christologie', p. 1738; also Pryor, *John*, pp. 119–20. On this and other terminology which Paul and John share, not because of direct influence on one another, but as part of their common Christian heritage, see Bultmann, *Theology vol. II*, p. 7. See too Rudolf Schnackenburg, *Das Johannesevangelium. IV. Teil. Ergänzende Ausle-gungen und Exkurse*, Freiburg: Herder, 1984, p. 104–6; Hans Weder, 'L'asymétrie du salut. Réflections sur Jean 3, 14–21 dans le cadre de la theologie johannique', in Jean-Daniel Kaestli, Jean-Michel Poffet and Jean Zumstein (eds.), *La Communauté Johannique et son Histoire. La trajectoire de l'évangile de Jean aux deux premiers*

literature where Jesus is portrayed as God's agent, it is not explicitly stated that his sending is qualitatively different from that of other messengers whom God sent.[37] However, it may be that in John, where Jesus is presented as the incarnation of one who previously pre-existed with God, the context may demand that we think of the Son having been sent *from heaven*.[38] Yet there is at least some evidence to suggest that John may have distinguished between 'Son' as a designation of Jesus, the Logos incarnate, and other designations appropriate to refer to the pre-existent state of the Logos.[39] Thus, while it seems that John has intensified earlier portraits of Christ as God's agent, it is not clear how the sending of the human person Jesus relates to the sending of the Logos from heaven. The relationship between the various aspects of John's distinctive Christology is a problematic and difficult subject, which we will return to towards the end of our study (chapter 15 below). Nonetheless, for now we may note that the sending of the Son is a far more central element in the Johannine portrait of Christ than it is in any of the other New Testament documents that we have, and Loader rightly regards it as part of the 'central structure' of the Christology of the Fourth Gospel.[40]

Jesus as the Son who reveals the Father

The similarity between the so-called 'bolt from the Johannine blue' in the Synoptics (Matt. 11.27; Luke 10.22) and John's presentation of Jesus is well known. Loader emphasizes that this Synoptic passage foreshadows central emphases found in John and may even represent their point of origin.[41] Thus the language of sonship and

siècles, Geneva: Labor et Fides, 1990, p. 164; Hagner, 'Paul's Christology', p. 21; de Jonge, 'Monotheism', p. 235.

[37] Cf. Bühner, *Gesandte*, pp. 374–433; Thompson, 'John', p. 378.

[38] On the understanding of sending in the Synoptics see Brown, *Introduction*, p. 205. Schnackenburg, *Johannesevangelium IV*, pp. 104–8 interprets the Pauline sending motif in terms of pre-existence, but in fact there is nothing in Paul (and perhaps not in John either) which explicitly links the designation 'Son of God' with pre-existence.

[39] See especially W. H. Cadman, *The Open Heaven. The Revelation of God in the Johannine Sayings of Jesus*, Oxford: Blackwell, 1969, pp. 11–13; also Dunn, *Partings*, pp. 228–9.

[40] William R. G. Loader, 'The Central Structure of Johannine Christology', *NTS* 30 (1984), 189–91; *Christology*, pp. 30–2.

[41] Loader, 'Central Structure', 204. See also Painter, *Quest*, p. 65; Maurits Sabbe, *Studia Neotestamentica. Collected Essays* (BETL, 98), Leuven: Leuven University Press, 1991, p. 407; Adelbert Denaux, 'The Q-Logion Mt 11, 27/Lk 10, 22 and the

even of revelation, while central in John, is not entirely absent from earlier Christian writings.[42] And while there is much more focus on the 'I' of Jesus in John, this is presumably because his role as God's agent and representative has become a more central concern.[43] Nevertheless, John's Gospel, as Barrett has emphasized, is focused on the Father, and on Jesus because he makes the Father known; it is theocentric as much as christocentric.[44] Here, as in the other aspects of Johannine Christology we have considered, a feature of earlier Christology appears in the Fourth Gospel in a much more fully developed form, and plays a far more central role in the overall portrait of Christ than it did in earlier writings.[45]

Jesus the bearer of the divine name

The bearing of the divine name by Jesus is connected with a number of the motifs we have already surveyed: divine agency, the exaltation of the Son of Man, and perhaps even with Moses typology.[46] There is clear evidence in Philippians 2.6–11 that the belief that Jesus bore the divine name is significantly earlier than John.[47] The author of this hymn is clearly applying to Christ an

Gospel of John', in A. Denaux (ed.), *John and the Synoptics* (BETL, 101), Leuven: Leuven University Press, 1992, pp. 187–8; Schnackenburg, 'Synoptische und Johanneische Christologie', pp. 1740–1.

[42] Moloney, 'Johannine Theology', p. 1422.

[43] Cf. Dunn, *Partings*, p. 314 n.58.

[44] C. K. Barrett, 'Christocentric or Theocentric? Observations on the Theological Method of the Fourth Gospel', *Essays on John*, London: SPCK, 1982, pp. 1–18; likewise Moloney, 'Johannine Theology', p. 1420; Loader, *Christology*, p. 171; see also Dunn, *Partings*, p. 314 n.56, for a comparison of the frequency of the designation 'Father' for God in the Synoptics and John. This topic was also addressed by Marianne Meye Thompson in her paper 'The Neglected Factor in Johannine Theology', presented at the 1997 SNTS conference in Birmingham.

[45] Cf. Loader, 'Central Structure', 190; *Christology*, pp. 32–3; Painter, *Quest*, p. 65; Sabbe, *Studia*, p. 407; Denaux, 'Q-Logion', pp. 187–8. On the earlier history of, and other issues relating to, the Q logion Matt. 11.27/Luke 10.22, see also S. Légasse, 'Le logion sur le Fils révélateur (Mt., XI, 27 par. Lc., X, 22): Essai d'analyse prérédactionnelle', in J. Coppens (ed.), *La Notion biblique de Dieu: Le Dieu de la Bible et le Dieu des philosophes* (BETL, 41), Leuven: Leuven University Press, 1976, pp. 245–74.

[46] There are numerous references in the Samaritan literature to Moses having been vested with the divine name. These can be conveniently found in Fossum, *Name of God*, pp. 87–94. See also Meeks, 'Moses as God and King', pp. 359–61.

[47] It is generally accepted that the 'name above every name' is the name of God. Cf. e.g. George Howard, 'Phil 2:6–11 and the Human Christ', *CBQ* 40 (1978), 381–6; Wright, *Climax*, pp. 93–4; Dunn, *Partings*, pp. 189–90; Hagner, 'Paul's Christology', pp. 25–6. Note also Heb. 1.4, 8, where, however, the name that is in mind may be 'Son' rather than 'Lord'.

acclamation that was, in Isaiah 45.23, attributed to God.[48] What is distinctive in John among the New Testament literature is the conviction that Jesus bore that name not as a result of his exaltation (which in John simply reveals what was already the case, namely that Jesus is 'I am'), but even during his earthly life.[49]

As the detailed study by Hurtado has shown, first-century Jewish monotheism had room for exalted figures who functioned as divine envoys or agents, and these figures could even bear the divine name.[50] Thus Paul's description of the exalted Christ in these terms need not indicate a departure from Jewish monotheism.[51] The safeguarding affirmation, 'to the glory of God the Father', made clear that Jesus' exalted lordship was not to be understood as detracting in any way from monotheism or from the glory due only to God himself.[52] For this reason we do not find Paul engaged in controversy over such exalted christological affirmations.[53] Such views did become controversial at a later stage, and in John we see controversy developing in precisely this area and in relation to precisely these concepts. We shall consider precisely what was controversial between John and his opponents in the chapters that follow. For the present, it will be sufficient to note that, in earlier Christian writings at least, such ideas were apparently not felt to be a threat to monotheism or other such key aspects of Jewish tradition and belief, and were regarded by Christians as an appropriate language to use in response to the unique eschatological action of God in and through Christ for the salvation of his people Israel and of all humankind. John's portrait of Jesus as one who

[48] Wright, *Climax*, pp. 93–4. Cf. also Dunn, *Partings*, pp. 190; 'Christology as an Aspect of Theology', in Abraham J. Malherbe and Wayne A. Meeks (eds.), *The Future of Christology. Essays in Honor of Leander E. Keck*, Minneapolis: Fortress, 1993, p. 205.

[49] See our discussion of John 8.28 below, ch. 5.

[50] Hurtado, *One God*, *passim*. See also the conclusion drawn by Alexander, 'Partings', pp. 19–20. Cf. the angel Yaoel in *Apoc. Abr.* 10.3–17. In later literature cf. the Samaritan work Memar Marqah 1.1, 3, 9, 12; 2.12; 4.7; 5.4; 6.6; 3 Enoch 12.5. The origin of this tradition is to be found in Exod. 23.21.

[51] Cf. Wright, *Climax*, p. 94.

[52] This is not to say that the author was even consciously aware that his christological affirmation could be in any way problematic. Nevertheless, the fact that this final statement was added may suggest that, if only at a subconscious level, the author wanted to make sure no misinterpretation of his striking language would ensue, perhaps in particular by Gentile readers. See also Kreitzer, *Jesus and God*, pp. 160–1; Steenburg, 'Worship', 100–1.

[53] Dunn, *Partings*, pp. 191, 205–6; see also G. B. Caird, *Paul's Letters from Prison*, Oxford: Clarendon, 1976, p. 124.

bears the divine name is best regarded as a development of earlier traditions of this sort.[54]

Jesus as God

The question whether Christians prior to John applied the designation 'God' (θεός) to Jesus is difficult to answer. Hebrews clearly does so (1.8), but the date of this work is uncertain.[55] The correct translation of 2 Peter 1.1 and Titus 2.13 is at best uncertain.[56] Similar ambiguity plagues almost all occurrences, but most scholars conclude that instances such as 2 Thessalonians 1.12 and Colossians 2.2 do not intend to refer to Jesus as 'God'.[57] That the Synoptics do not do so is clear, and if anything they distinguish clearly between Jesus and God.[58] Romans 9.5 is probably the only passage in the Pauline corpus for which a strong case can be made on grammatical grounds that Jesus is referred to as 'God'.[59] Nevertheless even here there is ambiguity. At least some early copyists,

---

[54] See further Apoc.Abr. 19.1–5, which makes clear that this author (who also engaged in speculation about a being who bears the divine name) was a monotheist. That the Samaritan version of this idea was understood to be monotheistic is clear from passages like Memar Marqah 4.7. For John as a first-century Jewish monotheist see ch. 3 below.

[55] This is the only non-Johannine occurrence which Brown regards as a clear and unambiguous use of θεός as a designation for Jesus (*Introduction*, pp. 185–7). So also Oscar Cullmann, *The Christology of the New Testament*, London: SCM, 1959, p. 310. On the significance of the application of the designation 'God' to Christ in Hebrews 1–2, see L. D. Hurst, 'The Christology of Hebrews 1 and 2', in L. D. Hurst and N. T. Wright (eds.), *The Glory of Christ in the New Testament. Studies in Christology in Memory of G. B. Caird*, Oxford: Clarendon, 1987, pp. 151–64; Murray J. Harris, *Jesus as God. The New Testament Use of Theos in Reference to Jesus*, Grand Rapids: Baker, 1992, pp. 200–2. D'Angelo's attempt (*Moses*, pp. 165–6, 186) to read Hebrews 3 as attributing to the Son the role of creator seems unlikely to be correct (cf. the preferable exegesis of Donald Guthrie, *Hebrews*, Leicester: IVP, 1983, p. 100; F. F. Bruce, *The Epistle to the Hebrews*, Grand Rapids: Eerdmans, 1990, pp. 92–3), and also fails to acknowledge the wider usage of the designation θεός in this period (cf. Hurst, 'Christology'; Harris, *Jesus as God*, pp. 200–2). She seems to be reading Hebrews' use of Wisdom/Logos imagery and ideas in light of John's use, but it is by no means clear that Hebrews represents a viewpoint as developed as John's (*contra* D'Angelo, *Moses*, p. 11).

[56] Although on the latter cf. Dunn, 'Christology as an Aspect of Theology', p. 206.

[57] Donald Guthrie, *New Testament Theology*, Leicester: IVP, 1981, p. 340; Harris, *Jesus as God*, pp. 263–6.

[58] Brown, *Introduction*, pp. 174–5. See also Cullmann, *Christology*, p. 308.

[59] Bruce M. Metzger, 'The Punctuation of Rom. 9:5', in Barnabas Lindars and Stephen S. Smalley (eds.), *Christ and Spirit in the New Testament*, Cambridge: Cambridge University Press, 1973, pp. 95–112. See also Cullmann, *Christology*, pp. 312–13; Dunn, *Partings*, p. 203; Harris, *Jesus as God*, p. 154.

when adding punctuation to this text, understood it *not* to be calling Christ God. In addition, many scholars feel that Paul, who elsewhere distinguishes between God and Christ, would not here break from his usual pattern.[60]

Yet even if it is allowed that Paul, like Hebrews and John later on, did call Jesus 'God', this does not immediately answer the question of what he might have meant by doing so. Even in the Jewish Christianity of later times, the use of the designation 'God' in reference to Jesus was accepted, provided this was understood in a broader sense current in Judaism which was not felt to conflict with monotheism.[61] We also have evidence in Jewish sources for the belief that Moses was exalted to the position of 'God and king', and that Adam, as the image of God, was regarded as functioning as God's agent and thus 'as God' over the earth.[62] It may thus be in this broader sense that Paul applies the term to Christ, if he does so at all. This would be consonant with his emphasis on Christ as the Last Adam, as well as with the contrast made between the glory of the covenant which came through Moses and that which came through Christ (as e.g. in 2 Cor. 3.7–18). It is interesting to note that, in the only instance where John hints that the application of the designation 'God' to Christ may have been an issue (10.33–5), an appeal is made to this broader use of the term 'God'.[63]

It is thus not clear whether the use of 'God' in reference to Christ is a Johannine innovation, nor whether Paul or any other writer before John's time applies the designation to Christ in anything more than this broader sense. The question of whether John's usage

[60] On this passage see further James D. G. Dunn, *Romans 9–16* (WBC, 38B), Dallas: Word, 1988, pp. 528–9; *Partings*, pp. 203–4; *Theology of Paul*, pp. 255–7. On all of these passages see also A. E. Harvey, *Constraints*, pp. 157, 176–8.

[61] Cf. Dunn, *Christology*, p. 45; 'Christology (NT)', p. 984. See also Harvey, *Constraints*, pp. 166, 172; 'Christ as Agent', pp. 249–50 and Thompson, 'John', p. 377, who suggest that the origins of the application of θεός to Jesus may perhaps be tied to the idea of Jesus as God's supreme agent or representative. On later Jewish Christianity see e.g. Ps.-Clem. *Recognitions* 2.41–2. See also McGrath, 'Johannine Christianity', 6.

[62] Meeks, 'Moses as God and King', is the main study of this theme in relation to Moses. See further Bruce D. Chilton, 'Typologies of memra and the fourth Gospel', in Paul V. M. Flesher (ed.), *Targum Studies. Volume One: Textual and Contextual Studies in the Pentateuchal Targums*, Atlanta: Scholars, 1992, p. 101, and also Philo, *Sac.* 9; *Quod Omn. Prob.* 43; *Som.* 2.189; *Mos.* 1.158; *Quaest in Ex.* 2.29. On Adam see Philo, *Op.* 83–84, 148; Sir. 49.16; 2 Enoch 31.3; 58.3–4; *Life of Adam and Eve* 11–16; *Apoc. Mos.* 20–21. See also *Gen. Rab.* 8.

[63] See our discussion below, ch. 6. In other places it is claiming the *status* of God, and not the *title*, that is at issue. See also Thompson, 'John', p. 377; de Jonge, 'Monotheism', p. 236.

marks a development beyond an earlier usage is also confronted with a further difficulty, namely the textual variants in John 1.18.[64] Nonetheless it seems certain that the risen Christ is called 'God' in 20.28; that Jesus is understood as the incarnation of the Logos who is God is also clear.[65] Further discussion of what use and developments of earlier tradition John may have made will have to await our fuller treatment below. For the present we may simply note that 'the Jews' in John are adamantly opposed to claims for Jesus which seem to attribute to him an equal *status* to God, but nowhere is the issue of *calling* Jesus 'God' explicitly raised, although it may be implied.[66]

Conclusion

As D. M. Smith rightly concludes, the major features of John's Christology are not completely absent from other early Christian literature. What is unique about John is the way that all these earlier ideas and perspectives are taken up and woven into a single narrative, in which each element remains continuously present at almost every stage throughout the story.[67] We shall have the opportunity to consider not only the ways that John has developed individual motifs in forming his distinctive Christology, but also the distinctive way he has related these various elements to one another, in the course of our discussion below. But for now, it is sufficient that we have shown through our rather brief survey that the Fourth Evangelist's key christological ideas are not entirely different from the motifs and imagery of other early Christian writers, and yet also that John has developed and used these elements of his Christian heritage in a distinctive way. In John, we

[64] On this passage, and particularly the text-critical discussion, see B. A. Mastin, 'A Neglected Feature of the Christology of the Fourth Gospel', *NTS* 22 (1975), 37–41; Margaret Davies, *Rhetoric and Reference in the Fourth Gospel* (JSNTS, 69), Sheffield: Sheffield Academic Press, 1992, pp. 123–4; Harris, *Jesus as God*, pp. 73–92; Bart D. Ehrman, *The Orthodox Corruption of Scripture. The Effect of Early Christological Controversy on the Text of the New Testament*, Oxford: Oxford University Press, 1993, pp. 78–82.

[65] See further Brown, *Introduction*, p. 188; Harris, *Jesus as God*, pp. 106–29. In 1.18 the risen and exalted Christ is probably in view – see our discussion in McGrath, 'Prologue', 106–8 and in ch.7 below.

[66] Cf. our further discussion of John 10.22–39 in ch. 6 below.

[67] D. M. Smith, *Johannine Christianity*, p. 187. See also Mealand, 'Christology', 466; Dunn, 'Let John Be John', pp. 321–2; Schnackenburg, 'Synoptische und Johanneische Christologie', pp. 1749–50.

have to do justice both to the continuity with tradition and to the uniquely Johannine developments of that tradition.[68] It is to the subject of *why* John developed the tradition in precisely the way that he did that we now turn. Our aim, as already stated, will be to attempt to trace the connections between issues in the conflict on the one hand, and developments in Christology on the other, to determine whether John's distinctive developments are part of his attempt to legitimate his community's beliefs about Jesus in response to objections which had been raised.

[68] Dunn, 'Let John be John', p. 321; see also his 'Christology (NT)', p. 987.

Part 2

JESUS AND GOD

3

ARE THERE 'TWO POWERS' IN JOHN?

In this second part of the book, we shall be focusing our attention on four key sections of the Gospel of John which concern the relationship between Jesus and God: the prologue and chapters 5, 8 and 10. However, before proceeding to our treatment of this theme, we need to consider one particular issue relating to the Jewish background that is often posited for these Johannine controversy passages. There has been a tendency in recent scholarship to read the Fourth Gospel in light of the evidence in rabbinic literature concerning heretics who claimed that 'there are two powers in heaven'.[1] This has been a helpful contribution, inasmuch as it has highlighted the fact that Johannine Christianity should be regarded as part of a much wider stream of *Jewish* thought which later orthodoxy excluded from its definition of Judaism. Alan Segal's study of this topic has shown that the ideas which the later rabbis polemicized against and rejected were probably widespread in first-century Judaism. However, he moves too quickly from the justified conclusion that the ideas were widespread in the New Testament period, to the much more hypothetical conclusion that the ideas were *already considered heretical* in the first century.[2]

Segal refers to a number of dialogues and discussions in the

[1] So e.g. Segal, *Two Powers*, p. 262; Meeks, 'Equal to God', p. 312; Dunn, *Partings*, pp. 224, 229; *Theology of Paul*, p. 253; Ashton, *Understanding*, pp. 144–6; Gaston, 'Lobsters', p. 122. See also Hurtado, *One God*, pp. 1–2, who relates this issue even to pre-Johannine Christianity; Jack T. Sanders, *Schismatics, Sectarians, Dissidents, Deviants. The First One Hundred Years of Jewish–Christian Relations*, London: SCM, 1993, pp. 65–6, who is more cautious than many, but still accepts much of Segal's case; Kanagaraj, *'Mysticism'*, pp. 147–9; de Jonge, 'Monotheism', p. 236 n.9. For a more detailed treatment of this topic and of many of the points made here, see my forthcoming study on this subject, co-authored with Jerry Truex.

[2] Segal also appears to assume that there was an orthodoxy in Judaism to make such a distinction (Alan F. Segal, *The Other Judaisms of Late Antiquity* (BJS, 127), Atlanta: Scholars, 1987, p. 17). We have already discussed the problems which such a view encounters (above, pp. 10–11, 14).

rabbinic literature which are attributed to tannaitic rabbis, as evidence of the views held during this period. However, there is apparently *no passage whatsoever* in the Mishnah that Segal could cite as mentioning the 'two powers' heresy. This is particularly striking in view of the fact that the Talmudim contain references to 'two powers' in places where the Mishnaic passage being commented on does not.[3] Similarly the Tosefta, composed *c.*220–300 CE, while it makes a number of references to Christians as *minim* ('heretics'), contains no explicit mention of 'two powers'.[4] All of the other sources that are cited by Segal are generally accepted to be later than the Mishnah and Tosefta, in some cases much, much later.[5] Of course, we are not attempting to deny that traditions found in later texts may nonetheless be much older than the written document in which they are found. However, complete silence on a particular *controversy* in earlier documents is often a reliable indicator that the topic or issue in question was not known or was not of particular importance in the earlier period. Thus, while the fact that a particular *exegetical tradition*, for example, is not mentioned earlier does not necessarily indicate that it is not in fact earlier, the fact that a particular *controversy* or *conflict* is not mentioned at all probably suggests that the controversy had not yet arisen, since heresy necessitates a response.[6] It therefore seems reasonable to expect controversies to leave some form of literary evidence of their existence in the literature of the period in question. And as there is no clear trace of the problem of 'two powers heresy' in the Mishnah or Tosefta, whereas there is in the rabbinic writings which date from later in the third century and thereafter, it seems most likely that this controversy arose in the third century, or perhaps the very late second century at the earliest. At the very least, it is, in view of the evidence, problematic to *assume* that this controversy provides the context of conflict in which the Gospel of John, and/or the material contained therein, was formed.

[3] Cf. Segal, *Two Powers*, pp. 98–9 for a clear example of this. Mishnah Sanhedrin 4.5 refers to some who say 'there are many ruling powers in heaven', but the context and the belief system referred to sound like polytheism, or perhaps Gnosticism. The reference is at any rate not to 'two powers in heaven'.

[4] Cf. George Foot Moore, *Judaism in the First Centuries of the Christian Era. The Age of the Tannaim. Volume I*, Cambridge, MA: Harvard University Press, 1927, p. 365 n.2, who notes that most debates with Christians about the unity of God are associated with rabbis from the third century.

[5] Cf. Günter Stemberger, *Introduction to the Talmud and Midrash*, Edinburgh: T&T Clark, 1996 on the dating of specific sources.

[6] Cf. Berger and Luckmann, *Social Construction*, pp. 123–34.

We may thus reiterate what a number of scholars have recently emphasized: a century was just as long in the ancient world as it is today, and for this reason it is simply unjustified to assume that what was controversial in the third and subsequent centuries was controversial in the first century. Thus, in much the same way that one would be cautious of reading the Synoptics in light of John, much less in light of the council of Nicaea, so one must be cautious of reading first-century sources in light of the views held by the rabbis of the third and subsequent centuries. It is thus to be stressed that there is *no evidence* from rabbinic sources that views such as those held by Philo and John were considered heretical or even objectionable in the first century – if anything, they are so widely attested as to appear to have been *normative* rather than 'heretical' in Judaism during this period.[7] Similarly, it should be stressed again that proving that views which were later deemed heretical *existed* in the first century is not to demonstrate that they were *already deemed heretical* then.[8]

Perhaps the closest that we can come to the period of the conflict reflected in John is in a discussion attributed to R. Akiba. In a Talmudic passage which purports to recount a debate between Akiba and R. Yosi the Galilean (*b.* Hag. 14a), Akiba interprets the plural thrones in Daniel 7.9 as 'one for God and one for David (i.e. for the Messiah)'. This interpretation is rejected by R. Yosi as

[7] Of course, *b.* Hag 15a dates the origins of 'two powers' to the apostasy of Aher in the first half of the second century, but as Segal admits, this is a late addition to the Babylonian Talmud (*Two Powers*, p. 60). See further L. Ginzberg, 'Elisha ben Abuyah', *Jewish Encyclopaedia* V (1903), p. 138; John Bowker, *The Targums and Rabbinic Literature. An Introduction to Jewish Interpretations of Scripture*, Cambridge: Cambridge University Press, 1969, p. 149; David J. Halperin, *The Merkabah in Rabbinic Literature*, New Haven: American Oriental Society, 1980, pp. 75–6; Ithamar Gruenwald, *From Apocalypticism to Gnosticism* (BEATJ, 14), Frankfurt am Main: Peter Lang, 1988, pp. 229–30, 242. Even if this tradition were reliable (which seems unlikely, as there are older accounts of Aher's apostasy which do not mention two powers), this would still give us a date in the second century, not the first. On the many intermediary figures and personified divine attributes found in Jewish literature in this period see especially Hurtado, *One God*; also Hengel, *Studies in Early Christology*, pp. 367–8; Bernard Lang, *Sacred Games: A History of Christian Worship*, New Haven and London: Yale University Press, 1997, pp. 107–8.

[8] Cf. Segal, *Two Powers*, pp. 27–8, 119–20, 173, 192, 260; Philip S. Alexander, 'Rabbinic Judaism and the New Testament', *ZNW* 74 (1983), 237–46; Gruenwald, *Apocalypticism*, p. 230 for cautionary remarks concerning dating and methodology. See too James D. G. Dunn, 'Was Christianity a Monotheistic Faith from the Beginning?', *SJT* 35 (1982), 322, and in relation to another set of later writings see Ashton, *Understanding*, pp. 295, whose remarks are equally applicable in the present context.

'profaning the Shekinah'.[9] The Synoptic Gospels appear to confirm that the interpretation of Daniel 7.9 in terms of the Messiah was already controversial prior to John's time, since, in their accounts of the trial of Jesus before the Sanhedrin, they portray the Jewish leaders as finding Jesus' affirmation concerning the 'Son of Man' objectionable and 'blasphemy'.[10] It is possible that the idea of a human being *sitting* enthroned in heaven was felt to be dangerous by some even at a fairly early stage.[11] However, there is no clear evidence that ideas such as Logos were felt to be unacceptable.[12]

[9] Dunn also notes that this is probably the earliest stratum of the material relating to the controversy (*Partings*, p. 224).

[10] Cf. Craig A. Evans, *Jesus and His Contemporaries. Comparative Studies* (AGAJU, 25), Leiden: Brill, 1995, pp. 210–11. That 'blasphemy' is not a category which first-century Jews associated exclusively with threats to monotheism is clear from Philo (*Spec. Leg.* 1.53) and Josephus (*Ant.* 4.207), who use the term in reference to insulting even the 'so-called gods' of the Gentiles. See further Darrell L. Bock, 'The Son of Man Seated at God's Right Hand and the Debate over Jesus' "Blasphemy"', in Joel B. Green and Max Turner (eds.), *Jesus of Nazareth: Lord and Christ. Essays on the Historical Jesus and New Testament Christology*, Grand Rapids: Eerdmans, 1994, pp. 184–5; Evans, *Jesus*, pp. 409–11; also A. E. Harvey, *Constraints*, pp. 170–1.

[11] On a human figure sitting in heaven as a recurring focus of debate see Bock, 'Son of Man', p. 189; Gruenwald, *Apocalypticism*, p. 238; see also below (esp. chs.7–8). It may in fact very well be the case that even sitting enthroned in heaven was not problematic in and of itself in this period (cf. the claims made in Ezekiel the Tragedian, *Exagoge* 68–86; 4Q427, 4Q491), but only when it was claimed of an apparently failed Messiah, both Jesus and Bar Kochba having been put to death by the Romans for their messianic claims. This is perhaps supported by Acts 7.56–7 (cf. 6.11), where even the vision of the Son of Man *standing* at God's side provokes Stephen's accusers to stone him. It would then be the attribution of an exalted status to a *particular type of figure*, rather than the exalted status *per se*, that is problematic. Given the difficulty scholars have had in determining exactly what was 'blasphemous' about the claims made by Jesus in the Synoptics (cf. E. P. Sanders, *Jewish Law*, pp. 60–7), we can do little more in this context than note three possibilities: (1) the claim to sit in heaven may have been blasphemous *per se*; (2) the claim may have been blasphemous when made for a failed Messiah; (3) the claim may have been blasphemous when claimed for oneself, but not when granted by God. There does not appear to be sufficient evidence to come down decisively in favour of one of these options.

[12] Even in later times many of the ideas that were supposedly 'heretical' are accepted without controversy by Jews. Cf. Justin Martyr's *Dialogue with Trypho*, 56, 60, where one of his interlocutors agrees from the outset that there is a 'second god', and Trypho is soon convinced as well. See also *b*. Sanh. 38b, which purports to recount a dialogue between R. Idi and a heretic – in the dialogue it is the rabbi and not the heretic who asserts the existence of Metatron. It was apparently not belief in any sort of heavenly viceroy that was controversial even in later times, but a particular type of belief about that figure. Cf. J. T. Sanders, *Schismatics*, pp. 93–4, who is unusual in recognizing that much of what has traditionally been felt to have been blasphemous in John was in fact not so when considered in the context of the Judaism of the time. However, he does insufficient justice to the fact that Messiah-

Their unacceptability in later times may have resulted from the fact that Christians made use of such ideas to support their position. We need to distinguish between ideas which were objectionable because they gave too much honour to a mere human being, and ideas which were objectionable because they were felt actually to involve a rejection of, or departure from, monotheism. There is no evidence that R. Akiba was felt to have departed from monotheism, however much his affirmation about the Messiah (whom he identified with Bar Kochba, which may have been part of the problem!) was felt to 'profane the Shekinah'.[13]

Other evidence suggests that the controversy within rabbinic Judaism about Logos and divine mediators in general may have been part of a more widespread philosophical discussion which arose in the third century not only for Jews, but for Christians as well. The issue that arose in this later period was where the line should be drawn which distinguishes the Creator from creation. In a recent paper, Frances Young has pointed out that there was a common cosmology accepted by nearly all, whether pagans, Jews or Christians, right through until at least the second century. The clearest evidence is perhaps the statement made by Maximus of Tyre in the second century CE: 'In spite of all this dissension [on other matters] one finds in the whole world a unanimous opinion and doctrine that there is one God, the king and father of everything, and many gods, God's co-regents. So says the Greek, so the barbarian.'[14] There was

ship would have been controversial in this period, not perhaps for theological reasons, but for its potential to create nationalistic fervour and thereby tension with the Roman authorities. Also, in the nationalism of the period between 70 and 135 CE the claim that a man who had threatened the Temple and been crucified by the Romans was the Messiah may have been particularly repugnant.

[13] Cf. Evans, *Jesus*, p. 208. Segal assumes (*Two Powers*, p. 49) that to assert in relation to an angelic figure what Akiba asserts concerning the Messiah would be even more offensive, but this is not necessarily the case. The passage in question makes equal sense as a reaction to a statement that is felt to give honour to the Messiah of which no human being is worthy. It also appears to be the case that things could be said about ancient biblical characters which many would be unwilling to say about a living, present-day figure. There is thus a 'psychological' aspect to this question that requires further study. It should also be mentioned that the attribution to Akiba of the view that Bar Kochba was the Messiah occurs only in significantly later writings. However, this is probably due to the situation immediately after the failed revolt, when it would have been advantageous for a number of reasons not to record facts of this sort. That Akiba's view was suppressed in earlier literature seems more likely than that later writers attributed this mistaken view to Akiba for no apparent reason.

[14] *Diss.* 11.5 (quoted Martin P. Nilsson, 'The High God and the Mediator', *HTR* 56/2 (1963), 106).

apparently widespread agreement that there was what might be termed a 'hierarchy of being', with God at the top, his Logos or powers next, then various divine or angelic beings, then humans, and so on.[15] Philo could therefore speak of the Logos as 'neither being uncreated as God, nor yet created as you, but being in the midst between these two extremities' (*Quis Her.* 206) and be understood, because it had not yet become necessary to draw a clear and unambiguous line separating creature and Creator. Or better, we should say that the Logos was the dividing line, overlapping or blurring into both sides. The boundary between God and creation was thus more like a river than a wall, inasmuch as the edges were not clearly defined while the existence of a distinction was nonetheless felt to be clear. The aforementioned ambiguity ('neither created nor uncreated') was an essential part of this cosmology.[16]

For most first-century Jews, the distinguishing factor between the one true God and other 'gods' and heavenly beings was apparently *worship*. Jews had a similar cosmology to other peoples and religions in their day, but offered cultic worship only to the high God, to the one God who was the source of all other beings and above all others.[17] Other figures who were not worshipped, whether

[15] Cf. Frances Young, 'Christology and Creation: Towards an Hermeneutic of Patristic Christology', paper read at the conference *The Myriad Christ*, Catholic University of Leuven, 21 November 1997 (forthcoming in BETL); Hurtado, 'First-Century Jewish Monotheism', pp. 365–7; also R. McL. Wilson, *The Gnostic Problem. A Study of the Relations between Hellenistic Judaism and the Gnostic Heresy*, London: Mowbray, 1958, pp. 36, 41, 46, 184; Grant, *Gods*, pp. 91, 157–8; Dunn, *Theology of Paul*, pp. 33–5; Lang, *Sacred Games*, pp. 107–8.

[16] See further Andrew Louth, *The Origins of the Christian Mystical Tradition. From Plato to Denys*, Oxford: Clarendon, 1981, pp. 75–7. On the lack of any 'gap' between God and creation in Philo see F. Gerald Downing, 'Ontological Asymmetry in Philo and Christological Realism in Paul, Hebrews and John', *JTS* 41/2 (October 1990), 423–40. Thus rather than speaking of Revelation placing Jesus 'on the divine side of the line which monotheism must draw between God and creatures' (Bauckham, 'Apocalyptic Christianity', 335), it is better to say that the close association of Jesus with the activity and worship of God in early Christianity was influential in determining, when such a line was eventually drawn, which side of the line Jesus would be placed on. The 'line' seems to have been drawn by Christians in the period leading up to the Arian controversy, when the doctrine of *creatio ex nihilo* developed (cf. Louth, *Origins*, pp. 75–6; Gerhard May, *Creatio ex Nihilo. The Doctrine of 'Creation out of Nothing' in Early Christian Thought*, Edinburgh: T&T Clark, 1994; Young, 'Christology and Creation'), and the Arian controversy was a debate precisely about on which side of the line the Son should be placed. Unfortunately space prevents further discussion of this topic here.

[17] Hurtado, 'First-Century Jewish Monotheism', pp. 360–5. See also Bauckham, 'Apocalyptic Christianity', 322, 324; Peter Hayman, 'Monotheism – A Misused Word in Jewish Studies?', *JJS* 42 (1991), 15; Barclay, *Jews*, pp. 429–32. By cultic worship we have in mind the sacrificial worship of the Temple; see further our

angelic messengers or personified divine attributes, could share in the sovereignty of God and perform divine acts as extensions of the sovereignty and activity of the one God.[18] This is significant for our study, as the focus in John (as we shall see below) is not the worship of Jesus, but Jesus' participation in the activity usually reserved for the one God.[19] Since other figures clearly could be regarded as legitimately carrying out such functions in what we know of first-century Judaism from the surviving literature, it may be necessary to rethink what exactly was at issue in John.

Without going into too much detail at this point, our research suggests that the Johannine conflict with 'the Jews' over Christology was not about Jesus performing divine functions *per se*. If Jesus was God's appointed, subordinate, obedient agent, then he could clearly do such things legitimately. The problem is that 'the Jews' do not recognize Jesus as God's agent. In their view, he is an upstart, one of a number of messianic pretenders and glory-seekers to appear on the scene during this period of Jewish history. If Jesus is the Messiah, then his actions are legitimate, because he is God's agent: this helps explain why John continues to summarize the key focus of his Christology in terms of belief that Jesus is the Messiah or Christ, even when he is discussing issues relating to Jesus' exercise of divine prerogatives and functions.[20] John's aim is to

discussion above, pp. 24–6. For later Christians, it was still frequently sacrificial worship that was the make or break issue of their identity and of the distinctiveness of their worship, even though they themselves did not practise sacrificial worship of their own God: cf. e.g. *Mart. Pol.* 8.2; *Acta S. Iustini* 5; Pliny, *Ep.* 10.96.5; see also the *libelli* which have survived from the persecution of Decius.

[18] Hurtado, 'First-Century Jewish Monotheism', p. 360. See also Christopher Rowland, *Christian Origins. An Account of the Setting and Character of the Most Important Messianic Sect of Judaism*, London: SPCK, 1985, p. 38; Markus Bockmuehl, *This Jesus: Martyr, Lord, Messiah*, Edinburgh: T&T Clark, 1994, p. 159.

[19] The 'worship' of Jesus is only mentioned in John 9.38, where it is mentioned in passing and provokes no controversy. The meaning is presumably the broader one of prostrating oneself before someone else, which is used of Jesus frequently (and without provoking controversy) in Matthew (see our discussion in ch.1 above). Thus against Martyn, *History*, pp. 72, 75, 78, it appears to have been *how* one worships rather than *whom* one worships that was at issue between the Johannine Christians and their Jewish opponents, a point rightly made by Marianne Meye Thompson in her lecture 'Reflections on Worship in the Gospel of John. The 1997–98 Alexander Thompson Lecture' given at Princeton Theological Seminary on 16 March 1998.

[20] Cf. Dodd, *Interpretation*, pp. 228–9; John A. T. Robinson, 'The Destination and Purpose of St. John's Gospel', *NTS* 6 (1959–60), 122–3; Pryor, *John*, pp. 133–5. That John has completely reinterpreted 'Christ' so that for him it carries little of its original Jewish connotations and instead signifies the developed Johannine Christology is argued by many (e.g. Francis J. Moloney, 'The Fourth Gospel's Presentation of Jesus as "The Christ" and J. A. T. Robinson's Redating', *Downside*

demonstrate that the behaviour and characteristics of Jesus are those of an obedient son and agent. Jesus does not seek his own glory, but that of the one who sent him. John is seeking to respond to Jewish objections by highlighting the aspects of Jesus' person and work which make clear that he is God's agent and sent one. The issue is therefore not 'equality with God' *per se*, but whether Jesus *makes himself* equal to God.[21] God could appoint agents, who would represent him and bear his full authority (examples include Moses, the judges and various principal angelic figures). It was only when someone who had not been appointed by God tried to put himself on a par with God (like Adam, Pharaoh or the king of Babylon in the Jewish Scriptures) that equality with God became problematic and even blasphemous; and it was into this latter category that 'the Jews' placed Jesus.[22] This will hopefully become clearer as we progress through our study. For the moment, it is sufficient to state that, in our view, the Johannine conflict with 'the

Review 95 (1977), 239–53; Segal, *Rebecca's Children*, p. 156; Dunn, 'Let John be John', pp. 303–5; Ashton, *Understanding*, p. 245; Loader, *Christology*, p. 213). However, one must do justice to John's choice of 'Messiah/Christ' to sum up his Christology at key points (most notably 20.31). See also the discussions in Painter, *Quest*, pp. 9–31; D. M. Smith, *Theology*, pp. 85–96. De Boer, *Johannine Perspectives*, pp. 66–7 rightly emphasizes that the *Messiahship* of Jesus was the issue that led to the expulsion of the Johannine Christians, although he continues to regard the issue which led to death threats as monotheism and the perception that the Johannine Christians worshipped 'two gods'.

If Jewish tradition is even remotely accurate, the Jamnian rabbis were allowed to meet there precisely because R. Yohanan was opposed to the Jewish revolt and 'a friend of Caesar' (cf. *b.* Git. 56ab; Abot R. Nat. A ch.4; see also Frédéric Manns, *John and Jamnia: How the Break Occurred Between Jews and Christians c. 80–100 A.D.*, Jerusalem: Franciscan, 1988, pp. 9–13). Josephus' success in the post-war period is described in similar terms (cf. e.g. *War* 3.400–404). It thus seems that in the post-70 period the rabbis may have been particularly cautious of any movements centred on messianic figures (cf. John 11.48). On the other hand, there is some evidence for an increase in messianic fervour in the post-70 period (cf. Joseph Klausner, *The Messianic Idea in Israel from Its Beginning to the Completion of the Mishnah*, London: George Allen and Unwin, 1956, pp. 396–8), in which context the belief that someone who was remembered for having threatened the Temple and having been executed by the Romans was the Messiah may have been understandably unpopular. It is true that John seeks to reinterpret Messiahship, but so do the Synoptics (see ch.13 below), and many aspects of John's distinctive portrait were in our view developed as part of the Evangelist's attempt to defend, among other things, his belief that Jesus was the Messiah.

[21] See Brown, *Community*, p. 47 n.80; Meeks, 'Equal to God', p. 310; Ashton, *Studying John*, p. 72; and ch.4 below.

[22] Cf. Beasley-Murray, *John*, p. 75; also Meeks, 'Divine Agent', p. 50. In a sense, the debate is about which of two kinds of 'equality' applies in the case of Jesus: the functional equivalence of a subordinate, obedient agent, or the self-appointed equality of hubris and rebelliousness.

Jews' did not concern a supposed abandonment of Jewish monotheism on the part of the Johannine Christians.[23] The Fourth Gospel never mentions the oneness of God in a polemical manner, and affirms it on one or two occasions in passing (John 17.3; also 5.44). Rather, the issue is whether Jesus is an agent carrying out God's will and purposes, or a blasphemer who is seeking glory and power for himself in a manner that detracts from the glory due to the only God. In the remainder of part 2 we shall seek to show that the issue in the relevant controversy material, rather than being about the oneness of God or monotheism, is consistently about whether Jesus is the Messiah, and about whether he '*makes himself God*' or '*makes himself equal to God*' (John 5.18; 10.33; cf. 8.53). John's development of Logos and other such ideas and motifs, we shall argue, represents the result of this conflict rather than its cause, part of John's attempt to show the legitimacy of the beliefs which Jewish opponents were calling into question.

[23] *Contra* Martyn, 'Glimpses', p. 162; *History*, p. 72; Brown, *Community*, p. 47; Dunn, 'Was Christianity a Monotheistic Faith', 330; 'Let John be John', pp. 316, 318–19; *Partings*, pp. 228–9; Loader, *Christology*, pp. 168, 228; D. M. Smith, *Theology*, p. 133. Although we disagree with Fennema, 'Jesus and God', p. 268 that the issue was *monotheism per se*, we nonetheless concur wholeheartedly that the reason that 'the Jews' found Jesus' claims blasphemous was their refusal to accept that he is God's agent. It must be admitted that even the present author previously accepted the scholarly consensus that monotheism was at issue in the Johannine conflict – cf. McGrath, 'Prologue', 105.

4

GOD'S EQUAL OR GOD'S AGENT? (JOHN 5)

John chapter 5 provides a natural starting point for an examination of Johannine Christology in relation to legitimation, as in this chapter one finds numerous indications both of some of the points at issue in the christological controversy, and of the ways the Fourth Evangelist sought to respond to them. Under the guise of 'the Jews', the contemporary opponents of the Johannine Christians are allowed to raise their objections.[1] As Loader points out, the accusations brought in this chapter 'are doubtless . . . real accusations hurled at the Johannine community by Jewish critics'.[2] The Johannine Jesus then provides a response to these Jewish objections, a defence or legitimation of Christology. These features have led a number of scholars to see an apologetic thrust here: the beliefs of the community are being 'put on trial' by Jewish objectors, and what is being mounted here is a defence of their understanding of Jesus, which is coupled with a denunciation of their opponents' unbelief (5.37–47).[3] There is much to support the conclusion that the whole passage (John 5.19–47) represents one of

[1] Cf. Lindars, *Gospel of John*, p. 219; Martyn, 'Glimpses', p. 162; *History*, p. 123; L. Th. Witkamp, 'The Use of Traditions in John 5:1–18', *JSNT* 25 (1985), 33; Meeks, 'Equal to God', p. 309; Loader, *Christology*, p. 161. This is not to say that this is a symbolic portrayal of an actual event in the community's history; rather, like Plato's account of the trial of Socrates, ideas are being defended via an ostensibly historical narrative. On ancient biographies and apologetic see Burridge, 'About People', pp. 122, 135–7.

[2] Loader, *Christology*, p. 161.

[3] Dodd, *Interpretation*, p. 327; Jürgen Becker, *Das Evangelium des Johannes. Kapitel 1–10*, Gütersloh: Gütersloher Verlagshaus Gerd Mohn/ Würzburg: Echter-Verlag, 1979, p. 249; Beasley-Murray, *John*, p. 80; Talbert, *Reading John*, p. 130; Witherington, *John's Wisdom*, p. 134. See also Carson, *John*, pp. 90–2; Pryor, *John*, p. 27; Francis J. Moloney, *Signs and Shadows: Reading John 5–12*, Minneapolis: Fortress, 1996, pp. 12, 28. On the trial motif in John see further A. E. Harvey, *Jesus on Trial. A Study in the Fourth Gospel*, London: SPCK, 1976; also Brown, *Community*, pp. 67–8; Loader, *Christology*, p. 165.

the clearest examples in John of the Evangelist engaging in legitimation, in the defence of his community's beliefs about Jesus.

The subject of the conflict

In order to ascertain exactly what is at issue in the conflict with 'the Jews' in John 5, we must consider the relationship between earlier tradition and the miracle story which John recounts in this chapter. As has already been emphasized, the relationship between the Johannine conflicts and those attested in earlier New Testament writings is crucial for our model of development.

The similarity between this Johannine miracle story and that found in Mark 2.1–12 (and parallels) is noted by most commentators.[4] These similarities do not necessitate that we posit a direct literary dependence by John on one or more of the Synoptic Gospels, but do at least suggest that here the Fourth Evangelist is dependent on a very similar tradition, and perhaps an independent version of the same basic story.[5] There is in fact much evidence to support this conclusion.

(1) In the Johannine narrative we have an invalid, someone who may well have been a paralytic in view of the reference to paralytics immediately prior to his being introduced, and also of his difficulty in getting into the water (John 5.3–7; cf. Mark 2.3).

(2) Jesus heals him by telling him to get up, pick up his mat and walk (John 5.8; Mark 2.9–11). The two Greek sentences are practically identical, the only difference between them being an additional καὶ in the Marcan version.

(3) In John this occurs on a Sabbath (John 5.9–10; cf. Mark 2.23–8; 3.1–4; Luke 13.10–16, which are not part of the same story but which nonetheless show that controversy

---

[4] So e.g. Brown, *Gospel*, pp. 208–9; Lindars, *Gospel of John*, pp. 52–3, 209; Joachim Gnilka, *Johannesevangelium*, Würzburg: Echter, 1983, p. 39; Beasley-Murray, *John*, pp. 71–2; Perkins, 'Gospel', p. 959; Painter, *Quest*, pp. 220–1; Frans Neirynck, 'John and the Synoptics: 1975–1990', in Adelbert Denaux (ed.), *John and the Synoptics*, (BETL, 101), Leuven: Leuven University Press, 1992, pp. 54–5; Pryor, *John*, pp. 25–6; see also Dodd, *Historical Tradition*, pp. 174–7; D. M. Smith, *Johannine Christianity*, pp. 116–22; Witkamp, 'Use of Traditions'; Peder Borgen, *Early Christianity and Hellenistic Judaism*, Edinburgh: T&T Clark, 1996, pp. 106–7.

[5] Cf. Dodd, *Historical Tradition*, pp. 174–80.

concerning healing on the Sabbath is also a traditional motif rather than a Johannine creation).[6]

(4)   Jesus is accused of blasphemy and/or of doing what only God can do (John 5.16–18; Mark 2.7).

(5)   He speaks with the man about sin and being made well (John 5.14; Mark 2.5–11).

(6)   It may also be significant that both Mark 2.10 and John 5.27 speak of the authority of the Son of Man.[7]

John thus seems to be familiar, if not with the same story as is narrated in Mark and the other Synoptics, then at the very least with a similar tradition.

Nevertheless, some commentators feel that the differences outweigh the similarities. For example, Brown considers that, apart from the basic fact that a lame man is told to stand, pick up his mat and walk, the two stories have almost nothing in common. He mentions three differences which he considers decisive in leading to the conclusion that the Johannine narrative and the Synoptic narratives do not refer to the same incident. These are the differences:

(1)   in setting: Capernaum vs. Jerusalem;

(2)   in local details: a man brought to a house by his friends and lowered through the roof vs. a man lying at the side of a pool;

(3)   in emphasis: a miracle illustrative of Jesus' power to heal sin vs. a healing with only a passing reference to sin (5.14).[8]

To this list may be added several additional points noted by Sanders (although Sanders only feels that these differences preclude direct literary dependence between John and Mark, and not the sort of dependence on divergent forms of the same original tradition which we are proposing):

(4)   In Mark the man has four friends, in John nobody.

---

[6] Peder Borgen, *Philo, John and Paul. New Perspectives on Judaism and Early Christianity* (BJS, 131), Atlanta: Scholars, 1987, p. 88; *Early Christianity*, pp. 140–4 notes that the Johannine Sabbath controversy in John 5 has the same form as is found in the Synoptics. Lindars (*Gospel of John*, p. 209) suggests that John was dependent on the whole section Mark 2.1–3.6, which was already known as a unit in the pre-Marcan tradition.

[7] See also the parallels of phraseology noted by Borgen, *Early Christianity*, pp. 143–4. See too Neirynck, 'John and the Synoptics', p. 54.

[8] Brown, *Gospel*, pp. 208–9.

(5) In Mark they take the initiative, in John Jesus does.

(6) In Mark Jesus sees their faith, in John faith is not mentioned.

(7) In Mark Jesus forgives the man before healing him, in John Jesus heals him and then warns him not to go on sinning.

(8) In Mark Jesus gives offence by telling the man he is forgiven, in John by breaking the Sabbath (not mentioned in Mark 2) and making himself equal to God (although Sanders notes that this last point is at least implied in Mark 2.7). [9]

Points (1) and (2) are rather easily explicable as changes made in order to allow the incident to occur in Jerusalem, as do the other Johannine accounts of conflicts with 'the Jews'; indeed, nearly the whole of the Fourth Gospel is set in Jerusalem. The third point (3) is weak, inasmuch as it is a similarity as much as a difference: although John's emphasis differs from that of the Synoptic story, not only does he mention sin and healing in connection with one another, but there is in addition a fundamental continuity in the issue being addressed by both the Johannine and Marcan narratives, namely the issue of whether Jesus blasphemously claims to do what only God can do. Dodd, in contrast to Sanders (point 6), feels that the Johannine account's discussion of the man's will to be healed, and participation in the healing process by responding to Jesus' call for him to get up and walk, parallels the calls for or discussions of faith in Mark 2 and other similar healing narratives.[10] Further, as Brown notes (point 3; compare Sanders, point 7), the question of the relationship between sin and suffering *is* addressed, albeit differently.

In connection with a number of the points raised, it should be noted that neither Brown nor Sanders considers the possibility that here John may perhaps be drawing on *more than one* traditional story, which he is then altering or conflating in order to be used as a foundation for a theological discourse. Lindars and Witkamp have argued that John is familiar not only with the story in Mark 2.1–12, but with the whole section Mark 2.1–3.6, which may have

---

[9] J. N. Sanders, *The Gospel According to Saint John*, London: A&C Black, 1968, pp. 160–1.

[10] Dodd, *Historical Tradition*, p. 177. See however Beasley-Murray, *John*, p. 74, who apparently interprets Dodd's meaning differently than I have.

already been linked in pre-Marcan tradition.[11] The Synoptics combine stories, and we should not be surprised to find the Fourth Evangelist doing so as well.

It is also likely that John will have edited his source material, rather than simply incorporating it *in toto* into his Gospel.[12] This may account for the remaining differences, since there is no reason to think that John's dependence upon tradition here can only be demonstrated if he made no alterations to the tradition which he inherited. As Barrett points out, 'disagreement does not prove lack of knowledge; all it proves is disagreement, and it often presupposes knowledge'.[13] John's version, where the man complains that he has no one to help him into the water (John 5.7), reads like an intentional contrast to Mark 2.3–4, where the man has friends to help him. Lindars rightly notes that the mention of the man's pallet (κράβαττόν) comes unexpectedly and is somewhat redundant in John, whereas it is central in the Marcan narrative. Its presence is best explained by supposing that John preserved it from a tradition he inherited, in which it was an essential part of Jesus' pronouncement.[14] Given that John is setting up a contrast with the healing story in chapter 9, many of the differences are explicable in terms of Johannine editorial activity aimed at bringing out the parallels between the two narratives. Culpepper notes the following as points of contact between the healing stories in John 5 and 9: Jesus taking the initiative, the presence of a pool, the Sabbath issue, the invitation of belief subsequent to the healing and the topic of the relation between sin and suffering. Given that these are key areas of difference between John and Mark, these elements are probably

[11] Cf. Lindars, *Gospel of John*, pp. 209–10; Witkamp, 'Use of Traditions'. See also D. M. Smith, *Johannine Christianity*, p. 117; Joanna Dewey, 'The Literary Structure of the Controversy Stories in Mark 2:1–3:6', in William Telford (ed.), *The Interpretation of Mark*, London: SPCK, 1985, p. 109–18.

[12] Cf. the discussion in Witkamp, 'Use of Traditions'; Borgen, *Early Christianity*, pp. 148–9. On John's creative use of his sources see also George L. Renner, 'The Life-World of the Johannine Community: An Investigation of the Social Dynamics which Resulted in the Composition of the Fourth Gospel', PhD dissertation, Boston University Graduate School, 1982, pp. 157–8, 162.

[13] C. K. Barrett, 'The Place of John and the Synoptics in the Early History of Christian Tradition', *Jesus and the Word and Other Essays*, Edinburgh: T&T Clark, 1995, p. 120. Whereas Barrett is here arguing for John's direct literary dependence on Mark, a suggestion I still find unconvincing, he is nonetheless right to emphasize that it is the character of the similarities rather than the differences which are crucial in determining dependence. Even if John *is* directly dependent on one or more of the Synoptics, this in no way weakens our case, and perhaps strengthens it even further.

[14] Lindars, *Gospel of John*, p. 210.

best regarded as the result of the editorial activity of the Fourth Evangelist.[15]

None of the objections raised proves that John was not dependent on a tradition akin to that preserved in Mark. The differences probably suggest that there was no direct literary dependence, but do not preclude an original common tradition lying behind both.[16] Thus given that, as Lindars notes, 'The verbal similarity between 5.8–9a and Mk. 2.9, 11–12a is so close that it can scarcely be doubted that an almost identical source lies behind them both',[17] it seems best to follow the majority of scholars in regarding John as dependent on traditional material similar to that found in Mark 2, and very probably traditions akin to those found elsewhere in the Synoptics as well.

The reason for discussing the relationship between John and earlier tradition at such length is that certain scholars regard the issue which is addressed here in John, in connection with the Sabbath healing, as fundamentally different from that addressed in John's source and in the Synoptics. In the view of Bultmann and Neyrey, for example, the earlier concern was with the sin of Sabbath breaking, whereas the Fourth Evangelist's concern is with blasphemy.[18] In other words, in the Synoptics, and in the pre-Johannine tradition known to the Fourth Evangelist, the concern is with a humanitarian principle, whereas the focus in John is christological. However, this line of argument ignores the fundamental similarity between the issue addressed on the basis of the miracle account in both John and the Synoptics. In the Marcan version (and parallels), Jesus is accused of *blasphemy* because he is claiming to forgive sins, something that in the objectors' opinion only God can do. In John, through the inclusion of the Sabbath motif, the issue is brought into focus by means of a claim that Jesus, like God, can work on the Sabbath.[19] The basic claim being made is

---

[15] R. Alan Culpepper, *Anatomy of the Fourth Gospel. A Study in Literary Design*, Minneapolis: Fortress, 1983, pp. 139–40.

[16] J. N. Sanders, *John*, p. 161.

[17] Lindars, *Gospel of John*, p. 209. Although see also Pryor, *John*, pp. 25–6.

[18] Rudolf Bultmann, *The Gospel of John. A Commentary*, Oxford: Blackwell, 1971, p. 247; Jerome H. Neyrey, ' "My Lord and My God": The Divinity of Jesus in John's Gospel', *SBL Seminar Paper Series*, 25, Atlanta: Scholars, 1986, pp. 154–5; *Ideology*, pp. 15–18. See also D. M. Smith, *Johannine Christianity*, p. 121; Painter, *Quest*, pp. 221–2; Herold Weiss, 'The Sabbath in the Fourth Gospel', *JBL* 110/2 (1991), 311; Pryor, *John*, p. 26.

[19] The background to this idea is discussed in sufficient detail elsewhere. See e.g. Dodd, *Interpretation*, pp. 320–2; Lindars, *Gospel of John*, p. 218; Moloney, *Johan-*

essentially identical, namely, that Jesus is capable of doing what only God can do, which 'the Jews' find objectionable.[20]

This element is an essential part of the tradition, and does not represent a Johannine alteration of an earlier tradition that did not address the question of Jesus claiming divine prerogatives.[21] What is different from the Synoptics is the fact that John provides a lengthy response to the objections, whereas in the Synoptics the miracle itself is deemed sufficient to silence opposition and legitimate Jesus' actions.[22] It seems likely, then, that the difficulties which some had with the claims made for Jesus by Christians, as are reflected already in the Synoptics, became even more problematic as time went on, so that John needed to address the issue in a fuller way.

The accusation of 'the Jews'

Before we can proceed, we must consider further the accusation that is brought by 'the Jews'.[23] Commentators seem to be more or less unanimously agreed that the phrase in 5.18, πατέρα ἴδιον ἔλεγεν τὸν θεὸν ἴσον ἑαυτὸν ποιῶν τῷ θεῷ, means something like, 'He was calling God his own Father, *thereby* making himself equal with God.'[24] However, while this is obviously a possible translation *grammatically*, from the perspective of cultural anthropology it is

nine *Son of Man*, pp. 69–70; Talbert, *Reading John*, pp. 123–4; Borgen, 'John and Hellenism', pp. 106–7. Primary sources include *Gen. Rab.* 11.10; *Exod. Rab.* 30.9; Philo, *Leg. All.* 1.5–7, 16–18; *Cher.* 86–90; *Mig.* 91; *Quis Her.* 170. An accusation of blasphemy is not explicitly made in John 5, although it is made elsewhere in John in passages closely related to this one (cf. 10.33; also 8.58–9). See further Fennema, 'Jesus and God', p. 266, and our treatment of these passages in chs. 5 and 6 below.

[20] On the similarity between John and Mark in the question of Jesus' authority cf. Lindars, *Gospel of John*, pp. 218–19. See also G. H. C. MacGregor, *The Gospel of John*, London: Hodder and Stoughton, 1928, pp. 173–4; de Boer, *Johannine Perspectives*, p. 59; and A. E. Harvey, *Constraints*, p. 171 on the charge of 'blasphemy' as a point of continuity between John and earlier Christian writings.

[21] Cf. Meeks, 'Equal to God', p. 309.

[22] On appeal to miracles to justify halakhic positions see Weiss, 'Sabbath', 314; Talbert, *Reading John*, pp. 123. John does not completely reject this approach: see 10.37–8. The issue in both Mark and John is Jesus' *authority* or *authorization by God* to do what he has done.

[23] Much of the following section has been published in another form as James F. McGrath, 'A Rebellious Son? Hugo Odeberg and the Interpretation of John 5.18', *NTS* 44 (1998), 470–3.

[24] Brown, *Gospel*, p. 212; Martyn, 'Mission', p. 310; Painter, *Quest*, p. 221. See also Lindars, *Gospel of John*, p. 219; Beasley-Murray, *John*, p. 74; Meeks, 'Equal to God', p. 310; Carson, *John*, p. 249.

low c extreme

extremely difficult to maintain. In first-century Jewish and other Mediterranean cultures, a claim to sonship would immediately imply obedience and dependence, not equality.[25]

We may note the following important texts as evidence. Epictetus, the first-century Stoic philosopher, wrote,

> Bear in mind that you are a son. A son's profession is to treat everything that is his as belonging to his father, to be obedient to him in all things, never to speak ill of him to anyone else, nor to say or do anything that will harm him, to give way to him in everything and yield him precedence, helping him to the utmost of his power.[26]

Ben Sira 3.6–16 says, 'Whoever glorifies his father will have long life . . . he will serve his parents as his masters . . . Do not glorify yourself by dishonouring your father, for your father's dishonour is no glory to you . . . Whoever forsakes his father is like a blasphemer.'[27] In a similar vein Philo asserts that 'men who neglect their parents should cover their faces in shame . . . For the children have nothing of their own which does not belong to the parents, who have either bestowed it upon them from their own substance, or have enabled them to acquire it by supplying them with the means'.[28] The Hebrew Scriptures share similar assumptions concerning sonship, as we see in Deuteronomy 21.18, where 'a rebellious son' is one 'who will not obey the voice of his father or the voice of his mother'.

To make an assertion of sonship would thus imply submission and obedience, and to make oneself equal to one's father (i.e. to claim the unique prerogatives of one's father and thereby detract from one's father's honour) would be to make oneself a rebellious son, one who was behaving in a way totally inappropriate to a son.[29]

---

[25] Cf. Davies, *Rhetoric*, pp. 129–31; Bruce J. Malina, *Windows on the World of Jesus. Time Travel to Ancient Judea*, Louisville: Westminster John Knox, 1993, pp. 2–4; also A. E. Harvey, *Constraints*, p. 159. See also Philo, *Conf.* 63, which is of great significance for our discussion (see further p. 93 below).

[26] Epictetus, *Dissertations* 2.7 (quoted M. Davies, *Rhetoric*, p. 130).

[27] Ben Sira 3.6–16.

[28] Philo, *Dec.* 118. The similarity between what is asserted here and John 5.19, 30 is also significant.

[29] Odeberg, *Fourth Gospel*, p. 203 claimed to cite rabbinic parallels which demonstrate that the rabbis designated a rebellious son as 'making himself equal to his father'. However, this expression does not actually appear anywhere in the early rabbinic corpus. For further discussion of this topic see McGrath, 'A Rebellious Son?'

It is thus better to take the participle ποιῶν in John 5.18 as a concessive participle, which would mean that the phrase as a whole be given a sense something like, 'He claimed that God was his[30] Father, although [he was] making himself equal with God.'[31] Jesus has claimed to be God's son; the Jews are accusing him of not behaving in a way appropriate to sonship, because he is claiming for himself his Father's unique prerogatives. In other words, what 'the Jews' find objectionable is not Jesus' claim to be God's son *per se*. Rather it is the fact that, while claiming this designation appropriate for one who submissively obeys God, he has nonetheless put himself in the place of God. 'The Jews' are thus accusing Jesus of behaving in a way that discredits or tells against his spoken claims. This suggestion fits well with what we find elsewhere in John. Similar accusations, which appeal to the actions of Jesus in order to discount his claims, can be found, for example, in John 8.13; 9.16,24; 10.33.[32] The interpretation we have suggested not only fits with the first-century Mediterranean cultural context, as we have already seen, but, as we shall demonstrate shortly, also coheres with the response which the Johannine Jesus goes on to give to the Jews' accusation.

Before proceeding, we may note some of the evidence that is available concerning Jewish views on human beings claiming equality with God. Even in the Old Testament, to grasp at equality with God was regarded as sinful hubris (cf. Gen. 3.5–6; 2 Chr. 24.24; Isa.14.13–15; 40.18, 25; Ezek. 28.2; 29.3). Philo expresses a similar opinion, as does the author of 2 Maccabees, who places these words in the mouth of a repentant Antiochus: 'It is right to be subject to God, and no mortal should think that he is equal to God.'[33] On the other hand, Beasley-Murray notes the Rabbinic

---

[30] In Koine Greek ἴδιον was often used in a reduced sense to mean simply 'his'. Cf. J. N. Sanders, *John*, pp. 99 n.3, 164 n.3.

[31] John 10.33 is an example of the use of a participle in a very similar way in a similar context. Even if the participle in 5.18 is taken as adverbial, it may have the sense of a temporal clause, meaning something like 'He made God his own Father *while* making himself equal to God', in which case the two may still be understood as in contrast to one another. See also John 19.7, where the same language is used as in 5.18 and 10.33: Jesus is accused of 'making himself', that is to say, of 'claiming to be' or 'putting himself in the place of', God's Son and agent, when in fact 'the Jews' are convinced that he is not (see further Meeks, 'Equal to God', p. 310).

[32] Note also 7.27, 41–2, 52, where accusations of a similar sort are made, based on a contrast between what seems to be implied by Jesus' actions/words, and his background.

[33] 2 Maccabees 9.12; Philo, *Leg. All.* 1.49. *Leg.* 114 is also of some relevance. See also Josephus, *Ant.* 19.1–16.

discussion of Pharaoh, where Moses is made 'as God' to Pharaoh, whereas because Pharaoh makes himself as God he must learn that he is nothing.[34] He concludes: 'It would seem that in their eyes God could exalt a man to be as God, but whoever *made himself* as God called down divine retribution on himself. They saw Jesus in the latter category.'[35]

To summarize, it appears that for *any* son to place himself on an equal standing with his *father* would be regarded as disrespectful. Thus for Jesus to claim to be *God's* son while also apparently *making himself equal* with God would have been wholly unacceptable to his Jewish interlocutors.[36] The key issue does not appear to have been equality with God *per se*, but whether Jesus is *making himself* equal with God. That is to say, 'the Jews' do not regard Jesus as someone appointed by God, who would thus bear God's authority and speak and act on his behalf, but as one who seeks his own glory, a messianic pretender who blasphemously puts himself on a par with God.

The Johannine response

(1) The obedient Son/agent

We now turn to the Johannine response to these objections, in the first part of which the Evangelist makes use of the imagery and categories of sonship and agency.[37] The presentation of Jesus as God's Son and agent was already part of Christian tradition prior to John, as we have already seen in chapter 2. It would seem that John is here drawing out the implications of the agency concept in a much fuller way than any of his predecessors, making the principle of agency (that the one sent is like the one who sent him) a *central christological theme* in a way that earlier writers did not do or did not do as fully. This motif is combined with the generally

[34] *Tanh. B* §12, on Exod. 7.1, cited in Beasley-Murray, *John*, p. 75.

[35] Beasley-Murray, *John*, p. 75. See also Carson, *John*, p. 249; Craig R. Koester, *Symbolism in the Fourth Gospel. Meaning, Mystery, Community*, Minneapolis: Fortress, 1995, p. 87.

[36] For a pagan parallel see Apollodorus (1.9.7), who writes concerning the hero Salmoneus, he 'was arrogant and wanted to make himself equal to Zeus, and because of his impiety he was punished; for he said that he was Zeus'. However, 'god-equal' can also have a positive sense in some non-Jewish literature; see Dodd, *Interpretation*, pp. 325–6.

[37] Cf. Meeks, *Prophet-King*, pp. 303–4; A. E. Harvey, *Jesus on Trial*, pp. 88–92; Létourneau, *Jésus*, pp. 233–55, 324.

accepted idea in contemporary culture that an obedient son will imitate his father and do what he sees his father doing.[38] The Evangelist argues on the basis of these concepts that Jesus is not a disobedient or rebellious son; the fact that he does what his Father does demonstrates not rebelliousness, but rather obedience.[39] The implication which is then drawn out of the traditional motifs which John uses here is that, as Son and Agent, Jesus can legitimately be regarded as carrying out functions which were traditionally considered to be divine prerogatives: working on the Sabbath, giving life, judging, and so on.[40] And whereas for a son to usurp the honour due to his father would be to become a rebellious son, because the son has been appointed as the father's agent, he is to be honoured, respected and obeyed as if he were the father himself. The one sent is to be regarded and honoured as the one who sent him.[41] John emphasizes these aspects of the Jesus tradition to make the point that Jesus resembles an agent appointed by God rather than a rebel against God, because he is constantly pointing attention away from himself to the Father who sent him.

In addition, John can reinforce the legitimacy of the attribution of various divine prerogatives to Jesus through appeal to the fact that, as many of his contemporaries would acknowledge, God had on occasion delegated the authority to carry out at least some of these acts. Prophetic figures like Elijah in the Hebrew Scriptures

[38] Some useful background texts are discussed by C. H. Dodd in 'A Hidden Parable in the Fourth Gospel', *More New Testament Studies*, Manchester: Manchester University Press, 1968, pp. 32–8. See also Harvey, *Constraints*, p. 160, and Philo, *Conf.* 63, which is quoted and discussed on p. 93 below.

[39] Cf. Brown, *Gospel*, p. 218 (commenting on verse 19).

[40] On giving life as a divine prerogative cf. R. H. Lightfoot, *St. John's Gospel: A Commentary*, Oxford: Oxford University Press, 1956, p. 142; Meeks, *Prophet-King*, p. 304; Lindars, *Gospel of John*, p. 222; Gnilka, *Johannesevangelium*, p. 42; Beasley-Murray, *John*, p. 76. See also e.g. 2 Kgs. 5.7, and Midrash on Psalm 78.5 (cited Meeks, *Prophet-King*, p. 304 n.1). On judgment as a divine prerogative cf. Brown, *Gospel*, p. 219. This of course refers to judgment in an ultimate, eschatological, final sense; the idea that human beings act as judges in a more limited sense is not at issue. See also Deut. 1.17, and n.56 below.

[41] See the discussion of sonship and agency in ch.2 above. The Johannine argument has been summarized well by a number of scholars: Jesus does not *make himself* equal with God, but he is equal (in authority) to God because *God* has made him so, by appointing him as his agent and sending him (so e.g. Brown, *Community*, p. 47 n.80; C. K. Barrett, '"The Father is Greater than I" (John 14:28). Subordinationist Christology in the New Testament', *Essays on John*, London: SPCK, 1982, 24; Neyrey, 'My Lord and My God', pp. 155–9; Loader, *Christology*, pp. 160–1; Pryor, *John*, p. 27; Ashton, *Studying John*, p. 72; de Boer, *Johannine Perspectives*, p. 59). See also Koester, *Symbolism*, p. 87.

were believed to have restored the dead to life through God's power,[42] and the apocalyptic figure of the Son of Man was thought of as judge.[43] The Fourth Evangelist does not appear to be arguing his point here strictly on the basis of certain unique christological claims, but also appeals to what is true in general of father–son relationships, and which could (in theory, at least) also apply to others, although the Evangelist would certainly have regarded Jesus as God's Son and Agent *par excellence*.[44] Yet although Jesus has been delegated an authority which may at least in theory be delegated at times to others, the Evangelist is broadening the area of authority being claimed for Jesus by including the idea of work on the Sabbath, which does not appear to have been claimed for any other figure in Israel's history anywhere in the extant litera-ture.[45] Even if the Evangelist's argument is based on a broad principle, there is nonetheless in this passage an accentuation and extension of earlier use of sonship and agency categories in relation to Jesus. The Evangelist is appealing to traditional images and/or generally accepted ideas, and although his argument would carry more weight for those who already accepted the Christian position that Jesus is God's Son and agent, the fact that the Fourth Evangel-ist bases his argument on general principles of agency and/or sonship suggests that even some non-Christian Jews may have found him persuasive, and at least concluded that there is nothing blasphemous or scandalous in the claims being made by the Johannine Christians for Jesus.[46]

---

[42] Although this was an exception rather than a rule; cf. Lindars, *Gospel of John*, p. 222. Neyrey notes later Jewish traditions that God granted to Elijah and Elisha three keys that he normally reserved to himself: the rain, the womb and the grave (*Ideology*, p. 75; cf. *b. Ta'an* 2a; *b. Sanh.* 113a; *Midr. Ps.* 78.5; also Barrett, *Commentary*, p. 260). Figures to whom God delegated his own prerogatives are the only ones of whom the term 'agent' (Heb. *shaliach*) is used by the later rabbis.

[43] Already in the Old Testament the Messiah had begun to be thought of as (eschatological) judge: see e.g. Isa. 11.1–5. Note also 1QSb 5.24–5 (cited by E. Earle Ellis, 'Deity-Christology in Mark 14:58', in Joel B. Green and Max Turner (eds.), *Jesus of Nazareth: Lord and Christ. Essays on the Historical Jesus and New Testament Christology*, Grand Rapids: Eerdmans, 1994, p. 196 n.22). We shall return to the Evangelist's use of the designation 'Son of Man' in 5.27 below.

[44] Dodd, 'Hidden Parable', pp. 31–2. *Contra* Beasley-Murray, *John*, p. 75, although a combination of the two approaches may be best: the Evangelist is using imagery which is true of sonship in general, but is clearly using it to argue a specifically christological point.

[45] Note the argument on the basis of David's action in Mark 2.23–8. Nonetheless, there is no hint of David having been thought to work on the Sabbath because God does. Cf. Weiss, 'Sabbath', 313.

[46] So rightly Michael Theobald, *Die Fleischwerdung des Logos. Studien zum*

The clearest indication that the Fourth Evangelist's appeal to tradition also represents a development of that tradition is to be found in the links between his conception of Jesus in terms of agency, and his understanding of Jesus as the Logos 'become flesh'. Although it may seem to some inappropriate to relate the concept of Logos, mentioned only in the prologue, to the imagery used in the present chapter, in fact there are a number of important conceptual links between them.[47] It must also be stressed that, inasmuch as the Gospel in its present form is concerned, the Evangelist would have expected his readers to be familiar with the prologue and the theology expressed therein. As Barrett and others have rightly stressed, John intends the whole of his Gospel to be read in light of the prologue.[48] The Fourth Evangelist would expect readers of this passage to think of Jesus not only as God's *human* agent, but also as God's unique agent, the Logos, 'become flesh'.

Even as early as Deutero-Isaiah, we find agency language associated with God's Word (Isa. 55.11). In later Jewish literature, Wisdom is presented in terms that are rightly regarded as falling within the sphere of agency categories, and the association is

Verhältnis des Johannesprologs zum Corpus des Evangeliums und zu 1 Joh, Münster: Aschendorffsche Verlagsbuchhandlung, 1988, pp. 377–8. See also Robin Scroggs, *Christology in Paul and John: The Reality and Revelation of God*, Philadelphia: Fortress, 1988, p. 68.

[47] Note esp. Peder Borgen, 'Creation, Logos and the Son: Observations on John 1:1–18 and 5:17–18', *Ex Auditu* 3 (1987), 88–97, who discusses a number of such aspects, including links with Jewish interpretations of Genesis, creation, agency, participation in divine activity and seeing God. So also Cadman, *Open Heaven*, p. 79; Paul S. Minear, 'Logos Affiliations in Johannine Thought', in Robert F. Berkey and Sarah A. Edwards (eds.), *Christology in Dialogue*, Cleveland: Pilgrim, 1993, pp. 143–4. Borgen (p. 92) also suggests that 1.1–18 may be understood as a demonstration that Moses wrote about Jesus (i.e. in Gen. 1–2; cf. John 5.46). For other connections between the prologue and the present passage see Eldon Jay Epp, 'Wisdom, Torah, Word: The Johannine Prologue and the Purpose of the Fourth Gospel', in Gerald F. Hawthorne (ed.), *Current Issues in Biblical and Patristic Interpretation. Studies in Honor of Merrill C. Tenney Presented by his Former Students*, Grand Rapids: Eerdmans, 1975, p. 142, who notes similar themes and material in connection with the following topics (among others): the witness of the Baptist, the contrast between Moses/Torah and Jesus, and God being unseen by human beings. Thomas L. Brodie (*The Gospel According to John: A Literary and Theological Commentary*, Oxford: Oxford University Press, 1993, p. 242) sees three divisions in both the prologue and the discourse in 5.16–47, namely creation, witness and glory, and even goes so far as to describe the latter as 'a variation on the prologue'.

[48] Barrett, *Commentary*, p. 156; Pryor, *John*, p. 7; Moloney, *Signs and Shadows*, p. 8. See also Minear, 'Logos Affiliations', p. 142 and p. 55 above.

particularly close in connection with creation.[49] That the role of the Logos in Philo can also be correctly brought under the heading of agency seems clear from the designations which Philo uses, such as 'mediator', 'angel/messenger', 'ruler' and 'governor or administrator'.[50] That many aspects of these contemporary Jewish portraits of God's Word or Wisdom in agency categories were familiar to the Evangelist is clear from the prologue.

Although there is no evidence that the Evangelist and his readers knew Philo's writings directly, nonetheless the similarities between what is said by Philo concerning the Logos and what the Fourth Evangelist writes in the prologue are so striking that most scholars consider the parallels to be significant and worth noting. The concepts, language and imagery are so similar that, even if there is no *direct* interdependence between the two, there is at the very least a shared 'world of ideas', a connection of environment or milieu, culture or tradition, which the two share in common with one another. This same point also applies to Philo's Logos concept as it relates to John 5. Most worthy of mention is *Conf.* 63, where the Logos is described as follows: 'For the Father of the universe has caused him to spring up as the eldest son, whom, in another passage, he calls the firstborn; and he who is thus born, *imitating the ways of his father*, has formed such and such species, looking to his archetypal patterns.' The significance of this statement is heightened still further when one also considers passages such as *Cher.* 77, where Philo writes, 'Who . . . could be a more determined enemy to the soul than he who out of arrogance appropriate[s] the especial attributes of the Deity to himself? Now it is an especial attribute of God to create, and this faculty it is impious to ascribe to any created being.'[51]

It is of course true, as so much recent research has stressed, that the Logos is for Philo none other than God himself in his interaction with the created order, depicted through means of personification.[52] Nonetheless, this in no way diminishes the significance of the fact that *Philo has chosen to describe the Logos as fulfilling this divine prerogative in terms of a son obediently imitating his father*. It

---

[49] See e.g. Wisd. 7.22; 8.4–6; 9.2. See further Hurtado, *One God*, pp. 42–4. Cf. too the depiction of Wisdom in Prov. 8.22–31.

[50] Cf. *Quaest in Ex.* 2.13; *Quaest in Gn.* 4.110–111; *Fug.* 94–105, 109; *Det.* 54. On Logos as agent in Philo see the helpful and brief discussion in Hurtado, *One God*, pp. 44–50.

[51] See also *Leg. All.* 3.99.

[52] Dunn, *Christology*, pp. 176, 230; Hurtado, *One God*, pp. 46–50.

is not impossible that the Fourth Evangelist and his community were aware of this (or some other similar) earlier use of father–son imagery in connection with the Logos, although this cannot be proved. However, it is at least clear from this passage that the principle that a son imitates his father was widely accepted – Philo does not argue for it, but simply appeals to it as the basis for his assertion about the creative activity of the Logos.[53] Philo's use of this principle in this context at the very least shows that to argue on this basis for the legitimacy of a particular figure's participation in divine activities or functions would not have appeared ludicrous, and would perhaps even have been reasonably convincing to those who shared certain presuppositions.

Thus, to sum up, the Fourth Evangelist has in this chapter taken up an element of earlier tradition, namely the idea that Jesus is God's Son and agent. In his use of it to defend the Christian view that Jesus carries out divine functions, the Evangelist has developed the motif(s) in a number of ways:

(1) In emphasizing that Jesus does these things precisely as God's agent and obedient Son, the Evangelist has stressed at the same time both the obedience and submission of the Son to the Father, and the equality of the authority of the Son (as agent) to that of the Father. The resulting portrait sets up a tension between equality language and subordination language that would exert a great influence on the course of later christological development. It also lays much greater stress on Jesus as life-giver and judge than did earlier works.

(2) The Evangelist has also brought the idea of the human Jesus as God's agent into connection with the idea of Jesus as the one as whom God's supreme agent, the Logos, has 'become flesh'. The concept of the Logos as agent was known in the community, and this would have lent still more weight to the Evangelist's argument: because the human being Jesus is one with the Logos, the attribution of divine activities to Jesus is not to be considered in any way more problematic than the similar assertions made by many Jews about God's Word/Wisdom/Spirit. This line of argument would have been most convincing to Christians, who already accepted that Jesus was the Messiah in whom

---

[53] And see also the parallels noted by Dodd, 'Hidden Parable', pp. 32–8.

God's Spirit, Word or Wisdom dwelt. Nonetheless, Jews who accepted the truthfulness of contemporary Jewish portraits of the Messiah as indwelt by God's Spirit or Wisdom may also have found John's portrayal convincing. At any rate, in John the agency motif is expanded and developed, and moved on to another plane by being integrated into the Evangelist's Logos Christology. Just how well integrated it was, and whether John had thought through in any detail the relationship between the sending of Jesus and the sending of the Logos from heaven, are interesting and important questions which we shall address later (in chapter 15 below).

(2)   The Son of Man as judge (5.27)

We may now proceed to consider the development made in this passage of another important motif, namely the use of the designation 'Son of Man'. Once again, we have already seen that John is aware of and has inherited aspects of earlier Jewish and Christian thought concerning the 'Son of Man'. On one level, it may seem that what the Evangelist does with the Son of Man motif here, while an attempt to legitimate a certain belief, is not particularly significant. The line of argument, on first reading, appears to be as follows: the apocalyptic Son of Man was widely accepted to carry out the role of judge, and if Jesus is the Son of Man, then he is rightly regarded as occupying the role of judge.[54] This is certainly part of what the Fourth Evangelist is arguing here, since the Evangelist is clearly appealing to the well-known apocalyptic traditions concerning the 'Son of Man'. This can hardly be denied, as in the immediate context we find:

(1)   the use of 'son of man' (the anarthrous form of which, in the view of some scholars, is a direct allusion to Daniel 7.13);[55]

[54] Cf. Joseph Coppens, *La Relève Apocalyptique du Messianisme Royal. III. Le Fils de l'Homme Néotestamentaire* (BETL, 55), Leuven: Leuven University Press, 1981, pp. 68–9. See also Létourneau, *Jésus*, pp. 324–5 on the connections between Sonship-Agency and Son of Man ideas here.

[55] Many commentators take the anarthrous 'Son of Man' to be a direct allusion to Daniel 7.13; so e.g. Brown, *Gospel*, p. 220; Barnabas Lindars, 'The Son of Man in the Johannine christology', in Barnabas Lindars and Stephen S. Smalley (eds.), *Christ and Spirit in the New Testament*, Cambridge: Cambridge University Press, 1973, pp. 51–2; Moloney, *Johannine Son of Man*, p. 81; Martyn, *History*, p. 139; Margaret Pamment, 'The Son of Man in the Fourth Gospel', *JTS* n.s. 36 (1985), 60;

(2)   reference to his being given authority (to judge);[56]
(3)   mention in the immediate context of the resurrection of some to life and others to condemnation;[57]

This makes it seem quite likely that the Fourth Evangelist has in mind the Danielic figure as he was understood in contemporary Judaism and Christianity, to which he could appeal to defend his belief that Jesus rightly and legitimately fulfils the divine prerogative of judgment.[58] However, there may be a further aspect to John's usage, as we shall now see.

E. M. Sidebottom and Robert Rhea have both made the interesting suggestion that John 5.27 shows knowledge of the Jewish work known as the *Testament of Abraham*.[59] In this work, Abel the 'son of Adam (= Man)' is presented as 'the frightful man who is seated on the throne . . . he sits here to judge the entire creation, examining both righteous and sinners'. The reasoning behind Abel fulfiling this role is given in the form of a statement attributed to God: 'For God said, "I do not judge you, but every man is judged by man"' (*T. Abr.* A 13.2–3). The attempt to relate

Perkins, 'Gospel', p. 960; Ashton, *Understanding*, p. 361; Carson, *John*, p. 259; M. Davies, *Rhetoric*, p. 190; Painter, 'Enigmatic', pp. 1873–4; de Boer, *Johannine Perspectives*, p. 152. Ashton (p. 357) notes that the allusion to Daniel 7.13 would be clear even if the designation υἱὸς ἀνθρώπου were not used. See also Smalley, 'Johannine Son of Man', 292.

[56] Cf. Martyn, *History*, p. 139; Painter, 'Enigmatic', p. 1872. Ashton (*Understanding*, p. 358) rightly notes that Daniel itself does not explicitly say that the authority which is given to the (one like a) son of man is authority *to judge*, and thus the Evangelist shows signs of awareness of the Synoptic-type tradition, in which this is made explicit, and perhaps also other Jewish traditions and writings (so also Smalley, 'Johannine Son of Man', 292–3; Moloney, *Johannine Son of Man*, pp. 81–2; de Boer, *Johannine Perspectives*, pp. 152–3). After reviewing the evidence, Ashton cautiously concludes that there is sufficient evidence to warrant the view that by the end of the first century CE Judaism (and Christianity) had begun to coalesce the Danielic figure of the 'son of man' and the Messiah-redeemer (*Understanding*, pp. 358–61).

[57] Lindars, 'Son of Man', p. 52 notes allusions to Danielic imagery (Dan. 12.2) in the two following verses, as do Moloney, *Johannine Son of Man*, p. 81; Painter, 'Enigmatic', p. 1872; de Boer, *Johannine Perspectives*, p. 152.

[58] Cf. Martyn, *History*, p. 139, who regards John 5.27 as 'In some respects . . . the most "traditional" Son of Man saying in the whole of the New Testament'; see also de Boer, *Johannine Perspectives*, p. 153. In the light of these allusions, Hare's view (*Son of Man*, p. 92) that there is no evidence of Danielic influence anywhere in John, much less in this context, cannot be sustained, although he may be correct that the anarthrous form of the phrase is not used specifically to allude to Daniel 7.13. See also Ragnar Leivestad, 'Exit the Apocalyptic Son of Man', *NTS* 18 (1972), 252.

[59] E. M. Sidebottom, *The Christ of the Fourth Gospel*, London: SPCK, 1961, pp. 94–5; Robert Rhea, *The Johannine Son of Man*, Theologischer Verlag Zürich, 1990, p. 71.

the Johannine use of the phrase υἱὸς ἀνθρώπου in this passage specifically to Abel, *ben Adam*, 'the Son of Man/Adam', seems unnecessarily far-fetched, given that there is no other evidence for the idea of Jesus as 'Abel reincarnate' in the Fourth Gospel.[60] Nonetheless, the principle that human beings shall be judged by a human being appears to antedate this work, since it is cited by the author not only as authoritative, but also as a divine oracle. The author of Acts may also show an awareness of this idea in Acts 17.31, where we find a similar emphasis on God demonstrating his justice by appointing a human being as judge.[61] Perhaps also relevant is Hebrews 2.17, where Jesus' high priesthood is related to his humanity, which makes him able to sympathize with those for whom he intercedes. In Hebrews 4.15–16, the *enthroned* Jesus is explicitly mentioned in connection with this idea, perhaps suggesting that the author was aware of a tradition concerning the human Jesus as righteous and merciful *judge*, which he has, for the most part, adapted to his own portrait of Christ in high priestly categories. It thus becomes plausible that the Evangelist may also have in mind here the most basic meaning of the designation 'son of man', i.e. human being, and be alluding to a tradition which held that God would judge humankind justly by allowing one of their own kind to judge them.[62]

This suggestion need not be understood to preclude the possibi-

[60] So rightly Delbert Burkett, *The Son of the Man in the Gospel of John* (JSNTS, 56), Sheffield: Sheffield Academic Press, 1991, pp. 25–6, criticizing the view of Wolfgang Roth, 'Jesus as the Son of Man: The Scriptural Identity of a Johannine Image', in Dennis E. Groh and Robert Jewett (eds.), *The Living Text: Essays in Honor of Ernest W. Saunders*, Lanham, MD: University Press of America, 1985, pp. 11–26. It should also be considered possible that T. Abr. has formulated its view of Abel in response to Christian claims for Jesus. See further E. P. Sanders, 'Testament of Abraham', in James H. Charlesworth (ed.), *The Old Testament Pseudepigrapha. Volume I: Apocalyptic Literature and Testaments*, New York: Doubleday, 1983, pp. 875, 888 n.11b, who notes that T. Abr. shows evidence of familiarity with some parts of the New Testament, while being nonetheless 'unmistakably Jewish'.

[61] F. F. Bruce, *The Book of the Acts*, Grand Rapids: Eerdmans, 1988, pp. 340–1 notes a three-way connection between John 5.27, Acts 17.31 and Dan. 7.13.

[62] It is perhaps also significant and worth noting that in both T. Abr. A 13.8 and John 5.31ff. (see also 8.17–18) there is a discussion of the legal requirement for the number of witnesses needed to confirm a legal matter. Hare, in rejecting the connections argued for here (*Son of Man*, p. 95), speaks of 'son of man' as a *poetic* way of saying 'man', but this is not correct: there is nothing intrinsically poetic about the phrase. Rather, 'human being' is its normal sense. See the examples cited in Maurice Casey's article, 'The Use of the Term (א)שנ(א) בר in the Aramaic Translations of the Hebrew Bible', *JSNT* 54 (1994), 87–118. Another interesting point of contact between T. Abr. and John is the use of descent/ascent language (cf. Talbert,

lity that the phrase here also refers to the figure of the 'Son of Man' known from apocalyptic literature.[63] In fact, in the case of *Testament of Abraham*, the reference to Abel as 'that . . . man' seated on a throne as judge surely intends to identify Abel with '*that* Son of Man', i.e. that specific, enthroned human figure of apocalyptic expectation. These were not two mutually exclusive traditions; rather, *Testament of Abraham* has Abraham ask the identity of the one Daniel and Enoch saw, and the answer which he is given is that 'that Son of Man' is Abel, the Son of Adam.[64] The Fourth Evangelist frequently used words and phrases with more than one shade of meaning, and thus it would not be surprising to find him doing so here, using 'Son of Man' with overtones of both apocalyptic expectation and humanity.[65] This would also explain the lack of the definite article, so distinctive of this verse, and a feature that a few scholars have interpreted to indicate an emphasis on Jesus' humanity.[66] The background which we have posited would also explain the fact that there is an imbalance in verse 27: whereas all the other functions mentioned in John 5.19–30 are *shared* by both Father and Son, judgment is *delegated wholly* to the Son.[67] The best explanation for this fact is our suggestion that John knew a tradition which said that God *would not judge*, but would entrust the judgment of human beings to a human being.

Thus while John has not excluded (and had no wish to exclude) the concept of the apocalyptic 'Son of Man' as judge, the Evangelist also appears to wish the reader to recall the principle that God will show his justice by appointing a human figure as judge. This would serve to further demonstrate the legitimacy of claiming such a role for Jesus: as a human being, and as that particular human being mentioned in Daniel 7 and subsequent writings, Jesus can rightly be regarded as God's designated judge. To claim that the human being Jesus will judge in no way represents an illegitimate appropriation

Reading John, pp. 270–1; Ashton, *Understanding*, p. 352 n.47). Cf. also Leivestad, 'Exit', 252.

[63] *Contra* Higgins, *Jesus and the Son of Man*, p. 167; Leivestad, 'Exit', 252.

[64] Cf. John 9.36; 12.34, where the Evangelist likewise addresses the contemporary question, 'Who is this Son of Man?'

[65] So rightly Moloney, *Johannine Son of Man*, pp. 80–1.

[66] So e.g. Burkett, *Son of the Man*, p. 42; Hare, *Son of Man*, pp. 90–6; Leivestad, 'Exit', 252; MacGregor, *John*, p. 179; Pamment, 'Son of Man', 60–1; Sidebottom, *Christ*, p. 93. Carson, *John*, accepts this as at least partially true. *Contra* Brown, Higgins, Lindars, Strachan.

[67] In John 5 at least. The issue is complicated slightly by the apparently contradictory point in 8.15, 50.

by him of a divine prerogative, because Jewish tradition provides justification for a human figure being appointed as judge, and one stream of tradition emphasizes that by doing this God demonstrates his justice.[68] In Carson's view, it is the fact that Jesus is both the apocalyptic Son of Man and a genuine human being that is here regarded as making him uniquely qualified to judge.[69]

It may be worth noting the echoes that are found in John 5.27 of other important New Testament christological statements. Showing particular affinity are Philippians 2.6–11 and Matthew 28.18.[70] The former is close in particular because it is the only other New Testament occurrence of the terminology of equality with God.[71] The latter is significant inasmuch as it also echoes the language of 'giving authority' found in Daniel 7.14.[72] For our purposes we may simply note that the Fourth Evangelist is here probably indebted to a strong current in earlier Christian tradition, one which emphasized that Jesus did not grasp at authority, but was given authority by God.[73] Thus John's portrait, while distinctive in important ways, is also strongly traditional. Were this not the case the Fourth Evangelist's attempt to legitimate his community's beliefs using these motifs would have been far less effective.[74]

To sum up, John has used the single phrase υἱὸς ἀνθρώπου to

[68] John's legitimation in this section is probably better understood when read in conjunction with the legitimatory/polemical thrust in 8.15, 17–18: whereas God's righteousness is shown through his appointing of Jesus as judge, and Jesus' righteousness is stressed through the description of him as wholly submitted to and obedient to the Father, 'the Jews' are presented in terms that sharply contrast with this: they judge wrongly, by human standards, and by misjudging the righteous judge, condemn themselves. Cf. also Moloney, *Signs and Shadows*, p. 28.

[69] Carson, *John*, p. 257.

[70] I am indebted at this point to a paper by Walter Moberly entitled 'The Way to Glory: Matthew and Philippians 2:6–11', read at the Durham Postgraduate New Testament Seminar on 28 April 1997.

[71] Cf. Morna D. Hooker, *From Adam to Christ. Essays on Paul*, Cambridge: Cambridge University Press, 1990, p. 97; Meeks, 'Equal to God', p. 309.

[72] So e.g. W. F. Albright and C. S. Mann, *Matthew*, Garden City: Doubleday, 1971, p. 362; David Hill, *The Gospel of Matthew*, Grand Rapids: Eerdmans/London: Marshall, Morgan and Scott, 1972, p. 361; France, *Matthew – Evangelist and Teacher*, pp. 291–2 (citing W. D. Davies); Ulrich Luz, *The Theology of the Gospel of Matthew*, Cambridge: Cambridge University Press, 1995, p. 139.

[73] The authority given to the Son at the end of Matthew is to be contrasted with the authority he refuses to take from Satan at the start of the Gospel (so Moberly, in the paper just cited above, n.70). See too our discussion in ch.5 below.

[74] A key difference is that John uses this imagery not in relation to an authority that Jesus receives after his exaltation, but rather to the authority he wields even during his earthly life. Cf. the helpful discussion of Hartman, 'Johannine Jesus-Belief', pp. 90–1.

make a double appeal: the author brings together two strands of authoritative tradition which could be used to defend the Christian standpoint that presented Jesus as carrying out the divine function of judgment. Perhaps the most significant development which is made in the process is the emphasis on the *humanity* of the one whom John elsewhere describes as *pre-existent*, and the connecting of these two emphases to the single designation, 'Son of Man'.[75] This development, while closely linked to earlier ideas about the Son of Man, nonetheless brought into sharp focus an uncertainty or difficulty which existed in this conceptuality, and which later christological formulations would need to seek to resolve. The Evangelist also uses motifs traditionally associated with the state of the *exalted* Jesus to defend the authority attributed to the *earthly* Jesus, thereby making another alteration to the tradition which represents a subtle but nonetheless significant development.[76]

(3)   Witnesses to Jesus as God's agent

John has thus far emphasized the legitimacy of the attribution of particular functions to an agent appointed by God. In 5.31–47 the Evangelist seeks to present arguments that Jesus is in fact God's agent. Witnesses are thus called in. John appeals to the witness of John the Baptist (who was apparently widely respected among Jews in the first century) and that of the Father (whose works Jesus does, thus making this an appeal to signs/miracles as evidence of his agency, as is also done in Mark 2.6–12). The testimony of the Scriptures is at the same time part of the witness of the Father (whose revelation it is) and of Moses (who wrote it). John thus

---

[75] The pre-existence of the Son of Man is not mentioned here, but is clearly part of John's understanding of who the Son of Man is (cf. 3.13; 6.62). The emphasis on Jesus being a human being through the use of the same words is thus clearly a linking of pre-existence and humanity which raises numerous difficult christological questions. On the paradox of humanity and heavenly origins in relation to the designation 'Son of Man', see William O. Walker, Jr, 'John 1.43–51 and "The Son of Man" in the Fourth Gospel', *JSNT* 56 (1994), 31–42.

[76] This is not, however, simply a move from an emphasis on futurist to realized eschatology, but also marks a transition from a Christology which emphasizes Jesus' authority as the exalted one to one which emphasizes his authority as the pre-existent one and in his earthly life as well. On Johannine eschatology see further Moloney, *Johannine Son of Man*, pp. 79–80; Kysar, 'Pursuing the Paradoxes', pp. 198–201; Nils A. Dahl, '"Do Not Wonder!" John 5:28–29 and Johannine Eschatology Once More', in Robert T. Fortna and Beverly R. Gaventa (eds.), *The Conversation Continues. Studies in Paul and John in Honor of J. Louis Martyn*, Nashville: Abingdon, 1990, pp. 322–36.

seeks to shift the onus back onto his opponents: have they taken seriously enough the evidence of the miracles attributed to Jesus, of the arguments from Scripture provided by Christians and of the positive witness which John the Baptist bore to Jesus? At least for the Johannine Christians, who already accept these testimonies, these points would strengthen the argument made here. Not only are the status and functions attributed to Jesus by Christians not blasphemous if attributed to God's appointed agent, but a sufficient number of witnesses attest to the fact that Jesus was in fact God's agent, thus – as far as the Evangelist is concerned – clinching the case and proving that Jesus is in fact who the Johannine Christians believe him to be.

Summary

To sum up our argument in this chapter on John 5:

(1) First, we examined the traditions which form the background to John 5.1–18, the narrative which provides the starting point for Jesus' monologue in 5.19–47, and found that the issue in the earlier traditions is essentially the same as that being discussed in John, namely that of Jesus doing what it has traditionally been believed that only God can or should do.

(2) Second, we considered the Johannine response to the objections raised by 'the Jews', and found that in them the traditional motifs of Jesus as God's Son and Agent, and of Jesus as the Son of Man, were developed in a number of distinctive ways. Aspects of these concepts were intensified. The idea of Jesus as agent was brought into connection with the idea of Jesus as the Word-made-flesh, and the agency aspect of this latter conceptuality was brought to the fore. Humanity and pre-existence were brought into direct relation with one another through their mutual connection with the designation 'Son of Man'.

(3) Third, we noted points of connection between the issue being addressed in this part of John and the specific developments made by the Evangelist. Given that these distinctive developments occur in the context of a response to Jewish objections, it is logical to conclude that the developments are the result of the process of legitimation.

The distinctive way John uses the traditions he inherited, the way he combines various traditional motifs and ideas, and the implications he draws from them, are the result of his use of them as part of an attempt to defend his community's beliefs about Jesus.

5

'I OBEY, THEREFORE "I AM"'
(JOHN 8.12–59)

This is a somewhat extensive passage, but as in the case of John 5, even though much of this passage is correctly regarded as an attempt to defend certain beliefs, not everything is relevant to our specific concern of how the legitimation in which the Fourth Evangelist engaged is linked to his development of inherited beliefs. The need to treat this section of the Gospel in our study is immediately indicated by its strong polemical thrust, which is noted by most scholars, as is its close relation to the Johannine disputes with the synagogue.[1] Neyrey regards the form of John 8 as 'an elaborate forensic procedure against Jesus'.[2] As in chapter 5, the Johannine Jesus is being 'put on trial' by 'the Jews', representing the accusation of the contemporaries of the Johannine community against them.[3] Becker classes 8.13–20 together with 5.31–47 and other passages which are about 'the legitimation of the one who has been sent'.[4] The focus of the dispute is the 'I am' statement by Jesus (which is clearly some sort of christological assertion, the meaning of which we will consider below): it is necessary for 'the Jews' to accept that Jesus is 'I am', or they will die in their sins (8.24); the 'lifting up' of Jesus will in some sense demonstrate that Jesus is in fact 'I am' (8.28); and in the end it is precisely as 'I am' that Jesus is rejected by 'the Jews' (8.59).[5] Much of the chapter, as we shall see, is devoted to demonstrating the legitimacy of Jesus' claims (and

[1] So e.g. J. N. Sanders, *John*, p. 229; Rudolf Schnackenburg, *The Gospel According to St. John. Volume II*, London: Burns and Oates, 1980, p. 205; Beasley-Murray, *John*, p. 133; Witherington, *John's Wisdom*, p. 169.

[2] Neyrey, *Ideology*, p. 39.

[3] Witherington, *John's Wisdom*, pp. 168–9 speaks of this chapter in terms of 'judicial proceedings', 'charges' and 'defence'.

[4] Becker, *Johannes*, p. 249.

[5] Neyrey, *Ideology*, p. 48. It is interesting, given the connection with the 'trial' of Jesus here, that the use of 'I am' in Deutero-Isaiah is in the context of Yahweh's 'lawsuit' against Israel. Cf. Schnackenburg, *John vol. II*, p. 200. Becker, *Johannes*, p. 250 feels that the Johannine trial motif is more Hellenistic than Jewish, focusing

thus the culpability of 'the Jews' for rejecting Jesus), and it therefore seems warranted to see an apologetic/legitimatory thrust in
this section.

The point at issue in the controversy

The christological focus of this part of the Fourth Gospel is
certainly to be found in its distinctive use of the absolute 'I am'.[6]
There has traditionally been a large amount of agreement among
scholars that this reflects the Jewish tradition, based in particular
on the Old Greek translation of Isaiah, that 'I am' is a unique way
in which God speaks, identifying and revealing himself in a way
that alludes to the divine name. Although this view has fallen into
disfavour in some circles in recent times, it is still nonetheless
almost certainly correct, and continues to be supported by the
majority of scholars.[7] In support it should be noted that Jesus is

on the defence of the accused rather than on witnesses. However, both personal
defence and appeal to witnesses are found in John.

[6] Three times in this chapter (8.24, 28, 58); elsewhere only in 13.19. The
occurrences in 6.20 and 18.5 may simply mean 'It is I' or 'That's me', although it is
arguable that in these instances too there may be at least some of the overtones of
the absolute Johannine usage. See further Pancaro, *Law*, p. 60, and also immediately
below.

[7] In addition to the scholars cited in ch.2, recent proponents of an Isaianic
background to the Johannine use of 'I am' include Dodd, *Interpretation*, p. 248 (see
also pp. 94, 377); Brown, *Gospel*, pp. 536–7; Smalley, 'Johannine Son of Man', 295;
Philip B. Harner, *The 'I Am' of the Fourth Gospel*, Philadelphia: Fortress, 1970,
passim; Pancaro, *Law*, p. 60; Howard, 'Phil 2:6–11', 385–6; Moloney, *Johannine Son
of Man*, pp. 131–2; *Signs and Shadows*, p. 99; Fennema, 'Jesus and God', pp. 270–1;
Schnackenburg, *John vol. II*, pp. 199–200; J. E. Morgan-Wynne, 'The Cross and the
Revelation of Jesus as εγω ειμι in the Fourth Gospel', in E. A. Livingstone (ed.),
*Studia Biblica 1978: II. Papers on the Gospels. Sixth International Congress on
Biblical Studies. Oxford 3–7 April 1978* (JSNTS, 2), Sheffield: JSOT, 1980, p. 220;
Gnilka, *Johannesevangelium*, pp. 68, 74; Mogens Müller, *Der Ausdruck 'Menschen-
sohn' in den Evangelien*, Leiden: Brill, 1984, p. 213; Hare, *Son of Man*, p. 102;
Burkett, *Son of the Man*, pp. 142–3; Carson, *John*, p. 343; Gary M. Burge, '"I Am"
Sayings', in Joel B. Green, Scot McKnight and I. Howard Marshall (eds.), *Dictionary
of Jesus and the Gospels*, Leicester: IVP, 1992, pp. 355–6; Pryor, *John*, p. 37; Talbert,
Reading John, p. 158; Graham H. Twelftree, 'Blasphemy', in Joel B. Green, Scot
McKnight, I. Howard Marshall (eds.), *Dictionary of Jesus and the Gospels*, Leicester:
IVP, 1992, p. 77; Létourneau, *Jésus*, pp. 411–17; Jarl A. Fossum, *The Image of the
Invisible God. Essays on the Influence of Jewish Mysticism on Early Christology*,
Freiburg: Universitätsverlag Freiberg/ Göttingen: Vandenhoeck & Ruprecht, 1995,
pp. 127–8; D. M. Smith, *Theology*, pp. 112–13; Witherington, *John's Wisdom*,
p. 175; David M. Ball, *'I Am' in John's Gospel. Literary Function, Background and
Theological Implications* (JSNTS, 124), Sheffield: Sheffield Academic Press, 1996,
passim. Neyrey, *Ideology*, pp. 213–17 focuses more on Exod. 3.14, but nonetheless
agrees that the Johannine use alludes to the name of God in the Jewish Scriptures.

explicitly stated in the Fourth Gospel to bear the divine name,[8] and that the attempt to stone him after he declares 'I am' is a reaction which suggests that, from the perspective of 'the Jews', Jesus has not only made an apparently implausible or even insane assertion concerning himself, but has also blasphemed.[9] 'The Jews' had already reached the conclusion that Jesus was mad, but without attempting to stone him for it, the reason presumably being that in the Jewish law, madness was not a capital crime, whereas blasphemy was. In John, attempts to kill Jesus are almost invariably linked with claims to unity with God or to divine authority, which are felt to be blasphemous.[10] It is also worth noting that the climactic objection in 10.33 makes better sense if it has been preceded not only by a discussion of whether Jesus is 'equal with God' (5.18), but also by a claim that Jesus is the 'I am'. There are also a number of traditional elements present in the narrative which elsewhere in the New Testament are closely connected with the bestowal of the divine name upon the exalted Christ, as we shall see below. All of this suggests that the absolute 'I am' is here an allusion to the divine name.

The most potent objection that has been raised against this view is probably that of Barrett. He writes concerning 8.28, 'It is simply intolerable that Jesus should be made to say, "I am God, the supreme God of the Old Testament, and being God I do as I am told."'[11] In response, it is necessary to consider the background to the Johannine use of 'I am'. When examined carefully, the Johannine 'I am' sayings do not appear to represent a direct assertion that Jesus is none other than the God of the Jewish Scriptures, so much as an allusive indication that he bears the divine name.[12] Similar claims had been made for other figures in at least some Jewish circles, although nothing in the extant parallels is quite as

---

Fossum, *Image*, p. 127 traces the LXX translation of Isaiah to the influence of Exod. 3.14.

[8] John 17.11–12. The connections between the Word and Name of God are also to be taken into consideration: on this see Sidebottom, *Christ*, pp. 39–44; Fossum, *Image*, pp. 113–21, 125–33.

[9] Cf. e.g. Harner, *'I Am'*, p. 39; Pancaro, *Law*, p. 56; Carson, *John*, p. 343; Brodie, *John*, p. 336. Pancaro also rightly points out that the attempt to stone Jesus *again* in 10.31, because he is regarded as having blasphemed, indicates clearly that here too Jesus is felt to have been guilty of blasphemy (p. 63).

[10] John 5.18; 7.1, 19–20, 25; 8.37, 40; 10.31.

[11] Barrett, 'The Father is Greater', p. 12.

[12] Cf. Hare, *Son of Man*, p. 102; also Howard, 'Phil 2:6–11', 384–6; Fennema, 'Jesus and God', pp. 271–2.

extravagant as what we find in John.[13] Nevertheless, when one considers the statement by the angel in Apoc. Abr. 10.8, 'I am Yaoel', in light of the application of the very same name to God in Apoc. Abr. 17.13, one can see how easily the statement of the angel could have been regarded by some as blasphemous, and misconstrued as a claim to be God himself.[14] But this use of the divine name by the angel does not represent a claim to be the God of the Old Testament, but to be the special, unique agent of God. The figure who bears the name of God does so as part of his empowering and commissioning as God's principal agent, and, as we have already seen, agency bestowed an equality of authority to, coupled with a complete submission to, the sender.[15]

Thus, if 'I am' on the lips of Jesus were synonymous with 'I am Yahweh' *tout court*, then Barrett's objection would be applicable. However, it appears more likely that the Johannine 'I am' represents something rather subtler and more carefully nuanced than this: it portrays Jesus as the bearer of the divine name, the agent upon whom God has bestowed his name.[16] John's portrait, understood in the way that we have suggested, makes excellent sense in the context of contemporary thought. Of course, it may be that 'the Jews' are presented here as (mis)understanding Jesus to be simply asserting 'I am Yahweh';[17] but it seems more likely that the heart of

[13] Cf. Meeks, *Prophet-King*, pp. 110–1, 193–4, 234–7, 302; Fossum, *Name of God*; Hurtado, *One God*, pp. 79–80.

[14] Just such an interpretation of Apoc. Abr. is offered by David B. Capes, *Old Testament Yahweh Texts in Paul's Christology* (WUNT 2, 47), Tübingen: Mohr-Siebeck, 1992, p. 171, who takes the inclusion of 'Yaoel' in the hymn in 17.8–14 as an indication that the angel is included in the worship of God. But 'Yaoel' in this context is the name of God, the name that the angel bears (so rightly Ashton, *Studying John*, p. 81). That this is the case is clear from 17.2, 7, which depicts the angel as kneeling with Abraham and reciting the hymn of worship with him. The angel is among the worshippers of God and not confused with God, even though, as God's agent, he bears the name of God himself.

[15] See our discussion of sonship and agency in chs.2 and 4 above. Thompson argues that the designations 'God' and 'I am' applied to Jesus in the Fourth Gospel indicate that he is God's principal agent who shares in God's status and functions ('John', p. 377). See also Fennema, 'Jesus and God', p. 288; Létourneau, *Jésus*, p. 415.

[16] See André Feuillet, 'Les ego eimi christologiques du quatrième Evangile', *RSR* 54 (1966) 235–6 and Thompson, 'John', p. 377, who argue that the Johannine use of 'I am', while a claim to divinity, is not simply equivalent to 'I am Yahweh'. The reason why 'the Jews' do not attempt to stone Jesus until verse 59 is that they did not understand what he was claiming; for example, in verses 24–5 they appear to have understood 'I am' as an incomplete sentence, and asked for a predicate (so Pancaro, *Law*, p. 62; Barrett, *Commentary*, p. 342; Burkett, *Son of the Man*, pp. 152–3).

[17] So e.g. Fennema, 'Jesus and God', pp. 269–71.

the problem for them was the claim that the human being Jesus bore the name of God and exercised the prerogatives of God. The issue, once again, is whether Jesus is God's appointed agent who bears God's name and authority, or an upstart who claims divinity for himself (or has it claimed for him by his followers), and who is thus misusing God's name and insulting God.

That the discussion focuses on an aspect of pre-Johannine Jesus-belief can be seen from a comparison with one earlier text in particular, namely Philippians 2.6–11. In this passage there are several points of contact with the section of John we are considering:

(1) Jesus does nothing on his own but obeys his Father (John 8.28–9; Phil. 2.6–8);
(2) this obedience is connected with his bearing of the divine name (John 8.28; Phil. 2.9);
(3) his bearing of the divine name is closely connected with his crucifixion and exaltation (John 8.28; Phil. 2.8–11).

The same traditional group of associations appears also to be attested in Hebrews 1.3–4, where we find a link between Jesus' death on the cross and his exaltation, coupled with his being granted a name greater than that of any other.[18] In the christological hymns of Revelation 5 many of these ideas and images are also present.[19] These points of contact suggest that John has not developed the idea of Jesus bearing the name of God 'from scratch', but is heir to earlier traditions akin to those preserved elsewhere in the New Testament. It thus seems likely that, even as other similar aspects of early Christian Jesus-belief became controversial with time, so too did the belief that Jesus bears the very name of God.[20]

[18] It has been suggested that the 'name' which is in mind here may be 'Son' rather than 'Lord', the name of God (so e.g. Bruce, *Hebrews*, pp. 50–1). However, although the context does immediately suggest 'Son', the fact that 'sons of God' was a frequent designation for angels in the Jewish Scriptures and other Jewish literature suggests that the author may perhaps have had a more distinctive name in mind (see also 2.10; 12.6–8, where 'sons' in the plural refers to Christians).

[19] So Martin Hengel, *Between Jesus and Paul. Studies in the Earliest History of Christianity*, London: SCM, 1983, p. 85. He notes the exaltation of Christ to the throne of God on the basis of his sacrificial death, and his receipt of the worship of all creation. To this we may add that Christ shares in the same designations as God (cf. e.g. 1.8 with 22.13), including (implicitly) 'God' in 22.9. See also the relevant parallels from other early hymnic fragments cited by Hengel (p. 86).

[20] Cf. Howard, 'Phil 2:6–11', 384–6; Kreitzer, *Jesus and God*, p. 161; also Caird, *Paul's Letters*, p. 124. It is possible that the Fourth Evangelist may have interpreted the 'I am' of Jesus when responding at his trial (Mark 14.62) or when crossing the

Closely related to this is the issue, which was also to the fore in John 5, of Jesus doing what only God is believed to be able or worthy to do. This issue, as we have already seen, is firmly rooted in the Synoptic tradition. Haenchen has made the interesting suggestion that John 8.51 may show knowledge of Mark 8.27–9.1.[21] Lindars reaches a very similar conclusion, asserting that this verse in John is based on the traditional saying that is attributed to Jesus in Matthew 16.28 (and parallels).[22] If these scholars are correct in their conclusions, then this would provide further corroboration that the debate in this section of John, about Jesus being the mediator or source of eternal life for believers, is closely linked to earlier christological traditions. John certainly shows a knowledge of the same or a closely related tradition in John 12.25, which is very close to Mark 8.35 and parallels.[23] In Mark 8.38–9.1, Jesus says that whoever is ashamed of him and his words, the Son of Man will be ashamed of that person when he comes in his Father's glory, and that there are among those present some who will not taste death before they see the kingdom of God come with power. The points of contact with the Johannine passage we are considering here are:

(1)   the reference to keeping/not being ashamed of Jesus' words (Mark 8.38; John 8.51);[24]

(2)   the consequence stated in terms of tasting/seeing death (Mark 9.1; John 8.51–2);[25]

sea (Mark 6.50) as a use of the divine name, which then formed the basis for his further development of the idea. In the former instance the theme that is brought in here, the 'lifting up' or crucifixion of the Son of Man, is closely interwoven. Cf. Brown, *Introduction*, pp. 139–40.

[21] Ernst Haenchen, *John*, Philadelphia: Fortress, 1984, vol. II p. 32. Becker recognizes the saying as traditional but is less convinced of the links with the saying preserved in Mark (*Johannes*, p. 309).

[22] Lindars, *Gospel of John*, p. 332. Cf. also J. Ramsey Michaels, *John*, Peabody, MA: Hendrickson, 1984, p. 154, who suggests a connection with the tradition found in Mark 12.27 and parallels.

[23] Cf. Dodd, *Historical Tradition*, pp. 338–43.

[24] Lindars, *Gospel of John*, p. 332 suggests that 'If anyone keeps my word' replaces 'there are some standing here', apparently failing to notice the link with the idea of remaining faithful to Jesus' word in the immediate context of the original tradition.

[25] Lindars, ibid., pp. 332–3 rightly notes that John has subtly altered the tradition, using his preferred language of 'eternal life' ('for ever') rather than the more traditional 'kingdom' language. Also significant is that the language of 'tasting death', while found in other Jewish and Christian writings, does not occur anywhere else in the Gospels outside these related passages. There is no reason to think, as

(3)   the closely related terminology of 'glory' and 'the Son of
       Man' (the glory is the Father's in both cases, although it is
       shared with the Son (of Man); Mark 8.38; John 8.28, 50,
       54).[26]

It thus seems likely that here, as in John 5, the christological debate
about who Jesus is and the claims made for him are based on, and
firmly rooted in, earlier Christian traditions which underlie the
narrative at many points, and which form the starting point both
for the debates themselves and for the responses given. The claims
made by Christians that Jesus bore the divine name, and was the
mediator or source of eternal life, were objected to by 'the Jews',
and the Fourth Gospel seeks to respond to those objections.

The Johannine response

The ultimate confirmation for the suggestions we have made above
will be if what the Evangelist has written here can be shown to
make good sense when interpreted as a response to Jewish objections to aspects of Christian belief such as the ones we have been
discussing. As we shall now see, there are strong indications that
this is in fact the case. The key alteration that the Evangelist
appears to have made to the tradition he inherited relates to *when*
Jesus bears the divine name. In John 8, Jesus is not going to be
given the divine name when he is exalted, but bears it already even
during his earthly life. His being 'lifted up' (crucified/exalted) will
simply demonstrate what is already the case.[27]

The significance of this as a response to the objections raised by
'the Jews' becomes clearer when we consider the relationship
between 'the Name' of God and 'the Word' of God in Judaism. In
Philo, both terms can designate the Logos, much in the same way
that Wisdom and Word are used interchangeably in some Jewish
literature. One very clear example is *Conf.* 146, where Philo writes:
'But if there be any as yet unfit to be called "son of God", let him
press to take his place under God's Firstborn, the Logos, who

---

Neyrey does (*Ideology*, p. 47), that the change from 'seeing' death to 'tasting' death
in 8.51–2 represents a Jewish misconstrual of Jesus' words.

[26] Also worth mentioning is that the designation 'Son of Man' is linked in the
Johannine passage with 'lifting up', a Johannine synonym for which is 'glorification'.

[27] One possible basis on which development may have been made is perhaps if the
author read the use of 'I am' on the lips of Jesus in the earlier Synoptic tradition in
light of the belief that (the exalting) Christ bears the divine name.

holds the eldership among the angels, their ruler as it were. And many names are his, for he is called "Beginning", and the *"Name of God"*, and his *"Logos"* . . . '[28] Similarly the *Prayer of Manasseh* 3 uses Word and Name in parallelism to one another:

> He who bound the sea and established it by the command
> of his *word*,
> He who closed the bottomless pit and sealed it by his
> powerful and glorious *name*.

In other contemporary and later literature similar statements of equivalence are made, and even where only one of the two terms appears, God's 'Word' and 'Name' repeatedly serve the same functions, such as having been with God in the beginning, and served as the agent or instrument of creation.[29] In view of this equivalence it seems justified, if not indeed necessary, to regard Jesus' claim in John 8 to be 'I am', i.e. to bear the divine name, as parallel or equivalent to the Johannine portrait of him as the Word 'made flesh'.[30]

In terms of Johannine legitimation, this equivalence would have been of great importance. Neyrey notes that a distinction was made in the ancient world between gods, who were truly immortal, and divinized human beings, who could be called 'gods' but were not divine in the fullest sense.[31] If this distinction was an important one for non-Jews, so much the more was it important for Jews, for whom God was unique and clearly superior to all other beings.[32] As far as 'the Jews' were concerned, for someone to claim for

[28] See also *Mig.* 174, where the Logos is described as the angel in whom God's name dwells, who is mentioned in Exod. 23.20.

[29] See the parallels compiled in Fossum, *Image*, pp. 117–20. See too Ball, *'I Am'*, pp. 279–82.

[30] See the point already made (above, p. 55), that the whole Gospel is to be read in light of the prologue. Burkett (*Son of the Man*, p. 151) notes another possible link with the imagery of the prologue through connection with Amos 8.11–12, where it is said that people will 'seek the Word of Yahweh, but they will not find it', a saying which appears to be echoed in 8.21 (see also 7.33–4). Also see Barrett's comments on 8.12 on the connection between light and Wisdom/Word (*Commentary*, pp. 336–7); also Boismard, *Prologue*, pp. 144–5 on a similar connection in relation to the prologue.

[31] Neyrey, *Ideology*, pp. 52–5, 218–19. He cites Plutarch, *Pelopidas* 16; *On the Malice of Herodotus* 857D; Diodorus of Sicily, *Library of History* VI.1.2.

[32] See Philo, *Virt.* 65; *Leg.* 118; *Dec.* 64–5; also ch.4 above, where we noted the unanimous disapproval of the Jewish tradition of any who 'made himself God'. In the case of 'divinized' figures like Moses, there was no question of there being any confusion between the Eternal and these other figures. Others could be called 'god(s)', but not in the fullest sense of being the eternal and only true God. The

himself the attributes of divinity was to rebel against the divine authority and deny the distinctiveness of the one true God. In responding to the objections raised, the Evangelist appears to have related the tradition that the exalted Christ was given the divine name to the tradition that he was indwelt by God's Word or Wisdom. From the combination of the two traditions he arrived at the conclusion that Jesus did not receive the divine name when he ascended to heaven, as a human being who has undergone an apotheosis, but is rather the human being whom the eternal, imperishable Name or Word became. In a sense, the claims of Jesus are justified because, rather than its being the case that Jesus bears the divine name, one might say that *the Name bears Jesus*.[33] The human Jesus is one with the Name of God, so that what can be predicated of the latter applies equally to the former. That this is the line of argument which the Evangelist is following is indicated by 8.23–4, where the need for 'the Jews' to believe that 'I am' is directly connected with a contrast between Jesus, who is 'from above/not of this world', and his opponents, who are 'from below/ of this world'.[34] We may thus suggest that the Evangelist is adapting the traditions he inherited in this way, in order to present Jesus as the one as whom the Name or Word has 'become flesh', one whose ultimate origin is heavenly rather than earthly and who is eternal by virtue of the divine name, and that the Evangelist seeks thereby to defend the legitimacy of Christian beliefs about Jesus.[35]

We must also note here the close connections with a theme which we have already considered at some length in connection with John 5, namely that of divine agency. In Jewish tradition, the one in whom God's name was caused to dwell was empowered and

distinction is also made very clearly in the Jewish-Christian Pseudo-Clementine *Recognitions* 2.42 (on which see further McGrath, 'Johannine Christianity', 6).

[33] See the similar point made by Brown (*Gospel*, p. 408) in connection with John 10 (quoted below, p. 000).

[34] Cadman (*Open Heaven*, p. 127) feels that the contrast is clearly moral rather than metaphysical (especially in view of 17.14, where the disciples are said to be 'not of this world' even as Jesus is 'not of this world'). Most likely, however, in the heavenly/earthly dualism moral and metaphysical categories at times overlap, so that the sense must be determined by the context. There can be no doubt that, at least as far as the Gospel in its present form is concerned, Jesus (or better the one incarnate as Jesus) has a literal heavenly origin, has 'come down from heaven'.

[35] For the relevance of the difficult verse 28 to the Johannine context, cf. further Moloney, *Johannine Son of Man*, pp. 137–8. It is clear that John hoped that the obedience of Jesus even unto death would demonstrate the validity of Jesus' claim, and that he did all things as God's obedient Son and agent; precisely *how* he hoped that all this would become clear to his Jewish interlocutors is uncertain.

authorized to serve as God's unique agent. The clearest example of this is the angel Yaoel in the *Apocalypse of Abraham* 10.8ff., who speaks of 'a power through the medium of his ineffable name in me', and then goes on to describe the various exalted functions which he carries out on God's behalf. Ashton notes that, while there are obvious differences, there are also important similarities between the presentation of Jesus in John and the portrayal of Yaoel in the *Apocalypse of Abraham* – in particular in relation to the motifs of sending and bearing the divine name.[36] Jesus functions as God's agent through the indwelling of God's name, and just as those who accepted the cultural principles of sonship and agency on which John's argument in chapter 5 depends would presumably have found his arguments sound, so here too those who accept that angelic figures (and perhaps others like Moses[37]) have been enabled by the indwelling of the divine name to perform unique tasks as God's envoy, would have found it difficult to deny the validity of John's argument. If Jesus has been commissioned by God in the way the Johannine Christians claim, then there is no reason to regard the assertions made about Jesus by the Johannine Christians as blasphemous.[38]

The Evangelist has thus developed the traditional Christian association between Jesus' obedience to death on a cross, and his subsequent exaltation and being given the name above all other names. The one who does these things had *already* become one with the Word, which is the Name, and it was this commissioning as God's agent which is *demonstrated* in his obedience to the Father, even to death on a cross. The exaltation then serves as a further demonstration, as the agent indwelt by the name returns to heaven. Through the use of the single phrase, 'lifting up', the

[36] Ashton, *Understanding*, p. 143. He cites at length Apoc. Abr. 10, where most of the parallels he is focusing on are found. As Ashton rightly notes, there is no question of direct dependence between the two works; rather, they represent parallel phenomena which can nonetheless illuminate one another.

[37] On the possible connections between the divine name in John and Moses-motifs see especially Meeks, ibid., pp. 290–1, 302, 304. See too the Samaritan sources cited in Meeks, *Prophet-King*, pp. 236–7; Fossum, *Name of God*, pp. 87–106. Possible evidence of similar traditions among the rabbis is provided by Meeks on pp. 193–5.

[38] The Johannine Christians may have also found biblical support for their linking of the divine name 'I am' and the sending of an agent, based on Isa. 48.12–16, where there is an absolute 'I am' followed by a statement of having been sent by 'my Lord Yahweh', without any indication of a change of speaker (so Burkett, *Son of the Man*, pp. 156–7).

Evangelist ties these various strands together into what appears to be a reasonably tidy system. However, in doing so he has once again altered the shape of the belief he inherited, the emphasis now being placed on the descent of the Name/Word from heaven and the subsequent return there, rather than on the exaltation of a human being.[39] This new emphasis makes the most sense if understood as part of the Evangelist's attempt to legitimate traditional beliefs. In doing so, the Evangelist has not simply repeated the tradition, nor has he created ideas and arguments out of thin air. Rather, in seeking to defend his and his community's beliefs, he has in the process developed them (and other traditions as well) in a number of significant ways.

One further point remains to be made. In its original context in Deutero-Isaiah, the 'I am (Yahweh)' declarations represent an affirmation of monotheism, of Israel's God as the only true God, against pagan polytheism and idolatry.[40] It may therefore seem ironic to some that John's Christology, which has been regarded by some as an abandonment of Jewish monotheism and assimilation to Gentile thought, makes use of such texts. However, it is unlikely that the Evangelist was unaware of such associations.[41] We are not to see here, as some have suggested, a traditional 'second God' that was carried over from pre-exilic Israelite belief.[42] Michaels rightly notes the relevance of Isaiah 47.8 and Zephaniah 2.15, where foreign nations arrogantly claim 'I am, and there is none beside me.' The conclusion that Michaels quite correctly draws from these passages is that for anyone other than Yahweh to make such a declaration was blasphemy.[43] However, it is important to note that the Evangelist's portrayal of these words on the lips of Jesus differs radically from these passages from the Hebrew Bible referred to by Michaels. Jesus as 'I am' does not say 'there is no other', but rather constantly affirms that there is another upon whom he is wholly

---

[39] We shall have opportunity in ch.7 to consider the prologue, where a similar logic and emphasis appears to be at work. See also chs.10 and 13 below.

[40] Cf. Feuillet, 'Ego eimi', 13, 217.

[41] Cf. Harner, 'I Am', p. 57.

[42] *Contra* Ashton, *Understanding*, p. 146, who too readily follows Barker's hypothesis (cf. Margaret Barker, *The Older Testament. The Survival of Themes from the Ancient Royal Cult in Sectarian Judaism and Early Christianity*, London: SPCK, 1987; also the criticisms in Hurtado, 'First-Century Jewish Monotheism', pp. 352–4).

[43] Michaels, *John*, p. 154.

dependent, the one whose name 'I am' he bears and on whose behalf he can thus speak with full authority.[44]

It is interesting that, whereas Ashton feels that interpreters would do well to be less concerned to defend the thesis that the Fourth Evangelist, 'like all good Jews, was a die-hard monotheist', others have reached the opposite conclusion, namely that monotheism is precisely what the Evangelist himself is seeking to defend.[45] The Evangelist explicitly asserts his monotheistic beliefs in 17.3 (and also in 5.44), and if objectors questioned his fidelity to this foundation stone of Jewish belief, he would certainly have stressed the monotheistic character of his beliefs. However, the issue does not appear to have been about whether the Johannine Christians were still monotheists, but about whether the one to whom they attributed various divine prerogatives and honours was God's appointed agent, or a rebel against God who sought to put himself in God's place. This discussion presupposes Jewish monotheism, but it does not appear that monotheism itself is the issue. The Fourth Evangelist works within the context of the dynamic monotheism of first-century Judaism, and makes use of many areas of flexibility within that monotheism to present Jesus as God's legitimate agent, the one whom he sent, who carries out his will and bears his name, and who is thus worthy to be respected and obeyed even as one would respect and obey God himself.

The 'I am' statements attributed to God in Deutero-Isaiah were spoken by the prophet, in the first person, on God's behalf. In later Jewish-Christian thought, the one who has now become incarnate as the human being Jesus is clearly considered to be the same one who previously spoke through the prophets.[46] As far as the Fourth Evangelist is concerned, the use of the divine name 'I am' by Jesus represents an appropriate expression of the Spirit or Word of God in and through the one with whom the Word/Spirit is now wholly at one: he can speak these words in a way that no other before him could. Nonetheless, presenting a human being as speaking these words not only on behalf of God and/or through the inspiration of God's Spirit, but as the Word *become flesh*, would eventually

---

[44] Cf. e.g. 5.19–30; 8.28–9; 12.48–9; 14.10–11. See also Harner, '*I Am*', p. 57.

[45] Cf. Ashton, *Understanding*, p. 146. Contrast Harner, '*I Am*', pp. 54, 57, 60–1; de Jonge, 'Monotheism', p. 236.

[46] Cf. e.g. Ps.-Clem. *Homilies* 3.20.13–14; Gospel according to the Hebrews (Jerome, *On Isa.* 11.2).

contribute to the extension of the boundaries of Christian monotheism and Christology.

Summary

To sum up our findings in this section, then, we have shown that, in
this part of the Gospel, John is dependent on earlier traditions
concerning Jesus as the one who bears God's name and who carries
out divine functions (such as giving, or being the source of, eternal
life). Such claims made for Jesus had, by the time John wrote at
least, come to be regarded by some as unacceptable and even
blasphemous. The Fourth Evangelist seeks to show that there is
nothing in these Christian beliefs which is not supported by Jewish
tradition and Scripture. In seeking to respond to the objections that
have been raised, the Evangelist relates the idea of Jesus as the
bearer of God's Name to the idea of Jesus as the one in whom
God's Word dwells. These two concepts had already been closely
related to one another in earlier Jewish writings. By exploiting this
connection, the Evangelist could argue that Jesus was not a
rebellious human being, nor even a divinized human being, but the
Word (or Name) become flesh. And because there was already
some precedent for God's agent to bear the divine name, the
Evangelist could tie the bearing of the divine name by Jesus into his
portrayal of Jesus as God's agent. In so doing, he undermined
certain possible objections, since if other figures, whether human or
angelic, could be thought of in these terms, then there was nothing
blasphemous about similar claims being made for Jesus. In taking
these steps, John was closely dependent on earlier tradition, and
once again we find that the Evangelist was not simply creating
arguments out of thin air. Had he done so, his arguments would
not have borne the weight they were required to.

Thus once again we can see how the steps which the Evangelist
took developed Christology in new directions. For John, as for
those who connected the divine name and the idea of agency with
figures like Moses or Yaoel, these ideas allowed the ultimate and
unique significance of a particular figure to be asserted. John's
portrait of Jesus was firmly within the boundaries of Jewish
monotheism as understood in his time. However, it is to a large
extent John's use of these ideas in the context of controversy and in
new and creative ways which raised many of the issues that would
confront Christian theology over the subsequent centuries. We may

thus conclude that by presenting Jesus in a manner that raised these issues, the Fourth Evangelist determined more than any other New Testament author the directions that the development of Christology would take and the issues with which the Church would, sooner or later, be confronted.

6

'YOU ARE GODS' – BUT WHO ARE 'YOU'?
(JOHN 10.22–39)

We shall now turn our attention to John 10. In this part of the
Fourth Gospel we have a clear example of an apologetic appeal to
Scripture in support of the christological claims made by the
Johannine Jesus.[1] Neyrey rightly classes verses 34–6 and verses
37–8 as apologies,[2] and Becker expresses a similar view in relation
to the whole of 10.22–5, 30–9.[3] There can be little doubt that the
Fourth Evangelist is here responding to the objections brought by
'the Jews', and seeking thereby to defend or legitimate the beliefs
that have come under fire.

The subject of the conflict and its relationship to earlier christological beliefs

The issue which is raised explicitly in this chapter is that Jesus, a
'mere human,' is 'making himself God,' and thus committing
'blasphemy.' As Talbert has noted, many aspects of this passage
closely resemble the main elements of the dialogue with the Jews in
John 5:[4]

(1) Jesus claims a functional unity with the Father. The Son
     does what the Father does (5.17, 19–21; 10.25–30, 37–8).[5]

[1] Cf. Carson, *John*, p. 397; Painter, *Quest*, p. 362; Talbert, *Reading John*,
pp. 169–70. The argument proceeds in a way that at times resembles later rabbinic
forms of exegesis (cf. Brown, *Gospel*, pp. lxx, 405, 409–10; Painter, *Quest*, p. 362).
[2] Neyrey, *Ideology*, pp. 72–7. Similarly one section of Neyrey's article '"I Said:
You are Gods": Psalm 82:6 and John 10', *JBL* 108/4 (1989), 653, is entitled 'Psalm
82 as Apologetic Response'.
[3] Becker, *Johannes*, pp. 249–50. See too Haenchen, *John vol.2*, p. 52.
[4] Talbert, *Reading John*, pp. 169–70.
[5] Most commentators agree that this is what ἕν means here, the neuter form
indicating that the meaning is 'united' rather than 'identical' or 'the same person'.
Cf. MacGregor, *John*, p. 241; Brown, *Gospel*, pp. 403, 407; Lindars, *Gospel of John*,
p. 370; Michaels, *John*, p. 187; Beasley-Murray, *John*, p. 174; Carson, *John*,
pp. 394–5; Brodie, *John*, p. 376; Witherington, *John's Wisdom*, p. 191.

(2) 'The Jews' misunderstand this in terms of Jesus making himself, as Son, equal to or identical with the Father (5.18; 10.33).

(3) As a direct consequence, 'the Jews' seek to kill Jesus (5.18; 10.31).

(4) An apologetic response is given, which appeals to Scripture as a support for the claims and actions of Jesus (5.39–40, 46–7; 10.34–5).

It thus seems justified to appeal to John 5 to help illuminate and clarify the meaning of the passage now under consideration.[6]

The reference to 'blasphemy' and the discussion of Jesus doing what God does, recall the tradition, found in the Synoptics, which lies behind John 5.1–18 (cf. Mark 2.1–12 and chapter 4 above). However, the accusation also recalls the Marcan trial narrative, where Jesus is condemned by the Sanhedrin for blasphemy (Mark 14.64). As Lindars points out, the direct question placed by 'the Jews' here concerning whether Jesus is the Christ reminds one of the Synoptic trial narratives.[7] Jesus' response in both instances posits a special relationship between him and God and claims for him an exalted status and role, which elicits an accusation of blasphemy and a decision to kill Jesus. [8]

It is not surprising to find the Evangelist using traditions from the trial narrative here, seeing as he has essentially replaced the traditional trial before the Jews (which follows Jesus' arrest in the Synoptics) with an 'extended trial narrative' that spans most or all of the public ministry.[9] Given the close links between the present passage and John 5, the tradition underlying it, and the Synoptic trial narrative, there is good reason to think that the issue of 'blasphemy' which the Fourth Evangelist is addressing here is closely related to the charge of blasphemy which had been brought against Jesus even in earlier times. As in the Synoptics, and also in

[6] So also rightly Beasley-Murray, *John*, p. 175.

[7] Lindars, *Gospel of John*, p. 368. See Mark 14.60–1, and the even more similar Luke 22.66–7, as George M. Smiga notes (*Pain and Polemic. Anti-Judaism in the Gospels*, Mahwah, NJ: Paulist, 1992, p. 156). See also Dodd, *Historical Tradition*, p. 91; Brown, *Gospel*, pp. 405–6; Pancaro, *Law*, p. 65; Beasley-Murray, *John*, p. 175; Brodie, *John*, p. 374.

[8] Cf. Pryor, *John*, p. 46. See also Sabbe, *Studia*, p. 447 who notes the similarity between the responses of Jesus recorded in John 10.25 and Luke 22.67.

[9] Brown, *Gospel*, p. 405; Pancaro, *Law*, pp. 7–8, 70–1; A. E. Harvey, *Jesus on Trial*, p. 17 (and *passim*); Sabbe, *Studia*, pp. 445–6; Andrew T. Lincoln, 'Trials, Plots and the Narrative of the Fourth Gospel', *JSNT* 56 (1994), 6.

John 5, Jesus is felt to blaspheme because he is putting himself in the place of God, claiming to carry out functions which are thought to be divine prerogatives (in this passage the giving of eternal life is the divine prerogative explicitly mentioned, in 10.28).[10] The objectionable character of what the Johannine Jesus says may possibly have been enhanced by a misunderstanding: 'the Jews' may have understood Jesus' assertion, 'I and the Father are one', in the sense of 'I am the Father' or 'I and the Father are one and the same person', rather than as a reference to the unity of the Father and Son.[11] Nonetheless, the claim of the Son to carry out divine prerogatives is the key issue, and thus it is the idea that the Son and Father are one in action that is in focus in the controversy described in this passage. [12] As in John 5, the issue is the claim that Jesus does what God does, and, more specifically, whether it is justified and legitimate to make such a claim for Jesus.

The unity of Father and Son (which is such a crucial issue in the controversy portrayed in John 10) is not a Johannine creation, although it is clearly emphasized in John in a way that it is not in earlier writings. In Q, there is a unique mutual knowledge shared between Father and Son (Matt. 11.27 and parallel). Elsewhere in early Christian tradition they share a glory (Mark 8.38 and parallels) and a kingdom (Luke 22.29–30; 23.42; 1 Cor. 15.24–8; Eph. 5.5; Col. 1.13). Paul calls the Gospel the 'Gospel of Christ' and 'Gospel of God' (e.g. Rom. 1.16; 15.16, 19, 29; 2 Cor. 9.13; 11.7). More directly relevant here is the gift from God of eternal

[10] Cf. Neyrey, *Ideology*, pp. 59, 70–1.

[11] Neyrey, ibid., pp. 69–70 suggests that ἕν in 10.30 means, in context, something like 'equal to' or 'on a par with'. Lindars, *Gospel of John*, p. 370 notes that the RSV renders ἕν as 'equal' in 1 Cor. 3.8. However, the Johannine Jesus nowhere else makes a direct claim to equality with God, and most commentators understand the saying of the Johannine Jesus as referring to the unity of action between Father and Son. This is confirmed by the use of the neuter ἕν and by verses 37–8.

[12] Neyrey, *Ideology*, pp. 69–70, 78 still seems to pose the alternatives too sharply: John is not simply claiming a moral unity with God (something which all Jews aspired to), so he must be claiming that Jesus is 'on a par with' God. However, the middle ground of agency once again seems to provide a better interpretation: Jesus bears equal authority to God and carries out divine activities, precisely as his agent who is subordinate to him. Cf. also Painter, *Quest*, p. 361, who suggests that John 'proposed an ontological equality and a functional subordination'. While John may have moved towards an ontological identification through his development of the Logos Christology, John thinks as well in terms of a *functional equality*, the equality of the agent's authority with that of him who sent him. Nonetheless we are largely in agreement with his conclusion that 'With the combination of functional and ontological sonship we find the distinctive Johannine christology, which is the result of a reinterpretation of the tradition' (p. 363).

life, which already in Paul's time is thought of as inseparable from and mediated by Christ (Rom. 5.17–18, 21; 8.2; cf. Col. 3.3–4).[13] The imagery and concepts are more sharply focused in John, presumably because they have become a point of controversy, but nonetheless it seems clear that the issue of the unity of action between Jesus and the Father, including the carrying out of divine prerogatives by the former, is what is in mind here, and this relates to a wider stream of early Christian beliefs not limited to the Johannine circle.

There is one other possible indication that what the Johannine Jesus is here debating with 'the Jews' is not monotheism, but whether Jesus is a blasphemous glory-seeker or an appointed obedient agent exercising divine prerogatives on God's behalf and with his authority. I am referring to the setting of the dialogue: the feast of Dedication or Hanukkah. Some scholars find no symbolic connection between the dialogue and the feast which provides the setting for it, while others have proposed links with what were, in later times at least, the lectionary readings for the feast, which are said to have been passages relating to the imagery of the shepherd or to blasphemy.[14] However, an even more direct link may exist.[15] Hanukkah celebrates the rededication of the Temple after it was profaned by Antiochus Epiphanes. The books of Maccabees – which would have been familiar to John if he used the Septuagint, as it appears he did – refer to blasphemy more frequently than any other book in the OT or apocrypha ('blasphemy' occurs three times in 1 Maccabees and twice in 2 Maccabees; 'blaspheme' occurs twice in 2 Maccabees; 'blasphemer' occurs three times in 2 Maccabees and 'blasphemous' twice in 2 Maccabees).[16] Thus over one third of

---

[13] By the time Revelation was written God and the Lamb were thought to share worship and a throne. On John's relationship to earlier Christian thought here see further Brown, *Gospel*, p. 408.

[14] Cf. Barrett, *Commentary*, p. 379; Schnackenburg, *John vol. II*, p. 305; Talbert, *Reading John*, pp. 168, 170–1; and the discussion of Guilding's views in Lindars, *Gospel of John*, pp. 366–7; James C. VanderKam, 'John 10 and the Feast of Dedication', in H. W. Attridge, J. J. Collins and T. H. Tobin (eds.), *Of Scribes and Scrolls: Studies on the Hebrew Bible, Intertestamental Judaism, and Christian Origins Presented to John Strugnell on the Occasion of His Sixtieth Birthday*, Lanham, MD: University Press of America, 1990, pp. 207–10.

[15] I am indebted to Jerry Truex for drawing my attention to this possibility. Cf. VanderKam, 'John 10', pp. 211–14; also Moloney, *Signs and Shadows*, pp. 149–50; Casey, *Is John's Gospel True?*, p. 135.

[16] 'Blaspheme' in various forms occurs a total of 16 other times in the whole of the OT and apocrypha. 'Blasphemer' occurs 2 other times and 'blasphemy' occurs 4 other times. On John's use of the LXX cf. Bruce G. Schuchard, *Scripture Within*

all occurrences of 'blasphemy' and related terms are found in the books of the Maccabees. Further, in 2 Maccabees 9.12, which describes Antiochus on his deathbed, Antiochus is depicted as repenting and asserting that 'no mortal should think that he is equal to God', a phrase which is not unlike the accusation here, 'You, although you are a human being, make yourself God' (see also John 5.18, where it is *equality* to God that is specifically mentioned). It thus seems highly plausible to suggest that John does intend his readers to recall something of the overtones and significance of this feast and of the scriptural texts that recount its origins. We may take this as probable further confirmation of what was at issue: Is Jesus making himself God or equal to God, as Antiochus Epiphanes and other blasphemers had done? Or was he, on the contrary, God's appointed agent, who obeyed God and as his agent bore the full authority of God himself? In view of the 'echoes of Scripture' which we have detected in this passage, it seems likely that we are correct to see this as having been at the heart of the issue in this debate between the Johannine Jesus and 'the Jews'. The debate over whether Jesus was the Christ or a blasphemous false messianic pretender is not distinctively Johannine, but arose prior to John. This encourages us to look for ways in which John is seeking to legitimate his belief that Jesus is the Messiah and, as such, legitimately carries out actions on God's behalf as his appointed agent.

The Johannine response

If it is relatively clear that the Evangelist was engaged in a debate concerning Christology and was seeking to defend his beliefs, it is in contrast surprisingly difficult to reach firm conclusions about exactly what the point is that the Evangelist wished to make in his defence, and how he was seeking to make it. It is clear that an appeal is being made to Scripture, but the precise force that the argument is likely to have had has been the subject of considerable debate.

The key to understanding John's apologetic argument here is his use of Psalm 82.6. There are a number of questions that need to be answered. For example, who are those who are called 'gods' to whom the Word of God came, and what is Jesus' relationship to them? And is the argument *a minori ad maius* (from the lesser to the greater) or *a maiori ad minus* (from the greater to the lesser)? That is to say, is Jesus presented as arguing 'If others can be called "gods", how much more can I' or 'If others can be called "gods", then what is wrong with my lesser claim to be God's son'?

Thus one major question which arises immediately is the significance of the change from 'gods' to 'son of God' in 10.35–6. In the preceding narrative, Jesus has spoken of himself and God in terms of Son and Father; there has been no explicit claim to the designation 'God'. Brown and Neyrey have pointed out that the move from 'gods' to 'Son of God' does not necessarily represent a lessening of the claim being made for Jesus: in Psalm 82, which John quotes, 'gods' and 'sons of the Most High' are equivalent, as is shown by their use in synonymous parallelism to one another.[17] Therefore we must determine who the Evangelist understood 'those to whom the word of God came', those referred to in the Psalm as 'gods' and as 'sons of the Most High', to be, in order to clarify in what sense Jesus is claiming to be 'Son of God' or 'God'.

Although it is worth noting that cases have been made for interpreting the reference as being to (a) angels; (b) judges; (c) prophets or (d) Israel at Sinai, only the last of these – Israel at Sinai – can be in mind in John, in view of the reference to the word of God having come to certain individuals, and also in view of the original context of the verse John cites, which emphasizes that those who are called 'gods' will nonetheless 'die like men'.[18] Angels and judges are not associated with the idea of the coming of the word of God, and the prophetic figures in the Jewish Scriptures were not singled out by God for judgment: only of Israel at Sinai can both be said.[19] This is also the interpretation that occurs most

[17] Brown, *Gospel*, p. 409; Neyrey, *Ideology*, p. 73.

[18] So rightly Beasley-Murray, *John*, pp. 176–7; Carson, *John*, p. 397. Cf. also W. Gary Phillips, 'An Apologetic Study of John 10:34–36', *Bibliotheca Sacra* 146 (1989), 410–1 n.13. Loader, *Christology*, p. 163 suggests that this interpretation would be a long way from what the author *usually* means by θεός in reference to Jesus, which seems an odd remark in view of the fact that the only other clear reference to Jesus as God is found in 20.28! The text in 1.18 is disputed (see Manns, *L'Evangile*, p. 22; Ehrman, *Orthodox Corruption*, pp. 78–82), and 1.1 refers to the pre-existent Logos, which is relevant for the status of Jesus but is not an example of the use of θεός in reference to the human being Jesus. See also our discussion of the prologue in ch.7 below.

[19] Of course, the false prophets are condemned, but precisely because they proclaimed their own words and had not received the Word of God or been sent by

frequently in the rabbinic literature.[20] Neyrey has greatly illuminated the passage by seeking to demonstrate that, rather than
having chosen this text in order to argue, in a very unsophisticated
and *ad hoc* way, that 'others are called "gods" so why not Jesus?',
the Evangelist probably chose it with its specific history of interpretation in mind.

In the most common form of rabbinic interpretation of Psalm
82.6, the Israelites are addressed as 'gods' at Sinai because, when
Torah was given, they became deathless, the Angel of Death being
restrained from affecting them any longer. But when they sinned,
they lost this privilege, with the result that they shall 'die like men'.
This was sometimes connected with the similar imagery applied to
Adam in Genesis 3: Adam could have had access to immortality,
but through his disobedience to the commandment, death gained
power over him. Neyrey suggests that it is because Jesus is holy or
consecrated, and has power over death, that this text is applied to
him.[21] In our view, there are even more fundamental issues in the
interpretation of the Psalm that the Evangelist has in mind and to
which he is appealing.

Before we can consider them, however, we must cautiously

him (cf. e.g. Jer. 1.14; 23.25–38; Ezek. 13.17). For this reason, Menken is forced to
posit that the Evangelist ignores the passage's original context, intending that the
reader think only of the citation given and no more, since the prophets would not be
an obvious group to which to apply the words, 'Yet you shall die like men' (Maarten
J. J. Menken, 'The Use of the Septuagint in Three Quotations in John. Jn 10, 34; 12,
38; 19, 24', in Christopher M. Tuckett (ed.), *The Scriptures in the Gospels* (BETL,
131), Leuven: Leuven University Press, 1997, pp. 376, 393). The evidence which
Menken gathers refers to agents appointed by God, which includes prophets but is a
much broader category, including e.g. the judges, Adam as God's viceroy and
probably even Israel at Sinai. This evidence is important, and if John's citation has
in mind agency in general rather than Israel at Sinai in particular, most of the points
made in this section will still retain their validity. His points about ascent to heaven
as part of the appointing of an agent are interesting in connection with our
discussion in ch.10 below. The argument of Boismard ('Jésus, le Prophète par
excellence, d'après Jean 10, 24–39', in Joachim Gnilka (ed.), *Neues Testament und
Kirche. Für Rudolf Schnackenburg*, Freiburg: Herder, 1974, p. 161) that 'word' in the
singular never refers to Torah is without foundation – cf. e.g. the frequent parallelism
between 'word' and 'law' throughout Ps. 119.

[20] Barrett, *Commentary*, p. 384. Cf. the texts conveniently collected and cited in
Neyrey, 'I Said: You are Gods', 655–8. Also A. J. M. Wedderburn, 'Adam in Paul's
Letter to the Romans', in E. A. Livingstone (ed.), *Studia Biblica 1978.III* (JSNTS, 3),
Sheffield: Sheffield Academic Press, 1978, pp. 414–5; Hanson, *Prophetic Gospel*,
pp. 144–5. Robin Scroggs, *The Last Adam: A Study in Pauline Anthropology*,
Philadelphia: Fortress/ Oxford: Blackwell, 1966, p. 53 acknowledges the existence of
this typology but seeks to play it down, presumably because he refuses to find
allusions to the story of Adam in Rom. 1 and 7.

[21] Neyrey, 'I Said: You are Gods', 659–63.

consider what evidence there is, if any, that the interpretation of this Psalm found in rabbinic exegesis could have its origins early enough for John to have known it. The most important piece of evidence is John's own testimony: in spite of the fact that the most obvious reference in the Psalm is to rulers (or possibly to heavenly beings), John seems clearly to identify those referred to in the Psalm as Israel at Sinai, 'those to whom the Word of God came'. The fact that John chooses this precise phrase, 'those to whom the Word of God came', is also significant, since this was precisely the point of contact between the Adam and Sinai narratives exploited by the later exegetes: both received the word or commandment of God.

That earlier Jewish authors had already drawn parallels of this sort between the Sinai and Eden narratives seems clear, even if it had not been formulated in exactly these terms. A number of early Jewish sources draw parallels between Adam and Israel with respect to their obedience (or otherwise) to God's law.[22] In fact, a good case can be made for some authors of the Hebrew Bible having intended such parallels to be drawn. In a number of places in the Jewish Scriptures the Exodus is thought of as a new creation, and the fulfilment of the promise to Abraham is portrayed as the reversal of Adam's sin; this is followed by the giving of a commandment, which in turn is followed by disobedience and punishment/curse which involves exclusion from the land.[23]

Early Christian writings prior to John also bear witness to similar ideas. At several points in Paul's letter to the Romans, the argument appears to assume that the stories of Adam receiving the commandment and Israel receiving Torah were already regarded as in some way parallel and comparable to one another.[24] And in the Synoptic temptation narratives, Jesus is portrayed as having

[22] So e.g. Ps.-Philo 13.8–10; Jub. 2.23; 3.31; Ben Sira 17; cf. Wisd. 10.1–2, 16. See also the slightly later but possibly pre-Johannine 4 Ezra 3.4–22; 7.72, 116–31. See too 2 Bar. 4.2–7. On points of similarity and contrast in 2 Bar.17–18 cf. John R. Levison, *Portraits of Adam in Early Judaism. From Sirach to 2 Baruch* (JSPS, 1), Sheffield: JSOT/ Sheffield Academic Press, 1988, pp. 133–4. Levison rightly stresses the diversity of early Jewish portraits of Adam, and we have no desire to deny this. The point which we are making here is simply that the ideas which we have suggested are presupposed by John's discussion can be traced back early enough to make John's knowledge of them plausible.

[23] Cf. Wright, *Climax*, pp. 24–5 for the relevant passages and their interpretation.

[24] Cf. Wedderburn, 'Adam', pp. 413–19; James D. G. Dunn, *Romans 1–8* (WBC, 38A), Dallas: Word, 1988, pp. 72–3; Hooker, *From Adam to Christ*, pp. 73–87 on Rom. 1.23; and Wedderburn, 'Adam', pp. 419–22; Dunn, *Romans*, pp. 378–9 on Rom. 7.7.

obeyed where Adam and/or Israel disobeyed, and as being himself at once the true Adam and the true Israel.[25] It might be suggested that John was the first to relate such ideas to Psalm 82.6 – this is possible, although it seems unlikely in view of the fact that this exegesis is so widely accepted in rabbinic sources. But even if John *was* the first to relate these parallels between Adam and Israel to Psalm 82.6, at the very least the conceptual basis for John's exegesis seems to have been well established by the time he wrote.

In the pre-Johannine (and probably pre-Pauline) passage Philippians 2.6–11, Jesus is portrayed as having been exalted to heaven and having received the divine name in a way that, at a later stage, 'the Jews' would find objectionable. John 8 appears to show awareness of the ideas found in the Philippians hymn and in other early Christian writings: Jesus as the one who bears the divine name in connection with his obedience to the Father, his death and his exaltation. In view of the points made by Neyrey, it is perhaps significant that this understanding of the exalted status of Christ was part of the presentation of him in terms of 'Adam Christology', i.e., as having obeyed as Adam should have and having been rewarded accordingly.[26] A fundamental connection thus appears to exist between the traditional interpretation within Judaism of Psalm 82 in terms of Israel/Adam typology, and aspects of the Christology which portrayed Jesus as exalted to heaven, serving as God's vice-regent and bearing his name, which were important issues in the Johannine conflict with 'the Jews'. This is unlikely to be a coincidence, and we must reflect on what the implications of John's appeal to this Psalm would have been for those aware of these traditional associations and interpretation.[27]

---

[25] Cf. James D. G. Dunn, *Baptism in the Holy Spirit. A Re-examination of the New Testament Teaching on the Gift of the Spirit in relation to Pentecostalism today*, London: SCM, 1970, pp. 29–31; Hill, *Matthew*, p. 101.

[26] Cf. Dunn, *Christology*, pp. 114–23; Wright, *Climax*, pp. 90–6. There is explicit evidence from Jewish and Christian authors (much of which is from a later date, but some of which dates from the first century) for the idea that Adam was appointed as God's viceroy and as 'god' over the earth, and/or that had he remained faithful and obedient, he would have been exalted and ruled (or continued to rule) as 'god' (that is, as God's agent) over the earth. See the widespread Jewish traditions on this subject, e.g. in Philo, *Op.* 148; *Life of Adam and Eve* 13–15; *b*. Hag. 12a; *b*. Sanh. 38b; Yalkut Shimeoni I §120. See also the other passages mentioned in our discussion of Jesus as God in ch.2 above, and in Scroggs, *Last Adam*, pp. 25–9; Steenburg, 'Worship', 96–8. Cf. also the various parallels cited by Fossum, *Name of God*, pp. 271–7, and also Theophilus, *Ad Autolycum* 2.24 (and the discussion thereof in Grant, *Gods*, p. 132).

[27] It should perhaps also be noted that this is not necessarily the only place in

As we have already seen, it appears quite certain that those whom John referred to as 'those to whom the word of God came' were the Israelites at Sinai and Adam. They had received God's commandment, and were set apart for him, to serve and obey him faithfully, and in so doing to act as his vice-regent(s), as 'god(s)' with dominion over the earth, to rule it on God's behalf.[28] These figures had been referred to as 'gods' in Scripture, and although they had failed in their appointed tasks and so lost this status, the general principle remains valid. It would seem that the Evangelist is arguing that those who receive God's commission to serve as his agents and/or vice-regents are rightly called by the name of him who sent or appointed them.[29]

These considerations appear to shed light on the question of the meaning of 'gods' and 'Son of God' here. Brown and Neyrey are correct: the two designations are indeed parallel to one another. The designation of the agent or viceroy of God as 'god', and the special relationship of sonship, go hand in hand. In Jewish tradition, both Israel and (less frequently) Adam are referred to as God's son.[30] This further elucidates the argument John is putting forward: sonship and agency are inextricably interconnected. To claim to be God's son – and at the same time to rule on his behalf, in complete unity with him, as his viceroy and agent, doing his work and wielding his authority, perhaps even being called by God's own name – is to be regarded as legitimate on the basis of

John where the Evangelist shows an interest in and awareness of Jewish exegesis of the Adam narratives. Borgen, *Philo*, pp. 90–2 connects the light/darkness imagery with 2 Bar. 17–18 and with rabbinic interpretations of Adam's fall. The prologue has also been suggested to reflect the 'Sinai myth' presupposed in rabbinic interpretation of Ps. 82 – see James S. Ackerman, 'The Rabbinic Interpretation of Psalm 82 and the Gospel of John', *HTR* 59 (1966), 188. However, the works Ackerman appeals to date from significantly later than John's time. See also Beasley-Murray (*John*, p. 177), who suggests that John reflects the Christian tradition of Jesus as the Son of God who represents Israel, the nation called to be God's son(s). See too Manns, *L'Evangile*, pp. 42–50; Hanson, *Prophetic Gospel*, p. 280; Carson, *John*, p. 398.

[28] On the covenant with Abraham and his descendants as a restoration of the original state of Adam, cf. Wright, *Climax*, pp. 21–3.

[29] In a similar vein Thompson, 'John', p. 377 makes the interesting suggestion that the use of 'God' in reference to Jesus/the Logos derives from the idea of agency, stressing that the agent rightly exercises divine prerogatives. See also Painter, *Quest*, p. 362; Loader, *Christology*, pp. 157–8, 160. See too the texts from the Jewish Scriptures cited in Phillips, 'Apologetic', 409 n.13.

[30] Although references to Israel as God's Son are relatively frequent (cf. Cullmann, *Christology*, p. 273), that this idea was associated with Adam is known only from occasional references, such as Philo, *Virt.* 204–5 and Luke 3.38.

the fact that the very same imagery is applied to Adam and Israel in Jewish tradition. There is thus nothing blasphemous about making similar claims for Jesus. In addition, in view of the polemical thrust found elsewhere in John against those who boast of their privileges because of their descent from Abraham or participation in the people of Israel, the implicit message may be that if God called Israel as a whole 'gods', even though they ultimately failed (and probably John would want to say *still fail*) to obey, how much more worthy is Jesus, who always does what pleases his Father (cf. 8.29).[31] As in John 5 and 8, the Evangelist is once again appealing to the concept of agency in order to defend the exalted status and functions attributed to Jesus by Christians.[32]

As with the other chapters that we have considered thus far in this part of the present study (that is, John 5 and 8), here too our interpretation is not complete until we allow the light of the prologue to shine here fully. Jesus is not simply a human agent, appointed, because of his obedience, to fulfil the role Adam forfeited. Rather, he is the one who was always with the Father, whom he consecrated and sent into the world: the Logos. The implication of this in the present context is grasped well by Brown: Jesus 'is not a man who makes himself God; he is the Word of God who has become man'.[33] The use of λόγος in verse 35 may be an intentional allusion to the prologue, with a contrast being made between 'those to whom the Word of God came' and the one *as whom* the Word of God came.[34] It seems reasonably likely that an attentive reader would have recalled in this discussion of the designation θεός the affirmation that θεός ἦν ὁ λογος in 1.1, and the words ὁ λόγος . . . ἐγένετο would likewise have recalled the phrase ὁ λόγος σὰρξ ἐγένετο in 1.14. The description of Jesus here as the one who pre-existed, was consecrated and was sent into the world must have the Logos in mind, making such a contrast even more likely to have been intended by the Evangelist. Thus here, as elsewhere, the argument is moved on to a higher plane through being brought into connection with the Evangelist's Logos Chris-

[31] As Michaels, *John*, p. 188 notes, the context of Ps. 82 as a whole emphasizes the failure and negative aspects of those who were called 'gods' in this way. See also John 1.11–13; 8.33–40.

[32] Brodie, *John*, p. 378 rightly notes that agency is implied by the reference in 10.36 to consecration and sending. See also Perkins, 'Gospel', p. 969.

[33] Brown, *Gospel*, p. 408.

[34] So e.g. Cadman, *Open Heaven*, p. 120; Hanson, *Prophetic Gospel*, pp. 146–9. See also Barrett, *Commentary*, p. 385; Phillips, 'Apologetic', 416.

tology: the argument is not simply that if other human beings have occupied this role or status then so can Jesus, but rather that if human beings such as Adam and the Israelites have been deemed worthy of this honour in their role as God's agents, then how much more worthy is the Word of God, and thus the Word-become-flesh, Jesus Christ, who is God's agent in the fullest sense, his heavenly agent become his earthly agent. In terms of the development of earlier Christology, we may put it sharply in the following terms: the Evangelist makes use of, appeals to and develops earlier Wisdom and agency Christology categories in order to defend an (equally early) Adam/exaltation Christology, and the related idea that Jesus carries out actions which were the prerogatives of God himself.

Summary

To sum up, the Evangelist in this section shows an awareness of earlier Christian ideas, which had – at least by the time of the writing of the Fourth Gospel, but in all probability even earlier – become controversial. This can be seen from the echoes of both John 5 (and the traditions and issues underlying it) and of the Synoptic trial tradition. It is also hinted at in the implicit connections with Adam Christology, with which the issues debated in John 8 (such as the exaltation of Jesus and his bearing the name of God) were connected from a very early stage. The Evangelist seeks to counter the objections that had been raised through one of the most basic forms of legitimation: an appeal to the Scriptures authoritative to both sides in the debate. The argument is not simply an *ad hoc* one, but evidences awareness of an interpretation of Psalm 82.6 which appears to have been current in at least some Jewish circles. One whom God set apart to be his viceroy and to rule over the earth could rightly be called both 'God' and 'son of God', sharing in an intimate relationship of obedience to God and yet wielding an authority like God's over the earth. If this was true of others who ultimately proved unworthy of this calling, how much more was it true of the Word-become-flesh, Jesus, who always obeyed and obeys his Father.

We may outline our interpretation of John 10.22–39 thus:

> *verses 22–3:* The setting of the debate is the Feast of Dedication. If, as elsewhere in John, there is a link between

the discourse and the Jewish religious institution against the backdrop of which it takes place, then the link here may be the downfall of Antiochus Epiphanes, who was remembered as having considered himself 'equal to God'.

verse 24: Jesus is asked to confess plainly whether he is the Christ. Jesus is on trial, and the Jews wish to convict him. As in the Synoptics, they do not believe that Jesus is the Christ, but wish for him to make an explicit claim on the basis of which they may convict him.

verses 25–30: Jesus claims that the miracles he does in the Father's name demonstrate who he is (God's appointed agent, the Messiah). Jesus is one with the Father in action, even giving eternal life.

verses 31–3: The Jews decide to stone Jesus for blasphemy. They do not accept his claims, and thus find his assertion that he is 'one' with God and does what God does blasphemous and insulting to God. He is a mere man, yet he *makes himself* God.

verses 34–6: Jesus defends the legitimacy of the agent of God being called 'Son of God' and even 'God' on the basis of Scripture. If this applies to earthly agents (Adam and Israel) who ultimately failed to obey God, how much more does it apply to God's heavenly agent, now become flesh, who always obeys God? If the Scriptures show something to be legitimate, there can be no denying it.

verses 37–8: The preceding argument depends on Jesus actually being the agent of God, and thus John reiterates once again that the miracles which he performs confirm his claim.

verses 39–42: The opponents reject him in spite of these arguments, but many others believe.

John's argument depends on the Scriptures and traditions of Judaism (and Christianity). Yet, as in the other parts of John, significant steps are being taken in certain directions. The emphasis is once again moved away from Jesus fulfiling divine functions as an exalted human being, and placed on the worthiness of him to do so as the pre-existent Word become flesh. The use of Wisdom motifs and imagery to describe Jesus was already part of the Christian tradition. John, by identifying Jesus and the Word or Wisdom even more closely, was able to legitimate the claims made for Jesus. If a human agent of God is worthy to receive honour and to act on God's behalf, how much more his supreme heavenly agent, the Word. And so, however one defines and nuances the extent and degree of the distinctively Johannine christological developments, the Fourth Evangelist appears to have made them as part of an attempt to draw out more fully the implications of the traditions which he inherited, in order to defend and legitimate the exalted status and functions which Christians attributed to Jesus.

Another extremely noteworthy development seen in John 10 is the defence of Jesus not only bearing the authority of God but even being called 'God.' The Fourth Evangelist clearly does apply the designation 'God' to the risen Jesus in 20.28 (and perhaps in 1.18), but nonetheless shows a great reticence – which his predecessors shared, to such an extent that it is not clear whether they intended to refer to Jesus as 'God' at all. In the period after John we notice a remarkable change: in Ignatius we already find a tendency to speak much more freely of Jesus as 'God,' and in later times even the Jewish-Christian Pseudo-Clementine literature defends this practice.[35] This is very likely a result of the fact that in John we find a scriptural support and basis being provided for this Christian practice of calling Jesus 'God.' Thus, in spite of his own restraint and reticence in referring to the human being Jesus as 'God,' by providing an argument which sought to demonstrate the legitimacy of using this language in reference to Jesus, the Evangelist apparently encouraged its wider usage, and this usage helped shape the course which later christological development followed and the conclusions which it reached. And so we see in John 10, as in the other passages we have considered thus far, evidence of the role legitimation played in the development of Johannine Christology.

[35] As we have noted elsewhere (McGrath, 'Johannine Christianity', 6), the argument in this chapter can be fruitfully compared with that found in the Jewish-Christian Pseudo-Clementine *Recognitions* 2.42, where the argument is that those who are rulers or agents on God's behalf can be called 'God'. Peter is depicted there as arguing: 'Therefore the name *God* is applied in three ways: either because he to whom it is given is truly God, or because he is the servant of him who is truly; and for the honour of the sender, that his authority may be full, he that is sent is called by the name of him who sends . . . '

7

IN THE BOSOM OF THE FATHER
(JOHN 1.1–18)

This part of our study would not be complete without a consideration of the prologue, since, as we have already stressed, the Evangelist intended the whole of his work to be read in light of it.[1] We have left it until last not due to any literary considerations, but because the evidence of *controversy* over Christology is much less explicit here than in the other passages we have considered.[2]

Nonetheless, a number of recent studies have emphasized that the conflicts and issues which are present in the rest of the Gospel are also reflected in the prologue. For example, as Kysar notes, light/darkness dualism is found in the prologue, symbolizing the acceptance and rejection of the Logos, which also runs throughout the Gospel and which is found in several of the conflict passages we have singled out for consideration in this book.[3] Closely connected with this is the prologue's polemical tone, emphasizing the Logos as the *true* (ἀληθινόν) light, and Jesus as the *unique* (μονογενὴς) Son of God. This, Kysar suggests, reflects 'a community under attack'.[4] This polemic Kysar connects with the issue of the revelations brought by Jesus and Moses.[5] Carter, however, also seeks to relate the prologue to the conflict we have been considering in this

[1] Barrett, *Commentary*, p. 156; Beasley-Murray, *John*, p. 5; Hartman, 'Johannine Jesus-Belief', pp. 96–7; Carson, *John*, p. 111; Dunn, 'Let John Be John', pp. 313, 317; Loader, *Christology*, p. 154; Pryor, *John*, p. 7; Witherington, *John's Wisdom*, p. 54. See also p. 55 above.

[2] This is not to ignore the difficult questions of whether the prologue is based on an earlier hymnic work, or of whether the Gospel ever circulated without the prologue. Nonetheless, the person(s) who put the Gospel in its present form clearly intended the whole work to be read through the 'lens' of the prologue.

[3] Kysar, 'Christology and Controversy', 354. See also Creech, 'Christology', pp. 206–17; Warren Carter, 'The Prologue and John's Gospel: Function, Symbol and the Definitive Word', *JSNT* 39 (1990), 38–9.

[4] Kysar, 'Christology and Controversy', 355.

[5] Ibid., 358–61. This topic will be treated further in ch.9 below.

chapter, that of the relationship between Jesus and God.[6] This is a conclusion which we have already hinted at, and which we shall seek to demonstrate in the present chapter. As the prologue shows indications of containing the same themes, and being concerned with the same issues, as the rest of the Gospel, it seems likely that here too we may find evidence of the Evangelist's use of traditional motifs and imagery for the purpose of legitimation.[7]

A point of controversy and its relation to earlier Christology

Although the prologue of the Fourth Gospel is often regarded as the peak or culmination of Johannine christological development, it would be a mistake to jump quickly to the conclusion that the prologue as a whole represents a very late, or even a very distinctively Johannine, development. In numerous respects the Johannine prologue resembles other early Christian expressions of wisdom Christology.[8] These earlier Christian wisdom ideas were themselves derived from modes of thought and expression which were fundamentally Jewish. In their Christian form, such ideas probably took shape in the context of reflection on the relationship between Jesus and God's earlier self-manifestation in the Torah.[9]

The earliest Christian hymns, including those that make use of wisdom language, were hymns about or to the *exalted* Christ.[10] This is significant for our purposes, since the claim that Christ had

---

[6] Carter, 'Prologue', 48 (see also pp. 38, 41).

[7] See too McGrath, 'Prologue', where we have sought to read the whole prologue in light of legitimation. On the close thematic relationship between the prologue and the rest of the Gospel see also John A. T. Robinson, 'The Relationship of the Prologue to the Gospel of St. John', *Twelve More New Testament Studies*, London: SCM, 1984, pp. 65–76; Carson, *John*, pp. 111, 135; Elizabeth Harris, *Prologue and Gospel. The Theology of the Fourth Evangelist* (JSNTS, 107), Sheffield: Sheffield Academic Press, 1994. See too Dunn, 'Let John Be John', p. 313 n.78.

[8] So e.g. Boismard, *Prologue*, p. 23; Kysar, 'Christology and Controversy', 348–51. See also Carson, *John*, pp. 135–6; McGrath, 'Change in Christology', 43–7. See further our discussion of this theme in ch.2 above.

[9] See e.g. W. D. Davies, *Paul and Rabbinic Judaism*, London: SPCK, 1955, pp. 147–76; Wright, *Climax*, p. 118. Wright also suggests that Colossians is using Wisdom imagery to address the issue of monotheism. However, there is no real evidence that this author's contemporaries regarded his Christology as in conflict with monotheism as understood in first-century Judaism.

[10] Those that we have either refer to Christ in his present exalted state, or end with the exaltation. See further Hengel, *Between Jesus and Paul*, pp. 85–6; also Paul Beasley-Murray, 'Colossians 1:15–20: An Early Christian Hymn Celebrating the Lordship of Christ', in D. A. Hagner and M. J. Harris (eds.), *Pauline Studies. Essays Presented to F. F. Bruce*, Exeter: Paternoster, 1980, pp. 169–83.

been exalted to heaven and was now seated at God's right hand seems to have been one of the aspects of earliest Christian belief that provoked objections and accusations of blasphemy.[11] The prologue to John's Gospel is sometimes regarded as an exception to this general tendency in early Christian hymns, since some scholars have suggested that the whole focus here is on the pre-existent Logos and the incarnation, with no mention of or interest in the exaltation of Christ.[12] This conclusion we believe to be mistaken for several reasons.

First, the structure of the hymn seems to imply that the place of Jesus with the Father in verse 18 refers to the ascended Christ. Most scholars agree that verses 1–2 and verse 18 parallel one another,[13] and seeing as we have the incarnation mentioned in between, the ending very likely refers to the Logos-become-flesh, Jesus Christ, having returned to heaven. If those scholars who find an inverted parallelism in the prologue are correct, this would lend even further support to our argument, although it does not depend on it.[14] Also noteworthy is that the reference in verse 18 is to the

[11] Cf. Mark 14.62–4. See further our discussion in ch.3 above.

[12] So e.g. Schnackenburg, *John vol. I*, p. 224 (hesitantly); Kysar, 'Christology and Controversy', 352; G. R. Beasley-Murray, *John*, p. 4; Witherington, *John's Wisdom*, p. 54.

[13] So e.g. Brown, *Gospel*, pp. 5, 36; John Painter, 'Christology and the History of the Johannine Community in the Prologue of the Fourth Gospel', *NTS* 30 (1984), 470; Marc Cholin, 'Le Prologue de L'Evangile selon Jean. Structure et Formation', *Science et Esprit* 41/2 (1989), 194–6; Jürgen Habermann, *Präexistenzaussagen im Neuen Testament*, Frankfurt am Main: Peter Lang, 1990, p. 400; Carson, *John*, p. 135; Manns, *L'Evangile*, p. 34; Loader, *Christology*, pp. 151, 158–9; E. Harris, *Prologue*, p. 115 n.2. The scholars mentioned in n.14 below who find a chiastic structure here by definition also discern a parallelism between the prologue's beginning and end.

[14] A chiastic structure is posited by Marie-Emile Boismard, *Prologue*, pp. 106–7; *Moise ou Jésus. Essai de Christologie Johannique* (BETL, 84), Leuven: Leuven University Press, 1988, p. 98; R. Alan Culpepper, 'The Pivot of John's Prologue', *NTS* 27 (1980–1), 16; Renner, 'Life-World', pp. 190–7; Paul Lamarche, 'The Prologue of John', in John Ashton (ed.), *The Interpretation of John*, Philadelphia: Fortress/ London: SPCK, 1986, pp. 43–5; Daniel J. Harrington, *John's Thought and Theology. An Introduction*, Wilmington, DE: Michael Glazier, 1990, p. 18; Talbert, *Reading John*, pp. 66–7; John W. Pryor, 'Jesus and Israel in the Fourth Gospel – John 1:11', *NovT* 32/3 (1990), 201–2; *John*, pp. 9–10; Mark W. G. Stibbe, *John*, Sheffield: Sheffield Academic Press, 1993, p. 30 (citing Staley); McGrath, 'Prologue', 101–3. The fact that the two subsequent sections also appear to be chiastically structured may lend further support to this view (cf. Elizabeth Danna, 'Which Side of the Line? A study of the characterization of non-Jewish characters in the Gospel of John', PhD dissertation, University of Durham, 1997, pp. 29–30). Borgen, *Philo*, p. 83 also proposes a chiastic structure, but one that is significantly different from that of the other scholars mentioned here.

μονογενής, which verse 14 makes clear refers to the Logos-become-flesh.[15]

Beasley-Murray, on the other hand, finds neither descent nor ascent in the prologue, and asserts that the Logos does not descend even for incarnation.[16] The main reason that he reads the prologue in this way is his explicit refusal to allow the later references to descent and ascent throughout the Gospel to illuminate the meaning of the prologue. This is a questionable methodology, since the readers of the Gospel would, for the most part at least, have been members of a church or churches that would be familiar with many of the narratives recorded therein before ever setting eyes on the written Gospel.[17] Beasley-Murray also does not consider the possibility that the event described here in terms of the Word becoming flesh would have been understood to be the same as that described in 1.32 in terms of the Spirit *descending* and remaining on him.[18] His argument that verse 18 cannot have the exalted Christ primarily in mind, because there is a reference to the revelation brought by the incarnate one while in the world, gives insufficient consideration to the fact that the aorist tense ἐξηγήσατο, used here in conjunction with the participle ὁ ὢν, may legitimately be translated as 'the one who is (*now*) in the bosom of the Father, he is the one who (previously, prior to his ascension) made God known'. We thus find more convincing the view of the majority of scholars, who see in John a parallelism between the beginning and end of the prologue, and this seems to imply that there is a move from heaven,

[15] See Cadman, *Open Heaven*, p. 17, who argues that sonship-terminology is reserved for the *incarnate* Logos. See too Colin Brown, 'Trinity and Incarnation: In Search of Contemporary Orthodoxy', *Ex Auditu* 7 (1991), 89; D. M. Smith, *Theology*, p. 101. We shall discuss this point further in ch.15 below.

[16] Beasley-Murray, *John*, p. 4.

[17] The Evangelist frequently assumes that the reader will recognize characters which have not been introduced and will be familiar with events not yet narrated (cf. Danna, 'Which Side', p. 63). Of course, it is correct first and foremost to read the Gospel in light of the prologue, rather than vice versa, but this need not mean that a less clear aspect of the prologue cannot legitimately be illuminated by motifs and emphases which are found throughout the remainder of the Gospel.

[18] Cf. Fuller, 'Incarnation'; Watson, 'Is John's Christology Adoptionist?'; Theobald, *Fleischwerdung*, pp. 408–18; Talbert, *Reading John*, pp. 74–7; 'And the Word Became Flesh'; McGrath, 'Johannine Christianity', 4–5; 'Prologue', 117–18. See also our discussion in ch.2 above. The imagery used in the Synoptics of the Spirit as a dove, if known by the Fourth Evangelist, might also have been felt to allude to the imagery of Genesis 1.2, connecting this event witnessed by the Baptist to the other imagery from Genesis 1 found in the prologue (cf. Calum M. Carmichael, *The Story of Creation. Its Origin and Its Interpretation in Philo and the Fourth Gospel*, Ithaca: Cornell University Press, 1996, pp. 44–5).

to earth for the incarnation, and back to heaven again. This lends support to our suggestion that the prologue ends with the exalted Christ in heaven alongside God, and will also shed light on the way John is interacting with this idea in the context of his work of legitimation.

Second, the idiom of being 'in the bosom' (εἰς τὸν κόλπον) of another person seems to refer to the position of *being seated next to* that person, especially if the other examples of the idiom in the New Testament are anything to go by (John 13.23; Luke 16.23). Many scholars have noted that the same idiom is used in John 1.18 and 13.23, but they have generally tended to read its use in reference to Jesus and the beloved disciple in 13.23 in light of its use in 1.18, suggesting that the main point of the idiom's use here is that the beloved disciple's intimate relationship with Jesus is akin to Jesus' relationship to the Father.[19] However, the meaning of the idiom is clearer in its use in the more prosaic contexts of John 13.23 and Luke 16.23, and it is more advisable to begin with these latter texts, which may then be used to elucidate 1.18.[20] Sanders does just that, and suggests that John's use of this idiom in 1.18 indicates 'their intimate relationship, as of friends reclining together at a banquet'.[21] Marsh makes a similar point, and writes of the phrase used in 1.18, 'This is the position given at a meal to the specially intimate guest.'[22] These scholars have made an important insight into the understanding of this text, the full implications of which for our study we will attempt to draw out below. Before proceeding, however, we should stress that there is no reason to think that this idiom referred exclusively to being seated alongside someone else *at a meal*. The fact that it is specified in John 13.23 that the beloved disciple was *reclining* (ἀνακείμενος) alongside Jesus (ἐν τῷ κόλπῳ τοῦ Ἰησοῦ) probably suggests that the idiom on its own simply means 'alongside', and does not *exclusively* refer to the position of *reclining at table*. A useful comparison may perhaps be made to the English idiom 'abreast'.[23]

---

[19] So e.g. MacGregor, *John*, p. 21; Lindars, *Gospel of John*, p. 99; G. R. Beasley-Murray, *John*, p. 238.

[20] *Contra* J. H. Bernard, *A Critical and Exegetical Commentary on the Gospel According to St. John*, Edinburgh: T&T Clark, 1928, p. 32.

[21] J. N. Sanders, *John*, p. 86.

[22] John Marsh, *The Gospel of St. John*, Harmondsworth: Penguin, 1968, p. 112.

[23] The EDNT article on κόλπος summarizes the meaning of the idiom ἐν τῷ κόλπῳ as 'a place of honor'. See also the papyrus fragment Preisigke Sammelbuch, 2034, and also *Const. Ap.* 8.41.2, both of which contain the phrase 'in the bosom of

John's reference to Jesus 'alongside' the Father would probably have conjured up in the minds of his hearers the image of the exalted Christ seated at God's right hand, in the place of honour alongside him in heaven. This appears to be how several scholars interpret the idiom, although they do not explicitly discuss it.[24] Taken together, (a) the evidence that Christian hymns consistently focus on or conclude with the exalted Christ, (b) the structure and parallelism of the prologue, and (c) the language and idioms used, all suggest that the prologue is best understood as ending with the exalted Christ seated alongside the Father in heaven, a concept which some had found blasphemous even in earlier times.[25]

The Johannine response

When considered in light of the points made in the previous section, the prologue takes on a new significance: it can be understood not only as a preliminary chorus, setting forth the themes of the Gospel and providing the author's perspective as a guide to understanding what follows, but also as a defence of the legitimacy of Christian belief concerning Jesus. The parallelism between the beginning and end of the prologue can be understood as an attempt to legitimate the place occupied by the exalted Christ. Jesus can occupy the highest place alongside God because he is the Word become flesh. God's Word or Wisdom had always rightfully occupied this place, as can be seen from passages such as Wisdom

Abraham, Isaac and Jacob', which must mean something like 'alongside', since it goes without saying that one cannot be leaning one's head on the breast of all three figures simultaneously. These and other relevant texts are available in Rudolf Meyer, ' κόλπος', *TDNT* III, pp. 824–6.

[24] Walther Eltester, 'Der Logos und Sein Prophet. Fragen zur heutigen Erklärung des johanneischen Prologs', in *Apophoreta. Festschrift für Ernst Haenchen* (BZNW, 30), Berlin: Alfred Töpelmann, 1964, p. 133; R. E. Brown, *Gospel*, p. 4. Brown (p. 17) also refers to 'others' who find a reference to the ascension here, but unfortunately without any explicit citation. MacGregor (*John*, p. 21) mentions the ascension in this context but makes nothing further of it. R. H. Strachan, *The Fourth Gospel. Its Significance and Environment*, London: SCM, 1941, pp. 108–9 recognizes that the phrase means something like 'sitting next to' in its other occurrences, but fails to apply this insight to John 1.18. David M. Hay, *Glory at the Right Hand. Psalm 110 in Early Christianity*, Nashville: Abingdon, 1973, p. 94 notes this phrase in John 1.18 as a possible allusion to Ps. 110.1b with its reference to sitting *at the right hand*. See also Loader, *Christology*, p. 151.

[25] Cf. our earlier discussion of the charge of blasphemy in the Synoptic trial narratives, which seems to be a response to Jesus' claim that he will be 'seated at the right hand of God' as the Son of Man (esp. ch.3 above).

9.4, which speaks of Wisdom sitting beside God's throne.[26] The Evangelist appeals to these traditions as a way of showing the legitimacy of this belief which he and his community hold dear. We shall now explore the interpretation we have suggested in further detail.

We have seen already that one major point that 'the Jews' seem to have been concerned with and to have found objectionable in Christian Christology was the claim that Jesus had been enthroned in heaven. As we have already noted, it is not entirely clear whether the issue was attributing too exalted a status to a human being, or rather the fact that the claims were being made specifically for Jesus. At any rate, we have already noted that in Judaism only God was eternal, and all others, even if they could be addressed as 'gods' in some sense, were lesser, created beings. Even outside of Judaism, in the wider Hellenistic world, it appears that the key difference between divinity in the truest sense and other lesser forms of divinity was *eternal existence*.[27] By presenting Jesus as the incarnation of one who was eternally worthy of this status alongside God, the Evangelist could legitimate his community's belief, by arguing that Jesus was not a blasphemous glory-seeker, nor even a divinized man, but one who, now incarnate, had returned to the place in heaven which was rightfully his.[28]

It is most likely as part of this legitimating presentation that John has (in contrast with earlier Christian writers) associated this exalted status, not with the designation Son of Man, but with Wisdom/Logos imagery.[29] Although the exalted place of the Son of Man was widely accepted in Christian tradition, and also among at least some first-century Jews, there is evidence from the later rabbinic literature of an uneasiness about such ideas in some

[26] Cf. Wisd. 9.10. See too Philo, *Fug.* 19.101, which may indicate that the Logos sits alongside God in his throne-chariot (so Evans, *Jesus*, p. 420).

[27] Neyrey, 'My Lord and My God', pp. 159–62; *Ideology*, pp. 218–20. See above p. 110.

[28] See also 3.13 and 6.62 on the place of the Son of Man in heaven as 'the place he was before', that is, the place which is rightfully his (see too 17.4). We shall have occasion to consider these Son of Man sayings below. Cf. also Painter, 'Christology', 470, who also understands the phrase εἰς τὸν κόλπον τοῦ πατρός to involve the return of the revealer to the situation in which the prologue began, namely his existence with God.

[29] Cf. esp. Mark 14.62 and pars.; Acts 7.56. Although the Evangelist elsewhere refers to the 'ascent' or exaltation of the Son of Man, there is no reference to Jesus specifically as 'Son of Man' in a position of honour alongside God in heaven. We shall consider the relationship between the 'Son of Man' and Wisdom/Logos in ch.15 below.

circles. It may also perhaps be noteworthy that problems only seem to have arisen for the rabbis in connection with figures other than God who *sit* enthroned in heaven. The Christian claim that Jesus sits 'at the right hand of God' was regarded as 'blasphemous', just as later so was the messianic interpretation of 'thrones' in Daniel 7.9 attributed to R. Akiba.[30] While it may be that controversy only arose over certain individuals for whom such claims were made, we must consider the possibility that some would have found it objectionable to make these sorts of exalted claims for any human being.

If some found it an insult to God to claim that a mere human being could sit in his presence, in contrast, the exalted place of Wisdom was far more widely accepted, whether in Christian circles, in the apocalyptic and sapiential literature, or in the later Targumic and rabbinic works. This was presumably because Wisdom was not strictly a figure *other than God*.[31] It seems plausible to suggest that John does not speak of Jesus as the *Son of Man* sitting at God's right hand because it is as the incarnation of Wisdom or the Logos that Jesus is to be understood to occupy this place, and thus to be worthy of divine honours and to exercise divine functions. In Wisdom 9.4, Wisdom is specifically said to '*sit* beside [God's] throne', and Proverbs 8.30 presents Wisdom at God's side.[32] It seems logical to suggest that this widely accepted status of Wisdom/ Logos in Judaism is being appealed to by the Fourth Evangelist as justification for the exalted status that Christians attributed to Christ.

Legitimation also helps explain why John, in contrast with all earlier Christian literature, takes the step of using the specific

---

[30] Cf. *b.* Hag. 15a. See also 3 Enoch 16 in relation to Metatron, whose status in heaven was problematic at least partly because Metatron *sits* in heaven. See also above, ch.3, esp. pp. 73–5, and Segal, *Two Powers*, pp. 60–6.

[31] Cf. Dunn, *Christology*, pp. 168–176. See also Kanagaraj, *'Mysticism'*, pp. 292–4.

[32] See also Wisd. 18.15, where the Word is implied to have been seated on the royal throne; also Wisd. 9.10; 1 Enoch 42.2. Cf. further Kanagaraj, *'Mysticism'*, pp. 298. Otfried Hofius, '»Der in des Vaters Schoß ist« Joh 1, 18', *ZNW* 80 (1989), 165 and Evans, *Word and Glory*, p. 91 refer to the MT of Prov. 8.30 as describing Wisdom as 'in God's bosom'. However, the meaning of this text is far from clear, and many interpret the difficult Hebrew word *'amon* as 'craftsman', which would make good sense in the context. The LXX also understood it differently, and thus we cannot be sure either that John knew this reading or that he understood it in this way. At any rate, this verse clearly refers to Wisdom 'at God's side', and therefore this imagery would be relevant to John's legitimation regardless of these other uncertainties.

designation λόγος. We have already noted that the term λόγος appears to have been more or less interchangeable with other terms (such as Wisdom) in Jewish literature of this period. However, if there is one feature which is, in the relevant Jewish literature, more clearly associated with the imagery of God's *Word* than with that of God's *Wisdom*, it is the clear and unambiguous assertion of the divinity of the Logos. For example, Barrett remarks that Wisdom 7.25 is the closest that any early Jewish work comes to asserting explicitly the divinity of Wisdom.[33] On the other hand, in Philo there are clear instances of the Logos being called 'God'.[34] The term Memra is also clearly used to denote the interaction of God himself with the world, and if this term was already being used in the Aramaic paraphrases of the Torah provided in the synagogue, then John's imagery of the 'Word' would carry even more weight, being given its authority within the synagogue itself.[35] However, the dating and origins of the ideas preserved in the Targums is a complex field, and certainty on this last point seems impossible.[36] It seems clear, however, that John emphasizes both the pre-existence prior to creation, and the full divinity, of the one who became incarnate in Christ, in a way (or at the very least to an extent) that no earlier Christian work did, and the most likely reason for this, we suggest, is that John is here appealing to and developing traditional language and motifs in order to defend his community's christological beliefs.

[33] Barrett, *Commentary*, p. 155.

[34] Such as *Somn.* 1.230; *Quaest in Gn.* 2.62; the Logos is also called 'divine' (θειος) in *Fug.* 97, 101; *Quaest in Ex.* 2.68; *Op.* 20; *Mig.* 174.

[35] See Martin McNamara, *Targum and Testament. Aramaic Paraphrases of the Hebrew Bible: A Light on the New Testament*, Shannon: Irish University Press, 1972, pp. 101–6; C. T. R. Hayward, 'The Holy Name of the God of Moses and the Prologue of St. John's Gospel', *NTS* 25/1 (1978), 16–32; Evans, *Word and Glory*, pp. 126–9; also Margaret Barker, *The Great Angel. A Study of Israel's Second God*, London: SPCK, 1992, pp. 134–48.

[36] Manns (*L'Evangile*, p. 41) is confident that John was aware of Targumic traditions. On the complex subject of dating the Targums see further Martin McNamara, *The New Testament and the Palestinian Targum to the Pentateuch*, Rome: Pontifical Biblical Institute, 1966, pp. 45–66; *Targum and Testament*, pp. 86–9; Bernard Grossfeld, *The Targum Onqelos to Genesis*, Edinburgh: T&T Clark, 1988, pp. 30–5. That some traditions found in the Targums are early is not disputed. If Memra *is* an early concept, then John's allusions in verse 14 to other similar terms and images, such as Shekinah, glory, and the image of tabernacling (used of Wisdom in Sir. 24.8) would reinforce his legitimating portrait of Jesus. See further Barker, *Great Angel*, p. 146–8, 158; Evans, *Word and Glory*, pp. 123–6 on the similarities between the Targumic Memra and Philo's Logos; cf. also McGrath, 'Prologue', 105–6.

The way in which the Evangelist is creating his legitimating portrait of Jesus out of earlier beliefs and ideas becomes clearer when we connect the prologue with the narrative which immediately follows it, namely John's description of the witness borne by John the Baptist to Jesus. In 1.32–3 we are told that the Spirit not only descended upon Jesus, but also *remained* on him. This is closely related to the description in 1.14 of the Word 'becoming flesh' or 'appearing on the human scene as flesh', suggesting a decisive new mode of existence which is different from previous appearances in human history, whether in the form of theophanies or in the inspiration of the prophets.[37] Here John is thus making use of a traditional point of Christian (and Jewish) belief, that the Messiah was (or would be) indwelt by God's Spirit/Wisdom, and drawing out from it that the Spirit has not only indwelt Jesus in a decisive and complete way, but has become wholly 'fused' with Jesus,[38] with the result that what could be attributed to Wisdom/Spirit could now also be attributed to Jesus. In other words, John here appeals to the traditional belief that Jesus the Messiah was indwelt by God's Spirit or Wisdom, in order to justify the exalted place attributed to Jesus by Christians. In so doing, he created a portrait of Jesus that identifies him much more completely with God's Word/Wisdom/Spirit than previous authors had. The differences between John and earlier Christian writings should not be exaggerated, but nonetheless there is a distinction to be made. And however one expresses the difference between Johannine Christology and that found in earlier writings, there can be no denying

[37] Cf. Dunn, *Christology*, pp. 243, 249; also J. N. Sanders, *John*, p. 80. Given the equivalence of Logos, Wisdom and Spirit which we have already noted above, it seems quite possible that the event described in John 1.14 as 'the Word becoming flesh' would have been understood by the earliest readers and hearers of the Fourth Gospel to refer to this event, which in the Synoptics is associated with Jesus' baptism. Cf. Fuller, 'Incarnation', pp. 61–6; Hartin, 'Community', 45; Schoonenberg, 'Sapiential reading', 405; Watson, 'Is John's Christology Adoptionist?'; Talbert, 'And the Word Became Flesh'; McGrath, 'Johannine Christianity', 4–5. See also ch.2 above.

[38] Watson, 'Is John's Christology Adoptionist?', pp. 118–19; Talbert, 'And the Word Became Flesh', pp. 50–1. This point appears to have been an issue among the 'secessionists' opposed by the author of the Johannine epistles, and also in later Gnostic writings. Cf. Elaine Pagels, *The Gnostic Gospels*, London: Penguin, 1979, chs. 2, 5; Theobald, *Fleischwerdung*, pp. 412–13; Hengel, *Johannine Question*, pp. 57–63. See also Dunn, *Christology*, p. 266 and Schoonenberg, 'Sapiential reading', 416–18 on the problems and prospects of the relationship between Christ, Wisdom and Spirit when attempting to bring together the various strands of New Testament Christology.

that John elaborated and developed the traditional understanding of the Messiah which he had inherited. We have seen evidence that his motivation for doing so was the need of his community for a defence of its beliefs against the objections raised by members of the local Jewish synagogue.[39]

It may also be significant that John the Baptist's witness to the Spirit's descent upon Jesus is linked in the tradition with the promise that Jesus will baptize with the Holy Spirit. Max Turner has suggested that the bestowal of the Spirit by Jesus was a clear instance of the exercising by Jesus of a divine function, which made a 'divine' Christology more or less inevitable.[40] To a certain extent we agree, but would want to stress that this feature of Christology made a development inevitable *because it became controversial*. Had certain Jews never raised objections to such Christian claims, these developments might never have been necessary. But as it is, John was compelled to legitimate his community's beliefs, and here we seem to have another example of this. Jesus is not just a human being, but the human being in whom the Spirit has come to dwell *permanently*, and this means that no one can receive the Spirit of God apart from Christ.[41] This is also directly connected to the issue of Christ's ascension, since it is the *risen* Christ who bestows the Spirit.[42] However, it must be stressed that it is not clear from the Fourth Gospel that this specific aspect of Christian belief – Jesus as the one who baptizes with the Holy Spirit – was at issue in the Johannine conflict with the synagogue. Nevertheless, the whole topic of Jesus carrying out divine functions clearly was an issue, and it is therefore possible that the specific issue of Jesus' agency in mediating the gift of the Spirit was important as part of this debate.

Before we conclude, we must mention one further aspect of John's portrait here – the possible use of θεός in verse 18 in reference to the exalted Christ. We saw earlier that it is not entirely

---

[39] This is not to say that the Evangelist would have understood himself to be making a major development. From his perspective, it probably seemed that he was merely drawing out the implications of what Christians had always believed.

[40] Max M. B. Turner, 'The Spirit of Christ and Christology', in Harold H. Rowdon (ed.), *Christ the Lord. Studies in Christology presented to Donal Guthrie*, Leicester: IVP, 1982, p. 183.

[41] Theobald, 'Gott, Logos und Pneuma', pp. 65–8. John 16.14–15 suggests that the Spirit's indwelling is closely related to Jesus' unity with God and his role as God's agent. See also Pryor, *John*, p. 13.

[42] Although 20.22 is somewhat ambiguous, the meaning of 7.39 seems clearly to indicate that it is only when Jesus is glorified that the Spirit is given. Cf. Dunn, *Baptism*, pp. 174, 177–8.

clear whether Jesus was called 'God' by Christians prior to John's time, and when this ambiguity is combined with that of the textual attestation of variant readings in this verse, it begins to appear extremely unwise to draw any hard and fast conclusions concerning John's development of earlier christological ideas in relation to this point and/or in connection with this part of the text.[43] Nonetheless, it is worth considering what implications John's use or non-use of θεός here would have had in the context of Johannine legitimation.

If John did not call the exalted Christ 'God' here, this is unlikely to have been because this was unacceptable to him, since in 20.28 it is generally agreed that the risen Christ is confessed as 'God'. Perhaps the Evangelist did not use his portrayal here to justify calling Jesus 'God' because he did not want to place an unnecessary stumbling block before readers who had not yet made up their minds concerning such Christian claims about Jesus, and were wavering between the arguments of the synagogue leaders and those of the Johannine Christians: he thus left this climactic confession until the end of his work, by which point the reader had been adequately prepared for it. Perhaps there is no reason – while the inclusion of the designation needs an explanation, its omission does not necessarily, since it may not even have occurred to the Evangelist to use the term here. On the other hand, if John did designate the exalted Christ as θεός here, it may have been to legitimate its use by earlier Christians: the exalted Jesus may be called 'God' not simply because he is the last Adam, or because he is the prophet like Moses and superior to Moses, but because he is the Word made flesh. Unfortunately, this important aspect of John's work of legitimation will continue to remain obscure due to the textual uncertainties in this verse.

What is certain, however, is that our study thus far has yielded important insights into the development of Johannine Christology and the work of legitimation which spurred it on. In the Johannine context, the exalted status attributed to Christ had come to the fore as an issue of contention between the Johannine Christians and the synagogue leaders. In order to defend his community's beliefs, the

---

[43] For differing assessments of the evidence see the discussions in Paul R. McReynolds, 'John 1:18 in Textual Variation and Translation', in Eldon Jay Epp and Gordon D. Fee (eds.), *New Testament Criticism: Its Significance for Exegesis. Essays in Honour of Bruce M. Metzger*, Oxford: Clarendon, 1981, pp. 105–30; Manns, *L'Evangile*, p. 22; M. J. Harris, *Jesus as God*, pp. 74–83; M. Davies, *Rhetoric*, pp. 123–4; Ehrman, *Orthodox Corruption*, pp. 78–82.

Evangelist appealed to authoritative traditions in order to prove that his faith was in accord with Judaism's (and Christianity's) Scriptures and traditions.[44] Thus here, at the very beginning of the Gospel, the Evangelist brought the traditional pictures of Jesus exalted to God's right hand, and of Jesus as the one in whom God's Wisdom/Spirit dwells, together, using the latter to justify the former. In doing so, John not only appealed to these traditions, but developed them, altering the imagery of the exalted Christ alongside God, and identifying the human being Jesus more fully and/or more explicitly with the Word, Wisdom or Spirit of God than had his predecessors. Legitimation, we may conclude, provides an explanation of what motivated John to take these important steps.

Summary

We have seen in this chapter, as had already been suggested by our treatment of other passages in the Gospel, that John is using traditional Wisdom ideas to legitimate the exalted status attributed to Jesus by Christians. In developing the tradition in the ways that he did, the Evangelist has taken an important step. In earlier Christian (and Jewish) tradition, we find Jesus (or in Jewish works the Messiah) clearly portrayed as indwelt by God's Wisdom or Spirit.[45] Earlier Christian writers like Paul and Matthew had depicted Jesus in Wisdom language and imagery, and had forged a close link between Jesus and the Spirit. John, however, appears to have moved beyond these earlier portraits of and reflections on the significance of Jesus. For the first time, we have a clear and unambiguous presentation of Jesus as the Logos incarnate. John's distinctive contributions should not be exaggerated, but neither should their significance be underestimated.

In earlier times, concepts such as Philo's Logos had served Judaism as a useful metaphor, a way of dealing with the problem of a transcendent God who interacts with the world. When John takes up such ideas and uses them to defend the legitimacy of his christological beliefs, he identifies this personification with a person. To a certain extent, it might be correct to say that it was

---

[44] Cf. Whitacre, *Johannine Polemic*, pp. 10–1, 25; Rowland, *Christian Origins*, pp. 246–8, 303; Theobald, 'Gott, Logos und Pneuma', pp. 59–63.

[45] See above ch.2; also Isa. 11.2; 61.1; 1 En. 49.3. Hartman, 'Johannine Jesus-Belief', p. 97, cites as a further relevant parallel Wisd. 7.27, which describes Wisdom's entrance into holy souls in each generation.

inevitable that this identification would push Christian belief away from monotheism in the strictest sense towards a binitarian or Trinitarian understanding of God. But we must be wary of speaking of 'inevitability' when we write with the benefit of hindsight, knowing which views and interpretations eventually prevailed.[46] At any rate, issues relating to monotheism do not appear to have arisen until well after John's time, and John could hardly have been aware of the implications which his adaptation of these traditional beliefs might have for future generations of Christians, who would read his Gospel in very different contexts from his own. It thus seems unwise to engage here in speculation as to what John might have said if he had lived in a later time, when these issues had been raised. For John, his legitimating portrait of Jesus was a solution to a different, immediately pressing problem, namely that of how to demonstrate that his community's beliefs about Jesus' exalted status in heaven, and about his role in the plan of God, should be adhered to faithfully by Christians and accepted by non-Christians.

[46] Cf. Ashton, *Studying John*, p. 89.

8

CONCLUSION TO PART 2

Having examined the main passages in the Fourth Gospel which relate to the conflict between the Johannine Christians and 'the Jews' over the relationship between Jesus and God, we may now seek to draw together the overall results and conclusions which arise from this part of our study.

First, we have found no reason to deny or qualify the Evangelist's statement of his purpose in 20.31. His aim is to convince people (whether those who already believe or unbelievers is irrelevant for our present purposes) that Jesus is the Christ, the Son of God. We have found no evidence that the Evangelist is seeking to defend the idea that Jesus is, for example, the Word-become-flesh. Rather, the Word/Wisdom imagery that we have encountered appears to serve as part of a defence of the Messiahship of Jesus as understood by many, if not indeed most or all, early Christians. The Evangelist seeks to defend and legitimate the Christian view of Jesus as the one to whom God has given authority as his agent and viceroy, who sits at God's right hand and even bears God's own name. All of these ideas are earlier than John, and the distinctively Johannine use of the imagery and ideas which he inherited from early Judaism and Christianity we have seen to be part of John's legitimation. John has used and adapted aspects of the traditions and ideas he inherited in order to enable or convince his readers to believe that Jesus is the Christ, the Son of God, and more specifically that the roles and status which Christians attribute to him as such are legitimate. In some cases, his arguments appear to have relied on Christian beliefs, which means that his portrait would have carried more weight as a defence of Christian beliefs for believers than as an attempt to convince non-Christian Jews to believe.

Second, it is interesting that in the three narratives which we considered (John 5, 8, 10) there was a degree of ambiguity present in the accusations made by 'the Jews'. In John 5 'the Jews' accuse Jesus of 'making himself equal to God', which represents a misunderstanding of what is being claimed for Jesus: he does not 'make himself' anything, but is rather God's Son and agent, wholly subordinate to the Father but bearing his full authority to do what he does and act on his behalf. In John 8, we saw that 'the Jews' may have understood Jesus' 'I am' to mean 'I am Yahweh', whereas the Johannine Jesus' claim seems to have been that he bears the divine name as God's agent. Likewise in John 10, we found that 'the Jews' may have interpreted Jesus' assertion, 'I and the Father are one' to mean 'I am the Father' or 'I am equal to the Father'.[1] The motif of misunderstanding is clearly a Johannine *literary* motif, but it may nonetheless also reflect an aspect of the relationship between the Johannine Christians and the synagogue. These Christians probably felt that their beliefs were not only being rejected, but were being rejected because they had been misunderstood. They perhaps even felt that their views were being maliciously misrepresented. The Evangelist's use of the motif of misunderstanding probably does not represent an attempt to convert 'the Jews', but to reinforce his own community's sense that their beliefs have been rejected wrongly, and that 'the Jews' are culpable for not having understood and believed things that the Johannine Christians felt should have been clear from Scripture and Jewish tradition.

It should also be mentioned that it appears difficult to define what was at issue in these passages more precisely than we have here. It is still not entirely clear whether the issue was (a) claiming too exalted a status for *any* human being – even if that human being is the Messiah, or (b) claiming an exalted status for one who was regarded as a false and failed Messiah. Further research into this question may help illuminate and clarify even further our understanding of the Fourth Gospel. However, there does appear to be sufficient evidence to justify our conclusion that the issue in the controversy was not the oneness of God, but rather the making of exalted claims for one whom the Jewish opponents of the Johannine Christians were convinced had not been appointed by

---

[1] Note also the parallel contrasts connected with these misunderstandings: In John 5, Jesus says he is God's Son, yet seems to make himself equal with God; in John 8, Jesus is not yet fifty years old, and yet claims to have seen (or been seen by) Abraham; In John 10, Jesus is a 'mere man', and yet apparently claims to be 'God'. On the motif of misunderstanding in John see further Létourneau, *Jésus*, pp. 381–95.

God. Ultimately, the question of whether, from the point of view of these opponents, to make such exalted claims for *any* human figure would have been equally objectionable, appears unanswerable. Nevertheless, the emphasis in these passages on the issue of whether Jesus was '*making himself*' certain things implies that the heart of the issue was whether Jesus had been appointed by God. The Jewish opponents did not believe Jesus had been appointed by God and thus regarded him as a political danger and a blasphemer. The Johannine Christians accepted that Jesus was God's appointed agent, and thus they sought to show both that Jesus was sent by God, and also that the claims being made for him were in no way blasphemous.

Let us sum up the findings of part 2. In all of the passages we examined, we found evidence that the debate with 'the Jews' reflected in John did not focus on the distinctive elements of Johannine Christology, but on earlier Christian beliefs. Of course, in the period after John was written, the conflict will very likely have continued, and may then have come to focus on the developments that John made. This period, however, lies beyond the scope of the present study.[2] In response to the objections raised, the Evangelist sought to defend his community's beliefs by appealing to various aspects of the Jewish and Christian Scriptures and traditions. In making use of these traditions in this way, his overall portrait and understanding of Christ was – at times subtly, but nonetheless significantly – altered, in ways that would eventually move Christian doctrine in directions that could not have been foreseen prior to this. The model of legitimation spurring on or producing development in doctrine thus seems to be able to illuminate the important question of *why* Johannine Christology developed along the lines that it did.

[2] Although the Evangelist (or a subsequent redactor) may perhaps give a brief glimpse into this period in chapter 6, and perhaps also in parts of chapter 8. See our discussion in ch.11 below.

Part 3

JESUS, MOSES AND TORAH

Jesus and Moses

We may now turn to the second major theme that we shall be considering in relation to the christological legitimation found in John's Gospel, the issue of the relationship between Jesus and Moses, and the revelation brought by each, as a point of controversy in the church-synagogue debates. Here – in contrast with part 2 – it will not be necessary to give extensive treatment to introductory matters, since we do not have any reason to disagree with the widely held view that the issue of the relationship between Jesus and Moses, and between their respective revelations, was an important issue in the controversy between the Johannine church and the synagogue.[1] In this section we shall once again consider four key passages which relate to this issue (the prologue and chapters 3, 6 and 9). Each will be discussed in turn, after which we shall attempt to tie together the findings from each section.

[1] See our discussion of John's relationship to earlier Christian tradition at this point in ch.2 above; see also Martyn, *History*, pp. 102–30; Boismard, *Moise*; D. M. Smith, *Theology*, p. 126.

9

THE WORD AND THE GLORY
(JOHN 1.1–18)

We have already reviewed in chapter 7 the indications that the prologue reflects a controversy setting and that it represents an attempt to legitimate certain beliefs, and thus we need not review this evidence again here. In order to avoid unnecessary repetition in this chapter we shall at times presuppose our earlier discussion of certain aspects of the prologue and the conclusions drawn there.

The focus of the conflict and its relation to earlier tradition

One of the debates which underlies the prologue of the Fourth Gospel is the issue of the relationship between Jesus and Moses and their respective revelations. This can be seen explicitly in 1.17, where some sort of contrast/comparison is made between Jesus and Moses. However, it is also implicit in a number of other features: the application to Christ of imagery connected with the Torah (with which Wisdom had been identified in Jewish tradition), and the allusions to traditions connected with Moses at Sinai (such as seeing God in 1.18, and grace and truth in 1.17).[1]

The imagery John uses, and his overall portrait of Jesus here, are based on earlier Christian approaches to this issue. In view of the poetic or hymnic character of the prologue, the closest New Testament parallel outside the Johannine corpus is probably Colossians 1.15–20. There we find Wisdom language and imagery being applied to Jesus, and this use of such imagery is best understood as a response to the application of similar imagery to Torah in Jewish writings. The message of this hymnic passage is that it is in Christ,

---

[1] Boismard, *Prologue*, p. 169. Anthony T. Hanson, *The New Testament Interpretation of Scripture*, London: SPCK, 1980, pp. 99–100 seems to have shown convincingly that the phrase is intended to reflect Exod. 34.6, the view also taken by most commentators. See also Loader, *Christology*, p. 159.

and not Torah, that God's Wisdom dwells in all its fullness.[2] The question of the place of the Jewish Law in the Christian life is one of the major themes addressed in Colossians.[3] Likewise in Hebrews, which focuses on the contrast between Jesus and Moses and their respective covenants, we find the epistle introduced with similar poetic Wisdom (and glory) imagery (1:1–3, where the immediate context is a contrast between God having spoken in partial ways in the past through prophets, of whom Moses is one, and the fuller revelation now given through Jesus).[4] John was not the first to discuss the relationship between Jesus and Moses, nor the first to apply Wisdom imagery to this subject.[5]

However, John does not contrast Jesus and Moses in exactly the same way that Paul and Hebrews do. The problems with reading 1.17, as it were, through Pauline spectacles, have been addressed by several scholars.[6] Wisdom imagery is not the exclusive possession

---

[2] Cf. e.g. W. D. Davies, *Paul and Rabbinic Judaism*, pp. 150–2; Wright, *Climax*, p. 118; McGrath, 'Change in Christology', 44–5. Eckhard J. Schnabel, *Law and Wisdom from Ben Sira to Paul: A Tradition Historical Enquiry into the Relation of Law, Wisdom, and Ethics* (WUNT 2, 16), Tübingen: Mohr-Siebeck, 1985, pp. 298–9 is correct to assert that for Paul Wisdom and Torah are no longer to be identified, but does insufficient justice to the fact that this former identification in Judaism provided at least part of the motivation for identifying Jesus as the embodiment of God's Wisdom. He provides very clear evidence that Paul was familiar with the earlier Jewish identification of Wisdom and Torah (pp. 233–4, 245, 264). The logical conclusion to draw is that, for Paul, the portrayal of Jesus in Wisdom categories was part of an attempt to provide a Jesus-centred rather than Torah-centred version of Judaism. This fits extremely well with what we know of Paul and of the issues he was most concerned with.

[3] Cf. Morna D. Hooker, 'Were There False Teachers in Colossae?', in Barnabas Lindars and Stephen S. Smalley (eds.), *Christ and Spirit in the New Testament. Studies in Honour of C. F. D. Moule*, Cambridge University Press, 1973, pp. 329–31; James D. G. Dunn, 'The Colossian Philosophy: A Confident Jewish Apologia', *Biblica* 76 (1995), 153–81; *The Epistles to the Colossians and to Philemon. A Commentary on the Greek Text*, Grand Rapids: Eerdmans/ Carlisle: Paternoster, 1996, pp. 34, 85, 89.

[4] Cf. D'Angelo, *Moses*, pp. 168–74.

[5] On the development of Wisdom Christology see further Hartmut Gese, 'Wisdom, Son of Man, and the Origins of Christology: The Consistent Development of Biblical Theology', *HBT* 3 (1981), 23–57; Ben Witherington III, *Jesus the Sage*, Minneapolis: Fortress Press/ Edinburgh: T&T Clark, 1994; and McGrath, 'Change in Christology' (as well as ch.2 above). De Boer, *Johannine Perspectives*, pp. 114, 116 does not appear to do justice to this link with tradition in John's use of Wisdom imagery, in contrast with his recognition on many other points that John is developing tradition in response to Jewish objections.

[6] Pancaro, *Law*, p. 537; Ruth B. Edwards, 'ΧΑΡΙΝ ΑΝΤΙ ΧΑΡΙΤΟΣ (John 1.16): Grace and Law in the Johannine Prologue', *JSNT* 32 (1988), 3–15; E. Harris, *Prologue*, pp. 64–5. See also McGrath, 'Johannine Christianity', 8–9. It is surely significant that the only text which Hanson, *New Testament Interpretation*, p. 104

of those who drew a sharp contrast between Jesus and Moses. Wisdom is also important for Matthew, who compares Jesus to Moses while holding a positive view of Torah.[7] The Hebrews and Colossians texts are very likely hymnic fragments quoted by the authors of these epistles, and may thus represent part of the wider heritage of the Church, affirmations of belief which different groups shared in common (but perhaps understood slightly differently). At any rate, John is clearly dealing with an issue which was widespread in early Christianity, and which was not limited to the 'Torah-free' Pauline circle of churches.

The language of 'glory' (John 1.14) was also important in this context. This language was used in the transfiguration account in Luke, and as we shall see later, there are a number of reasons to believe that John was familiar with the transfiguration story in some form.[8] A similar comparison between the glory of Moses' face when he came from meeting with God, and the glory of Jesus, is also to be found in one of Paul's letters, 2 Corinthians 3.7–18. We do not need to discuss Paul's 'midrash' in detail here;[9] for our purposes it is sufficient that once again we have clear evidence that the issues John is discussing and the terminology he is using are in fact pre-Johannine. John is, in the prologue to his Gospel, addressing the issue, which had arisen much earlier, of the relationship between Jesus and Moses, and in doing so he also makes use of much traditional imagery.

The Johannine response

As we have seen, John's use of Wisdom categories to interpret the significance of Christ in comparison/contrast to that of Moses/Torah is closely related to similar approaches taken by earlier New Testament authors. John presents Jesus as the embodiment, as the appearance in human history, of that which 'the Jews' claimed was

cites to support his view that in John 1.17 the Torah is regarded as something temporary, obsolete, and indirect is *Galatians* 3.19!

[7] Cf. Suggs, *Wisdom, passim*; M. D. Johnson, 'Reflections on a Wisdom Approach'; France, *Matthew: Evangelist and Teacher*, p. 304; Allison, *New Moses*, pp. 229–30.

[8] See below, pp. 165–6.

[9] For further discussion of this passage see Dunn, *Christology*, pp. 143–4; *Unity and Diversity*, pp. 88, 91.

to be found in Torah, namely Wisdom and light.[10] Jewish thought had already presented this Wisdom (which was identified with Torah) as the instrument of creation (cf. e.g. Prov. 8.22–31; Wisd. 6.12–11.1), and the early Christians responded by applying such language to Christ. John takes this up from earlier Christianity, presenting Jesus in the language of Wisdom, the Word of creation.

What, then, is distinctive about John? Has the ongoing debate on this subject in the intervening period led John to go beyond what these other authors did? The answer to the latter question is to be answered in the affirmative, and as we have already suggested, the distinctive aspect of John's Wisdom Christology is to be found in his complete identification of Jesus with Wisdom. Earlier writers applied Wisdom imagery to Jesus, which John also does; but John goes further, identifying the Word with Jesus in a fuller way than earlier writers had. John thus places his Wisdom-hymn at the beginning of the Gospel, so that everything else may be read through its lens. Wisdom imagery and motifs also pervade and undergird the entire Gospel, as part of the fundamental substructure of its Christology.[11] This is in marked contrast to all other New Testament authors. For Paul, while we cannot enter into the ongoing debate about centre and periphery in Paul, it seems clear that Wisdom is less central than other more frequently occurring christological motifs, such as, for example, those connected with Adam. For Hebrews, the central christological idea is almost certainly the idea of Jesus as High Priest, and perhaps also the contrast with Moses; although Hebrews begins with Wisdom language, it cannot be said to pervade the entire portrait in the same way that it does in John. Moses typology seems to be central for Matthew, while Wisdom imagery is a peripheral element that appears only in isolated passages.[12]

The ways in which moving this traditional imagery to the centre of his christological portrait of Jesus would have benefited his legitimation need to be considered. For one thing, by identifying Jesus as the human being whom Wisdom became, John was able to

---

[10] For the Jewish background cf. Sir. 24.23, 25; Bar. 3.36–4.4; also Wisd. 6.18. On light and word as connected with Torah cf. Borgen, *Philo*, pp. 87–8. See too Boismard, *Prologue*, pp. 144–5; Dunn, 'Let John Be John', pp. 315–16; de Boer, *Johannine Perspectives*, pp. 114–16.

[11] Cf. esp. Willett, *Wisdom, passim*.

[12] Cf. W. D. Davies, *Setting*, pp. 25ff (who rightly notes that Mosaic categories do not exhaust Matthew's Christology); Johnson, 'Reflections on a Wisdom Approach', 64; Allison, *New Moses, passim*.

give Jesus a priority of place and authority which was beyond that of Moses. Rather than simply suggesting that the fullest expression of God's wisdom or glory is found in Jesus rather than Torah, as earlier authors had also clearly done, John presents Jesus as God's Word, Wisdom and Glory *become flesh*. Although Paul does at one point assert in passing that Christ is 'the Wisdom of God' (1 Cor. 1.24), this does not come close to John's developed 'metaphysical' portrait. In the Gospel of John, as in the work of no earlier author, the reader is left in no doubt whatsoever that Jesus is not merely the demonstration that God is wise, but the incarnation of personified Wisdom. By placing the term 'glory' alongside the language of Logos and 'tabernacling', John has turned it into a metaphysical category of sorts, and thereby strengthened even further the total unity between Jesus and God that he presents in his Gospel.

In this way, John was able to stress the superiority of Jesus over Moses: he claims, in effect, that the one who has now 'become flesh' as the human being Jesus Christ is the one whom Moses may have caught a glimpse of, but whose glory is now fully revealed to Christians. Hanson reaches this conclusion on the basis of internal considerations alone: since John asserts that no one had ever seen God, but that the only begotten has made him known, then John must be interpreting the apparent visions of God in the Jewish Scriptures as visions of the pre-existent Logos.[13] Further confirmation of this is found in the description of Christ in the same language as is used to describe the theophany to Moses on Sinai: 'glory', 'full of grace and truth'.[14] In addition, there is also external evidence that supports such an interpretation. Philo suggests that Moses 'saw God', but since this is impossible, he must in fact have seen the Logos, who is the 'visible' of the invisible God, God made known.[15] The Targums also refer to Moses as having met or spoken, not directly with God himself, but with the Word or Spirit of God.[16] Several scholars have presented the similarities between these passages and ideas reflected in early Christianity, and while it is admittedly impossible to assume an early date for Targumic traditions, this is one of many cases where the similarities with

[13] Hanson, *New Testament Interpretation*, pp. 102–4.
[14] Anthony T. Hanson, *Jesus Christ in the Old Testament*, London: SPCK, 1965, pp. 110–11; *New Testament Interpretation*, pp. 99–100.
[15] Cf. *Spec. Leg.* 1.47; *Post.* 13, 15. See further D'Angelo, *Moses*, pp. 180–6.
[16] Cf. the texts cited in McNamara, *The New Testament and the Palestinian Targum*, p. 182–8; *Targum and Testament*, pp. 108–12.

ideas found in early Christianity and early Judaism suggest that these particular Targumic traditions may reflect a widespread, relatively early approach to the interpretation of Scripture.

John appears to have in mind here in the prologue the Exodus/ Sinai traditions in the Jewish Scriptures.[17] Just as in John 3 it is denied that Moses ascended, so here it is denied that Moses actually saw God: Moses, it is implied, saw the Logos, the one who alone can see God. The difference between Jesus and Moses is thus one of kind rather than degree: the Word *spoke to* Moses, but *became* Jesus. Or to paraphrase Johannine terminology, the Word *gave* revelation through Moses, but *appeared on the scene of human history* as the human being Jesus.[18] John is thus using traditional Wisdom categories, but has identified Jesus and Wisdom more fully and completely than any other before him, thus altering in subtle but extremely important ways his understanding of Jesus.

Summary

The issue of the relationship between Jesus and Moses is only one of the issues addressed in the prologue, as we have already seen. In relation to the issue being discussed in the present chapter, we have seen (1) that John is closely related here to earlier Jewish and Christian traditions, and (2) that he is developing those traditions in response to a specific issue in the debates between the Johannine Christians and 'the Jews'. Here John's approach is particularly close to that of his predecessors, although there are also important differences from and developments beyond them. John makes use of traditional Wisdom categories in order to emphasize the superiority of Jesus and his revelation in contrast to Moses: the one whom Moses revealed has now appeared on the scene of human history as a human being, as Jesus Christ. Legitimation is once again an important key to understanding the emphases and concerns of the Evangelist, and thereby also the ways in which he developed the traditions he inherited, and the factors which motivated him to do so.

---

[17] Most scholars agree that John is here interacting with Exod. 33–34 (cf. in particular Hanson, *New Testament Interpretation*, pp. 97–109).

[18] Cf. John 1.17; Barrett, *Commentary*, p. 165. On a possible similar emphasis in Hebrews see D'Angelo, *Moses*, pp. 174–99, although note the reservations we voiced earlier.

10

DESCENT AND ASCENT (JOHN 3.1–21)

There is a large amount of agreement that, on one level at least, the dialogue with Nicodemus in John 3.1–21 reflects the discussions and debates which took place between one or more Christian and Jewish communities.[1] Although the language used in this section is in some ways less openly hostile than that used in some other parts of the Gospel, there is still a strong polemical dualism present, distinguishing between 'us' and 'you' (3.7, 11), belief and unbelief (3.12, 15, 18), light and darkness (3.19–21).[2] These themes suggest that John is engaging here in debate or dialogue with 'the Jews', and that we may thus expect him also to provide legitimation for points that were at issue in this controversy.

The point at issue in the conflict

Since Odeberg's work on this passage, it has become more and more widely accepted that John 3.13 reflects a polemic against claims made for other figures to have ascended into heaven, whether figures like Moses and Elijah, or Merkabah mystics.[3] As

---

[1] Meeks, *Prophet-King*, pp. 298–9; J. N. Sanders, *John*, p. 126; Martyn, *History*, p. 131; Haenchen, *John*, I, p. 202; Borgen, *Philo*, pp. 103–4 (= 'Some Jewish Exegetical Traditions as Background for the Son of Man Sayings in John's Gospel (John 3:13–14 and context)', in M. de Jonge (ed.), *L'Evangile de Jean. Sources, Rédaction, Théologie* (BETL, 44), Leuven: Leuven University Press, 1977, pp. 263–4).

[2] Cf. Godfrey C. Nicholson, *Death as Departure: The Johannine Descent-Ascent Schema* (SBLDS, 63), Chico, CA: Scholars, 1983, pp. 86–90.

[3] Odeberg, *Fourth Gospel*, p. 72. Also Meeks, *Prophet-King*, pp. 297–9, 301; 'Man from Heaven', p. 147; Lindars, *Gospel of John*, p. 156; R. G. Hamerton-Kelly, *Pre-Existence, Wisdom, and the Son of Man. A Study in the Idea of Pre-Existence in the New Testament* (SNTSMS, 21), Cambridge: Cambridge University Press, 1973, p. 230; Moloney, *Johannine Son of Man*, pp. 54–7; Alan F. Segal, 'Ruler of this World: Attitudes about Mediator Figures and the Importance of Sociology for Self-Definition', in E. P. Sanders, A. I. Baumgarten and Alan Mendelson (eds.), *Jewish and Christian Self-Definition. Volume Two: Aspects of Judaism in the Graeco-Roman*

we have already seen, the question of the relative value of the revelations brought by Jesus and Moses was an important one in the community's debates with the synagogue, and it is therefore likely to be Moses in particular who is in view here.[4] In many streams of Jewish tradition, Moses was believed to have ascended to heaven to receive the Torah. Philo speaks of Moses having 'entered into the darkness where God was; that is to say, into the invisible, and shapeless, and incorporeal world, the essence, which is the model of all existing things, where he beheld things invisible to mortal nature' (*Mos.* I.158). Another clear piece of evidence, roughly contemporary with John, that Moses' ascent up Sinai was understood as in some sense an ascent to heaven is found in Pseudo-Philo, who describes Moses' descent from the mountain as a descent to 'the place where the light of the sun and moon are' (12.1), implying that he had previously been above this region in the heavenly realm. The well-known rabbinic polemic against the idea that Moses ascended into heaven also provides evidence that this view was widespread, since it is clearly arguing against a generally accepted position. 'The polemic presupposes practice.'[5]

The statement of Nicodemus which opens this chapter may also indicate that the dialogue which follows will focus on the theme of Jesus as the 'Prophet like Moses', since he speaks of Jesus as a teacher sent by God whose commission is confirmed by miraculous signs.[6] However, Brown is correct to caution that Nicodemus' faith was probably not so profound, for if he had indeed recognized Jesus as the 'Prophet like Moses' his statement would have been

Period, London: SCM, 1981, pp. 255–6; Nicholson, *Death as Departure*, pp. 91–2; Borgen, *Philo*, pp. 103–4; Hare, *Son of Man*, pp. 85–6; Ashton, *Understanding*, p. 350; Carson, *John*, pp. 200–1; Dunn, 'Let John Be John', pp. 307, 310; Painter, 'Enigmatic', p. 1879; Kanagaraj, '*Mysticism*', pp. 199, 203–5; also A. D. A. Moses, *Matthew's Transfiguration Story and Jewish-Christian Controversy* (JSNTS, 122), Sheffield: Sheffield Academic Press, 1996, pp. 222–3. Burkett, *Son of the Man*, pp. 78–82 argues against this view, but his attempt to limit the ἐπουράνια to 'the heavenly aspects of salvation' is unconvincing.

[4] So e.g. Moloney, *Johannine Son of Man*, p. 57; Martyn, *History*, p. 142; Ashton, *Understanding*, pp. 353–4; Carson, *John*, pp. 200–1; Witherington, *John's Wisdom*, p. 100. On other figures who were believed to have ascended to heaven see Odeberg, *Fourth Gospel*, pp. 72–3.

[5] The quotation is from Meeks, *Prophet-King*, p. 141, in connection with a similar polemic in Josephus. For further discussion of this topic and the evidence for it see ibid., pp. 205–9. See too *b*. Sukkah 5a; *Mek.* Exod. 19, 20.

[6] See esp. Pryor, *John*, p. 19. Moloney, *Johannine Son of Man*, p. 47 draws attention to LXX Exod. 3.12. On signs as part of the Mosaic typology see ch.12 below.

responded to more favourably.[7] Nonetheless it seems to be the case that the language used by Nicodemus alludes to this aspect of Jesus' identity, even though Nicodemus has not grasped the full implications of these things for his understanding of who Jesus is.[8] When these points are considered together with the explicit and implicit comparisons with Moses in 3.13–14, there is good reason to conclude that this is the issue with which the Evangelist is concerned here.

Several scholars have suggested that the grammar and logic of John 3.13 indicate that Jesus was thought to have made an ascent to heaven *already prior to the time that he is speaking to Nicodemus*.[9] That is to say, Jesus was thought to have made an ascent to heaven not only at the end of his life, after the resurrection, but also during the course of his lifetime.[10] The grammar seems to imply this both in its use of the perfect tense ἀναβέβηκεν and through the use of εἰ μὴ ('except'), which seems to suggest that the one who has descended is an exception to the rule and has (already, previously) ascended.[11] Before reaching a conclusion, two alternative interpretations of this evidence need to be considered.

First, it has been suggested that John is making Jesus speak from his own post-resurrection perspective.[12] However, while the occasional insertion by the Evangelist of a phrase such as 'and now is' (cf. 4.23; 5.25) may perhaps refer to the present post-resurrection

---

[7] R.E. Brown, *Gospel*, p. 137.

[8] See also Carson, *John*, p. 187.

[9] Cf. Bühner, *Gesandte*, pp. 374–99, 422–33; Roth, 'Jesus as the Son of Man', p. 12; Borgen, *Philo*, pp. 107–8; Ashton, *Understanding*, pp. 349–56; Morton Smith, 'Two Ascended to Heaven – Jesus and the Author of 4Q491', in James H. Charlesworth (ed.), *Jesus and the Dead Sea Scrolls*, New York: Doubleday, 1992, p. 294. Borgen's understanding of the prior ascent as a *heavenly installation into office* rather than an ascent to heaven from earth is more problematic. See some of the valid criticisms made in Burkett, *Son of the Man*, pp. 34–5; also Kanagaraj, *'Mysticism'*, pp. 195–6.

[10] Note the similarity with the Moses tradition here, which held that Moses ascended on Sinai and also at the end of his life, the latter in at least one tradition (alluded to in Jude 9) apparently involving an ascent after death somewhat akin to a resurrection. See further Meeks, *Prophet-King*, pp. 124, 209–11.

[11] See also Létourneau, *Jésus*, pp. 170–3, who nonetheless reaches a different conclusion than mine. *Contra* Arie W. Zwiep, *The Ascension of the Messiah in Lukan Christology* (NovTSup, 87), Leiden: Brill, 1997, p. 135, the perfect tense need not necessarily mean 'ascended and is still there'.

[12] So e.g. Hamerton-Kelly, *Pre-Existence*, pp. 230–1; Barrett, *Commentary*, p. 213; Nicholson, *Death as Departure*, pp. 95–6; Painter, *Quest*, pp. 329–30; John W. Pryor, 'The Johannine Son of Man and the Descent-Ascent Motif', *JETS* 34/3 (1991), 349–50; Zwiep, *Ascension*, p. 135. *Contra* Moloney, *Johannine Son of Man*, p. 54.

situation of his community, these may also be, like 13.31, assertions that the decisive hour has arrived, even if all is not completely
and finally accomplished. It is of course true that the dialogue
between Jesus and Nicodemus to a large extent represents and
reflects the discussions that took place between Christians and
Jews in a later period. But given that the denial of ascent is a
polemic against the ascent of figures, in particular Moses, concerning whom it was claimed by John's opponents that they had
ascended to heaven to bring back revelation, this is the meaning
which should be given to the verb ἀναβέβηκεν in the exception
clause, unless there are very strong indications that such a rendering
would be inappropriate.

The phrase ὁ ὢν ἐν τῷ οὐρανῷ found in some manuscripts is
regarded as original by some scholars, but it is more likely an
addition made due to the difficulty which later Christians, no
longer familiar with the idea of an ascent made by Jesus prior to
the resurrection, found in attributing the words in verse 13 to
the earthly Jesus, and an attempt to make them refer to the
post-resurrection ascension. If it is a later addition, it must have
been inserted relatively early. Nonetheless, Nestle-Aland's decision not to include the phrase seems to be based on a sound
judgment as to the relative weight of the textual evidence.[13] If
this phrase was original, it may be that, as Ashton suggests, it
was a Johannine addition to an earlier tradition.[14] In that case
John would be abandoning the view that Jesus ascended during
his earthly career, and placing the complete focus on descent.[15]
At any rate, the structure of the saying appears to confirm both
that the latter phrase is not integral to the saying, and that the
author intends to contrast the Son of Man with those figures for
whom claims of ascent were made. The following structure has
been proposed:[16]

---

[13] Cf. Moloney, *Johannine Son of Man*, p. 59. See also Nicholson, *Death as
Departure*, pp. 97–8, whose assessment of the evidence is fair and balanced, even
though he reaches a different conclusion. See also Painter, 'Enigmatic', pp. 1878–9.

[14] Ashton, *Understanding*, pp. 349, 354.

[15] It seems quite clear that the Evangelist intended to move the focus from ascent
to descent. Cf. Kanagaraj, *'Mysticism'*, p. 196. Nonetheless, it is difficult to know
with any certainty whether he simply changed the emphasis, or whether he
abandoned entirely the idea of Jesus having made an ascent during the course of his
earthly life. See further below, n.17 and n.47, and ch.13.

[16] Pryor, 'Johannine Son of Man', 346, following Moloney, *Johannine Son of
Man*, p. 56.

A οὐδεὶς
  B ἀναβέβηκεν
    C εἰς τὸν οὐρανὸν
      εἰ μὴ
    C' ὁ ἐκ τοῦ οὐρανοῦ
  B' καταβάς,
A' ὁ υἱὸς τοῦ ἀνθρώπου.

This seems quite likely to be correct, as it fits the text admirably and in no way appears forced. We thus see that the Son of Man is directly contrasted with the 'no one': the Son of Man is the exclusive revealer of heavenly things. The basis for his revelation is also contrasted: descent from heaven rather than ascent into heaven. The context and structure suggest that the ascent attributed to the Son of Man is of the same sort as that which is being polemized against in the case of other figures, rather than a reference to Jesus' post-resurrection ascension.[17]

However, these considerations do not exclude the second alternative translation, which we must now consider. On the basis of Revelation 21.27, Sidebottom suggests that John 3.13 may be rendered, 'No one has ascended into heaven but one has descended'. However, it must be observed that Rev. 21.27, like the other examples of this idiom in the New Testament, excludes one group from doing something that a second group does. 'None of category X shall enter, but only those of category Y (shall enter)' is the sense of the example from Revelation. If this grammar is applied to John, we get the same result: 'No one has ascended into heaven, but only the one who descended (has ascended).' Thus, as Ashton rightly points out, the example cited in favour of Sidebottom's rendering in fact discounts it.[18] It is preferable, therefore,

---

[17] Context must be given priority in interpretation. Zwiep, *Ascension*, p. 135 draws attention to the fact that the only other occurrence of the perfect tense ἀναβέβηκεν in the NT is in John 20.17, where the Johannine Jesus stresses that he 'has not yet ascended'. There the context clearly refers to the post-resurrection ascension, whereas the context in 3.13 relates to a different sort of ascent. Nonetheless, it may be that John disagrees with his source and no longer holds that Jesus made an ascent akin to that of Moses – at any rate John clearly emphasizes that it is due to *descent* rather than *ascent* that Jesus can reveal what no other can (cf. Painter, 'Enigmatic', p. 1879). John's exact position is difficult to pin down, because his assessment of the ascent tradition we are discussing here is unclear; nonetheless his basic emphasis seems clear enough. See further ch.13 below.

[18] Ashton, *Understanding*, p. 350 n.37. See also Coppens, *Relève Apocalyptique*, pp. 63–4. Hare's appeal (*Son of Man*, p. 87) to Gal. 1.19 likewise seems clearly to represent the citation of a verse in support of his case which actually favours the

on the grounds of both syntax and context, to interpret John 3.13 along these lines: No one has ascended to heaven to bring back revelation from there, but the one who descended from heaven – the Son of Man – has ascended to heaven to do just that. Both the claim being denied (ascent to heaven to bring back revelation) and the exception clause (Jesus, the Son of Man, has done what these others have not) suggest that John knows a tradition which claims that Jesus, in comparison with or contrast to Moses, has at some point in the course of his life ascended into heaven and returned.[19]

If we are correct to suggest that John is aware of a tradition which attributed to Jesus a heavenly journey akin to that made by Moses,[20] then the next question is whether there is any evidence for such a view in the pre-Johannine Christian literature available to us.[21] An affirmative answer to this question has been reached by Fossum and Chilton, in connection with the narratives in the Synoptic Gospels concerning the transfiguration of Jesus.[22] The parallels between the Synoptic transfiguration accounts and the

rendering he is arguing against (see also Carson, *John*, p. 200, who recognizes the difficulty but still attempts to maintain this sort of interpretation). See further the detailed criticisms raised by Nicholson, *Death as Departure*, pp. 93–6, whose arguments are not answered by Hare's restatement of Sidebottom's position.

[19] This may also be implied by John's reference to 'birth from above', especially if Philo's understanding of Moses' ascent at Sinai as both a 'second birth' and a 'calling above' had a wider currency and/or was known to John, and if, as some have suggested, it is primarily *Jesus* who is thought of as 'born from above' (so e.g. Meeks, *Prophet-King*, pp. 298–9; 'Man from Heaven', p. 147; Nicholson, *Death as Departure*, pp. 81–4).

[20] The Evangelist seems to be working with a tradition here, which he is altering, placing the focus on descent rather than ascent. A number of statements made by the Johannine Jesus would fit very well within the context of a view of his having ascended to heaven in a way similar to Moses (cf. especially 8.38, 40; see further Bühner, *Gesandte*, pp. 375–7).

[21] The only objection raised by Burkett (*Son of the Man*, pp. 36–7) to Bühner's thesis which affects the present study in any significant way is the question of evidence for Jesus having ascended to heaven or received a prophetic 'call vision'. We hope to show evidence for at least one clear instance in the tradition where an ascent is implicit, namely the transfiguration. Bühner seems to assume (on his 'anabatic-prophetic' model) that the ascent would have taken place at the call of the prophet, which leaves him open to Burkett's criticism at this point; but in connection with the Mosaic typology found in the Gospels and in particular the transfiguration accounts, it should be noted that Moses' call took place at the burning bush, prior to the ascent and receipt of Torah at Sinai, and thus on a Mosaic typology or understanding of Jesus' mission, his call would not necessarily have involved an ascent.

[22] Fossum, *Image*, pp. 71–94; Bruce D. Chilton, 'The Transfiguration: Dominical Assurance and Apostolic Vision', *NTS* 27 (1981), 121. See also Morton Smith, 'The Origin and History of the Transfiguration Story', *USQR* 36 (1980), 41–2; 'Ascent to the Heavens and the Beginnings of Christianity', *Eranos* 50 (1981), 420–1.

traditions concerning Moses on Sinai have been discussed on numerous occasions and need only be mentioned briefly here: the high mountain, the cloud and the voice which speaks from it, the radiance of Moses/Jesus, the fear of those who saw, the mention of a special group of three and the reference to six days.[23] However, there is no explicit mention of an ascent to heaven, and we must thus consider the possible evidence that a heavenly journey of some sort is implied in the narrative.

Among the features of the transfiguration stories which are noted by Fossum and Chilton as having parallels in Jewish traditions of heavenly journeys are the following:

(1) Mountains were frequently the starting places for ascent to heaven. This is not only true of the Moses-Sinai traditions: in numerous ancient worldviews, mountains were considered close to heaven, and were often regarded as meeting places between heaven and earth.[24]

(2) The transformation of a figure's clothing and/or appearance, including their becoming luminous, is frequently among the results of the ascents described in Jewish sources.[25]

[23] Chilton, 'Transfiguration', 120–2; William Richard Stegner, *Narrative Theology in Early Jewish Christianity*, Louisville: Westminster John Knox, 1989, pp. 86–93; Joel Marcus, *The Way of the Lord. Christological Exegesis of the Old Testament in the Gospel of Mark*, Louisville: Westminster John Knox/ Edinburgh: T&T Clark, 1992, pp. 81–4; Allison, *New Moses*, pp. 243–8; Moses, *Matthew's Transfiguration Story*, pp. 43–4, 53–4, 84. Cf. also Boismard, *Prologue*, pp. 168–9; W. D. Davies, *Setting*, p. 50; Vernon H. Kooy, 'The Transfiguration Motif in the Gospel of John', in James I. Cook (ed.), *Saved by Hope. Essays in Honor of Richard C. Oudersluys*, Grand Rapids: Eerdmans, 1978, pp. 66–7; Fossum, *Image*, pp. 78, 84–5; Moses, *Matthew's Transfiguration Story*, pp. 45–8, 114–60. The voice from the cloud also seems to echo the command to heed the prophet like Moses in Deut. 18.15 (so e.g. Davies, *Setting*, p. 50; Hill, *Matthew*, p. 268; Moses, *Matthew's Transfiguration Story*, p. 145). D'Angelo (*Moses*, p. 192 n.85) rightly interprets the transfiguration against a Mosaic background, but reads too 'high' a Christology into the Marcan version when she suggests that already in Mark Jesus is thought of as the one who appeared to Moses and Elijah on the mountain. This interpretation was given to the narrative in the subsequent centuries, and is very possibly the way John himself read the narrative, but there is no real evidence that the very earliest readers of Mark would have understood his narrative in this way. Cf. the more balanced interpretation of Marcus, *Way*, pp. 80–93.

[24] Fossum, *Image*, pp. 72–6. On this as a typical feature in post-Biblical apocalyptic works describing ascent to heaven see Mary Dean-Otting, *Heavenly Journeys. A Study of the Motif in Hellenistic Jewish Literature*, Frankfurt am Main: Peter Lang, 1984, pp. 267–9. Chilton ('Transfiguration', 120) notes the similarity with the experience of the apocalyptic visionary in Rev. 21.10.

[25] Fossum, *Image*, pp. 82–6. Chilton ('Transfiguration', 120) notes Rev. 3.5, 18; 4.4 as relevant parallels. The ascent is also closely connected with the commissioning

(3) The appearance of two heavenly figures to accompany the one who is ascending is a standard feature of ascent accounts.[26]

(4) There may be some evidence for a six-day period preceding an ascent or the receipt of a revelation as a recurrent motif in some Jewish literature.[27]

(5) The statement by Peter that 'it is good for us to be here' may imply a realization that he has entered a heavenly realm. The language of 'tabernacles/dwellings' is also sometimes connected with heavenly existence.[28]

These features on their own may appear inconclusive, but combined with the Moses-Sinai imagery which we have already noted to be present in the passage, and the widespread tradition that Moses ascended to heaven on Sinai, it seems quite probable that the transfiguration tradition intended to present Jesus as having made a 'heavenly ascent' of some sort.[29] This connects in an obvious way with John 3, where the relationship between Jesus and Moses and the issue of ascent are also to the fore.[30]

---

of the one who ascends as God's agent (cf. Dean-Otting, *Heavenly Journeys*, pp. 278–9).

[26] Fossum, *Image*, pp. 88–9. See also Sabbe, *Studia*, p. 70 on this as a feature of apocalyptic writings. J. G. Davies (*He Ascended into Heaven. A Study in the History of Doctrine*, London: Lutterworth, 1958, p. 40) notes that Luke uses the phrase καὶ ἰδοὺ ἄνδρες δύο both in the transfiguration account (Luke 9.30) and the account of the post-resurrection ascension (Acts 1.10). See further the table of parallels in ibid., p. 186.

[27] Cf. Fossum, *Image*, pp. 79–82.

[28] Ibid., pp. 89–91. See also Chilton, 'Transfiguration', 118, 121, who also notes the motif of fear in visionary experiences as important here.

[29] It should also be noted that in much of the literature which provides evidence of belief in Moses' ascent to heaven, the ascent is implied or assumed rather than explicitly asserted or argued for (as Allison, *New Moses*, p. 177 notes). Pseudo-Philo's *Biblical Antiquities* 12.1 says that Moses went down again 'to the place where the light of the sun and moon is', without having previously said that he ascended. See also Meeks, *Prophet-King*, p. 158, who notes that 2 Baruch 4.2–7 describes the things revealed to Moses in terms very close to the description of the revelation to Enoch in 1 Enoch 17–36, but without ever stating that Moses ascended. See also Ezekiel the Tragedian, *Exagoge* 68–89; *b*. Shab. 88b. The fact that the Sinai accounts were so widely interpreted in this way, in spite of the lack of explicit reference to the ascent of Moses into heaven, indicates that allusions to the narratives of Moses on Sinai may have been sufficient to suggest that the transfiguration of Jesus be interpreted in a similar manner. Cf. further Meeks, *Prophet-King*, pp. 122–5, 156–9, 205–9, 241–4.

[30] See further Moses, *Matthew's Transfiguration Story*, pp. 221–4, who recognizes the affinity between John 3.13 and the Matthean transfiguration account that is the focus of his study.

Although John does not record the transfiguration of Jesus, it has nonetheless been suggested that he knew this tradition. The verse that has been the focus of most attention in this regard is John 1.14, where the Evangelist affirms that 'we beheld his glory'. Luke 9.32 explicitly describes the transfiguration as a vision of Jesus' *glory*.[31] Both in the transfiguration narratives and in John 1.14, Jesus is affirmed as God's 'beloved/only Son'.[32] The language of 'tabernacle' is also present in both, as is imagery evocative of Moses on Sinai.[33] Brown, having reviewed all this evidence, cautiously affirms that there is much to support the idea that the second part of John 1.14 echoes the transfiguration story.[34]

In addition, the centrality of the designation of Jesus as 'Son of Man' in John 3.13 is another possible connection between John and the transfiguration accounts. Although not all aspects of A. Moses' attempt to relate Matthew's transfiguration account to the imagery of Daniel 7 are entirely convincing, he rightly notes that (in Matthew more emphatically, but already in Mark) the transfiguration story is bracketed on both sides by references to the 'Son of Man'.[35] Matthew and the other Synoptic Evangelists obviously do not make as much of this as John does, but it certainly seems possible that John felt able to relate the traditions about the Son of Man to the question of ascent in the way that he did because the two had already been brought into close proximity in the traditions he inherited. One of the 'Son of Man' sayings recorded in close proximity to the transfiguration accounts in the Synoptics is the first passion prediction, and this is perhaps significant in view of the fact that the first saying which asserts that 'the Son of Man must be lifted up' occurs in this section of John (3.14). Also noteworthy is the centrality of the language of 'seeing the kingdom of God',

---

[31] On glory as a key theme in ascent narratives see further Dean-Otting, *Heavenly Journeys*, pp. 280–4, 286–8.

[32] Boismard, *Prologue*, pp. 71–2; Moses, *Matthew's Transfiguration Story*, pp. 214–21.

[33] Boismard *Prologue*, p. 169.

[34] R. E. Brown, *Gospel*, p. 34. See also T. Francis Glasson, *Moses in the Fourth Gospel*, London: SCM, 1963, pp. 65–73; Kooy, 'Transfiguration'.

[35] Moses, *Matthew's Transfiguration Story*, pp. 91–9. For suggested parallels with Daniel see Sabbe, *Studia*, pp. 65–77; Moses, *Matthew's Transfiguration Story*, pp. 100–13; of these the most convincing are the points of contact with Dan. 10 noted by Sabbe, *Studia*, pp. 66–7. On close connections between Luke's account of the transfiguration and the figure of the Son of Man, see Allison A. Trites, 'The Transfiguration in the Theology of Luke: Some Redactional Links', in L. D. Hurst and N. T. Wright (eds.), *The Glory of Christ in the New Testament. Studies in Christology in Memory of G. B. Caird*, Oxford: Clarendon, 1987, p. 80.

which is also closely connected with the transfiguration (Mark 9.1 and parallels).[36]

We have thus seen evidence suggesting that (1) John is concerned here with polemic against claims that Moses ascended to heaven; (2) John has inherited a tradition which asserts or suggests that Jesus ascended to heaven; (3) the Synoptic transfiguration accounts imply that Jesus ascended to heaven and relate this to the imagery of Moses at Sinai. All in all, then, it seems quite plausible to suggest that John is dependent here on some form of transfiguration account, which had already been related to the issue of the relationship between Jesus and Moses.[37] John is thus addressing the same issue as these earlier texts, the relationship between Jesus and Moses, but in a more explicit and developed way. By John's time, the focus had come to be more explicitly on the question of Jesus' *qualifications* to reveal God as compared with Moses (cf. John 9.29).[38] Earlier it had been sufficient to allude to similarities and differences between Jesus and Moses, whereas by the time John wrote the debates over this issue had progressed, and John had to address the same basic issue more explicitly and directly.

The Johannine response

The Fourth Evangelist's response is two-pronged. He argues that, on the one hand, no one has ever ascended to heaven to bring back revelation, whether Moses, Enoch or others, while on the other hand, the one who came down from heaven has brought such heavenly knowledge.[39] As we have already seen, John has probably inherited a tradition which *compared* Jesus' experience on a moun-

---

[36] Cf. Chilton, 'Transfiguration', 123.

[37] We will suggest possible reasons why John did not include an account of the transfiguration in his Gospel below. For further discussion of John's possible knowledge of such traditions see Kooy, 'Transfiguration'; Moses, *Matthew's Transfiguration Story*, pp. 214–24. See also Stegner, *Narrative*, pp. 83–103; Marcus, *Way*, p. 93.

[38] John 9 is discussed in ch.12 below. It is unclear why Nicholson (*Death as Departure*, pp. 91–3) opposes this idea, in view of the large amount of evidence which he surveys that seems to support it. See also M. Davies, *Rhetoric*, pp. 71–2, who notes that there are similarities and differences between the use of ascent/descent language for Moses and for Jesus. Moses ascends the mountain and descends again, whereas Jesus descends from heaven and ascends again, but both descend in order to make God known.

[39] Cf. William C. Grese, '"Unless One is Born Again": The Use of a Heavenly Journey in John 3', *JBL* 107 (1988), 687; Moloney, *Johannine Son of Man*, p. 54; Borgen, 'John and Hellenism', p. 103.

tain with that of Moses. However, the ascent of Moses was widely accepted, whereas that of Jesus was difficult to demonstrate to those who were not already believers. John had to find some way of demonstrating the *superiority* of Jesus' qualifications to be the revealer, over against those of Moses.

In discussing this passage in John, commentators frequently note that a denial of heavenly ascent is also found in the Babylonian Talmud, in a saying attributed to R. Jose b. Halaphta: 'The presence of God did not descend to earth, nor did Moses and Elijah ascend on high' (*b*. Suk. 5a). This was certainly not the position of the majority of rabbis, who seem to have accepted the possibility of heavenly ascent, both in connection with Moses and also in their own day for Merkabah mystics. Nonetheless, there is some evidence from sources dated close to the time of John which suggest that there may have been hesitation in some Jewish circles, even in the first century, to believe that any human figure had ascended to heaven and either seen God or entered the very presence of God.[40] There was a tension in Jewish tradition between the belief that God could not be seen and the belief that he had been seen and made known. The Fourth Evangelist is not ruling out the possibility of 'seeing/entering the kingdom of God' or of knowing heavenly things. Rather, he is emphasizing one of these two dialectical strands, with the aim of making an exclusive claim for Jesus as revealer. What is being denied is not so much any claim to have received revelation apart from Jesus, as the possibility of a revelation superior to that of Jesus.[41] The force of this

[40] Although the Talmudic tradition cited, which raises such concerns explicitly, is obviously of a date much later than John, we have seen evidence that may suggest that there was concern in some circles, even in the first century, about claiming that a human being ascended to heaven to be enthroned there (esp. in chs. 3 and 7 above). Thus it is not impossible that other ideas of heavenly ascent, while generally accepted, had been objected to by some, perhaps a small minority, even as early as John's time (cf. esp. Josephus, *Ant*. 4.326). Barrett (*Commentary*, p. 212) relates this to the many early Jewish texts which express caution about mysticism and scepticism about human claims to know or understand heavenly things (cf. e.g. Prov. 30.4; 4 Ezra 4.10–11). If such concerns existed in John's time, then it may be that John was appealing to the position of some Jews or Jewish authorities over against others.

[41] John can reject the claim that Moses or any other ascended to heaven, since the Sinai narratives nowhere explicitly state that Moses ascended. Even in the case of Enoch and Elijah, it could be argued that they did not ascend to the highest heavens, to really have access to God and heavenly things in the fullest sense; and it could be further pointed out that at any rate they are not said in the scriptural accounts to have returned with revelation. However, John may well not have intended to deny the possibility of some sort of postmortem unidirectional ascent even for others.

claim is only felt when it is coupled with the second prong of the Johannine defence.

In this chapter, John moves from a discussion of issues related to Moses and/or the Prophet-like-Moses, to the Son of Man. Since, as Martyn points out, this pattern occurs several times in the Gospel, of which this is the first, the pattern must certainly be significant.[42] John is using the Son of Man category he has inherited to address the issues raised by the debate over Jesus' relation to Moses, in ways that we shall now consider.

Whereas it could be denied that any human figure, ancient or contemporary, had in fact ascended to heaven (or at least to the highest heaven, the very presence of God), what could not be denied by Jews who accepted the authority of the book of Daniel was that a particular human or human-like figure was, had been or could be in heaven in the presence of God. The '(one like a) son of man' in Daniel 7 appears to have been understood by many Jews – at least towards the end of the first century if not earlier – as a messianic figure, as is clearly the case in the Similitudes of Enoch and IV Ezra, as well as in at least some streams of the later rabbinic tradition.[43] In the case of the Similitudes in particular, this messianic figure is described in the language of pre-existence, as a means of expressing his eternal place in the plan of God. As we have already noted, the Fourth Evangelist appears to be the first to draw out from this tradition the implication that the Son of Man, because he pre-existed in heaven, can reveal the heavenly things he saw there.[44] The first assertion in the Gospel of the pre-existence of Jesus as Son of Man occurs in the present context (John 3.13), and may be expected to shed light on precisely why this development took place.

The Fourth Evangelist is here developing traditional motifs in order to respond to Jewish objections. 'The Jews' regarded the revelation brought by Moses as sufficient, and thus felt they had no

[42] Martyn, *History*, pp. 131–4. See also below, p. 190 (and also ch.13), in relation to the similar pattern in John 9.

[43] Cf. especially 1 Enoch 37–71; IV Ezra 13; also the later *b*. Sanh. 38b; 98a; Hag. 14a. Once again it must be stressed that our concern is not to demonstrate that such an understanding of Daniel 7 is pre-Christian, but pre-Johannine. It is very likely that at least some Jews interpreted Daniel 7 in messianic terms even before the first century; it is certain that towards the end of the first century a number of different authors espouse this view. See further Dunn, *Christology*, p. 72.

[44] See further our discussion of this theme in ch. 2 above, and also McGrath, 'Change in Christology', 45–6.

need for Jesus' revelation, which at any rate they found it difficult to verify as being of divine origin (cf. John 9.29). In this context, the Fourth Evangelist was able to appeal to the view of at least some of his Jewish contemporaries that the Son of Man is the Messiah, and the Christian view that Jesus was the Messiah and Son of Man.[45] On the basis of these traditions, which had also begun to use pre-existence language, the Evangelist was able to draw the conclusion that, as one who pre-existed in heaven, Jesus (the Son of Man) was superior to all others for whom claims had been made of heavenly journeys and revelations: they had not truly made such journeys, but even if they had, their fleeting visits would be nothing in comparison to the revelation which could be brought by one who had dwelt in heaven before appearing on earth.

Our discussion thus far suggests a plausible reason why the Fourth Evangelist, who emphasizes throughout his Gospel the glory of Jesus, has not included an account of the transfiguration, in spite of the fact that he probably knew this tradition. The usual reason proposed by scholars is that John omitted it in order to present the whole of Jesus' ministry as a revelation of glory, a glory that was beheld by all of Jesus' followers and not simply a small elite circle.[46] This is very probably correct, but an additional and perhaps more pressing reason would seem to have been the debates over Jesus' relationship to Moses: Jesus does not reveal God on the basis of such heavenly visits, but rather on the basis of the descent of the Son of Man, who knows heavenly things because of his pre-existence in heaven. It is not entirely clear whether John still maintained that Jesus ascended to heaven and returned, or whether he has abandoned this view in order to place full weight on the descent.[47] The latter seems more probable, but in either case, John

[45] Dunn is rightly cautious about using the Similitudes of Enoch, IV Ezra and/or the rabbinic tradition as evidence for Jewish thought in *pre-Christian* times (*Christology*, pp. 75–82). However, our interest is not in pre-Christian Jewish thought, but merely pre-*Johannine*, and in response to this question the concurrence of 1 Enoch and IV Ezra, which are temporally close to the Fourth Gospel, together with the rabbinic evidence, makes it seem likely that by John's time not only Christians but many Jews as well would have understood the Danielic 'son of man' to be a messianic figure. On the history of the phrase among Christians see e.g. Higgins, *Jesus and the Son of Man*, pp. 153, 157–71; E. P. Sanders, *Jesus and Judaism*, pp. 142–6; John Dominic Crossan, *The Historical Jesus. The Life of a Mediterranean Jewish Peasant*, Edinburgh: T&T Clark, 1991, pp. 238–59.

[46] So e.g. J. N. Sanders, *John*, p. 82; Kooy, 'Transfiguration', pp. 65–6, 72.

[47] In which case Ashton would be correct in his suggestion that John 3.13 contains overtones of an earlier meaning which the Evangelist did not continue to hold (*Understanding*, pp. 354–5).

is emphasizing the descent of the heavenly pre-existent one, over against ascent, as the basis of Jesus' revelation.[48] John's emphasis on descent over ascent follows the logic implicit in the Jesus tradition itself: the fundamental event in the revelation given to, in and through Jesus was not the transfiguration (and any ascent connected with it), but the earlier descent, when Jesus was empowered and indwelt by the Spirit, who John emphasizes became completely united with Jesus.[49] At the very least, it provided a firm basis in the tradition for the view that descent precedes ascent in the case of Jesus.[50]

The Evangelist's development of the tradition has a number of striking implications, which later Christology was left to wrestle with. Of these the most obvious and most difficult is the apparent implication that not simply God's Word, but *Jesus* the Messiah as a personal individual, pre-existed in some sense. Of course, this may in fact be a misreading of John, but a decision on this matter will have to await our later discussion of the coherence of the various images and ideas which John uses in his legitimation. An assessment of how the pre-existence of the Son of Man relates to the pre-existence of the Logos will also have to await this later discussion (see chapter 15 below). However, it seems justified to suggest that the Johannine emphasis on pre-existence and descent over any claim to ascent, whether before or after the resurrection, was a key factor which shaped one of the fundamental emphases of subsequent Christology, and that John has presented Jesus in these terms in order to legitimate his christological beliefs.

Summary

In this section we have once again seen John to be taking part in the ongoing debate over an issue that arose earlier, the relationship between Jesus and Moses, here specifically considered in terms of their respective qualifications to reveal heavenly things. John

[48] Cf. above n.15, n.17, and n.47; also our discussion in ch.13 below.

[49] See our discussions above, esp. in ch.7. See too Boismard, *Moise*, pp. 78–9; Michèle Morgen, *Afin Que Le Monde Soit Sauvé*, Paris: Cerf, 1993, pp. 59–61 on possible allusions to Wisdom language here, and pp. 76–7 on connections with Philo's exegesis of Exodus (see also Kanagaraj, '*Mysticism*', pp. 197–8, 201). On the relationship between the concepts of Word, Wisdom and Spirit, see ch.2 above.

[50] Another reason for omitting the transfiguration account may be the Johannine view of Jesus as not merely like Moses on Sinai, but as the incarnation of the one who spoke to Moses on Sinai. See ch.9 above.

appears to be dependent on earlier streams of tradition, in particular one that presented Jesus on the mountain as having been
transfigured in the same way as Moses was, due to a similar
experience of ascent into heaven. The traditions concerning the
revelation at Sinai and Moses' ascent to heaven had thus been
brought by Jewish opponents into comparison with the claims
Christians were making for Jesus. The conclusion which these
opponents reached was that one could be certain of Moses'
qualifications and of the revelation which he brought in a way that
one could not be concerning the parallel claims made by Christians
concerning Jesus.

In response, John takes up the traditional chronology of the
events in the life of Jesus, together with traditions concerning the
Son of Man in both Christianity and Judaism. On the basis of
these, John draws the conclusion that Jesus' revelation was not
based on an ascent to heaven, but on the descent of one who had
pre-existed in heaven. John goes so far as to claim that no one had
in fact ascended to heaven in order to bring back knowledge of
heavenly things, except for the one whose revelation was based not
on the ascent of a human being into heaven, but on the descent of
one who pre-existed in heaven to tell of what he saw and experienced there. This is clearly a significant development, but from the
perspective of the Fourth Evangelist, this was probably felt to be
simply drawing out the implications of the traditions he inherited.
Earlier tradition had presented the descent of the Spirit on Jesus,
and had referred to Jesus as 'Son of Man', a designation which in
contemporary literature was associated with the language of pre-
existence. However, no one had previously suggested that the Son
of Man would come and tell about what he saw in heaven.[51] John
was apparently the first to draw the sorts of conclusions that he did
from the application of this sort of language and imagery to Jesus.
It seems quite likely that he did so because of his need to defend or
legitimate Jesus' qualifications to reveal God. The debate over this
issue provoked him to draw out the implications of the traditions
he inherited, resulting in significant developments to them.

[51] It is impossible to determine with any certainty how a first-century Jew would
have answered the question whether he or she distinguished different types or uses of
the language of pre-existence. It seems clear however that the use of pre-existence
language in reference to the Son of Man in pre-Johannine literature did not lead
anyone to explicitly draw the sort of implications that John drew.

11

BREAD FROM HEAVEN (JOHN 6)

The next segment of John's Gospel that we will be considering in this part of our study is the bread of life discourse in John 6. Here John presents yet another dialogue between Jesus and 'the Jews'.[1] That the conflict setting of the Johannine community has influenced this text is suggested by the way 'the Jews' respond to what Jesus says: they ask for a miraculous sign (6.30–1),[2] and grumble and argue in response to his words (6.41, 52). The result is that even many of his disciples turn back from following him (6.66). This may indicate that we have to do here with a later conflict, an inner-Christian one, a possibility to which we shall return our attention later in the present chapter. Nonetheless, the fact that the opponents are here referred to as 'the Jews' suggests that, whomever else the author may have had in mind, the same opponents that were in view in the other passages we have been examining are still in view here. These factors, as well as many features of the text that we shall consider below, suggest that the bread of life discourse will prove relevant to our study.

The focus of the conflict

The focal point of the narrative, which provides its starting point and most of its imagery, is the Jewish manna tradition.[3] The crowd asks Jesus for a miraculous sign to demonstrate his claims, just as Moses' claims were confirmed by the miracles he accomplished.[4] The mention of the specific miracle of the provision of *manna* is

[1] Note the similarity in form with other texts reflecting the church–synagogue conversations presented in Martyn, *History*, pp. 131–3.

[2] Cf. ibid., p. 114.

[3] Cf. Peder Borgen, *Bread from Heaven. An Exegetical Study of the Concept of Manna in the Gospel of John and the Writings of Philo* (NovTSup, 10), Leiden: Brill, 1965.

[4] See our discussion of this theme in relation to John 9 in ch.12 below.

significant. There is evidence that around the time John wrote his Gospel there was an expectation in at least some Jewish circles of an eschatological provision of manna in the Messianic age.[5] Thus, although 'the Jews' do not ask specifically for bread from heaven, but for a miracle which will prove Jesus' claims just as Moses' claims were proved by miracles, nevertheless the fact that their request for a sign mentions the provision of manna in Moses' time suggests that the issue is whether Jesus is the eschatological redeemer, the one about whom Moses wrote.[6] The question being asked by the crowd is whether Jesus meets the criteria which the Jewish Scriptures and traditions lay down for the redeemer, Messiah or prophet like Moses.

The bread of life discourse is frequently read as having a sacramental rather than a christological emphasis. While there is no reason to deny that the imagery used here would have recalled for Christians the Eucharistic meal, to recognize that a particular type of imagery is present in this section of John is not necessarily to determine the chief emphases on which the Evangelist wished to focus through his use of that imagery.[7] The dialogue with 'the Jews' may begin with a discussion of food, but this is quickly interpreted in terms of believing on the one whom God has sent (6.29). As in the dialogue with the Samaritan woman, which has a very similar form,[8] the conversation is taking place on two levels. Jesus'

[5] 2 Baruch 29.8 (probably *c.*100 CE). See also Sib.Or. 7.149; *Mek. Ex.* 16.25. See further Dodd, *Interpretation*, p. 335; R. E. Brown, *Gospel*, pp. 265–6; Lindars, *Gospel of John*, p. 255; Barrett, *Commentary*, pp. 288–9; Carson, *John*, p. 286. In a much later rabbinic tradition which is frequently cited by scholars in discussing John 6 (*Eccles. Rab.* 1.9), R. Berechiah says in the name of R. Isaac (*c.*300 CE): 'As was the first redeemer so is the latter redeemer . . . as the first redeemer brought down the manna, so also will the latter redeemer bring down the manna.' This statement occurs in the context of a comparison between the first redeemer, Moses, and the latter redeemer (the eschatological Messiah or prophet like Moses). This rabbinic tradition in fact mentions three activities which are common to both redeemers: the provision of manna, the provision of water and riding on a donkey, and it is striking that only John of all the Gospels presents Jesus as doing all three of these things (John 6.32–5; 4.10–14; 7.37–8; 12.14–15). However, the late date of this work prevents certainty about whether Jewish expectations took anything like this form in John's time. Cf. further G. R. Beasley-Murray, 'Mission', p. 1858. On the relationship between John 6 and the expectation of a 'prophet like Moses' see further Schnackenburg, *John vol. II*, pp. 19–20, 24. On the Jewish views of Moses that may lie behind this chapter, see Menken, *Old Testament Quotations*, pp. 54–63.

[6] Lindars, *Gospel of John*, pp. 233–4 regards John 6 as a demonstration of the statement in 5.46–7, namely that Moses wrote about Jesus.

[7] Cf. James D. G. Dunn, 'John VI – A Eucharistic Discourse?', *NTS* 17 (1970–1), 336; G. R. Beasley-Murray, *John*, p. 95.

[8] Cf. R. E. Brown, *Gospel*, p. 267.

interlocutors are thinking of some form of very special, but none-theless literal, food or drink, whereas Jesus is offering *himself*. The issue in this passage is not whether the Christian Eucharist is the bread of life, but whether Jesus himself is the bread of life (6.35, 48). The need of 'the Jews', as far as the author of John is concerned, is to believe in Jesus and thereby to receive eternal life (6.40, 47). Of course, belief in Jesus would involve becoming part of the Christian community, and thus partaking in their communal meals. The point is not that there is no Eucharistic imagery here, but that this imagery is used primarily to make a christological point, namely to present Jesus himself as the true bread from heaven, manna, and bread of life.

The focus on the issue of Jesus' relationship to Moses and the Sinai revelation is also indicated by the use of language similar to that found in 1.18; 3.13; 5.37-8. Here John states that 'No one has ever seen the Father except the one who is from God; only he has seen the Father' (6.46).[9] This indicates that in this chapter, as in these other passages, one issue that is to the fore is the claim made for Moses/Israel at Sinai to have seen God. This suggests that, once again, John is contrasting aspects of the Moses/Sinai tradition with the claims he is making for Jesus as revealer.[10]

The relationship of John 6 to earlier tradition is relatively easy to demonstrate, given the Evangelist's use of a story that has a clear parallel in the Synoptics. So much has been written on the relationship between the Johannine and Synoptic accounts of the feeding of the multitude and the subsequent crossing of the sea that it is unnecessary to discuss the parallels in detail here.[11] John is dependent on a tradition known also to Mark and the other Evangelists, and in the view of the present author most likely

---

[9] The parallel with 1.18 is particularly close. Cf. Theobald, *Fleischwerdung*, pp. 367-8.

[10] See further Borgen, *Bread*, pp. 148-54 on the links with the Sinai tradition.

[11] See e.g. Dodd, *Historical Tradition*, pp. 196-222; R. E. Brown, *Gospel*, pp. 236-50; J. N. Sanders, *John*, pp. 9-10, 175-200; Barrett, *Commentary*, p. 271; Schnackenburg, *John vol. II*, pp. 20-3; E. Ruckstuhl, 'Die Speisung des Volkes durch Jesus und die Seeüberfahrt der Jünger nach Joh 6, 1-25 im Vergleich zu den Synoptischen Parallelen', in F. van Segbroeck, C. M. Tuckett, G. van Belle and J. Verheyden (eds.), *The Four Gospels 1992. Festschrift Frans Neirynck. Volume 3* (BETL, 100), Leuven: Leuven University Press, 1992, pp. 2001-19; Francois Vouga, 'Le quatrième évangile comme interprète de la tradition synoptique: Jean 6', in Adelbert Denaux (ed.), *John and the Synoptics* (BETL, 101), Leuven: Leuven University Press, 1992, pp. 261-79; Borgen, *Early Christianity*, pp. 206-7.

knows it independently of them.[12] The important question for our purposes is whether the issue of the relationship between Jesus and Moses, or of the provision of manna, is connected with this particular narrative not only in John, but already even in the earlier tradition. Stegner, considering the Marcan account, concludes that its symbolism does indeed focus on the manna tradition.[13] In Mark, one finds several allusions to the narratives of Israel's wilderness wanderings, which provided the setting for the Exodus manna story. First, there is the organization of the people into hundreds and fifties. This parallels the organization of Israel in the wilderness (Exod. 18.21), and is found again in the Qumran community, who intentionally patterned themselves on Israel in the wilderness.[14] Second, the reference to the crowd as 'like sheep without a shepherd' recalls Moses' prayer that God appoint a new leader, so that Israel will not be 'as sheep who have no shepherd'.[15] Both feeding accounts in Mark are set in a 'wilderness place' (ἔρημον), which uses the same word as the Greek versions of the Pentateuchal accounts of Israel's wanderings in the wilderness.[16] It may also be significant that the feeding is closely connected with the crossing of the sea, which may recall the crossing of the Sea of Reeds in the Exodus tradition.[17] There is also evidence from Paul (1 Cor. 10.3) that at a very early stage the Christian Eucharist was associated with the manna, and since many commentators find Eucharistic overtones in the feeding narrative(s), a close connection with the manna tradition would not be surprising.[18] Other additional parallels noted by Allison include the fact that both Mark

[12] Cf. Dodd, *Historical Tradition*, pp. 196–222; Christian Riniker, 'Jean 6, 1–21 et les Evangiles Synoptiques', in Jean-Daniel Kaestli, Jean-Michel Poffet and Jean Zumstein (eds.), *La Communauté Johannique et Son Histoire. La trajectoire de l'évangile de Jean aux deux premiers siècles*, Geneva: Labor et Fides, 1990, pp. 52–3, 58–9 and *passim*.

[13] Stegner, *Narrative*, p. 56.

[14] Cf. 1QS 2.21–2; CD 13.1–2. See also Stegner, *Narrative*, p. 57; M. Davies, *Rhetoric*, p. 239.

[15] Stegner, *Narrative*, p. 58 (citing Num. 27.17). See too Carson, *John*, p. 383; also Meeks, *Prophet-King*, pp. 196–7, 202–3, 295, 307, 311–313 on Moses as shepherd in Jewish tradition.

[16] Dennis E. Nineham, *Saint Mark*, Harmondsworth: Penguin, 1963, pp. 178, 182. For other possible verbal echoes of the scriptural narratives, see Stegner, *Narrative*, pp. 63, 70; Allison, *New Moses*, p. 239.

[17] This may explain why the two narratives became inseparably linked to one another, so that both the Synoptics and John recount the two together.

[18] Stegner, *Narrative*, pp. 58–9. Cf. Nineham, *Mark*, pp. 179, 183; also Davies, *Setting*, pp. 48–9.

and the Pentateuch have two accounts (Mark 6.30–44; 8.1–10; Exod. 16; Num. 11), and the fact that the provision of the 'bread' takes place late in the day/in the evening.[19]

In view of these numerous points of similarity, it seems quite likely that the Marcan version of the feeding of the multitude had already associated the events described with the story in the Jewish Scriptures of Israel being provided with manna in the wilderness.[20] It therefore seems reasonable to conclude that John is here taking up this earlier tradition about the feeding of the multitude because it already formed part of the early Jewish-Christian discussion of the relationship between Jesus and Moses. The issue of how Jesus compared with Moses, and how his miracles compared with those worked in Moses' day, antedates John, and John is thus addressing an issue that was not unique to his time or his community.

The Johannine response

John presents Jesus as the 'true bread from heaven', i.e. the true manna. On one level, this may be John's way of answering the objection that Jesus did not actually provide bread from heaven in the way that some Jews seem to have expected the Messiah, or the prophet like Moses, to do. As far as the Fourth Evangelist is concerned, Jesus did fulfil the expectation of an eschatological return of the manna, because *he himself* was the manna. Further, Jesus' 'manna' provides eternal life, whereas the manna which was eaten in the wilderness – and which 'the Jews' continue to expect – does not. John could make such claims on the basis of traditions he inherited, especially the traditions concerning Jesus' final meal with his disciples, which included an identification between Jesus' body and bread.[21] The tradition of Jesus feeding the multitude not only recalls the manna tradition, but also contains Eucharistic allusions, even in its earliest known form.[22] This allowed a three-way connection to be made between this narrative, the identification of Jesus' body with the Eucharistic bread, and manna. Similarly, there were traditions identifying Jesus very closely with God's Wisdom, in

[19] Allison, *New Moses*, p. 239.

[20] For possible indications that Matthew understood the story this way see Allison, *New Moses*, pp. 240–2.

[21] Mark 14.22 and pars. Note also the Passover setting, which also provides a link with the manna traditions.

[22] Mark 6.30–52. Cf. Nineham, *Mark*, p. 179.

contrast with Torah, which is significant since both were linked to the imagery of manna in Jewish tradition.[23] It is probably on the basis of these various but interconnected traditions that John took the step of identifying Jesus as the manna, the bread from heaven. John drew out the implications which he did from the traditions he inherited, at least partially in response to Jewish objections that Jesus could not be the eschatological revealer/redeemer because he had not provided manna.[24]

The main thrust of John's portrait only becomes clear when we take into consideration the three-way identification between manna, Wisdom and Torah that is attested in Jewish literature. There can be little doubt that this identification predates John: it already appears to be implied in Deuteronomy 8.3, and is made more explicit in numerous subsequent Jewish writings.[25] Thus John is not only contrasting Jesus with the manna, but is also contrasting him, through his use of Wisdom/Word imagery, with the revelation brought by Moses in the Torah, much as he did in the prologue.[26]

The issue of the relationship between Jesus and Moses/Torah was also to the fore in the dialogue with Nicodemus in John 3, where it was addressed in connection with the descent/ascent of the Son of Man, and with the theme of knowledge of heavenly things. It is probably significant that a reference to ascent and an allusion to the descent of the Son of Man are given in the present passage as well (6.62). There has been much discussion of and disagreement

[23] On manna and Wisdom/Torah see immediately below. Note also 1 Cor. 10.3–4, where Christ is identified with the rock that followed Israel in the Wilderness, which some Jewish writings identify as a symbol of Wisdom and which is closely connected to the manna tradition. Cf. Dunn, *Christology*, pp. 183–4; *Theology of Paul*, pp. 279–80.

[24] And of course, given the account of a feeding miracle which is provided in the immediate context, there is also the argument that Jesus did miraculously provide bread, even if it did not fall from the heavens, and the failure of 'the Jews' to heed him is due to their failure to recognize or acknowledge the signs which Jesus has in fact accomplished. Cf. Martyn, *History*, pp. 125–6.

[25] Cf. Dodd, *Interpretation*, p. 336; Barrett, *Commentary*, pp. 288–9; Pryor, *John*, p. 31. Philo, *Mut.* 259–60; *Leg. All.* 3.162, 169–76; See also Neh. 9.20; *Mek. Ex.* 13.17; *Ex. Rab.* 25.7. Jos. and Asen. 16 may also indicate that manna was identified with the Jewish Torah/Wisdom (which the proselyte to Judaism must accept), and also referred to as 'bread of life' in connection with the imagery of the tree of life in Genesis. If this work could be shown to predate John, then it would provide an even clearer indication that the whole of his imagery may derive from this sort of background.

[26] See ch.9 above. In addition to the Wisdom parallels, there are also echoes of the description of the Word of God in Isa. 55.1–11. Cf. Burkett, *Son of the Man*, pp. 129–34.

over the meaning of this verse, with most commentators arguing over whether seeing Jesus ascend would make the situation better or worse for those who saw him do so.[27] In our view, the most convincing interpretation is that of Moloney. He suggests that the question being asked in John 6.62 is what Jesus must do in order for his revelation as the one that has come down from heaven to be accepted – must he go so far as to ascend to where he was before? Moloney suggests that here (as in 3.13) Jesus is being contrasted with figures who were thought to have ascended to heaven to bring back revelation. 'To ask that he ascend is completely to misunderstand his origin. It is because of his origin "with God" that his revelation is true; he has no need to ascend.'[28] This clearly ties in very well with the emphases we have discerned in other parts of the Fourth Gospel. Nonetheless, Moloney does insufficient justice to the fact that, although Jesus' revelation is based on descent rather than ascent, nonetheless Jesus *will* ascend when he returns to the Father, and this exaltation will confirm his revelation, precisely as a vindication of the one whose origin is in heaven, and who therefore has no need to ascend in order to bring back knowledge of heavenly secrets.[29]

John 6 combines the two key images which John has used prior to this in his Gospel to legitimate his view of the relationship between Jesus and Moses: Wisdom and Son of Man. Discussion of the question of how Wisdom relates to the Son of Man we must once again postpone until a later chapter. But we may note briefly that John identifies Jesus both as the true bread from heaven, the bread of life (6.35, 48), and also the source of this food which gives eternal life (6.27; presumably in unity with his Father, since in 6.32–3 the Father gives the bread, which is Jesus). Jesus seems to be both the giver and the gift! Vermes has suggested that this may be connected with a rabbinic tradition which identified Moses with the bread from heaven,[30] but given the late date of the work cited

---

[27] Cf. e.g. Barrett, *Commentary*, p. 303.

[28] Moloney, *Johannine Son of Man*, pp. 122–3.

[29] There may be an element of Johannine irony here: those who recognize that his origins are in heaven have no need to see him ascend in order to learn of heavenly things, and yet they *will* see his identity confirmed when he returns to the Father; those who refuse to recognize him as one whose origin is in heaven will also object to the idea that he has ascended to heaven (cf. our discussion of the controversy over Jesus' exalted status in chs.3 and 7 above).

[30] Geza Vermes, 'He is the Bread. Targum Neofiti Exodus 16:15', in E. Earle Ellis and Max Wilcox (eds.), *Neotestamentica et Semitica. Studies in Honour of Matthew Black*, Edinburgh: T&T Clark, 1969, pp. 256–63.

and the lack of attestation for the idea in any earlier source, no argument can be made for John's dependence on such ideas. This paradox will be examined further in our penultimate chapter. For our present purposes, it is sufficient that we have seen that the discourse concerning the bread of life in John 6 confirms what we have already suggested in connection with the prologue and the dialogue with Nicodemus: John made creative use of traditions concerning Jesus as Wisdom and Son of Man in order to answer Jewish objections to his christological claims, in order to defend Jesus' qualifications not only to reveal God, but to do so in a way that none other, not even Moses, was able to. We shall return later to the question of whether John formed the developments that arose out of these into a coherent and unified christological portrait of Jesus.

John 6 and inner-Christian conflict

The motifs used here echo those used elsewhere in John to respond to the issue of the relation between Jesus and Moses. But what is striking is that, in contrast to the other passages we have considered thus far, we actually find evidence in John 6 of conflict *about the distinctive Johannine developments*.[31] In other words, John 6 records not only the developments that resulted from the conflict with the synagogue, but also the further conflicts resulting from those developments. Here the heavenly origin claimed for the Son of Man does provoke a direct, negative response. This is very possibly due to the fact that, as Lindars suggests, John 6 was added to the Fourth Gospel after much of the earlier material had already been produced.[32] The difference in content suggests this, but an even clearer indication of this is the way John 6 clearly interrupts the

---

[31] The only possible exception is John 8.31ff., where there is conflict with 'the Jews who believed in him', and here too there is some evidence that conflict about the distinctive Johannine Christology has been worked into earlier material (there is a strong objection to Jesus' claim to pre-existence). This may reflect a revision of the Gospel at a later time, perhaps around the time when the Johannine epistles were written (cf. de Boer, *Johannine Perspectives*, p. 82). Space does not permit us to attempt to discern an earlier version of John to which later material has been added, but it is at least possible that in parts of John 6 and 8 we have evidence of a subsequent revision of the Gospel in order to apply it to new issues.

[32] Lindars, *Gospel of John*, p. 50. Cp. Painter, *Quest*, pp. 254–5, 284–5. In our view, it seems clear both that the majority of John 6 reflects conflict with 'the Jews', and also that the story has been reshaped so as to address later, inner-Christian debates, and in that form has been placed between John 5 and 7.

continuity between chapter 5 and chapter 7.[33] Further, the result which follows from the distinctive Johannine developments is not simply further conflict with 'the Jews', but also that some of Jesus' own disciples turn back and no longer follow him, a feature which is found almost nowhere else in John apart from in this passage.[34] It thus seems that, whatever its literary history, this passage gives us insight into the 'aftermath' of Johannine legitimation, and it is thus worth reflecting at least briefly on this point.[35]

The claim that Jesus is the bread of life which came down from heaven is found objectionable, since Jesus is clearly 'the son of Joseph' (6.41); so is the demand that people eat his flesh (6.52). There are two key reasons why caution must be exercised in interpreting this latter point. One is that the Johannine motif of *misunderstanding* is present: what Jesus' interlocutors take literally should in fact be given some form of 'spiritual' interpretation (6.63). The other is that the imagery of the complaints, like the christological imagery applied by the Johannine Jesus to himself, has been influenced by the Exodus narratives. This may be true even in 6.52, where Lindars has suggested there is an allusion to the traditions concerning Israel's request for 'meat' (σάρξ) in the wilderness.[36] The whole discourse is an exposition of the Jewish Scriptures, and its imagery is derived from there.[37]

We may thus cautiously suggest that the author felt that those Christians who objected to the implications he was drawing from traditional beliefs, and to the developments he was making, were misunderstanding the Scriptures and the teaching of Jesus. In his view, the ascent of the Son of Man demonstrates that he was in fact of heavenly origin (6.62). The only one who could rightly be exalted as Jesus had been was one who was eternally worthy of that status. Yet it was the spirit which was important, and not the flesh. The descent of Jesus did not refer to the descent of a fully formed, flesh-and-blood human being from heaven; this would obviously have contradicted the natural birth that Jesus was known to have had. Rather, what is in view is the descent of the heavenly one who became incarnate as the human being Jesus.

Likewise some Jewish Christians may have objected to the

---

[33] Cf. Lindars, *Gospel of John*, pp. 277–8.
[34] The exception once again being John 8 (see n.31 above).
[35] On this subject see also Anderson, *Christology*, p. 218.
[36] Lindars, *Gospel of John*, p. 267.
[37] Cf. Borgen, *Bread*, pp. 59–98; Lindars, *Gospel of John*, pp. 250–3.

language of eating and drinking Jesus' flesh and blood which had become associated with the Christian Eucharist. However, the author does not make any direct reference to the practice of the Eucharist, but rather uses its imagery as a symbol of coming to faith in Jesus. The author responds to these objections by stating that those who cannot grasp Jesus' teaching have not been drawn by God – that is, they have not responded correctly to the teaching of Scripture (6.44–45 – on which see further pp. 201–2 below). As Rensberger has pointed out in connection with the baptismal imagery in John 3, distinctive Christian practices would have served a sociological function, clarifying the borders between Christianity and other forms of Judaism.[38] To believe in Jesus meant to join the Christian community, even though that meant rejection by the Jewish leaders and synagogue authorities. Those who reject the Johannine developments, like those who reject Jesus, are portrayed as unwilling to listen to God (and to the voice of the Spirit-Paraclete, as the author will make clear in 14.15–31; 16.5–15). The author emphasizes that the scandal of belief in Jesus is one that has always been attached to obedience to God, and it is this scandal that those who wish to have eternal life must overcome.

Summary

In John 6, we have once again seen John portraying Christ in comparison/contrast to Moses, and taking up Wisdom and Son of Man imagery in order to legitimate his beliefs concerning Jesus. He thus makes use of a number of traditions in order to portray Jesus as having fulfiled the expectation of an eschatological gift of manna: Jesus himself is the manna, the true bread from heaven, which gives eternal life. John also uses these traditional images to contrast Jesus with Torah. Yet there is an unusual aspect to this part of John. Here the focus is not only on the objections of 'the Jews' (to which the Evangelist's distinctive developments were a response), but also on the response which *followed on from those developments*. That is to say, we are allowed a glimpse of the issues that arose subsequently in the community, as a direct result of the developments we have been studying. As we might have expected, the developments were controversial, and were not accepted by all.

---

[38] David Rensberger, *Overcoming the World: Politics and Community in the Gospel of John*, London: SPCK, 1989, pp. 54–61.

The means were already in place for the author to legitimate his beliefs against these further conflicts, as many of the features that enabled him to defend his beliefs against Jewish objections could also be turned against Christians who objected. The imagery he had at his disposal in the tradition enabled him to legitimate his beliefs in light of the rejection of those beliefs by 'the Jews', and also by some Christians as well.

12

LEGITIMATING SIGNS (JOHN 9)

John 9 has particular relevance for our study, as it was taken by Martyn as the starting point for his interpretation of the Gospel on two levels, one reflecting Jesus and his ministry, the other reflecting the needs and experiences of Christians in conflict with the synagogue.[1] There seems to be a large amount of agreement that the conflict and debate portrayed in John 9 reflect those which were taking place between certain Christians and opponents in their local Jewish community or communities.[2] It is thus a logical place to look for evidence of the Evangelist's legitimating activity.

The point at issue in the conflict

John 9 contains one of the clearest and most straightforward examples of the sort of objections which were being raised by the Johannine Christians' Jewish opponents: 'We know that God spoke to Moses, but as for this man, we do not know where he comes from' (John 9.29). This objection is coupled with an expression of the view that Jesus is a sinner and therefore cannot be from God. The point is that, whereas Moses' credentials are indisputable, the Jewish authorities regard Jesus as a lawbreaker, and take this as

[1] Martyn, *History*, pp. 30, 39 and *passim*.
[2] Meeks, *Prophet-King*, pp. 292–3; Pancaro, *Law*, pp. 24–5; Schnackenburg, *John vol. II*, pp. 238–9; Painter, *Quest*, pp. 7, 305ff.; Brodie, *John*, p. 343. See also Dodd, *Historical Tradition*, p. 188; Barrett, *Commentary*, p. 355. Meeks suggests that the trial of the man parallels Jesus' trial before Pilate. However, it is perhaps more accurate to suggest that this incident ties in to the motif in John of 'Jesus on Trial' (cf. A. E. Harvey, *Jesus on Trial*, pp. 76, 85, 89, 93), with Jesus being tried here *in absentia* through the trial of a man who has become Jesus' disciple. Meeks does not regard the man as a representative of the Christian community, but of individuals within Judaism who have been confronted with the Christian message, but the fact that the man asks whether the Pharisees wish to become Jesus' disciples *also* (9.27) suggests that the man who had been blind is portrayed by the Evangelist as already a Christian disciple. See further Pancaro, *Law*, pp. 24–6, 105–6.

definitive evidence against his claim to reveal God and speak authoritatively on God's behalf. As Martyn observes, the theme of 'Jesus versus Moses' is one that occurs repeatedly in the Fourth Gospel, and represents a key point of conflict between church and synagogue with which John himself wrestled.[3]

Since we have already touched on this subject in chapter 2 and in the chapters immediately preceding this one, little needs to be said concerning the evidence that the relationship between Jesus and Moses (and the revelations brought by each) was an issue in pre-Johannine times. This issue obviously has a direct connection to the issue of whether Jesus' teaching is in accord with the Mosaic law, which is to the fore in instances where Jesus is presented, as he is in John 9, as healing on the Sabbath. In the Synoptic Gospels, Jesus is presented as having been accused of breaking the Sabbath on a number of occasions (e.g. Mark 2.23–8; 3.2–4; Luke 13.10–16; 14.1–6).[4]

We may narrow the focus still further, since the healing narrated in this chapter is considered by a number of scholars to be closely related to a similar story attested in the Synoptic tradition, that found in Mark 8.22–6,[5] and/or to the only other detailed Synoptic account of the healing of a blind man, the story of Bartimaeus (Mark 10.46–52, paralleled in Matt. 9.27–31; 20.29–34; Luke 18.35–46).[6] Brown and Schnackenburg feel that the points of contact between John and these alleged Synoptic parallels are not as significant as the differences in setting and the fact that the man in John's narrative was *born* blind.[7] But Barrett is clearly correct to emphasize not only that the story was traditional in some form (a point with which Brown and Schnackenburg also agree),[8] but also

[3] Martyn, *History*, p. 39 n.44.

[4] Note also the traditions of his associating with sinners, which was presumably felt by Jesus' opponents to indicate that he belonged in the same category. See further A. E. Harvey, *Jesus on Trial*, pp. 67–77.

[5] So e.g. Moloney, *Johannine Son of Man*, pp. 158–9; Martyn, *History*, p. 24 n.7.

[6] Lindars, *Gospel of John*, p. 341. Martyn, *History*, p. 24 n.7 notes these latter passages, but feels that John is closer to the story in Mark 8. Michaels, *John*, p. 161, on the other hand, feels that the Johannine account recalls both of the Marcan stories. See also Dodd, *Historical Tradition*, p. 185; Haenchen, *John* II, p. 41. Brief mentions of the blind being healed are found in Matt. 11.5 = Luke 7.21–2; Matt. 15.29–30; 21.14 (noted by Schnackenburg, *John vol. II*, p. 244; see also the list given by R. E. Brown, *Gospel*, p. 378).

[7] Brown, *Gospel*, pp. 378–9; Schnackenburg, *John vol.2*, p. 244.

[8] So also Pancaro, *Law*, pp. 17–8; Robert T. Fortna, *The Fourth Gospel and its Predecessor. From Narrative Source to Present Gospel*, Philadelphia: Fortress, 1988, pp. 109–10.

that the issues which are to the fore in the Johannine narrative (Sabbath healing and Torah observance; the spiritual blindness of Jesus' hearers; the ministry of Jesus as a test by which all men stand or fall) are also traditional.[9]

We must stress again that we are not attempting to argue for John's direct literary dependence upon Mark or any of the Synoptic Gospels.[10] However, the attempt to prove that John does not show direct literary dependence on the other Gospels has frequently led to an overemphasis on the differences between the Johannine and Synoptic narratives of similar incidents. For our purposes, we need only demonstrate that the central motifs and interests of the Johannine narrative did not originate from the Evangelist, but are paralleled in earlier Christian literature. Having made this point, it is nonetheless certainly striking that in Mark 8.22–32 we have the healing of a blind man, followed immediately by a discussion of whether Jesus is a prophet, or the Messiah, which is in turn followed by a depiction of Jesus interpreting himself through the designation 'Son of Man'.[11] Immediately before this in Mark Jesus refers to having eyes but not seeing (Mark 8.17–18), and immediately after (Mark 9.1ff.) there is material on (spiritual?) seeing, and the transfiguration account which contrasts Jesus with Moses.[12]

For convenience we may set out the parallels between John 9 and Mark 8–9 as follows:

(1) A blind man is healed through the use of spittle and touching (John 9.6; Mark 8.23).

(2) The imagery of the blind seeing and the sighted not seeing is exploited as a symbol of responsiveness to Christ, in connection with reference to the Pharisees (John 9.39–41; Mark 8.15, 17–18).[13]

(3) The designations prophet, Christ and finally Son of Man

---

[9] Barrett, *Commentary*, pp. 354–5. See also R. E. Brown, *Gospel*, pp. 378–9.

[10] Cf. ch.1 n.118 above.

[11] Cf. Schnider, *Jesus der Prophet*, pp. 183–7 on Jesus as prophet in this Marcan pericope.

[12] Cf. ibid., pp. 100–1, who notes that the command to 'hear him' recalls Deut. 18.15 LXX, which refers to the promised 'prophet like Moses'. See also Moloney, *Johannine Son of Man*, pp. 158–9.

[13] Note also that in Mark 8.11–12 the Pharisees ask for a sign; perhaps if John knew this material as a unit he adapted the healing story as a response, providing them with a sign which only showed even more clearly their blindness and hardness of heart.

are mentioned in that order (John 9.17, 22, 35; Mark 8.28–31).

(4)   The relationship of Jesus to Moses is addressed or alluded to (John 9.28–9; Mark 9.2–7).

Thus it is certainly not impossible that John not only had earlier issues in view, but knew as a unit something akin to this Marcan healing narrative and the material which now surrounds it, material which compared Jesus to the prophets of old and discussed the topics of Jesus as Son of Man and of spiritual vision in connection with a comparison between Jesus and Moses. If so, John has reworked the tradition in a number of ways in order to bring certain elements to the foreground of the narrative: he has integrated the discussions of (spiritual) sight into the more immediate context of the healing narrative, so that the narrative functions more clearly as a symbolic illustration of this point; he has placed the healing on a Sabbath, so as to enable the issues of Moses and Torah to be addressed more directly through the healing account;[14] he has perhaps also brought in elements from the other Synoptic account of the healing of a blind man, namely that found in Mark 10 and parallels.[15]

At any rate, it is certainly indisputable that John is dependent on earlier tradition here, and that the key motifs (healing a blind man who was sitting and begging, using spittle, healing on a Sabbath) are traditional in some form.[16] This means that the issue which John uses this healing narrative to address is also traditional, one that had arisen prior to the time in which John was written, namely the relationship of Jesus' healing activity, carried out on the Sabbath day, to the prohibitions which the Mosaic law placed on Sabbath activity. John has clearly adapted the tradition he inherited in order to bring certain issues into focus.[17] Regardless of whether

[14] Cf. also Painter, *Quest*, pp. 310, 313–14.

[15] That John has reworked the traditional stories is not surprising for another reason: the 'partial healing' that takes place at first was regarded as difficult by the other Evangelists, who do not repeat Mark's story. Likewise John, concerned to present Jesus in the best possible light, can be expected to make use of other traditions more suitable for his purpose, which could 'improve' the story while still remaining as faithful as possible to tradition. In fact, it is possible that the Fourth Evangelist has 'spiritualized' this difficult traditional story preserved in Mark, in his narration of the gradual growth of the man's (symbolic) sight as he increasingly recognizes more and more concerning who Jesus is.

[16] Cf. again Barrett, *Commentary*, pp. 354–5.

[17] Cp. Matthew's redaction of the similar tradition in Matt. 9.27–34.

John is dependent on the Synoptics or on an independent account
of the same narrative or narratives that are found in the Synoptics,
what is important for our purposes is that it is clear that the issues
which he brings to the fore through his use of this traditional story
are *equally traditional*. They did not originate with John, but were
topics of concern even earlier.

The Johannine response

The man who had been born blind represents the standpoint of
Christians.[18] He gives priority to the evidently miraculous works
Jesus does, and on the basis of them concludes that Jesus cannot
possibly be a sinner, since God would not listen to him in this way
if he were.[19] Given the question of the relationship between Jesus
and Moses which is to the fore in this part (and others) of John,
there is good reason to think that the Johannine emphasis on *signs*
reflects the fact that God is said in the Jewish Scriptures to have
worked signs (LXX has the same Greek word σημεῖον) to confirm
that Moses was sent by him.[20] Allison's recent book on Moses
typology notes a number of post-Johannine works that explicitly
make this connection.[21] While John is by no means the first to
compare or contrast Jesus with Moses, he appears to have been the
first to make explicit use of the category of *signs* in this way, and to
seek to defend Jesus' authority over against the arguments of a
Moses-centred Judaism by appeal to his signs. The Evangelist has
thus taken up the tradition of Jesus as a miracle worker, and
altered slightly the significance which those miracles had by making
them a testimony to the truthfulness of the claims of Jesus as a
direct part of a comparison between Jesus and Moses.[22]

   In doing so, John could present the rejection of Jesus by the

---

[18] Cf. Martyn, *History*, pp. 30–1, although we would not go so far as to say that
this is the portrayal of an actual event in the history of the community; it is better
understood as a reflection in narrative form of the type of debates that took place
and the issues which were important in them.

[19] Cf. A. E. Harvey, *Jesus on Trial*, pp. 93–4.

[20] Cf. e.g. Exod. 4.8; 8.23. See also Létourneau, *Jésus*, p. 282.

[21] Allison, *New Moses*, p. 207, citing *Acts of Pilate* 5.1; Ps.-Clem. *Recognitions*
1.57; Eusebius, *Dem. Ev.* 3.2.

[22] Cf. Painter, *Quest*, p. 15 (and on John's closeness to tradition in his use of
'legitimating signs' see pp. 20–1). On the signs and Mosaic-Prophet/Messianic
typologies, see also W. Nicol, *The Semeia in the Fourth Gospel. Tradition and
Redaction* (NovTSup, 32), Leiden: Brill, 1972, pp. 79–90, and also our discussion of
the concept of the Prophet like Moses in ch.2 above and the works cited there.

Pharisees on the basis of their alleged loyalty to Moses in an ironic fashion. When the Jewish Scriptures narrate how Moses was sent by God to deliver the people of Israel from Egypt, Moses is presented as fearful that the people would not believe him. The signs God gave him to perform were given to him with an apologetic function, to demonstrate that he was truly sent by God.[23] The Pharisees are unable to prove that Jesus has not accomplished a sign, yet they reject him in spite of that sign on the basis of an appeal to their fidelity to Moses. Yet Moses' status was demonstrated by the accomplishment of signs that, in the view of the Evangelist, were less spectacular than those of Jesus (cf. 9.32: 'Nobody has ever heard of opening the eyes of a man born blind'). Those who are open to the signs of Jesus and their meaning come to recognize that Jesus' actions have not in fact violated the Sabbath or any other aspect of the Mosaic law. 'The Jews' are thus presented as hardening their hearts towards Jesus, as being unwilling to see, for if they were willing to consider his signs, they would realize where he comes from: from God (9.30–3; also 5.36–40).

John also very likely had in mind the Jewish expectation of a 'prophet like Moses' based on Deuteronomy 18.15, 18–19.[24] In light of the earlier presentations in the Fourth Gospel of Jesus as the one 'concerning whom Moses wrote' (John 5.46–7), and in terms of the signs connected with Moses (John 6.30ff.), it seems likely that such ideas are in view in the present passage as well. Jesus is not a false prophet, to be rejected on the basis of fidelity to Moses, but the true prophet, the prophet like Moses, who must be heeded by those who take Moses' teaching as authoritative (Deut. 18.19).

What would John's emphasis on Jesus' fulfilment of this role have added to his legitimation? As we have already noted, Moses was accepted on the basis of signs, and yet while there were some (in later times at least) who felt that miracles confirmed the validity of a prophet's message,[25] there was also a warning in the Jewish Scriptures (Deut. 13.1–5) that even one who performs signs and miracles is not to be heeded if he leads people away from Yahweh. Thus the issue of miracles or signs was not necessarily decisive. For

---

[23] So rightly Boismard, *Moise*, p. 60.

[24] Meeks, *Prophet-King*, pp. 294–5. See also Boismard, *Moise*, p. 25.

[25] See the texts cited by Nicol, *Semeia*, p. 83; Sifre Deut. 13.3; 18.19; *b*.Sanh. 89b, 90a, 98a.

this reason, John not only presents Jesus as performing a miracle that was felt to be unprecedented, but also presents him as the prophet like Moses. Moses came performing signs that were meant to confirm his commissioning by God, but the people frequently did not listen to him. By presenting Jesus in the way that he does, John turns the tables on his opponents. Rather than the onus being on the Christians to demonstrate their claims for Jesus, the onus is placed on 'the Jews': will they imitate their forefathers and reject the one whom God has sent to them, even though God has confirmed him through many signs? John's portrait of them as refusing even to accept that a miracle has taken place is intended to show them to be culpable. As far as the Fourth Evangelist is concerned, the reason why Jesus is rejected by 'the Jews' is not the inadequacy of his signs or the character of his teaching, but the refusal of 'the Jews' to listen to him, even as they so often refused to listen to Moses and the later prophets.

Also of interest is the question the Johannine Jesus asks the healed blind man in John 9.35. This saying is particularly striking and undeniably unique, since in none of the Synoptic Gospels or other early Christian literature is Jesus presented as calling for faith in the Son of Man.[26] Even if it were to be suggested that 'Son of Man' is here a circumlocution for 'I',[27] there is still no parallel outside of John: Jesus did call for faith, but he is never presented as asking someone to believe in him in such a direct fashion. The saying does not represent a traditional saying, but rather expresses the church's desire for people to accept that Jesus is the Son of Man. However, there is a similarity with earlier use of the Son of Man title in one respect. Jesus is presented as using 'Son of Man' to carry his own distinctive self-understanding, and thus to correct other understandings associated with other designations and titles.[28] In this chapter Jesus has already been described in a number of different ways, and the subsequent identification of him as Son of Man is at least somewhat similar to the Synoptic usage. However, it is not immediately clear what content the portrayal of Jesus in these terms bears in contrast to the

[26] Cf. Higgins, *Jesus and the Son of Man*, p. 155; Martyn, *History*, p. 140; Rhea, *Johannine Son of Man*, p. 44.

[27] This has been suggested – in the view of the present author, unconvincingly – by Mogens Müller, ' "Have You Faith in the Son of Man?" (John 9.35)', *NTS* 37 (1991), 291–4. For an evaluation of this suggestion cf. Painter, *Quest*, pp. 319–20.

[28] See esp. Mark 8.29–31; the use in John 1.35–51 in some ways also resembles the use to which the designation is put in 9.35.

titles already used.[29] The only feature which gives an indication
that John has in mind something of the traditional use of Son of
Man imagery is the reference to judgment in verse 39, although
here too the language is distinctly Johannine, and the judgment is
not eschatological but present.[30]

This chapter is full of Johannine irony, and it may be that the
unusual use of the Son of Man imagery here can be explained in
terms of the pointed irony which the Evangelist often uses in
polemical contexts. Earlier in the Gospel, the status of Jesus, and
his carrying out of divine functions such as judgment, were seen to
be a point of controversy in the debate with 'the Jews.' This chapter
represents a similar debate, albeit one which focuses on the issue of
Jesus' relationship to Moses and Torah rather than his relationship
to God. On the one hand, Jesus' identity is borne witness to by the
signs he accomplishes, while on the other hand Jesus appears to
break the Sabbath, and a lawless man cannot meet with God's
approval. In this verse and its immediate context, John calls for
faith from one who has begun to recognize that Jesus has been sent
by God, and expresses that call for faith in terms of the Son of
Man. Ironically, the one who recognizes that Jesus is the Son of
Man, God's agent, will have no difficulty in accepting that he
carries out divine acts, such as judgment or even healing on the
Sabbath. Yet those who fail to perceive that he is the Son of Man
fail to discern who Jesus is and regard his actions and claims as
blasphemous. Thus, in a sense, recognizing Jesus as the Son of Man
who is appointed by God as rightful judge saves one from
judgment, but failing to recognize him as such leads to judgment.[31]

Finally, we may mention once again the movement from traditional titles relating to Jesus as prophet (like Moses) to an affirmation concerning him as Son of Man.[32] By the time the reader
arrived at chapter 9, the designation Son of Man would have
carried with it an emphasis on the superior qualifications of Jesus
to be the revealer of heavenly things, over against the claims being
made for Moses by the opponents of the Johannine Christians. The
fact that this chapter would have been read in the light of passages
which occur prior to it in the Gospel in its present form means that

[29] Contrast 1.51. Cf. Rhea, *Johannine Son of Man*, p. 47.

[30] Cf. Moloney, *Johannine Son of Man*, pp. 152, 156.

[31] See further our treatment of Jesus as agent and Son of Man in ch.4 above.

[32] This movement occurs in several passages in the Gospel. See Martyn, *History*,
pp. 130–5; Moloney, *Johannine Son of Man*, p. 157.

the reader would be familiar with material which would have made clear to him or her the relevance to this issue of faith in Jesus as, and recognition of him as, the Son of Man. To recognize Jesus as the Son of Man is to recognize him as the one with authority even to heal on the Sabbath, and with qualifications superior even to those of Moses to reveal heavenly things.

Summary

In this section of John, we have found John to be discussing issues which are also found in pre-Johannine Christian writings, such as the relationship between Jesus and Moses, and the question of how Jesus' claims and actions correspond to the demands of the Torah. This is connected with one or more earlier accounts of Jesus healing a blind man, perhaps an independent version or versions of stories recorded in the Synoptics. John uses the traditional motif of healing on the Sabbath to pose the issue in the sharpest possible form. If Jesus has broken the Sabbath, how can he possibly be from God? On the other hand, if he is from God, what does this imply with regard to the Sabbath, or at least contemporary Jewish under-standing of the Sabbath? In order to answer the possible objections that could be raised, John does not argue that Jesus did not break the Sabbath, but poses the issue differently. If Jesus were the prophet like Moses, then it would not be surprising if God (a) confirmed his ministry through signs, and (b) offered new insight into the meaning of Torah. It would also not be surprising if (c) God's own people, who claim to be faithful to Moses, in fact behaved towards the 'prophet like Moses' as the Israelites in the Pentateuchal narratives did towards Moses himself. John adapts the Christian miracle tradition to this purpose. The miracles performed by Jesus actually serve the same function as the signs that God gave to Moses to confirm his divine accreditation and commissioning. Belief in Jesus as the Son of Man is also mentioned allusively in this chapter, and in view of our earlier treatments of some of the other instances where this designation appears in the Fourth Gospel, it will hopefully be clear that, in mentioning the need to recognize Jesus as the Son of Man, John is tying in his presentation of Jesus here to other aspects of his christological portrait, which develop the traditions which he inherited in order to emphasize Jesus' superior revelation.

The development to which John 9 bears witness is perhaps less striking than that evidenced in many of the other passages we have discussed thus far. Nonetheless, it plays an important role in John's Gospel as one of the distinctive aspects of his presentation of Jesus in relation to Moses, as he addresses the issue of how Jesus relates to him. Thus once again we see legitimation involving development, as this issue affects the way the author of the Fourth Gospel develops, configures and reworks the traditions he inherited.

13

CONCLUSION TO PART 3

In part 3 we have seen nothing that would cause us to modify the conclusions which we reached in part 2, and have found much further evidence to support our case. In connection with the issue of how Jesus' revelation relates to that of Moses, as in connection with the issue of the relationship between Jesus and God, the Fourth Evangelist engaged in legitimation, attempting to defend his beliefs. In order to do so, he developed the traditions he inherited. The idea of pre-existence was of particular importance, as it allowed John to attribute to Jesus as Son of Man a knowledge of heavenly things which could not be attributed to any other figure. In his use of Wisdom categories, John is particularly close to earlier writers, as they too made use of Wisdom language and imagery in order to present Christ as superior to Moses/Torah. Nonetheless, John's portrait is more developed than these. This may be due in part to the 'knock-on effects' of the developments we traced in part 2. Once John began to rethink the relationship between Wisdom and the human Jesus, further implications for the issue of the relation between Jesus and Moses would have become apparent. Yet we have not seen any firm evidence that John's legitimation of Christology against charges of 'blasphemy' is presupposed in his legitimation of his Christology in relation to the Moses issue, nor any real indication that the reverse is true. This being the case, it may be that these issues were both important ones in the conflict which the author was involved in, and that the two issues worked together simultaneously to shape the thinking of the Evangelist and his community.

One key feature of John's use of the traditional depiction of Jesus as Son of Man is his use of this designation to reinterpret others, such as Messiah/Christ, king of Israel, and prophet.[1] This

---

[1] Moloney, *Johannine Son of Man*, p. 109; Martyn, *History*, pp. 130–5; Painter, 'Enigmatic', p. 1870.

use of 'Son of Man' to a large extent resembles its use in the Synoptics. As a designation which was not already filled with a clearly defined content to the same extent as others, it could serve as the medium to communicate the distinctiveness of Jesus, and the fact that he does not merely fulfil traditional expectations, but also transcends them (cf. Mark 8.27–31; 14.61–2). Jesus as the Messiah and Son of Man fulfils the expectations that pointed to him, but he is not to be limited to those traditional categories. Rather, traditional concepts of Messiahship must be redefined in order to incorporate, and do justice to, who the Messiah in fact turned out to be. In stressing this point, John stands in a close relation to earlier writers, and makes use of a legitimating portrait of Jesus as the Son of Man which others before him had begun to construct. John was not the only one for whom traditional designations such as 'prophet' and 'Messiah' were inadequate. Already in Mark the process of attempting to redefine Messiahship in terms of Jesus, rather than force Jesus into the mould of traditional expectation, had begun. By bringing in pre-existence, with the implications John drew from it, John developed the Son of Man tradition in response to issues in the controversy with the synagogue. But the idea that Jesus was greater than Moses, than the prophets, than even traditional expectations concerning the Messiah, was an idea John inherited. He did not invent it, but rather sought to defend this traditional perspective on Jesus, which was part of the foundation of the faith that he and other Christians shared.[2]

Finally, we may return to the issue that was raised by our treatment of John 3.13 and 6.62. We have suggested that John knew a tradition that presented Jesus on the mountain as having made an ascent of some sort, to meet with God and be affirmed by him in his role as mediator of the new covenant. The imagery used compared Jesus with Moses, who was also believed by many to have made an ascent of this sort at Sinai. It seems quite likely that early Christians may have argued that, if Moses had had such an experience on the mountain, then surely Jesus must have also had such an experience of ascent. By the time John wrote, however, there had been a response from 'the Jews', emphasizing that while it was clear that God had spoken to Moses, it was not at all clear that this was true of Jesus. The Evangelist thus felt the need not simply

[2] As Martyn, *History*, pp. 130–5 rightly notes, the chief focus in John's use of Son of Man to reinterpret traditional categories is the Prophetic/Mosaic expectation.

to compare Jesus with Moses or present him as similar to Moses, but to stress his superiority to Moses. He did this by bringing to the fore other aspects of the tradition which he inherited, such as the presentation of Jesus in the imagery of the apocalyptic Son of Man, and also the traditional viewpoint that the decisive moment in the career of Jesus is the descent of the Spirit upon him, rather than an ascent to heaven. The Evangelist was thus able to assert that Jesus as the Son of Man and Word-become-flesh was not merely a human being who had ascended to receive revelation, but the incarnation of one who had pre-existed in heaven, and who on this basis could reveal what he saw there in a way that no other could.

With these considerations in view, it seems unlikely that John continued to maintain that Jesus made an ascent akin to the ascent of Moses during his lifetime. But regardless of whether the mention of a Moses-like ascent by Jesus in John 3.13 is simply part of a tradition which was insufficiently redacted by the Evangelist, or is something the Evangelist did not deny but merely 'de-emphasized', it is clear that the Evangelist placed all the emphasis on *descent*.[3] The importance of this in terms of the present work is that the Evangelist's reasons for doing so are best understood in terms of legitimation. The Evangelist creatively adapted aspects of the traditions he inherited in order to defend his community's belief in Jesus as the supreme revealer, and to respond to objections raised by Jewish opponents. The developments made as part of this legitimation played an important role in influencing the shape of subsequent Christology.

[3] Our reason for hesitating to assume that John has abandoned the view that Jesus ascended to heaven during his lifetime in a manner similar to Moses is a lack of certainty as to the authority this idea had. If it was not an authoritative traditional belief, John may have abandoned it; if it was authoritative and he did not feel that he could do this, he may simply have downplayed it.

Part 4

OTHER ISSUES AND CONCLUSION

14

OTHER POSSIBLE ISSUES

In the previous two parts of this book we have considered what are very likely to be the two issues in the conflict between church and synagogue which had the greatest influence on the development of Johannine Christology. They were not the only ones, however, and in this chapter we will attempt to survey some of the other issues which may have been important to the Evangelist and led to the development by him of various earlier christological motifs.

The rejection of Jesus

The fact that the majority of Jews did not accept Jesus to be the Messiah promised in the Jewish Scriptures was a major problem, which called into question the validity of, and undermined the plausibility structure of, the beliefs of the early Christians. John is convinced that there are in fact many believers among the Jewish people and even among the leaders, who are afraid to admit this because they are afraid of the authorities (cf. 7.12–13; 9.22; 12.42–3). Yet he also places the objection on the lips of the Pharisees, 'Has any of the rulers or of the Pharisees believed in him? No! But this mob that knows nothing of the law, there is a curse on them' (John 7.48). It appears likely that some opponents felt that only those who were ignorant of the Jewish Scriptures would be persuaded to believe in Jesus. John makes use of several traditional motifs in order to legitimate belief in Jesus in spite of his rejection by the majority of 'the Jews'.

One way in which John sought to demonstrate that the failure of so many Jews to believe did not invalidate the claims made by Christians was to appeal to Jewish traditions about Moses. In the wilderness, Israel had grumbled against Moses; likewise in Jesus' day 'the Jews' grumbled against the one whom God had sent to them (6.41, 52). The Israelites in the wilderness saw the *signs* which God performed through Moses, and yet even so they did not believe in him and grumbled against him; likewise in Jesus' day, 'the Jews' refused to believe in spite of the many signs which he performed (12.37). This last instance is also linked with direct citations from Isaiah, which speak of the stubbornness of God's people. By presenting Jesus in this way, John is able to argue that the rejection of Jesus by his Jewish contemporaries did not discredit the faith of Christians, because God's own people had refused to listen to Moses, and it is thus not surprising that they should refuse to listen to the 'prophet like Moses' as well. John is here making use of the traditions which we considered at many points in part 3, which present Jesus as the prophet like Moses or describe him in Mosaic imagery and categories.

We have already seen how John made use of Wisdom traditions in relation to two other issues in his community's conflict with the synagogue. John shows awareness of and interest in another aspect of the Wisdom tradition, namely, the rejection of Wisdom (which, significantly, is followed by her return to heaven). In 1 Enoch 42.1–2, we are told that 'Wisdom went out to dwell with the children of the people, but she found no dwelling place. (So) Wisdom returned to her place,' an idea which is alluded to in John 1.10–11. Even in the Hebrew Scriptures, it is recognized that some Israelites do not heed Wisdom's call (cf. e.g. Prov. 1.22–33; 9.13–18). A clear allusion to Proverbs 1.28 is found in John 7.34. The presentation of Jesus as Wisdom incarnate thus helped to provide an explanation of why the majority of Jews had not accepted Jesus. They had already in the past rejected God's Wisdom, and the present instance was just one more example of this wider phenomenon recorded in Israel's Scriptures and traditions.

Another way that the author of the Fourth Gospel appeals to tradition in order to legitimate his beliefs, in response to the rejection of Christian claims by most Jews, is to link this rejection to disobedience to God himself as he has revealed himself in Israel's history and Scriptures. This theme is obviously very closely linked to the other two we have just considered, since the rejection of God's spokesperson or of his Wisdom is ultimately a rejection of God himself. In John 5.37, Jesus claims that the Father himself testifies concerning him. This very likely includes the witness of Jesus' signs (5.36), but the focus is probably primarily on the witness of the Father in the Jewish Scriptures.[1] If 'the Jews' responded as they should to their own Scriptures, which they study so intently, they would come to Jesus (5.38–40). As it is, they cannot appeal to Moses in their defence, because Moses wrote about Jesus and yet they refuse to accept him (5.45–7). The writings of Moses are the revelation of God, the witness of the Father.

In John 6 a similar approach is taken. John blames the refusal of 'the Jews' to believe in Jesus on the fact that they have not been 'drawn by God' (6.44). This is very frequently interpreted as a predestinarian emphasis,[2] which is understandable given the clear examples, particularly in the Dead Sea Scrolls, of the use of predestination as a form of legitimation, as a way of explaining why the majority has not accepted the sect's message.[3] However, the emphasis in John seems to lie elsewhere. The assertion that 'the Jews' do not believe in Jesus because they have not been drawn by the Father appears to function similarly to Exodus 16.8, where Moses is presented as rebuking the Israelites by saying, 'You are not grumbling against us, but against Yahweh.'[4] It is not an assertion that 'the Jews' cannot believe because they have not been predestined, so much as an accusation of 'the Jews' for not having learned from God, through the Scriptures, the revealed truths which would have enabled them to recognize Jesus as the Messiah. The verses that immediately follow John 6.44 seem to support our interpretation. It is those who have been open to learn from the Father, presumably as he has revealed himself in the Jewish Scriptures, who will come to Jesus.[5] The rejection of Jesus by 'the Jews' is presented as a symptom of a wrong attitude to God and an

[1] Note the reference in the immediate context to God's Word and the Scriptures, as well as the reference to seeing and hearing which recalls the Sinai revelation.

[2] So e.g. R. E. Brown, *Gospel*, p. 277; Barrett, *Commentary*, p. 295; Schnackenburg, *John vol. II*, p. 50; Haenchen, *John* I, pp. 292–3; Carson, *John*, p. 293; Painter, *Quest*, p. 277. See also Lindars, *Gospel of John*, p. 263 (who denies a predestinarian meaning while still referring this drawing to an inward work of God); Brodie, *John*, p. 284.

[3] Cf. e.g. 1QS 3.15–4.26; 4Q186; 4Q534.

[4] Cf. Moloney, *Signs and Shadows*, p. 51.

[5] Cf. e.g. J. N. Sanders, *John*, pp. 192–3; Moloney, *Signs and Shadows*, p. 51. See also Lindars, *Gospel of John*, p. 495 on John 15.24. The Father of Jesus in John is always the God of Israel revealed in the Jewish Scriptures. Cf. esp. 8.54; also 4.21; 5.17. Barrett, *Commentary*, p. 296 takes the reference to be to an inner teaching by God, but it is difficult to imagine a Jewish reader who would not immediately associate the teaching of God with the Jewish Scriptures. Schnackenburg, *John vol. II*, p. 51 recognizes this, but nonetheless rejects this interpretation.

unwillingness to listen to him, particularly as he has spoken in Scripture.[6]

John thus puts the onus back on his opponents. Are they certain that they have correctly understood what the Scriptures teach about the coming one? The Johannine Christians, who were already convinced that Jesus was the one promised in Scripture, would have found such arguments convincing and an encouragement to their faith; whether any of John's opponents would have been convinced is less clear. But certainly by blaming the refusal of 'the Jews' to believe on their refusal to listen to God, a refusal which could be traced back to the people of Israel throughout their history as portrayed in Scripture, John was able to legitimate his community's beliefs. In John's view, rejection by the majority is just what one would expect from the people of God, when one is familiar with the accounts of Israel's history of disobedience in the Jewish Scriptures.[7]

Jesus and John the Baptist

Another issue that may possibly have influenced the development of Johannine Christology is the debate about the relationship between Jesus and John the Baptist, which many scholars have suggested lies behind the Fourth Gospel. The emphatic assertions,

[6] Cf. Marianne Meye Thompson, *The Humanity of Jesus in the Fourth Gospel*, Philadelphia: Fortress, 1988, pp. 126–7. The reference to Isa. 54.13 in this context by the Johannine Jesus may have carried important intertextual echoes. The original context refers to the restoration of Jerusalem after the exile. Because of the ongoing state of domination by foreigners, many Jews seem to have regarded the exile as something which was continuing (cf. Paul Garnet, 'Jesus and the Exilic Soteriology', in E. A. Livingstone (ed.), *Studia Biblica 1978, II* (JSNTS, 2), Sheffield: Sheffield Academic Press, 1980; N. T. Wright, *The New Testament and the People of God (Christian Origins and the Question of God: Volume I)*, London: SPCK, 1992, p. 269; James M. Scott, ' "For as Many as are of Works of the Law are under a Curse" (Galatians 3.10)', in C. A. Evans and J. A. Sanders (eds.), *Paul and the Scriptures of Israel* (JSNTS, 83), Sheffield: Sheffield Academic Press, 1993, pp. 187–221). The present situation in which the Jewish nation found itself would have worked together with these echoes in order to reinforce the message that Israel's disobedience to God continues even into the present. The close proximity to Isa. 55.1–11 would also help the reader to understand that the use of the imagery of eating and drinking, and the identification of Jesus as the bread which comes down from heaven, are really an identification of him as the Word of God (see further ch.9 above). On the Isaiah citation see further Menken, *Old Testament Quotations*, pp. 67–77.

[7] On the relevance of the above-below and ascent-descent ideas to the legitimation of the rejected community's beliefs and status see Meeks, 'Man from Heaven' (and also Rensberger, *Overcoming*, pp. 119–20), although see too the important criticisms in Holmberg, *Sociology*, pp. 127–8 and Barton, 'Gospel Audiences', 189–93.

such as 'He himself was not the light' (John 1.8) and 'He confessed and did not deny and confessed that he is not the Christ' (1.20), seem to be clear indications of polemic, which implies that some held to the views which are being denied.[8] There is evidence of continuing groups of followers of John the Baptist from Acts 18.25; 19.1–4, and also from the Pseudo-Clementine literature (*Recognitions* 1.54, 60). Unfortunately, we have very little information about the claims which were made by such groups, but if it is legitimate to 'mirror read' the Fourth Gospel, then they claimed that John was superior to Jesus, and very likely described John as 'Messiah' and even 'the Light'. John makes use of the traditions available to him in order to reject such claims.

One way John does this is to expand on the traditions concerning John's testimony about Jesus. To begin with, he omits any mention of the fact that the initial testimony was given on the occasion of Jesus' *baptism* by John.[9] The fact that Jesus was baptized by John caused difficulty for many early Christians, as can be seen from the way other Gospel writers altered the basic Marcan account.[10] The Fourth Evangelist also attributes more emphatic testimony to John the Baptist, which is placed on the lips of the Baptist himself, which 'clarifies' the Baptist's own understanding of the relation between himself and Jesus (1.19–36; 3.22–30). John thus adapts the traditions concerning Jesus' baptism by John and John's witness to the descent of the Spirit, making more explicit what he understood to already be implied therein, namely the superiority of Jesus over John.

Another way the Evangelist emphasizes Jesus' superiority compared to John is to emphasize his *temporal priority* and *heavenly*

[8] Cf. R. E. Brown, *Gospel*, pp. lxvii–lxx, 46–54; Edwin D. Freed, 'Jn 1, 19–27 in Light of Related Passages in John, the Synoptics, and Acts', in F. Van Segbroeck, C. M. Tuckett, G. Van Belle and J. Verheyden (eds.), *The Four Gospels 1992. Festschrift Frans Neirynck. Volume 3* (BETL, 100), Leuven: Leuven University Press, 1992, pp. 1951, 1960–1.

[9] Cf. Dowell, 'Jews and Christians', 26, who also notes another significant omission by John (if he knew the Synoptic Gospels), namely the doubts expressed therein by John the Baptist when he was in prison (Matt. 11.2–3).

[10] Matthew makes John object and assert that he needs to be baptized by Jesus (Matt. 3.14–15). Luke places the baptism of Jesus *after* the mention of John's imprisonment (Luke 3.20–1) and makes John's testimony about the coming one a direct answer to the question of whether he is the Christ (3.15–16). Later writers went further still, as can be seen particularly clearly in the Gospel of the Hebrews, where Jesus is presented as being invited by his family to come with them to be baptized by John, to which Jesus is made to reply, 'Wherein have I sinned, that I should go and be baptized of him?'.

origins. Jesus, in his pre-existence as the Word, was before John (1.15, 30), just as he was before Abraham (8.58). As the incarnation of the Logos, Jesus had more claim to the designation 'the Light' than did any other, since the imagery of light was already closely associated with God's Word and Wisdom.[11] And whereas John is of earthly origin, the human being Jesus is the Word become flesh, and thus is of heavenly origin (3.31).[12]

Our lack of direct knowledge concerning the claims made by the followers of John the Baptist, and the paucity of even second-hand information, make it unwise to speculate too far concerning the details of the conflict and of the development which it may have caused. Nonetheless, it does seem clear that both conflict and the development of earlier tradition can be connected with this issue in the Gospel of John.[13]

Jesus and other figures

Jesus is also contrasted explicitly with two other key figures in the history of Israel: just as we have already seen that Jesus was compared with Moses and John the Baptist, we also have the question raised of whether Jesus is greater than either 'our father Abraham' or 'our father Jacob' (4.12; 8.53). What precisely was at issue here is difficult to determine, but at the very least we may suggest that, since it was being claimed that Jesus is the Messiah and/or prophet like Moses, arguably the most decisive figure to have appeared in Israel's history, then he must be shown to have characteristics which demonstrate his superiority in comparison with other key figures in Israel's history.

Jesus and Abraham

In connection with the question of Jesus' relation to Abraham, mention is made of the divine 'I am' and of Abraham 'seeing Jesus' day'. The latter phrase must refer to a vision during Abraham's lifetime, since John says that Abraham 'saw' his day, not that he 'has seen' or 'sees' it. There are two possible events that may be in

---

[11] See above, p. 55, p. 110 n.30, and p. 154 n.10.
[12] Cf. Dowell, 'Jews and Christians', 25.
[13] See further Dodd, *Interpretation*, pp. 115–30; R. E. Brown, *Gospel*, p. lxviii. On the relationship of these narratives to their Synoptic counterparts see also Painter, *Quest*, pp. 166–78.

mind. One is the interpretation of Genesis that understood Abraham to have been given a vision of the future, including the days of the Messiah.[14] The other is the meeting with three 'men', understood to be Yahweh and/or his angels.[15] It seems impossible to settle the matter definitively, but the references to 'rejoicing' and 'believing what was heard from God' do appear to favour the latter interpretation.[16] That John thought of the one who was now incarnate in Christ as having been the one who appeared in the theophanies recorded in the Jewish Scriptures seems clear from a number of indications: (1) John also speaks of Isaiah having seen Jesus' glory (John 12.41);[17] (2) John denies that anyone has ever seen God (apart from the Word/Son), suggesting that (as in Philo) it was in fact the Word that was seen by various figures in the Jewish Scriptures; (3) the grammar of 9.5 may imply that he has been in the world before, since the Greek literally reads '*Whenever* (ὅταν) I am in the world, I am the light of the world';[18] (4) the point which is made is not about Abraham's foreknowledge concerning the Messiah, but the eternal 'I am'. Thus the emphasis here is not on Jesus as the Messiah, but on Jesus as the incarnation of the Word. As the incarnation of the one through whom the promises were made to Abraham, Jesus' superiority to Abraham is felt to be clear and indisputable.[19]

Jesus and Jacob-Israel

The comparison with Jacob (4.12) is in a similar vein. We may begin with the imagery of meeting at a well, which is a familiar motif in the patriarchal narratives.[20] The closest parallel, which is

---

[14] Cf. Barrett, *Commentary*, pp. 351–2; also R. E. Brown, *Gospel*, p. 360; G. R. Beasley-Murray, *John*, pp. 138–9. Midrash Rabbah 44.22, 28 attributes this interpretation to tannaitic sages, which may be correct in view of the similar idea found in 4 Ezra 3.14.

[15] So e.g. Hanson, *Prophetic Gospel*, pp. 126–7.

[16] Cf. Hanson, *Jesus Christ*, pp. 123–6; *Prophetic Gospel*, pp. 126–31.

[17] The reference is presumably to the vision in the Temple mentioned in Isa. 6. Cf. Schnackenburg, *John vol. II*, p. 222.

[18] So Burkett, *Son of the Man*, p. 165.

[19] Alternatively, it might be suggested that Jesus is the promised seed, of whom the true Father is God (something which Philo asserts concerning Isaac in *Mut.* 131–2; see also *Cher.*, 40–52; Hanson, *Prophetic Gospel*, pp. 125–31), and thus in witnessing the birth of Isaac, Abraham witnessed the beginning of the fulfilment of the promises of God concerning his 'seed'. Nevertheless, the interpretation we have offered in the text seems more cogent.

[20] Cf. e.g. Gen. 24.11ff.; 29.2ff.; also Exod. 2.15ff.

particularly relevant because of the explicit mention of Jacob and his well in this context, is the meeting between Jacob and Rachel described in Genesis 29.2–7, a meeting that also took place at midday.[21] While we cannot discuss in this context some of the more difficult interpretative problems relating to the dialogue between Jesus and the Samaritan woman, it seems legitimate to suggest that Jesus is here portrayed as creating a new, restored, eschatological Samaria/Israel, who will worship in spirit and truth through Jesus himself, who is the true temple (2.21; 4.23–4). Jesus is also the source of living water that provides eternal life, rather than water that merely quenches one's literal thirst temporarily. As such, Jesus is 'greater than our father Jacob'.

The imagery John uses in 1.51 is also related to this theme. This verse is more or less unanimously accepted to be taking up the imagery of Jacob's vision in Genesis 28.12–13,[22] and while it may not be dependent on early rabbinic exegesis of that text, it at the very least takes a similar approach in interpreting it, as we shall see below. This passage is also linked by some scholars to the church–synagogue controversy, which adds to its potential interest for our study.[23]

There are a number of indications that this verse was not composed by the Evangelist for use in its present setting, but already existed in some form prior to being made use of here. Most frequently noted are the fact that there is a change from singular (ὄψῃ) to plural (ὄψεσθε) and the superfluous 'and he said to him'.[24] The view that the differences between this verse and its present context are because it is a later addition to the Gospel seems less likely than that it is due to the Evangelist's use here of a tradition which had a prior history as an independent logion.[25] Yet we are not to think of the Evangelist simply inserting a preformed saying into a narrative which once existed without it, but rather of

[21] Cf. Carmichael, *Story of Creation*, p. 105.

[22] Cf. e.g. Dodd, *Interpretation*, p. 246; Higgins, *Jesus and the Son of Man*, pp. 158–61; R. E. Brown, *Gospel*, pp. 89–91; Jerome H. Neyrey, 'The Jacob Allusions in John 1:51', *CBQ* 44 (1982), 589; Ashton, *Understanding*, p. 342; Létourneau, *Jésus*, p. 312; Kanagaraj, *'Mysticism'*, p. 188–9; Casey, *Is John's Gospel True?*, pp. 60, 106.

[23] So e.g. Haenchen, *John* I, p. 167; Hanson, *Prophetic Gospel*, p. 38.

[24] Higgins, *Jesus and the Son of Man*, p. 160; R. E. Brown, *Gospel*, pp. 88–9; Painter, *Quest*, p. 187; 'Enigmatic', p. 1873 (although note the objections in Carson, *John*, pp. 165–6, which do not demonstrate that Brown is wrong, but at least caution that the prehistory of the verse cannot be known with certainty).

[25] Cf. Neyrey, 'Jacob Allusions', 586–9.

the *adaptation* of a saying, or at the very least of imagery and language, which the Evangelist inherited.[26]

Higgins attempts to distinguish between Johannine Son of Man sayings which are of a Synoptic type and those which are not, and this verse is placed in the former category. The reasons which he gives are as follows: (1) Jesus is not explicitly identified as the Son of Man; (2) 'amen' is used in connection with a reference to the future glory of the Son of Man; (3) there is association with angels; and (4) reference is made to heaven being opened.[27] Several scholars note a similarity with Matthew 26.64, a similarity which was apparently noticed already by some of the early copyists and scribes, who added to the Johannine saying the words 'from now on' from the Matthean logion.[28] There seem to be good reasons, then, for regarding this Son of Man saying as bearing a close relationship to its Synoptic counterparts. It promises in the future a vision of the heavens opened, and of the glorified Son of Man in the presence of angels.[29]

What is John doing with this traditional Son of Man language here, and how is he relating it to the issue of the relationship between Jesus and Jacob? The answer that seems most probable to the present author is that here, as in John 6.25–59, the Evangelist is developing traditional christological motifs by relating them to passages in the Jewish Scriptures by means of rabbinic-type exegesis. John is appealing both to the Jesus tradition and to the Jewish

---

[26] Lindars, 'Son of Man', pp. 46–7; Loader, *Christology*, pp. 271–2. *Contra* Neyrey, 'Jacob Allusions', 587–8.

[27] Higgins, *Jesus and the Son of Man*, pp. 157–8; he notes in connection with the last point the similar language used in Acts 7.56. Contrast Ashton, *Understanding*, p. 342, who too quickly dismisses the possibility of any connection with the Synoptic tradition.

[28] R. E. Brown, *Gospel*, p. 84; Lindars, *Gospel of John*, p. 121; Létourneau, *Jésus*, pp. 313–14. Neyrey, 'Jacob Allusions', 599–600 also notes similarities (and differences) between this verse and Mark 14.62 (see also Smalley, 'Johannine Son of Man', 287–8). Kanagaraj, *'Mysticism'*, pp. 187–8 argues against these parallels in favour of an interpretation of this verse in light of early Jewish mysticism. However, I see no reason why the two must be mutually exclusive.

[29] When this vision of the Son of Man will be granted is not specified; however, no fulfilment is recounted in the course of the Gospel, and it would thus appear that, like its Synoptic counterparts, it promises the glorification of the Son of Man after his exaltation. Cf. the discussion in William R. G. Loader, 'John 1:50–51 and the "Greater Things" of Johannine Christology', in Cilliers Breytenbach and Henning Paulsen (eds.), *Anfänge der Christologie. Festschrift für Ferdinand Hahn zum 65. Geburtstag*, Göttingen: Vandenhoeck and Ruprecht, 1991, pp. 255–74; de Boer, *Johannine Perspectives*, p. 161.

Scriptures in order to demonstrate Jesus' superiority, in ways that we shall now consider.

In rabbinic exegesis of Genesis 28.12, the Hebrew word *bô* was recognized to be ambiguous: it could mean either 'on it' (i.e., on the ladder) or 'on him'. The latter understanding could be understood to mean that the angels were ascending and descending 'on Jacob'.[30] This interpretation may well stem from as early as the time of John, but whether or not this is the case does not affect our argument – John's reading of the Genesis text may simply represent an independent interpretation of the passage in a 'rabbinic' fashion, i.e. using techniques of exegesis which were the same as or similar to those used by the later rabbis.[31] That John should engage in such exegesis in the context of a debate with the synagogue seems *a priori* likely, and it seems necessary to disagree with the conclusion reached by Martyn that the Fourth Evangelist was opposed to midrash and exegesis as a means of debate with his Jewish opponents.[32] On the contrary, the Jewish Scriptures were an authoritative source for the Johannine Christians, and would, when interpreted 'correctly', support the legitimacy of the community's beliefs, because the Scriptures testify to Jesus.[33]

As we have noted, it was the ambiguity of the Hebrew word *bô* that made possible the interpretation 'on him' rather than 'on it'. However, it does not seem that John read the text as meaning that the angels ascended and descended upon Jacob;[34] in John 1.47 it is Nathaniel who is presented in the role of the 'true Israelite' and who is promised a vision like Jacob's.[35] The Evangelist appears to be reading the text christologically. The angels ascended and descended on *him*, but that him is not Jacob, but the Son of Man.

Neyrey has suggested that the Son of Man here is identified with or takes the place of neither the ladder nor Jacob, but rather the figure of 'the Lord' who stood atop the ladder. This, as he points out, would fit well with the Evangelist's high Logos Christology, which represents the one incarnate in Christ as the Word or Glory

[30] For this interpretation see *Gen. Rab.* 68.12; also Targums Neofiti and Ps.-Jon. to Gen. 28.12. Cf. also Ernest G. Clarke, 'Jacob's Dream at Bethel as Interpreted in the Targums and the New Testament', *SR* 4 (1974–5), 374.

[31] Cf. Higgins, *Jesus and the Son of Man*, p. 159.

[32] Cf. e.g. Martyn, *History*, pp. 127–8, 134.

[33] John 5.39. Cf. Whitacre, *Johannine Polemic*, pp. 25, 32–3; also Pancaro, *Law*, pp. 83, 116.

[34] *Contra* Dodd, *Interpretation*, p. 245; Clarke, 'Jacob's Dream', 374.

[35] Neyrey, 'Jacob Allusions', 589; Ashton, *Understanding*, p. 348.

of God, which was what Old Testament figures saw when it says that God appeared to them. However, the fact that a particular reading appears to cohere well with Johannine theology does not decisively determine that that reading is the best one. In none of the Jewish traditions which are available to us are the angels represented as having ascended and descended upon Yahweh; it is always either upon the ladder or Jacob. Attempts to suggest that the author means that the angels ascended (and descended?) *to* the Son of Man are unconvincing and do insufficient justice to the wording which the Evangelist has chosen to use.[36] In John, the figure atop the ladder is not mentioned, and it may be that the author read the Genesis passage as indicating that the Lord was atop the ladder, in heaven, but was not able to be seen by Jacob – or possibly was alongside the ladder, as we shall suggest below. At any rate, although the ladder is not mentioned, and neither is Jacob, all of the indications suggest that the Son of Man was understood by the Evangelist to fulfil the role of the *ladder* in Jacob's vision.

We should now ask whether there was any feature in the Genesis text that encouraged its use in connection with the figure of the Son of Man. The similar imagery of heavenly visions involving angels would have provided one crucial point of contact. Another feature which may have aided the identification of Jesus, as the exalted Son of Man seated alongside God in heaven, with the ladder of Jacob's vision, was the fact that the Hebrew of Genesis 28.13 could be understood to mean that the Ancient of Days was standing *beside* the ladder, which would of course mean that the ladder was alongside God in the position that was ascribed by Christians to the Son of Man.[37] Yahweh is presented in the Hebrew Bible as enthroned in heaven, but resting his feet upon the earth as a footstool,[38] and this would be appropriate alongside a heavenly ladder the foot of which rests upon the earth. This suggestion cannot be proved, since in this

[36] Neyrey, 'Jacob Allusions', 590, 598 and Loader, 'John 1:50–51', pp. 271–2 do not adequately address this point.

[37] Cf. Hengel, *Studies in Early Christology*, p. 136, who notes the interchangeability between reference to someone being at God's right hand and reference to God being at that person's right hand, as e.g. in Ps. 110.1, 5. See also our discussion of John 1.18 above.

[38] Isa. 66.1; also implicitly 1 Chr. 28.2 (the ark, which rests on the earth, is the footstool of Yahweh, who sits enthroned in heaven); 2 Esd. 6.4. See also Ps. 99.5; 132.7; Lam. 2.1. That this idea was current in New Testament times is clear from Matt. 5.35; Acts 7.49.

instance we can only hypothesize how the Evangelist read and interpreted this particular text in the Jewish Scriptures. However, given that he exploited the ambiguity of *bô*, it would not be surprising that he should notice and exploit the ambiguity of another Hebrew word in the text. Further support for this suggestion may perhaps be found in the fact that Targums Neofiti and Ps.-Jon. read at Genesis 28.13 that the Lord (or an angel or the glory of the Lord) stood *beside* him (i.e., Jacob). In the Targums which exploit the ambiguity of the Hebrew *bô* (and also in Genesis Rabbah 69.3), the ambiguity of the Hebrew *'alâw* is also exploited.[39]

In the Johannine christological reading and exegesis of the Genesis passage, therefore, Jesus does not appear to be identified with Jacob-Israel, or we should say with the earthly figure of Jacob-Israel. It may be suggested, however, that John was aware of the idea of a heavenly counterpart to the earthly Israel, which could then be identified with the messianic Son of Man who embodies the identity of Israel.[40] The rabbinic texts do not provide sufficient evidence, at least on their own, to allow us to date the exegesis of Genesis 28.12 in terms of the earthly and heavenly Israel earlier than the third century CE.[41] However, Philo (among others) already thinks of 'Israel' as the name of a heavenly being, namely the Logos.[42] Further, it cannot be without significance that the function of the 'one like a son of man' in Daniel 7 is to represent the 'saints of the most high', the faithful Israelites upon the earth.[43] Perhaps the promise made to Nathaniel is that he, as a 'true Israelite', will see the vision which Jacob/Israel saw, and (unlike him?) will recognize the ladder to be none other than the heavenly Israel, the Son of Man. Such a correspondence is given further credence when it is noted that in several streams of tradition 'Israel' is interpreted as deriving from the Hebrew *'ish ro'eh 'el* or *'a man*

---

[39] Cf. Clarke, 'Jacob's Dream', 377 n.18. If this suggestion is correct, it fits well with the view of Loader, 'John 1:50–51', p. 272 that the vision is of the heavenly status of the exalted Son of Man. See also Neyrey, 'Jacob Allusions', 600.

[40] Cf. Fossum, *Image*, pp. 135–51; also Casey, *Is John's Gospel True?*, p. 60.

[41] As R. E. Brown, *Gospel*, p. 90 rightly points out.

[42] Cf. Philo, *Conf.* 146; see also J. Z. Smith, 'The Prayer of Joseph', in Jacob Neusner (ed.), *Religions in Antiquity: Essays in Memory of E. R. Goodenough*, Leiden: Brill, 1968, pp. 262–8. Note also the striking description of God's Word in Wisd. 18.14–16 as having his head touching heaven and his feet upon the earth.

[43] We are not necessarily saying that the 'one like a son of man' in Daniel *was* the saints of the most high, but simply that the figure, whether intended as a real human or angelic figure or as merely a symbol, *represents* them.

who sees God'.[44] The 'true Israelite' is granted a vision of the Son of Man; and the Son of Man, the heavenly Israel, is the link between heaven and earth, and the one who alone is truly 'a man who sees God' in the fullest sense and is thus able to reveal him. This identification also fits in well with the emphasis in John on Jesus, the Son of Man, as the bringer of revelation of heavenly things.[45]

Whatever this pericope's prehistory before being placed in its present context in John, it is included here in the context of Jesus' supernatural knowledge about Nathaniel, which evokes from him a confession of Jesus as 'Son of God' and 'King of Israel'. Jesus' response promising a vision of the Son of Man can be expected to relate to these themes. The future vision will not only confirm that Jesus is the Messiah and King of Israel, but will also offer a far greater demonstration of his ability to reveal things which no other person can.[46] The Son of Man shall be seen alongside God, in a position which is both rightfully that of the Davidic Messiah, and also a demonstration that Jesus is far greater than the expectations held by many about who the Messiah would be. He is the true 'man who sees God', and thus is in fact 'greater than our father Jacob', as the one who is the revealer *par excellence* and who thus links heaven and earth, as the one who inspired such awe in Jacob when he was seen by him in his dream. There are indications that the Evangelist is seeking to demonstrate certain aspects of Christian belief about Jesus – not only in response to the question of the relationship between Jesus and Jacob, but also in relation to the issues of his qualifications to be revealer and of his exalted status.[47] In order to do so he develops the traditions that were authoritative for him and his community, in particular by relating a scriptural 'proof text' to the Son of Man tradition.

[44] See the texts and references helpfully compiled in J. Z. Smith, 'Prayer of Joseph', pp. 265–268.

[45] There is an obvious tension between Jesus as the one who sees God and the one whom to see is to see God. This is a tension that pervades the Gospel and is not limited to the present passage. See further our discussion of the tensions in John below, ch.15.

[46] In Philo's exegesis of the passage (*On Dreams* 1.147–8), the angels who ascend and descend on the ladder are God's words. The references in Gen. 28.17 to the place as 'the house of God' and 'the gate of heaven' also link in to christological motifs found later in John.

[47] In view of the controversy discussed in part 2, this presentation of Jesus as the Son of Man alongside God in relation to imagery found in the Jewish Scriptures may have helped legitimate that idea.

Before concluding we may perhaps mention that the fulfilment of the promise which is made to Nathaniel is nowhere recorded in the Gospel;[48] the same is true of the challenge to Nicodemus to be born again and so 'see the Kingdom of God', and of the related promise of the gift of living water made in 4.10–14 and 7.37–9. This last passage appears to provide an explanation of why the spiritual and visionary experiences of the Christian community are not recounted: they were not possible until the pouring out of the Spirit upon Jesus' followers subsequent to the glorification of Jesus. The Johannine Christians have themselves presumably experienced those things which provide the capstone of this attempt to legitimate their beliefs; to their Jewish opponents, these things remain a mystery to which they do not have access, and no concessions will be made to their unbelief. If they will not accept what the community claims about earthly things, no attempt will be made to convince them by telling them of heavenly things (John 3.11–12).[49]

A crucified Messiah

It is widely recognized that the idea of a crucified Messiah was one that Judaism on the whole found objectionable.[50] In pre-Johannine writings, Christians appeal to the necessity of the event because it was foreordained in God's plan and in Scripture, and John also inherited this approach to the issue.[51] However, John nonetheless presents Jewish objections to this idea more explicitly than other writers do: 'We have heard from the Law that the Christ will

[48] Although those familiar with the Synoptic accounts of Jesus' baptism might have recalled the witness of the Baptist to heaven opening and the Spirit descending. Cf. Lindars, 'Son of Man', p. 46; Ashton, *Understanding*, p. 346.

[49] A connection with John 14.18–22 is also possible. The Synoptic account of Jesus' response at his Jewish trial suggests that his adversaries will see him enthroned in heaven. John may have dealt with the problem of the lack of fulfilment of this prediction by reinterpreting the prediction in terms of a spiritual seeing which only those who believe can experience. Nonetheless, John seems to expect that Jesus' adversaries will recognize who Jesus is subsequent to his crucifixion and exaltation (cf. 8.28).

[50] See in particular Paul's references to the cross as a 'stumbling block' (1 Cor. 1.23), and Mark's presentation of the inability of even the disciples to understand (Mark 8.31–2; 9.31–2; 10.32–4).

[51] See e.g. Luke 24.26–7; 1 Cor. 15.3–4. These authors show clear evidence of a conviction that these things were foretold in Scripture, but what passages they had in mind is unclear. Cp. John 2.22; 3.14 (where the traditional 'must' (δει) is found, and where John attempts to see in the lifting up of the bronze serpent by Moses a prefiguring of the crucifixion). See also Whitacre, *Johannine Polemic*, p. 40.

remain for ever, so how can you say, "The Son of Man must be lifted up"? Who is this "Son of Man"?' (John 12.34).[52] It is thus worth considering whether there is any evidence that the Fourth Evangelist further developed the traditions he inherited, in response to questions and objections raised concerning the death of Jesus.[53]

John, like the Synoptics, presents the passion predictions in terms of the Son of Man. It is apparently the messianic overtones of 'Son of Man' which lead to objections. The Son of Man about whom 'the Jews' have read in the Scriptures is the victorious apocalyptic figure, messianically interpreted.[54] It was thus the use of 'Son of Man' not only in reference to Jesus' apocalyptic parousia, but also to his suffering, which was felt to be objectionable, and this is clearly an aspect of Christian belief that predates John.[55] John, we may suggest, found a way to appeal to Jewish tradition in order to present the death of the Son of Man on the cross as not only scriptural, but also a victory over the forces of evil, which is therefore not incompatible with the claim that he is the Messiah.

[52] Nicholson (*Death as Departure*, p. 139) denies that the issue here is that of the crucified Messiah. Nicholson's interpretation frequently does insufficient justice to the *crucifixion* aspect of the 'lifting up' sayings. Cf. the balanced criticisms of Carson, *John*, p. 437. Moloney (*Signs and Shadows*, p. 193 n.56) goes too far in the other direction. See also Barrett, *Commentary*, p. 428; Hare, *Son of Man*, p. 108; Létourneau, *Jésus*, p. 334.

[53] For reasons of space we shall focus our discussion on the passion predictions. See further Dodd, *Historical Tradition*, pp. 121–36; Raymond E. Brown, *The Gospel According to John (XIII-XXI)* (AB, 29A), New York: Doubleday, 1970, pp. 787–91; Paul S. Minear, 'Diversity and Unity: A Johannine Case Study', in Ulrich Luz and Hans Weder (eds.), *Die Mitte des Neuen Testaments. Einheit und Vielfalt neutestamentlicher Theologie. Festschrift für Eduard Schweizer zum siebzigsten Geburtstag*, Göttingen: Vandenhoeck and Ruprecht, 1983, pp. 162–75; Robinson, *Priority*, pp. 275–81; Pryor, *John*, pp. 72–3, 109–11; de Boer, *Johannine Perspectives*. De Boer's book was unavailable to me until my own book was essentially complete. Many of his points concerning the reinterpretation of Jesus' death in relation to new circumstances agree with our own conclusions, although we have not sought to discern different stages of development in John's view of the death of Jesus corresponding to different editions of the Gospel.

[54] Carson, *John*, pp. 445–6; see also the texts cited in Judith L. Kovacs, ' "Now Shall the Ruler of this World be Driven Out": Jesus' Death as Cosmic Battle in John 12:20–36', *JBL* 114/2 (1995), 236–46. Even outside of the apocalyptic literature the Messiah's kingdom was expected to remain for ever; cf. Schnackenburg, *John vol. II*, p. 394; Michaels, *John*, p. 230; G. R. Beasley-Murray, *John*, p. 215; Hanson, *Prophetic Gospel*, p. 165. See also Lindars, *Gospel of John*, pp. 434–5; Kenneth Grayston, *The Gospel of John*, London: Epworth, 1990, p. 101; Létourneau, *Jésus*, pp. 294–5; Witherington, *John's Wisdom*, pp. 225–6.

[55] Cf. Kovacs, 'Now Shall the Ruler', 240–2.

In Colossians, we already find the idea that Christ's death was in some sense a victory over evil spiritual forces (Col. 2.15). This idea, as it is found in John, may thus perhaps represent an earlier apologetic that John is continuing, rather than implications which he was the first to draw. If there is a distinctive emphasis in John, it is the presentation of the crucifixion in terms of 'lifting up' and 'glorification'. The cross is the first step of the Son of Man in his return to heaven, but more than that, the cross is in itself somehow paradoxically the glorification or enthronement of the Son of Man.[56] The use of 'glory' (δόξα) language in connection with the Son of Man most naturally recalls the traditions concerning the Son of Man seated in heaven upon his *throne of glory*.[57] The lifting up to heaven on or via the cross represents the taking of the power and authority given to him by God, and this follows directly from his obedience even unto death.[58] The enthronement of the Son of Man indicates his victory, and the victory of the people of God, over the forces of evil which oppose him/them (Dan. 7).[59] The power of the 'ruler of this world' is then overcome, so that he is cast down from the heavenly places.[60]

Thus Kovacs rightly considers that John has developed his own distinctive understanding of Jesus' death by developing and making use of earlier traditions.[61] All that needs to be added is that this development out of and on the basis of earlier tradition is part of the legitimation in which the Fourth Evangelist is engaging, attempting to defend and demonstrate the validity of the beliefs he inherited in response to objections raised against them. By developing the idea of the suffering Son of Man in relation to the apocalyptic worldview which forms the background for the

[56] So e.g. Barrett, *Commentary*, pp. 423, 427. *Contra* Nicholson, *Death as Departure*, pp. 141–4. See also Lindars, *Gospel of John*, p. 427.

[57] Kovacs, 'Now Shall the Ruler', 244–5.

[58] Cf. Phil. 2.6–11; Matt. 28.18 (on which see also above, p. 99); Rev. 5; Heb. 1.3–4; 2.9.

[59] Cf. Létourneau, *Jésus*, p. 295.

[60] I am grateful for this insight to the paper read by Ron Piper at the New Testament Conference in Aberdeen in September 1996, entitled 'Satan, Demons and the Absence of Exorcisms in the Fourth Gospel'. Regardless of whether it is the original reading, the interpretation of 12.31 in terms of 'casting *down*' is very likely correct. For John as for many other contemporary writers, heaven is the place of God whereas the lower world is under the influence of baneful spiritual powers (cp. the similar idea in Rev. 12.7ff.). For a slightly different interpretation cf. Witherington, *John's Wisdom*, p. 224.

[61] Kovacs, 'Now Shall the Ruler', 246–7.

idea of the heavenly Son of Man, John was able to present the crucifixion of Jesus the Messiah not merely as a scandal foreordained in Scripture, but as the expected victory of the Son of Man.[62]

A contrived Messiah?

Another possible objection that may have been raised is that the supposed fulfilment of Scripture and messianic expectations by Jesus was in fact contrived. That is to say, some may have suggested that Jesus arranged things, with the help of his disciples, so as to be able to perform acts which would make him appear to be the Messiah. Objections of this sort were raised prior to John, as we can see for example from Matthew 27–8, where the resurrection is attributed by Jewish opponents to the theft of the body by the disciples. Whereas Matthew responds to this objection simply by portraying it as false, John takes a different approach, and draws on the traditional motif of the failure of Jesus' disciples to understand him. John thus emphasizes that Jesus' followers did not understand Jesus' words foretelling his resurrection until after the event (2.21–2). Likewise the entry into Jerusalem on a donkey was not recognized as having messianic significance until afterwards (12.16). The implication is that, if the disciples did not understand these things at the time, then they could not have been involved in an elaborate plot to make Jesus appear to be the Messiah. The same is true of John the Baptist: his testimony concerning Jesus was not prearranged, but was a response to a revelation received from God. If such accusations as these were made, then it may be suggested that John adapts the traditions which he inherited in such a way as to emphasize that Jesus' fulfilment of Scripture was

---

[62] Cf. Nicholson, *Death as Departure*, pp. 143–4, who also discerns in the distinctive Johannine portrait indications that John is responding to objections. See also Ashton, *Understanding*, p. 496. If the references to 'lifting up' and 'glorification' derive from the portrait of the Servant in Deutero-Isaiah, this too would provide a clearer scriptural basis for the idea that a figure who could be interpreted messianically could suffer. John's portrait of Jesus in 1.33–6 as the chosen one of God, as the lamb of God and as the one on whom the Spirit descends all recall the portrait of the Servant in Isa. 42.1 (cf. Boismard, *Prologue*, p. 161). The traditions in Jewish literature concerning the martyrs overcoming God's/Israel's enemies through their suffering and death may also have played a crucial role. In each of these cases we are dealing with traditional Jewish ideas which are alluded to in connection with these issues prior to John, but which are developed more fully by him.

genuine and the result of God's action, rather than being the result of a plot by Jesus and his friends.[63]

Summary

In this chapter, as in the previous ones, we have seen the Fourth Evangelist facing objections and questions from his Jewish interlocutors. In response, he seeks to demonstrate the superiority of Jesus to other figures in Israel's history, and to show why the failure of the majority of his Jewish contemporaries to accept Jesus as the Messiah does not discredit the faith of Christians. This he does, once again, by engaging in legitimation, adapting the traditions he inherited and drawing out new implications from them. The evidence surveyed in this chapter thus fits with and supports the overall hypothesis for which we have been arguing thus far.

[63] For a fuller discussion of this topic see James F. McGrath, 'Uncontrived Messiah or Passover Plot? A Study of a Johannine Apologetic Motif', *IBS* 19 (1997), 2–16.

15

PUTTING THE PIECES TOGETHER

The coherence of John's portrait

The question that we shall be addressing in this chapter is whether John, as he adapted various traditions in response to a number of different issues, integrated the developments he made into a coherent portrait of Christ. One important point needs to be made from the outset: it must be recognized that what seems incoherent to a reader today may not have seemed so to an ancient reader.[1] In other words, our task will by definition contain a measure of anachronism. Nonetheless, it still seems worthwhile to note, wherever possible, indications that may help us to understand the underlying thought-world that harmonized elements that appear to us today to be in tension, or to recognize where, even in John's time, certain ideas would have been perceived as incompatible.

It may be useful to distinguish between two 'types' of tension that may exist in the Fourth Gospel. Anderson has recently emphasized that the tensions which modern readers perceive in Johannine thought may be either *internal* or *external* to the Evangelist. In other words, the tensions in the Evangelist's literary work may represent either tensions in his own thought, or tensions between unharmonized elements of different literary strata.[2] This distinction is an important one. However, in terms of our reading of John it is entirely possible to reach the conclusion that, in a sense, both are true. Given that we are looking at John in terms of the development of earlier tradition, it seems very possible that John may have developed elements of the tradition, which created

---

[1] Kysar ('Pursuing the Paradoxes', p. 203) notes this problem, but nonetheless takes the view that we should assume that what is paradoxical or contradictory to us would likewise have been so to the Evangelist and his readers, until we have clear evidence to the contrary. See also Hengel, *Johannine Question*, p. 103.

[2] Anderson, *Christology*, pp. 4–15.

tension between these elements and others that were not developed along similar lines. However, John may nonetheless have been aware of these tensions and felt that they were 'mysteries' which he and his community could be content to live with. We shall hopefully be better able to answer the question of what sort of tension is found in John once we have looked at aspects of John's Christology which are often felt to be in tension with one another. In view of the multi-faceted character of Johannine Christology, in this chapter we will have to content ourselves with looking at but a few of the major themes, motifs and emphases which previous scholarship has felt to be inconsistent, and/or which are open to more than one possible interpretation. A helpful guide to discerning questions that were left unanswered by the Evangelist will be the debates which took place subsequent to the writing of the Fourth Gospel, whether in the Johannine epistles or even later.[3]

Son of Man and Logos

Perhaps one of the most obvious and most puzzling issues is the relationship between the pre-existent Son of Man and the pre-existent Logos, or more precisely, the pre-existence of the Son of Man and that of the Logos. Are the two figures identical? If one refers to the pre-existent human Messiah and the other to God, then were they united even prior to the incarnation? Did they both come down from heaven at the same time? And most importantly, was John even aware that such questions would need an answer?

A good place to begin is with the suggestion, which has been made by several scholars in recent times, that John did not think of the Son of Man as a figure who descends and ascends. Among these is Pryor, who is clearly right to emphasize that John 1.51 has often been wrongly used to demonstrate such a connection, since in this verse it is the *angels* who ascend and descend, rather than the Son of Man.[4] However, he fails to do justice to the reference in 6.62 to the Son of Man ascending to *where he was before*. The key difficulty

---

[3] It is the view of most scholars that the epistles were written after the Gospel. Cf. R. E. Brown, *Epistles*, pp. 32–5 (and also 69ff.); also Talbert, *Reading John*, p. 3, who notes this as the majority view even though he opposes it. It is of course possible that the Gospel was redacted in relation to the later controversies reflected in the epistles, which might explain the presence of Christians who do not believe in John 6 and 8.

[4] Pryor, 'Johannine Son of Man', 341–2. See also Lindars, 'Son of Man', p. 48 n.16; de Boer, *Johannine Perspectives*, p. 174.

with Pryor's article is that he is polemizing. As he clarifies slightly later, he is not attempting to deny that there is a descent–ascent motif in John, but merely that this motif (and in particular descent) is connected in a special way to the designation 'Son of Man'.[5]

What needs to be stressed in response to these objections is that, inasmuch as John's understanding of Jesus as Son of Man is firmly rooted in earlier Christian tradition, the key emphases associated with this designation are not descent–ascent, but crucifixion and exaltation (which John combines through his use of the term 'lifting up'). Nonetheless, John has also clearly taken up and developed the incipient pre-existence conceptuality which, by the time he wrote, had become linked to the figure of the Son of Man. For John, the Son of Man was a figure who had pre-existed in heaven, and who had now come to earth, and this was of crucial importance for the Evangelist, inasmuch as this way of thinking about the Son of Man enabled him to defend the superior qualifications of Jesus to reveal God.[6] However much one may feel the need to qualify possible previous overemphasis on the Son of Man as a figure who descends and ascends, in the two passages in John where the concepts of Son of Man and pre-existence/ascent–descent are linked, they play a vital role in John's legitimation. The fact that the link is made explicitly only in two passages simply demonstrates John's close dependence on tradition, while the fact that he develops the traditional imagery in the way that he does shows that these further developments were deemed by him to be important and necessary.[7]

Having clarified our understanding of John's position and emphases in this area, we may now move on to another important point, namely that the issue of the relationship between the pre-existence of the Son of Man and the pre-existence of God's

---

[5] Pryor, 'Johannine Son of Man', 348. See also de Boer, *Johannine Perspectives*, pp. 159–62.

[6] See our discussion above, ch.10. We thus disagree with de Boer, *Johannine Perspectives*, pp. 174–5 inasmuch as we see pre-existence as of crucial importance in John's motivation for developing the Son of Man tradition in the way that he did.

[7] The view of Leivestad, 'Exit', 253 (cf. also Lindars, 'Son of Man', p. 48 n.16; Moloney, *Johannine Son of Man*, p. 122; Hare, *Son of Man*, p. 111), namely that 'Son of Man' refers to the incarnate Logos and never to the pre-existent one, cannot be maintained. It is of course true that in John the Son of Man *is* the incarnate Logos, Jesus of Nazareth, and for the most part the designation bears connotations which are traditional and which carry no overtones of pre-existence. Nonetheless, John has developed the traditional view, in a similar way to – and probably under the influence of – other contemporary writers, so that he now clearly thinks of the Son of Man as having come down from heaven. See further Painter, 'Enigmatic', pp. 1879–80 n.46.

Wisdom/Word/Spirit is an issue which was already implicitly raised by the tradition which John inherited. In the Similitudes of Enoch, the pre-existent Son of Man is portrayed as already being indwelt by God's Spirit of wisdom (1 Enoch 49.3), and as revealing God's wisdom to the righteous (1 Enoch 48.7).[8] Shall the Son of Man be born already 'full of wisdom'? And will the Son of Man remember his earlier existence in heaven? Such questions are not reflected on in the Similitudes of Enoch; they are nonetheless raised at least implicitly by this author's portrayal of the Son of Man, although they are not the subject of any further reflection or discussion. This ambiguity was therefore present in the tradition that John is likely to have inherited. John does give an explicit answer to the question implicitly raised by the Enochic tradition, as to whether the Son of Man on earth will remember his earlier existence in heaven. The Evangelist's answer is an affirmative one: whatever the precise relationship between Jesus as Wisdom incarnate and Jesus as Son of Man, the earthly Jesus remembered a prior existence in heaven on the basis of which he could reveal heavenly things to others. However, John does not address what implications this might have for Jesus' knowledge, for example, as an infant, presumably because he had other more pressing concerns.

It is thus not entirely clear what answer John gave (or would have given) to the question of the relationship between the Son of Man and Wisdom/Logos. This is also due at least in part to the fusing of the Enochic/apocalyptic traditions concerning the pre-existent Son of Man who is indwelt by God's Spirit, with the Jesus tradition, which presented the Spirit as coming upon Jesus at his baptism. In John's portrait, it is clear that once the incarnation has taken place, the human Jesus, the Son of Man and the Word or Wisdom of God are no longer to be regarded as 'separate entities'. But what about before the incarnation?[9]

One possible answer is that John identified the pre-existent figures of the Son of Man and Wisdom/Logos. John may have

---

[8] See also Theobald, *Fleischwerdung*, pp. 396–7, who notes possible evidence of the influence of the portrait of Wisdom in Wisd. 8.23–6 on the portrait of the Son of Man in 1 Enoch 48.3, 6.

[9] A comparable problem arises in Luke's portrait of Jesus and John the Baptist. The Baptist is said to be filled with the Holy Spirit even from birth (Luke 1.15). If Jesus did not receive the Spirit until his baptism, does this make him inferior to John? And if his conception through the power of the Spirit means that he was filled with the Spirit from birth, then what is the meaning of the descent of the Spirit upon him at his baptism?

found a basis for such an identification in the Old Greek reading in Daniel 7.13, which speaks of the Son of Man coming '*as* the ancient of days' (ὡς παλαιὸς ἡμερῶν).[10] If John was familiar with this reading, then the description of the Son of Man as a heavenly figure, who is both separate from God and yet ultimately none other than God himself, may have enabled him to identify the Son of Man with Wisdom/Logos.[11] However, at this point certainty appears impossible, since John does not give any explicit indication that he made such an identification, much less that he made it on this basis.

It appears that John has left an element of ambiguity in his portrait, although as we have already pointed out, the ambiguity of his *literary* presentation does not necessarily indicate an ambiguity in his own thought. Yet we must also give serious consideration to the possibility that the questions which we are raising may not have occurred to the Evangelist or his earliest readers. In the Prayer of Joseph, Israel is presented as being (or becoming) aware of actually being an angelic figure. Such a portrait, like that of John, raises certain questions (for us, at least), such as whether Jacob 'is' the angelic figure, or whether the angelic figure is the heavenly equivalent or parallel to the human, earthly Jacob. It also leads us to ask when the angel 'became' the human figure of Jacob – was it at birth or at some later point? And if it was at birth, did the human Jacob always remember his prior existence, or did the memory return at a later point?[12] Such questions that may be raised do not appear to have been given an explicit answer (although we cannot be certain, given the extremely fragmentary nature of our knowledge of this work), and yet this is not felt to spoil the story or detract from its plausibility. Both John's portrait of Jesus and the Prayer of

[10] On this reading see Loren T. Stuckenbruck, '"One Like a Son of Man as the Ancient of Days" in the Old Greek Recension of Daniel 7, 13: Scribal Error or Theological Translation?', *ZNW* 86 (1995), 268–76. For arguments in favour of John having known the Old Greek version of the Jewish Scriptures, see Schuchard, *Scripture*; Menken, *Old Testament Quotations*.

[11] For possible evidence that an identification between the heavenly (Son of) Man and Wisdom/Logos was also made by other authors than John, see the references in Coppens, *Relève Apocalyptique*, p. 93 n.165. See also Theobald, *Fleischwerdung*, pp. 396–8; Painter, 'Enigmatic', pp. 1879–80 n.46.

[12] The existing text suggests the latter, but it is not clear whether this represents Origen's interpretation of the original text or something that was made explicit therein. See J. Z. Smith, 'Prayer of Joseph. A New Translation with Introduction', in James H. Charlesworth (ed.), *The Old Testament Pseudepigrapha. Vol. II*, Garden City, NY: Doubleday, 1985, pp. 704, 714.

Joseph's portrait of Jacob use a variety of imagery and metaphors in order to speak of divine and/or metaphysical realities which cannot be accessed or spoken of directly.[13] John may have been 'inconsistent' by modern standards, but it is not clear that this type of consistency is to be expected in an ancient work such as the Fourth Gospel.

Ultimately, the Son of Man and Wisdom are to be identified, because they are both now to be identified with the person of Jesus.[14] At least by the time John 6 was composed, this tension appears to have been internalized by the Evangelist. There, Jesus is presented both as the giver of the bread of life (i.e. the Son of Man; cf. 6.27) and as the bread of life itself (i.e. Wisdom; cf. 6.35, 48).[15] The tension which we have noticed to be a feature of the Gospel as a whole is crystallized here, but it is not resolved, and no explicit answer is given to the question of how the Son of Man and Wisdom related to one another prior to their union as the human being Jesus. Both have come down from heaven, and both are now to be identified with Jesus. Beyond that, John gives no indication of what views, if any, he may have held on this matter.[16]

The Son who is sent and pre-existence

One frequently reads in works of Johannine scholarship of the Johannine concept of the Son who is sent from heaven.[17] However, a number of scholars have stressed that this is in fact precisely what John does *not* say. He refers to the pre-existent one as Logos and Son of Man, but not (at least directly or explicitly) as *Son*.[18] John clearly uses the language of sending in connection with 'the Son', but such language is traditional, and there is no clear evidence to

[13] Cf. Ashton, *Understanding*, p. 345; McGrath, 'Going up'.

[14] Cf. Painter, 'Enigmatic', p. 1883, who makes a similar point concerning Son of God and Son of Man language in John.

[15] See further our discussion in ch.11 above. On the unity and disunity of Johannine Christology with particular focus on John 6, see Anderson, *Christology*, pp. 72–89, 167 and *passim*.

[16] It is interesting to note that Origen found it necessary to speak of the pre-existence of Jesus' soul, which was united with the Logos even in its pre-existence. Although space will not permit a discussion here, it would be interesting to explore further whether this is an attempt to harmonize various aspects of New Testament Christology, or whether such an idea could have been in the Evangelist's mind.

[17] So e.g. Watson, 'Is John's Christology Adoptionist?', pp. 121–2; G. R. Beasley-Murray, 'Mission', p. 1865.

[18] So e.g. Cadman, *Open Heaven*, pp. 11–12; C. Brown, 'Trinity and Incarnation', 89–90.

indicate that it was understood to imply pre-existence in its traditional, pre-Johannine use.[19] The question we must therefore ask is whether John actually refers to Jesus as *the Son* in connection with pre-existence, indicating a development of this earlier tradition. The answer appears to be negative. The fact that Jesus begins to be referred to in terms of sonship only from the incarnation, at which point the term Logos also disappears, seems to provide an answer: λόγος is a designation appropriate only in reference to the pre-existent one, and μονογενής (υἱός) is a designation not of the pre-existent one, but of the Word-become-flesh, Jesus Christ (1.14).

The reason for this, it has been suggested, is that John is concerned to maintain the monotheistic character of his christological beliefs. To speak of an eternal *Son* would, it is argued, give the appearance of belief in a 'second power in heaven', in a way that the use of less personal categories (such as Word) would not.[20] Yet we have found reason to question whether 'two powers' was an issue in the period when John wrote (see chapter 3 above). This aspect of John's portrait can be explained equally well by the fact that John found support in the traditions which he inherited for referring to the Son of Man and to God's Word/Wisdom as pre-existent, but did not find such ideas associated with the designation 'Son of God'. Legitimation depends to a very large extent on appeal to authoritative sources and traditions, and for this reason there may have been insufficient motivation to – or sufficient motivation not to – connect the imagery of sonship with pre-existence.

Of course, these considerations in no way make it impossible to suggest that John took the final step of identifying *all* of these designations with the pre-existent one. However, we have no evidence that he did so, and certainty once again proves elusive. What is clear is that John felt that all of these designations and figures were ultimately to be identified with the human being Jesus, and this identification was John's distinctive contribution, which paved the way for the fuller identification that was made by Christians in later times between these various figures and designations even prior to the incarnation. In the Fourth Gospel, 'Christ' still appears to maintain its traditional character as a messianic title, closely connected with the messianic sense of 'Son

---

[19] Cf. Dunn, *Christology*, pp. 39–40, 44–5; Robinson, *Priority*, p. 383.

[20] So e.g. C. Brown, 'Trinity and Incarnation', 89–90; see also Dunn, 'Let John Be John', pp. 318–9.

of God',[21] whereas in the Johannine epistles 'Christ' appears to refer at times to the pre-existent one, perhaps suggesting that this transfer of titles was a further development made out of and on the basis of John's portrait.[22] This in turn suggests that John did not completely harmonize these various elements. Both the Word and the Son are sent, but the former designates the divine agent sent from heaven, whereas the latter designates the human agent whom the Word becomes. The Son is the Messiah/Son of Man,[23] and yet whereas the one who is now designated as 'Son' pre-existed, John refrains from designating the pre-incarnate one as 'Son'. This left tensions in his portrait which even very early readers appear to have felt the need to resolve.

The commissioning: descending Logos and/or ascending seer?

Closely related to the previous two topics is the suggestion, which we had the opportunity to consider briefly earlier in this study, that Jesus is thought of as having ascended to heaven to receive revelation. Our study suggests that John did in fact inherit such an idea, and it is possible that, while he may have altered its emphasis somewhat, he did not completely repudiate it. The question we must consider here is whether this concept will provide the harmony that has eluded us in our previous two avenues of approach. To raise the question directly, will the view that Jesus ascended to heaven and subsequently descended enable us to

[21] Cf. John 1.49; 10.24, 36; 11.27; 20.31. The references to 'coming into the world' need not imply pre-existence (cf. Robinson, *Priority*, p. 370), but even if not originally intended by the Evangelist, such an understanding probably arose quite quickly, under the influence of the pre-existence motifs in John. Ashton (*Understanding*, p. 207 n.5) is unnecessarily dismissive of Robinson's point.

[22] When 1 John was written the pre-existent one appears to have been designated as 'Christ' and 'Son of God' (cf. Painter, *Quest*, p. 460). This is an early interpretation of John, but may not represent the nuances and precise views of the author of the Gospel when he wrote the Gospel. Whether the author's views developed in a new context of a different conflict, or whether others developed his ideas, is difficult to tell, as it is unclear how much time elapsed between the relevant strata of the Gospel and the writing of 1 John, just as it is uncertain whether the same author is responsible for both.

[23] That during his earthly life Jesus is to be identified as both Son and Son of Man is clear from passages such as John 5.27. See also the close connection between the description of Jesus as the Son who is sent and as the Son of Man in John 3.13ff.; ch.6; and 8.28.

somehow clarify the relationship between the descent of the Son of Man and the descent of Wisdom/Logos in John's thought?

Bühner has recently argued the case for understanding the Johannine Jesus in terms of his ascent to heaven to become identified with a heavenly figure. But as promising as this suggestion might seem to some as a means of resolving a number of the tensions and difficulties in John's portrait of Jesus, there are nonetheless strong reasons for rejecting it. The biggest difficulty is that it is based on the assumption that there was a Jewish tradition in John's time which presented the seer as ascending to heaven and there being identified with a pre-existent heavenly figure.[24] The concept of the transformation of Enoch into a heavenly being is found in 2 Enoch 22.8, which may date from around the time of John, but this is not the same as the identification between Enoch and Metatron in 3 Enoch 4, which is much later. The interpretation of 1 Enoch 71.14 in terms of an identification of Enoch with the heavenly Son of Man appears to be much more difficult to maintain than the suggestion that 'son of man' (a different Ethiopic idiom than the one used elsewhere in 1 Enoch) here simply has its generic sense, 'human being', and does not intend to identify Enoch with the figure he has seen in his visions. This is especially the case given that Enoch and the Son of Man are clearly distinguished elsewhere in the Similitudes.[25] We thus feel compelled to reject Bühner's interpretation of 1 Enoch.

However, the weakness of the argument based on the evidence of 1 Enoch does not completely rule out the possibility that *John* thought of the Son of Man as a figure who ascends and descends rather than descends and ascends. Nevertheless, this seems unlikely, not only because John shows himself to be aware of the apocalyptic traditions concerning the pre-existence of the Son of Man, but also because it appears to be the *descent* which, in 3.13, provides the focus of attention and emphasis, rather than ascent. John's emphasis is on the descent of the pre-existent Son of Man and of

---

[24] This interpretation of the Enochic tradition is central to Bühner's thesis (*Gesandte*, pp. 385–99), but we feel it is of questionable relevance to the study of John's ascent-descent schema. The other texts Bühner adduces (*Gesandte*, pp. 388–391) are not evidence for this conceptuality, unless read in light of 1 Enoch interpreted in the way he proposes.

[25] See further John J. Collins, 'The Son of Man in First-Century Judaism', *NTS* 38 (1992), 451–3. On the different idiom see E. Isaac, '1 (Ethiopic Apocalypse of) ENOCH', in James H. Charlesworth (ed.), *The Old Testament Pseudepigrapha, vol. I*, New York: Doubleday, 1983, p. 50.

God's Word/Wisdom/Spirit, which for him provides the basis for Jesus' revelation. Thus, while Bühner's interpretation cannot be ruled out absolutely, it seems less likely and less preferable than the one we have adopted.

In light of these considerations, it is interesting to note that, in John 3.13, John has not completely eliminated every trace of the ascent tradition which he inherited, even though its role was made redundant by his emphasis on and reinterpretation of the pre-existence and descent traditions. Here too, then, we find a tension which John has not finally resolved, and in this particular instance there is no evidence that we are dealing with a tension that the Evangelist was content to retain, rather than an unintentional one resulting from his adaptation of a traditional saying or concept. Nonetheless the overall direction in which John developed Christology seems clear. In earlier tradition, Jesus was described for the most part as the human agent of God, who had been exalted by God and could now be described in the language of heavenly agency. In John, it is clearly the heavenly agent that has descended to be identified with the human agent. Both the continuity, and at the same time the change of emphasis, are not difficult to discern.

The human Jesus and the divine Logos

The question of the exact relationship between the humanity and divinity of Christ was not given a clear answer by John, as the debates of the subsequent centuries show.[26] Nonetheless, it is worth considering at least briefly the indications John gives of what views, if any, he held on this subject. It seems clear that he believed that, from the moment of incarnation onwards, the human being Jesus and the divine Logos were to be identified, to such an extent that what could be predicated of the Logos could now also be predicated of the human being Jesus, the Word-become-flesh. This, as we have already seen, was an important point in terms of his legitimating portrait of Jesus. Did this mean that two 'persons' had now become one 'person'? John does not make explicit his views on the 'personality' of the Logos, nor on the relationship between the personality of the Logos and that of the human being Jesus – indeed, it is unclear whether he had given any thought to the

---

[26] Cf. R. P. C. Hanson, *The Search for the Christian Doctrine of God: The Arian controversy 318–381*, Edinburgh: T&T Clark, 1988, and our discussion in ch. 1 above.

matter. In fact, it is probably misleading to ask such questions, since for us the terminology of 'persons' has both a technical theological meaning and a transformed secular meaning, neither of which existed in John's time.[27] John's portrait eventually resulted in the affirmation that Christ was one person with two natures, but the formulation of such a definition is an attempt to answer questions which John's portrait raises, but does not answer.

Before concluding, we should mention Fennema's work on John's development of earlier tradition. He rightly emphasizes that, in his portrait of Jesus, the Fourth Evangelist has merged the ideas and motifs connected with heavenly and earthly agents of God, in a way that removes the limitations which were an inherent part of each conceptuality.[28] Thus Jesus (unlike the prophetic agents described in the Jewish Scriptures) was wholly and unquestioningly obedient to the one who sent him. Yet on the other hand, he is clearly a separate individual from God, and not just a personified extension of his own being, sovereignty and will. While we do not agree with Fennema's characterization of John's aims in terms of the defence of monotheism, he has nonetheless summarized clearly and succinctly an important aspect of John's portrait of Jesus, one which would have the effect of driving on the further development of Christology and of providing the basis on which a Christian redefinition and reaffirmation of monotheism would take place.[29]

[27] On some of the debates which ensued on this matter in the post-Johannine church cf. Maurice Wiles, 'Person or Personification? A Patristic Debate about Logos', in L. D. Hurst and N. T. Wright (eds.), *The Glory of Christ in the New Testament*, Oxford: Clarendon, 1987, pp. 281–9.

[28] Fennema, 'Jesus and God', pp. 294–5.

[29] Fennema's point about John's combination and identification of the heavenly and earthly agent ideas probably answers the question raised by Rainbow ('Jewish Monotheism', 86) in response to Hurtado: if belief in divine agents did not represent a departure from Jewish monotheism, how can it help explain the way Christians redefined monotheism? The answer seems to be that it was not the idea of heavenly or human agents of God *per se* that caused Christians to eventually redefine monotheism, but the identification of God's earthly agent and his personified attribute(s) in a way and/or to an extent that had not previously been done within Judaism. This suggests that Hurtado is correct in his emphasis on Jewish concepts of agency to account for early christological categories, and that Fennema is correct to conclude that the complete identification of Jesus by the Fourth Evangelist as both heavenly and earthly agent at the same time is John's distinctive contribution which would influence the direction of future christological development.

Conclusion

We have not seen anything in our study that would suggest that the different strands of Johannine theology can be separated simply along the lines of the subject headings we have chosen for our different chapters. On the contrary, we have found all the key motifs of Johannine theology, such as Wisdom/Logos, Son of Man and agency, to have been used and developed by the Evangelist in relation to *various* issues in the conflict with the synagogue. And further, although we have seen a great many points of contact with earlier tradition, nothing gave a clear and unambiguous indication that John made direct literary use of any other New Testament document. The most likely reason for this is perhaps that John's development of the traditions he inherited – whether these were one or more of the Synoptic Gospels, a written Signs Source or Gospel, or oral tradition – took place *prior to the writing of the Gospel*. The Gospel is the product of this development, incorporating within itself the responses that certain early Christians made to objections that had been raised against them. In it, the traditions John inherited and the developments he made are interwoven. This is not to say that pre-Johannine traditions cannot be detected underlying the present form of the Gospel at many points, but simply that it seems that, even if John has not woven these points into a completely unified picture, neither has he merely allowed early and late, tradition and interpretation, to simply stand unaltered side by side. The model of legitimation helps us to understand how and why John developed the traditions that he inherited in the ways that he did, but it does not allow us to reconstruct the exact form of those traditions in detail.

We must also recognize that it is somewhat unrealistic to expect total consistency in a document formed in the context of an intense conflict. The reason for this is that these developments were, for John and his readers, solutions to very pressing problems and issues. John is therefore unlikely to have had the leisure of reflecting on what issues might arise from his portrait over the next decades and even centuries, once the immediate conflict in which he was engaged had come to an end. Rather than disparage his inconsistency, a sympathetic reading will more likely be amazed at the degree of consistency achieved in spite of these circumstances. As we have also seen, many aspects of John's portrait that appear to us to be in tension would not necessarily have appeared so to the

Evangelist and his readers. Nonetheless, there is evidence that at least some of the tensions which are present in the text are a result of the developments which John made as part of his legitimation. We should thus conclude that John attempted to answer the issues of his day by appealing to traditional beliefs and drawing the necessary implications from them. This resulted in a portrait of Jesus composed of numerous interwoven strands. These strands were developed to answer questions and issues raised in the conflict with the synagogue. For John, they were simply the implications of the traditions he inherited, expounded and elaborated in response to pressing issues facing Christians in his time. For us, they are part of a problem, a text that forms part of the Christian canon, yet which is full of unresolved tensions, the implications of which Christian theologians continue to wrestle with.[30]

To sum up then, we agree with Kysar's assessment of the 'dialectical' thought of the Fourth Evangelist in terms of the dialogue between his own views and those of the traditions he inherited. This dialogue represents the Evangelist's theological method, as he and the Christians for whom he wrote wrestled with the significance of the authoritative traditions that they inherited in light of the issues confronting them in the present.[31] To this we would simply add that the dialectical tension exists not only between tradition and interpretation, but also between different elements of the interpretation as well. And whereas these tensions may have been the *result* of the process of legitimation and development that we have been tracing, there is no need to conclude that John did a poor editing job, leaving contradictions that he would have avoided had he been more careful. Rather, John's 'dialectical thought' is the product of an ongoing dialogue between past and present, between tradition and experience.[32]

[30] For differing interpretations of John in the early church see Peter Hofrichter, 'Logoslehre und Gottesbild bei Apologeten, Modalisten und Gnostikern. Johanneische Christologie im Lichte ihrer frühesten Rezeption', in Hans-Josef Klauck (ed.), *Monotheismus und Christologie. Zur Gottesfrage im Hellenistischen Judentum und im Urchristentum*, Freiberg: Herder, 1992, pp. 186–217; Wiles, 'Person or Personification?'. See also R. P. C. Hanson, *Search*, on the later Arian controversy.

[31] Kysar, 'Pursuing the Paradoxes', p. 190.

[32] Ibid., pp. 202–3. See also de Boer, *Johannine Perspectives*, pp. 314–15.

16

CONCLUSION

It remains only for us to summarize our findings and to attempt to reflect on what implications this study may have for future Johannine scholarship and for the use of John in contemporary theology.

Summary

In our first chapter, we saw that there are a number of possible solutions to the problem of *why* Johannine Christology developed along the distinctive lines that it did. We found it necessary to reject the approaches which we categorized under the rubric of 'History of Religions', since these did insufficient justice to the Jewishness of Johannine thought and its close continuity with earlier Christian ideas and motifs. The suggestion that John's Christology developed organically out of earlier traditions was given a more positive evaluation, but was nonetheless felt to do insufficient justice to the extent of the developments, and the need for some sort of catalyst or explanatory factor in order to understand the development. The suggestion that a particular individual's insight shaped the Johannine portrait of Christ was not denied, but we nonetheless felt it necessary to look for a different level of explanation, one which gave greater attention to the setting in which the author wrote and the factors which inspired or stimulated him to write as he did. We thus adopted a sociological approach, suggesting, in line with Berger and Luckmann's model of legitimation, that the Fourth Evangelist adapted and developed the traditions which he inherited as part of a defence of his (and his community's) beliefs against objections raised by Jewish opponents.

After this we proceeded to set forth in our second chapter some of the evidence for the conflict setting which we have posited for the Gospel, and the points of continuity and further development between John and earlier Christian writings. In part 2, we considered the influence of one key theme in the conflict, namely that of the relationship between Jesus and God. There we saw that John developed a number of earlier ideas, drawing out new and further implications from them in response to objections that had been raised. John thus identified Jesus more fully and/or explicitly with God's Word/Wisdom/Spirit than had earlier authors. John also appealed to the category of agency and the identification of Jesus as the Son of Man in order to defend the Christian belief that Jesus exercises divine prerogatives. The parallelism between the Word of God and the Name of God in Jewish writings was utilized in order to present Jesus not as a man who received the divine name when he was exalted, but as the person whom the Name/Word became, and as whom the Word/Name returned to heaven. By appealing to these and other traditions, John sought to defend the exalted status and functions attributed to Jesus by Christians.

In part 3 we examined the issue of the relationship between Jesus and Moses and their respective revelations. John was seen to have developed the miracle tradition in order to present Jesus' miracles as *signs* similar to those of Moses. He also drew the new implication from the Son of Man tradition that, as the pre-existent Son of Man, Jesus could reveal heavenly things in a way that no other could. Jesus was also more fully identified with Wisdom than was the case in earlier writings, the one who had been glimpsed by Moses having now appeared on the human scene 'in the flesh'. Jesus had, in line with Jewish expectations, provided bread miraculously, and was himself the 'bread from heaven' which was expected to be provided in the last days. In chapter 14 we considered a number of other possible issues in the conflict, such as the relationship between Jesus and John the Baptist (and also other figures from Israel's Scriptures), the scandal of the cross and the rejection of Jesus by the majority of Jews. In each case we found our initial hypothesis confirmed. The Fourth Evangelist's development of the traditions he inherited is best explained in terms of legitimation, his attempt to provide an answer to objections and issues raised in the conflict with the synagogue.

Finally, we considered briefly whether the various developments made by John had been integrated by him into a coherent portrait of Jesus. We were forced to conclude that, while many aspects of his portrait would not have been as problematic for his contemporaries as they are for us today, at many points John did not have the luxury of reflecting on further implications which others after him might draw from his portrait. John's portrait was a *response* to a particular problem, and in the intensity of the conflict setting in which he wrote, it is not surprising that he did not reflect on problems and difficulties which those who came after him might find. From the Evangelist's perspective, he was simply drawing out the implications of the authoritative traditions which he inherited, as a response and solution to the pressing problem of the objections raised by 'the Jews'.

Implications for Johannine studies

A number of implications appear to arise out of the present study. Above all, we have seen reasons to situate and interpret John against a predominantly Jewish background, and to reject appeals to non-Jewish influences as the key to explaining the development of Johannine Christology. This supports those scholars and approaches which emphasize the need to interpret John not simply against the broad background of first-century Hellenism, but rather against the more narrow background of first-century Hellenistic Judaism. A corollary is that the methodologies employed to study John should do justice to this background, as indeed we have sought to do in this present study through the use of Berger and Luckmann's model of legitimation. Hopefully this study will have helped clarify some of the methodological possibilities available in approaching the issue of doctrinal development.

Another important conclusion arising out of our study is that the debate between the Johannine Christians and the local synagogue was over *pre-Johannine* christological beliefs. The distinctive Johannine beliefs were seen to be an attempt to defend or legitimate earlier beliefs. This helps to bring a greater measure of clarity to the issue of whether Johannine Christology was the *cause* or the *result* of the conflict with the synagogue. It has become popular to give the answer 'both', but hopefully the present study has shed some light on what such an answer might mean in practice. As certain influential strands of post-70 Judaism sought to draw in the boundaries of Judaism by enforcing their own definition thereof, Christians came under fire for the christological beliefs which they held. This conflict, and the legitimation it necessitated, resulted in many of the distinctive Johannine formulations. Christology is thus both cause and effect, but it is the pre-Johannine Christology which is the cause, and the distinctive Johannine developments which are the effect. It is thus to be hoped that this study will have helped to clarify some of the issues relating to method, and to questions of 'before and after', in the study of Johannine Christology.

In our study, we have focused on John's development of earlier *traditions* and *motifs*, and avoided any attempt to reconstruct the sources which were used by the Evangelist in creating his Gospel. While not opposed to such reconstructions, it is hoped that the methodology used in this study will provide a more secure basis for tracing the development of Johannine thought about Jesus than previous attempts based on hypothetical source-reconstructions. Hopefully any future attempts at source criticism of the Fourth Gospel will take as their starting point John's relationship to traditions known from other sources, traditions with which John appears to have been familiar, and will use the trajectory reconstructed by the use of this methodology as the basis for attempting to discern source and redaction in John. The fact that we have not engaged in source criticism here should not be taken to indicate a complete rejection of this method, but merely reflects the conviction that the approach adopted here will provide a useful supplement, which can shed light on a number of unanswered questions in Johannine scholarship.

Johannine Christology, Trinitarianism and monotheism

We saw in part 2 that John's aim was not, as many scholars have thought, to defend monotheism. Yet this was not because John denied monotheism, but rather because John's Christology fit within the bounds of first-century Jewish monotheism. Within this context, it was possible to think of God's Logos or other mediating figures as extensions of God's own sovereignty and activity, and thus 'neither created nor uncreated', 'both God and distinct from God'. This paradox came to be at the heart of the christological debates that took place in the centuries that followed. It is presumably also a key reason why defenders of a strict or monistic monotheism and defenders of a Trinitarian monotheism have both found themselves able to appeal to John for support. Those theologians who regard John's portrait as an authoritative basis for any contemporary reformulation will presumably want to do justice both to the fact that John understood himself to be a monotheist and formulated his Christology within the context of first-century Jewish monotheism, and also to the fact that John's creative use of tradition ultimately – when considered in terms of its long-term impact – expanded the boundaries of what could be regarded as monotheism.[1] John's Gospel, when read in the light of issues and questions raised in subsequent centuries, pulls in two directions, because the one who is said to have been incarnate as the human person Jesus is regarded both as God himself, and as separate from and subordinate to God. The paradox of Johannine Christology is an aspect of John's development of traditions he inherited, utilizing motifs current in his day and age, and it is with this paradoxical portrait of Jesus that the Church of all subsequent centuries has had to wrestle.

John's approach to his task and ours

I have argued elsewhere that we share a common task with the New Testament authors, namely the task of taking up, adapting and applying the traditions which we have inherited, in response to the needs, issues and setting of our contemporary Christian communities.[2] This suggests that an attempt to simply repeat John's portrait would in fact be less faithful to the spirit and emphases of John than is often thought to be the case. John did not seek to resolve every possible christological issue for all time, but to give as convincing an answer as possible to questions raised in his own day. Presumably we would do well to do likewise, attempting to make the Christian tradition which we have inherited, including the Fourth Gospel, just as meaningful and relevant to our own setting and issues. Allowing John to speak today will mean speaking on his behalf, giving him a new voice to address new issues, drawing out new implications from his Gospel, and thus seeking to be as relevant to our day as he was to his.[3]

---

[1] Yet it must also be considered that it may well have been a prior redefinition of monotheism (in terms of *creatio ex nihilo*) which led to the reinterpretation of John, and thus to the further redefinition of monotheism along Trinitarian lines. Cf. further ch.3 above.

[2] McGrath, 'Change in Christology', 47–50. See also my 'Christology on Two Fronts: A New Testament Model for Doing Christology in a Pluralistic Context', *Religion and Theology* 6/1 (1999), 74–5.

[3] Cf. the similar conclusion reached by Esler at the conclusion of his work applying Berger and Luckmann's model of legitimation to Luke-Acts (*Community and Gospel*, p. 223).

And finally . . .

Our study cannot give an answer to the question of whether John's Gospel is a faithful exposition of the implications of earlier tradition, or whether it goes beyond anything that Jesus himself would have been happy with. But what it does suggest is that, whereas one can 'do' Christology or theology, the task of theology is never finally 'done', as long as human history continues and new situations and needs, new worldviews, questions and ideas, continue to arise. And we can say that, if John had not adapted the traditions he inherited in the way that he did, Christianity would very possibly have found itself reabsorbed into Judaism, unable to defend the legitimacy of its beliefs and thus finding that the plausibility structure of its worldview had dropped out from under it. We thus have the ironic situation that, in order to *preserve* the original gospel message, one may be required to *alter* it, that in order to remain faithful to Jesus, one may have to say something other than what Jesus himself said. The implications of this may seem radical, but in fact this is nothing more than a call to do what Christians throughout history have always sought to do: to relate their beliefs and heritage to the life-setting in which they found themselves, without losing their distinctive emphases and meaning. This is the challenge that confronts the reader of the Fourth Gospel even today.

BIBLIOGRAPHY

Primary sources and translations

Aland, K., Black, M., et al., *Nestle-Aland Novum Testamentum Graece*, Stuttgart: Deutsche Bibelgesellschaft, 1979.

Charlesworth, James H. (ed.), *The Old Testament Pseudepigrapha* (2 vols.), New York: Doubleday, 1983.

Colson, F. H., Whitaker, G. H., et al., *Philo* (Loeb Classical Library, 12 vols.), Cambridge, MA: Harvard University Press, 1979–93.

Danby, H., *The Mishnah*, Oxford: Clarendon Press, 1933.

Epstein, I. (ed.), *The Babylonian Talmud*, London: Soncino Press, 1935–52.

Grossfeld, Bernard, *The Targum Onqelos to Genesis* (The Aramaic Bible, 6), Edinburgh: T&T Clark, 1988.

James, Montague Rhodes, *The Apocryphal New Testament*, Oxford: Clarendon Press, 1924.

Maher, Michael, *Targum Pseudo-Jonathan: Genesis* (The Aramaic Bible, 18), Edinburgh: T&T Clark, 1992.

McNamara, Martin, *Targum Neofiti 1: Genesis* (The Aramaic Bible, 1A), Edinburgh: T&T Clark, 1992.

Stevenson, J., *A New Eusebius. Documents Illustrative of the History of the Church to A.D. 337*, London: SPCK, 1968.

Streane, A. W., *A Translation of the Treatise Chagigah from the Babylonian Talmud*, Cambridge: Cambridge University Press, 1891.

Vermes, Geza, *The Dead Sea Scrolls in English* (fourth edition), London: Penguin, 1995.

Whiston, William, *The Works of Josephus*, 1736, reprinted Peabody, MA: Hendrickson, 1986.

Yonge, C. C., *The Works of Philo*, Peabody, MA: Hendrickson, 1993.

Secondary literature

Ackerman, James S., 'The Rabbinic Interpretation of Psalm 82 and the Gospel of John', *HTR* 59 (1966), 186–91.

Albright, W. F. and C. S. Mann, *Matthew* (AB, 26), Garden City, NY: Doubleday, 1971.

Alexander, Loveday, 'Ancient Book Production and the Circulation of the Gospels', in Richard Bauckham (ed.), *The Gospels for all Christians*, Edinburgh: T&T Clark, 1998, pp. 71–105.

Alexander, Philip S., 'Rabbinic Judaism and the New Testament', *ZNW* 74 (1983), 237–46.
'"The Partings of the Ways" from the Perspective of Rabbinic Judaism', in James D. G. Dunn (ed.), *Jews and Christians. The Partings of the Ways A. D. 70 to 135* (WUNT 2, 66), Tübingen: J. C. B. Mohr (Paul Siebeck), 1992, pp. 1–25.
Allison, Dale C., *The New Moses. A Matthean Typology*, Minneapolis: Fortress Press/ Edinburgh: T&T Clark, 1993.
Anderson, Paul N., *The Christology of the Fourth Gospel: Its Unity and Disunity in the Light of John 6* (WUNT 2, 78), Tübingen: J. C. B. Mohr (Paul Siebeck), 1996.
Ashton, John, *Understanding the Fourth Gospel*, Oxford: Clarendon Press, 1991.
Studying John. Approaches to the Fourth Gospel, Oxford: Clarendon Press, 1994.
Aune, David E., *The Cultic Setting of Realized Eschatology in Early Christianity* (NovTSup, 28), Leiden: E. J. Brill, 1972.
'Orthodoxy in First Century Judaism? A Response to N. J. McEleney', *JSJ* 7/1 (1976), 1–10.
Prophecy in Early Christianity and the Ancient Mediterranean World, Grand Rapids: Eerdmans, 1983.
Revelation 1–5 (Word Biblical Commentary, 52), Dallas: Word, 1997.
Bailey, Kenneth E., *Poet and Peasant and Through Peasant Eyes. A Literary-Cultural Approach to the Parables in Luke* (Combined Edition), Grand Rapids: Eerdmans, 1983.
Balchin, John F., 'Paul, Wisdom and Christ', in Harold H. Rowdon (ed.), *Christ the Lord. Studies in Christology Presented to Donald Guthrie*, Leicester: IVP, 1982, pp. 204–19.
Ball, David Mark, *'I Am' in John's Gospel. Literary Function, Background and Theological Implications* (JSNTS, 124), Sheffield: Sheffield Academic Press, 1996.
Barclay, John M. G., *Jews in the Mediterranean Diaspora. From Alexander to Trajan (323 BCE–117 CE)*, Edinburgh: T&T Clark, 1996.
Barker, Margaret, *The Older Testament. The Survival of Themes from the Ancient Royal Cult in Sectarian Judaism and Early Christianity*, London: SPCK, 1987.
The Great Angel. A Study of Israel's Second God, London: SPCK, 1992.
Barrett, C. K., *The Gospel of John and Judaism. The Franz Delitzsch Lectures, University of Münster, 1967*, London: SPCK, 1975.
The Gospel According to St. John. An Introduction with Commentary and Notes on the Greek Text, London: SPCK (second edition), 1978.
'Christocentric or Theocentric? Observations on the Theological Method of the Fourth Gospel', *Essays on John*, London: SPCK, 1982, pp. 1–18.
'"The Father is Greater than I" (John 14:28). Subordinationist Christology in the New Testament', *Essays on John*, London: SPCK, 1982, pp. 19–36.
'The Place of John and the Synoptics in the Early History of Christian

Tradition', *Jesus and the Word and Other Essays*, Edinburgh: T&T Clark, 1995, pp. 119–34.

Bartlett, John R., *Jews in the Hellenistic World. Josephus, Aristeas, The Sibylline Oracles, Eupolemus* (Cambridge Commentaries on Writings of the Jewish & Christian World 200 BC to AD 200, 1), Cambridge: Cambridge University Press, 1985.

Barton, Stephen C., 'The Communal Dimension of Earliest Christianity: A Critical Survey of the Field', *JTS* n.s. 43/2 (October 1992), 399–427.

'Early Christianity and the Sociology of the Sect' in Francis Watson (ed.), *The Open Text. New Directions for Biblical Studies*, London: SCM Press, 1993, pp. 140–62.

'Historical Criticism and Social-Scientific Study in New Testament Study', in Joel B. Green (ed.), *Hearing the New Testament. Strategies for Interpretation*, Carlisle: Paternoster/ Grand Rapids: Eerdmans, 1995, pp. 61–89.

'Can We Identify the Gospel Audiences?', Richard Bauckham, ed., in *The Gospels for All Christians. Rethinking the Gospel Audiences*, Edinburgh: T&T Clark, 1998, pp. 173–94.

Bauckham, Richard, 'The Worship of Jesus in Apocalyptic Christianity', *NTS* 27 (1980–1), pp. 322–41.

'The Worship of Jesus', in David Noel Freedman (ed.), *The Anchor Bible Dictionary, Vol. III, H–J*, New York: Doubleday and Co., 1992, pp. 812–19.

'For Whom Were Gospels Written?', in Richard Bauckham (ed.), *The Gospels for All Christians. Rethinking the Gospel Audiences*, Edinburgh: T&T Clark, 1998, pp. 9–48.

Beasley-Murray, George R., *Revelation* (New Century Bible Commentary), Grand Rapids: Eerdmans/ London: Marshall, Morgan & Scott, 1974.

John (Word Biblical Commentary, 36), Dallas: Word, 1987.

'The Mission of the Logos-Son', in F. Van Segbroeck, C. M. Tuckett, G. Van Belle and J. Verheyden (eds.), *The Four Gospels 1992. Festschrift Frans Neirynck. Volume 3* (BETL, 100), Leuven: Leuven University Press, 1992, pp. 1855–64.

Beasley-Murray, Paul, 'Colossians 1:15–20: An Early Christian Hymn Celebrating the Lordship of Christ', in D. A. Hagner and M. J. Harris (eds.), *Pauline Studies. Essays Presented to F. F. Bruce*, Exeter: Paternoster Press, 1980, pp. 169–83.

Becker, Jürgen, *Das Evangelium des Johannes. Kapitel 1–10* (Ökumenischer Taschenbuch-Kommentar zum Neuen Testament 4/1), Gütersloh: Gütersloher Verlagshaus Gerd Mohn/ Würzburg: Echter-Verlag, 1979.

Berger, Peter, *The Sacred Canopy. Elements of a Sociological Theory of Religion*, New York: Doubleday, 1967.

Berger, Peter and Luckmann, Thomas, *The Social Construction of Reality. A Treatise in the Sociology of Knowledge*, London: Allen Lane/ Penguin Press, 1967.

Bernard, J. H., *A Critical and Exegetical Commentary on the Gospel According to St. John* (2 volumes), Edinburgh: T&T Clark, 1928.

Bock, Darrell L., 'The Son of Man Seated at God's Right Hand and the

Debate over Jesus' "Blasphemy"', in Joel B. Green and Max Turner (eds.), *Jesus of Nazareth: Lord and Christ. Essays on the Historical Jesus and New Testament Christology*, Grand Rapids: Eerdmans, 1994, pp. 181–91.

Bockmuehl, Markus, *This Jesus: Martyr, Lord, Messiah*, Edinburgh: T&T Clark, 1994.

Boismard, Marie-Emile, *Le Prologue de Saint Jean* (Lectio Divina, 11), Paris: Les Editions du Cerf, 1953.

'Jésus, le Prophète par excellence, d'après Jean 10,24–39', in Joachim Gnilka (ed.), *Neues Testament und Kirche. Für Rudolf Schnackenburg*, Freiburg: Herder, 1974, pp. 160–171.

Moise ou Jésus. Essai de Christologie Johannique (BETL, 84), Leuven: Leuven University Press, 1988.

Borgen, Peder, 'The Unity of the Discourse in John 6', *ZNW* 60 (1959): 277–8.

Bread from Heaven. An Exegetical Study of the Concept of Manna in the Gospel of John and the Writings of Philo (NovTSup, 10), Leiden: E. J. Brill, 1965.

'Some Jewish Exegetical Traditions as Background for the Son of Man Sayings in John's Gospel (John 3:13–14 and context)', in M. de Jonge, ed., *L'Evangile de Jean. Sources, Rédaction, Théologie* (BETL, 44), Leuven: Leuven University Press, 1977, pp. 243–56.

'Bread from Heaven. Aspects of Debates on Expository Method and Form', *Logos was the True Light and other essays on the Gospel of John*, Trondheim: Tapir Publishers, 1983, pp. 32–46.

'God's Agent in the Fourth Gospel', in John Ashton (ed.), *The Interpretation of John* (IRT, 9), Philadelphia: Fortress Press/ London: SPCK, 1986, pp. 67–78.

Philo, John and Paul. New Perspectives on Judaism and Early Christianity (Brown Judaic Studies, 131), Atlanta: Scholars Press, 1987.

'Creation, Logos and the Son: Observations on John 1:1–18 and 5:17–18', *Ex Auditu* 3 (1987), 88–97.

Early Christianity and Hellenistic Judaism, Edinburgh: T&T Clark, 1996.

'The Gospel of John and Hellenism. Some Observations', in R. Alan Culpepper and C. Clifton Black (eds.), *Exploring the Gospel of John. In Honor of D. Moody Smith*, Louisville: Westminster John Knox Press, 1996, pp. 98–123.

Bowker, John, *The Targums and Rabbinic Literature. An Introduction to Jewish Interpretations of Scripture*, Cambridge: Cambridge University Press, 1969.

Bowman, John, *The Samaritan Problem. Studies in the Relationships of Samaritanism, Judaism, and Early Christianity* (Pittsburgh Theological Monograph Series, 4), Pittsburgh: Pickwick Press, 1975.

Brodie, Thomas L., *The Gospel According to John: A Literary and Theological Commentary*, Oxford: Oxford University Press, 1993.

Brown, Colin, 'Trinity and Incarnation: In Search of Contemporary Orthodoxy', *Ex Auditu* 7 (1991), 83–100.

Brown, Raymond E., *The Gospel According to John (I–XII)* (Anchor Bible, 29), New York: Doubleday, 1966.

The Gospel According to John (XIII–XXI) (Anchor Bible, 29A), New York: Doubleday, 1970.

The Community of the Beloved Disciple, London: Geoffrey Chapman, 1979.

The Epistles of John (Anchor Bible, 30), New York: Doubleday and Co, 1982.

An Introduction to New Testament Christology, London: Geoffrey Chapman, 1994.

Bruce, F. F., *The Book of the Acts* (NICNT), revised edition, Grand Rapids: Eerdmans, 1988.

The Epistle to the Hebrews (NICNT), Grand Rapids: Eerdmans, revised edition 1990.

Buchanan, George Wesley, 'The Samaritan Origin of the Gospel of John', in Jacob Neusner (ed.), *Religions in Antiquity. Essays in Memory of Erwin Ramsell Goodenough*, Leiden: E. J. Brill, 1968, pp. 149–75.

'Apostolic Christology', in K. H. Richards (ed.), *Society of Biblical Literature Seminar Papers 1986*, Atlanta: Scholars Press, 1986, pp. 172–82.

Bühner, J.-A., *Der Gesandte und sein Weg im viertem Evangelium: Die kultur- und religionsgeschichtlichen Grundlagen der johanneischen Sendungschristologie sowie ihre traditionsgeschichtliche Entwicklung*, Tübingen: J. C. B. Mohr (Paul Siebeck), 1977.

Bultmann, Rudolf, *Theology of the New Testament. Vol. I*, New York: Charles Scribner's Sons, 1951.

Theology of the New Testament. Vol. II, London: SCM Press, 1955.

The Gospel of John. A Commentary, Oxford: Basil Blackwell, 1971.

'The History of Religions Background to the Prologue to the Gospel of John', in John Ashton (ed.), *The Interpretation of John* (IRT, 9), Philadelphia: Fortress Press/ London: SPCK, 1986, pp. 18–35.

Burge, Gary M., '"I Am" Sayings', in Joel B. Green, Scot McKnight and I. Howard Marshall (eds.), *Dictionary of Jesus and the Gospels*, Leicester: IVP, 1992, pp. 354–6.

Burkett, Delbert, *The Son of the Man in the Gospel of John* (JSNTS, 56), Sheffield: Sheffield Academic Press, 1991.

Burridge, Richard A., 'About People, by People, for People: Gospel Genre and Audiences', in Richard Bauckham (ed.), *The Gospels for All Christians. Rethinking the Gospel Audiences*, Edinburgh: T&T Clark, 1998, pp. 113–45.

Cadman, W. H., *The Open Heaven. The Revelation of God in the Johannine Sayings of Jesus*, Oxford: Blackwell, 1969.

Caird, G. B., *Paul's Letters from Prison* (New Clarendon Bible) Oxford: Clarendon Press, 1976.

Capes, David B., *Old Testament Yahweh Texts in Paul's Christology* (WUNT 2, 47), Tübingen: J. C. B. Mohr (Paul Siebeck), 1992.

Carmichael, Calum M., *The Story of Creation. Its Origin and Its Interpretation in Philo and the Fourth Gospel*, Ithaca: Cornell University Press, 1996.

Carson, D. A., *The Gospel According to John*, Leicester: IVP/ Grand Rapids: Eerdmans, 1991.

Carter, Warren, 'The Prologue and John's Gospel: Function, Symbol and the Definitive Word', *JSNT* 39 (1990), 35–58.

Casey, Maurice, *From Jewish Prophet to Gentile God. The Origins and Development of New Testament Christology. The Edward Cadbury Lectures at the University of Birmingham, 1985–86*, Cambridge: James Clarke and Co., 1991.

'The Use of the Term (א)נש(א) בר in the Aramaic Translations of the Hebrew Bible', *JSNT* 54 (1994), 87–118.

Is John's Gospel True?, London: Routledge, 1996.

Charlesworth, James H., 'A Critical Comparison of the Dualism in 1 QS 3:13–4:26 and the "Dualism" Contained in the Gospel of John', in James H. Charlesworth (ed.), *John and the Dead Sea Scrolls*, London: Geoffrey Chapman, 1972, pp. 76–106.

Chilton, Bruce D., 'The Transfiguration: Dominical Assurance and Apostolic Vision', *NTS* 27 (1981), 115–24.

'Typologies of memra and the fourth Gospel', in Paul V. M. Flesher (ed.), *Targum Studies. Volume One: Textual and Contextual Studies in the Pentateuchal Targums* (South Florida Studies in the History of Judaism, 55), Atlanta: Scholars Press, 1992, pp. 89–100.

Cholin, Marc, 'Le Prologue de L'Evangile selon Jean. Structure et Formation', *Science et Esprit* 41/2 (1989), 189–205.

Clarke, Ernest G., 'Jacob's Dream at Bethel as Interpreted in the Targums and the New Testament', *SR* 4 (1974–5), 367–77.

Cohen, Shaye J. D., 'Epigraphical Rabbis', *JQR* n.s. 72 (1981), 1–17.

Collins, Adela Yarbro, 'Crisis and Community in John's Gospel', *TD* 27/4 (Winter 1979), 313–21.

Collins, John J., 'The Son of Man in First-Century Judaism', *NTS* 38 (1992), 448–66.

Coppens, Joseph, *La Relève Apocalyptique du Messianisme Royal. III. Le Fils de l'Homme Néotestamentaire* (BETL, 55), Leuven: Leuven University Press, 1981.

Court, John M., *Revelation* (New Testament Guides), Sheffield: Sheffield Academic Press, 1994.

Creech, Richard Robert, 'Christology and Conflict: A Comparative Study of Two Central Themes in the Johannine Literature and the Apocalypse', PhD dissertation, Baylor University, 1984.

Crossan, John Dominic, *The Historical Jesus. The Life of a Mediterranean Jewish Peasant*, Edinburgh: T&T Clark, 1991.

Cullmann, Oscar, *The Christology of the New Testament*, London: SCM Press, 1959.

The Johannine Circle. Its place in Judaism, among the disciples of Jesus and in early Christianity, London: SCM Press, 1976.

Culpepper, R. Alan, 'The Pivot of John's Prologue', *NTS* 27 (1980–1), 1–31.

Anatomy of the Fourth Gospel. A Study in Literary Design, Minneapolis: Fortress Press, 1983.

Dahl, Nils Alstrup, 'The Johannine Church and History', in John Ashton (ed.), *The Interpretation of John* (IRT, 9), Philadelphia: Fortress Press/London: SPCK, 1986, pp. 122–40.

'"Do Not Wonder!" John 5:28–29 and Johannine Eschatology Once More', in Robert T. Fortna and Beverly R. Gaventa (eds.), *The Conversation Continues. Studies in Paul and John in Honor of J. Louis Martyn*, Nashville: Abingdon Press, 1990, pp. 322–36.

D'Angelo, Mary Rose, *Moses in the Letter to the Hebrews* (SBLDS, 42), Missoula: Scholars Press, 1979.

Daniélou, Jean, *The Theology of Jewish Christianity (A History of early Christian doctrine before the council of Nicaea; v.1)*, London: Darton, Longman and Todd, 1964.

Danna, Elizabeth, 'Which Side of the Line? A study of the characterization of non-Jewish characters in the Gospel of John', PhD dissertation, University of Durham, 1997.

Davies, J. G., *He Ascended into Heaven. A Study in the History of Doctrine* (Bampton Lectures 1958), London: Lutterworth Press, 1958.

Davies, Margaret, *Rhetoric and Reference in the Fourth Gospel* (JSNTS, 69), Sheffield: Sheffield Academic Press, 1992.

Davies, W. D., *Paul and Rabbinic Judaism* (second edition), London: SPCK, 1955.

The Setting of the Sermon on the Mount, Cambridge: Cambridge University Press, 1964.

de Boer, Martinus C., *Johannine Perspectives on the Death of Jesus* (Contributions to Biblical Exegesis and Theology, 17), Kampen: Kok Pharos, 1996.

de Jonge, Marinus, 'Monotheism and Christology', in John Barclay and John Sweet (eds.), *Early Christian Thought in its Jewish Context*, Cambridge University Press, 1996, pp. 225–37.

de la Potterie, Ignace, 'Structure du Prologue de Saint Jean', *NTS* 30 (1984), 354–81.

'«C'est lui qui a ouvert la voie». La finale du prologue johannique', *Biblica* 69 (1988), 340–70.

Dean-Otting, Mary, *Heavenly Journeys. A Study of the Motif in Hellenistic Jewish Literature* (Judentum und Umwelt, 8), Frankfurt am Main: Verlag Peter Lang, 1984.

Denaux, Adelbert, 'The Q-Logion Mt 11,27/Lk 10,22 and the Gospel of John', in Adelbert Denaux (ed.), *John and the Synoptics* (BETL, 101), Leuven: Leuven University Press, 1992, pp. 163–99.

Dewey, Joanna, 'The Literary Structure of the Controversy Stories in Mark 2:1–3:6', in William Telford (ed.), *The Interpretation of Mark* (IRT, 7), London: SPCK, 1985, pp. 109–18.

Dodd, C. H., *The Interpretation of the Fourth Gospel*, Cambridge: Cambridge University Press, 1953.

Historical Tradition in the Fourth Gospel, Cambridge: Cambridge University Press, 1963.

'A Hidden Parable in the Fourth Gospel', *More New Testament Studies*, Manchester: Manchester University Press, 1968, pp. 30–40.

Domeris, Bill, 'Christology and Community: A Study of the Social Matrix of the Fourth Gospel', *Journal of Theology for Southern Africa* 64 (1988), 49–56.

Dowell, Thomas M., 'Jews and Christians in Conflict: Why the Fourth

Gospel Changed the Synoptic Tradition', *Louvain Studies* 15 (1990), 19–37.

'Why John Rewrote the Synoptics', in Adelbert Denaux (ed.), *John and the Synoptics* (BETL, 101), Leuven: Leuven University Press, 1992, pp. 453–7.

Downing, F. Gerald, 'Ontological Asymmetry in Philo and Christological Realism in Paul, Hebrews and John', *JTS* 41/2 (October 1990), 423–40.

Dunn, James D. G., *Baptism in the Holy Spirit. A Re-examination of the New Testament Teaching on the Gift of the Spirit in relation to Pentecostalism today*, London: SCM Press, 1970.

'John VI – A Eucharistic Discourse?', *NTS* 17 (1970–1), 328–38.

'Was Christianity a Monotheistic Faith from the Beginning?', *SJT* 35 (1982), 303–36.

'Some Clarifications on Issues of Method: A Reply to Holliday and Segal', *Semeia* 30 (1984), 97–104.

Romans 1–8, 9–16 (Word Biblical Commentary 38A, 38B; two volumes), Dallas: Word, 1988.

Christology in the Making. An Inquiry into the Origins of the Doctrine of the Incarnation (second edition), London: SCM Press, 1989.

Unity and Diversity in the New Testament. An Inquiry into the Character of Earliest Christianity (second edition), London: SCM Press, 1990.

Jesus, Paul and the Law. Studies in Mark and Galatians, London: SPCK, 1990.

'Let John Be John: A Gospel for Its Time', in Peter Stuhlmacher (ed.), *The Gospel and the Gospels*, Grand Rapids: Eerdmans, 1991, pp. 293–322.

The Partings of the Ways Between Judaism and Christianity and their Significance for the Character of Christianity, London: SCM Press, 1991.

'John and the Oral Gospel Tradition', in Henry Wansbrough (ed.), *Jesus and the Oral Gospel Tradition* (JSNTS, 64), Sheffield: Sheffield Academic Press, 1991, pp. 351–79.

'Christology (NT)', in David N. Freedman (ed.), *The Anchor Bible Dictionary. Vol.I, A–C*, New York: Doubleday, 1992, pp. 978–91.

'Incarnation', in David N. Freedman (ed.), *The Anchor Bible Dictionary. Vol.III, H–J*, New York: Doubleday, 1992, pp. 397–404.

'Christology as an Aspect of Theology', in Abraham J. Malherbe and Wayne A. Meeks (eds.), *The Future of Christology. Essays in Honor of Leander E. Keck*, Minneapolis: Fortress Press, 1993, pp. 202–12.

'The Making of Christology – Evolution or Unfolding?', in Joel B. Green and Max Turner (eds.), *Jesus of Nazareth: Lord and Christ. Essays on the Historical Jesus and New Testament Christology*, Grand Rapids: Eerdmans, 1994, pp. 437–52.

'The Colossian Philosophy: A Confident Jewish Apologia', *Biblica* 76 (1995), 153–81.

The Epistles to the Colossians and to Philemon. A Commentary on the Greek Text (New International Greek Testament Commentary), Grand Rapids: Eerdmans/ Carlisle: Paternoster, 1996.

The Theology of Paul the Apostle, Grand Rapids: Eerdmans/ Edinburgh: T&T Clark, 1998.

Edwards, Ruth B., 'ΧΑΡΙΝ ΑΝΤΙ ΧΑΡΙΤΟΣ (John 1.16): Grace and Law in the Johannine Prologue', JSNT 32 (1988), 3–15.

Ehrman, Bart D., The Orthodox Corruption of Scripture. The Effect of Early Christological Controversy on the Text of the New Testament, Oxford: Oxford University Press, 1993.

Ellis, E. Earle, 'Deity-Christology in Mark 14:58', in Joel B. Green and Max Turner (eds.), Jesus of Nazareth: Lord and Christ. Essays on the Historical Jesus and New Testament Christology, Grand Rapids: Eerdmans, 1994, pp. 192–203.

Eltester, Walther, 'Der Logos und Sein Prophet. Fragen zur heutigen Erklärung des johanneischen Prologs', in Apophoreta. Festschrift für Ernst Haenchen (BZNW, 30), Berlin: Alfred Töpelmann, 1964, pp. 109–34.

Epp, Eldon Jay, 'Wisdom, Torah, Word: The Johannine Prologue and the Purpose of the Fourth Gospel', in Gerald F. Hawthorne (ed.), Current Issues in Biblical and Patristic Interpretation. Studies in Honor of Merrill C. Tenney Presented by his Former Students, Grand Rapids: Eerdmans, 1975, pp. 128–46.

Esler, Philip F., Community and Gospel in Luke-Acts (SNTSMS, 57), Cambridge: Cambridge University Press, 1987.

The First Christians in their Social Worlds. Social-scientific approaches to New Testament interpretation, London and New York: Routledge, 1994.

Evans, Craig A., Word and Glory. On the Exegetical and Theological Background of John's Prologue (JSNTS, 89), Sheffield: Sheffield Academic Press, 1993.

Jesus and His Contemporaries. Comparative Studies (AGAJU, 25), Leiden: E. J. Brill, 1995.

Feuillet, André, 'Les ego eimi christologiques du quatrième Evangile', RSR 54 (1996), 5–22, 213–40.

Fennema, D. A., 'Jesus and God According to John. An Analysis of the Fourth Gospel's Father/Son Christology', PhD dissertation, Duke University, 1979.

'John 1.18: "God the Only Son"', NTS 31 (1985), 124–35.

Fortna, Robert T., The Fourth Gospel and its Predecessor. From Narrative Source to Present Gospel, Philadelphia: Fortress Press, 1988 (Edinburgh: T&T Clark 1989).

Fossum, Jarl E., The Name of God and the Angel of the Lord. Samaritan and Jewish Concepts of Intermediation and the Origin of Gnosticism (WUNT 2, 36), Tübingen: J. C. B. Mohr (Paul Siebeck), 1985.

The Image of the Invisible God. Essays on the Influence of Jewish Mysticism on Early Christology (Novum Testamentum et orbis antiquus, 30), Freiburg: Universitätsverlag Freiberg/ Göttingen: Vandenhoeck & Ruprecht, 1995.

France, R. T., 'The Worship of Jesus: A Neglected Factor in Christological Debate?', in Harold H. Rowdon (ed.), Christ the Lord. Studies in Christology Presented to Donald Guthrie, Leicester: IVP, 1982, pp. 17–36.

Matthew – Evangelist and Teacher, Carlisle: Paternoster Press, 1989.

'Development in New Testament Christology', in William R. Farmer (ed.), *Crisis in Christology. Essays in Quest of Resolution*, Livonia, MN: Dove Booksellers, 1995, pp. 63–82.

Freed, Edwin D., 'Jn 1,19–27 in Light of Related Passages in John, the Synoptics, and Acts', in F. Van Segbroeck, C. M. Tuckett, G. Van Belle and J. Verheyden (eds.), *The Four Gospels 1992. Festschrift Frans Neirynck. Volume 3* (BETL, 100), Leuven: Leuven University Press, 1992, pp. 1943–61.

Freyne, Sean, 'Vilifying the Other and Defining the Self: Matthew's and John's Anti-Jewish Polemic in Focus', in Jacob Neusner and Ernest S. Frerichs (eds.), *'To See Ourselves as Others See Us'. Christians, Jews, 'Others' in Late Antiquity*, Chico, CA: Scholars Press, 1985, pp. 117–43.

Fuller, Reginald H., *The Foundations of New Testament Christology*, New York: Scribners, 1965.

'The Incarnation in Historical Perspective', in W. Taylor Stevenson (ed.), *Theology and Culture. Essays in Honor of A. T. Mollegen and C. L. Stanley* (Anglican Theological Review Supplementary Series, 7), November 1976, pp. 57–66.

'Lower and Higher Christology in the Fourth Gospel', in R. T. Fortna and B. R. Gaventa (eds.), *The Conversation Continues. Studies in Paul and John in Honor of J. Louis Martyn*, Nashville: Abingdon Press, 1990, pp. 357–65.

Garnet, Paul, 'Jesus and the Exilic Soteriology', in E. A. Livingstone (ed.), *Studia Biblica 1978, II* (JSNTS, 2), Sheffield: Sheffield Academic Press, 1980.

Gaston, Lloyd, 'Lobsters in the Fourth Gospel', in Jacob Neusner (ed.), *Approaches to Ancient Judaism. New Series. Volume IV*, Atlanta: Scholars Press, 1993, pp. 115–23.

Gese, Hartmut, 'Wisdom, Son of Man, and the Origins of Christology: The Consistent Development of Biblical Theology', *HBT* 3 (1981), 23–57.

Ginzberg, L., 'Elisha ben Abuyah', *Jewish Encyclopaedia* V (1903), pp. 138–9.

Glasson, T. Francis, *Moses in the Fourth Gospel* (SBT, 40), London: SCM Press, 1963.

Gnilka, Joachim, *Johannesevangelium* (Die Neue Echter-Bibel), Würzburg: Echter Verlag, 1983.

Goldstein, Jonathan A., 'Jewish Acceptance and Rejection of Hellenism', in E. P. Sanders, A. I. Baumgarten and Alan Mendelson (eds.), *Jewish and Christian Self-Definition. Volume 2: Aspects of Judaism in the Greco-Roman Period*, London: SCM Press, 1981, pp. 64–87.

Goodenough, Erwin R., *Jewish Symbols in the Greco-Roman Period* (edited and abridged by Jacob Neusner from the original 13 volumes) (Mythos: The Princeton/Bollingen Series in World Mythology, 37), Princeton: Princeton University Press, 1988.

Goulder, Michael, 'The Two Roots of the Christian Myth', in John Hick (ed.), *The Myth of God Incarnate*, London: SCM Press, 1977, pp. 64–86.

Grabbe, Lester L., 'Orthodoxy in First Century Judaism. What Are the Issues?', *JSJ* 8/2 (1977), 149–53.

Grant, Robert M., *Gods and the One God*, Philadelphia: Westminster, 1986.

Grayston, Kenneth, *The Gospel of John* (Epworth Commentaries), London: Epworth Press, 1990.

Grese, William C., '"Unless One is Born Again": The Use of a Heavenly Journey in John 3', *JBL* 107 (1988), 677–93.

Grossfeld, Bernard, *The Targum Onqelos to Genesis* (The Aramaic Bible, 6), Edinburgh: T&T Clark, 1988.

Gruenwald, Ithamar, *From Apocalypticism to Gnosticism* (Beiträge zur Erforschung des Alten Testaments und des antiken Judentums, 14), Frankfurt am Main: Peter Lang, 1988.

Guthrie, Donald, *New Testament Theology*, Leicester: IVP, 1981.

Hebrews (Tyndale NT Commentaries), Leicester: IVP, 1983.

Habermann, Jürgen, *Präexistenzaussagen im Neuen Testament* (Europäische Hochschulschriften, Reihe 23 Theologie, Bd.362), Frankfurt am Main: Peter Lang, 1990.

Haenchen, Ernst, *John* (Hermeneia; two volumes), Philadelphia: Fortress Press, 1984.

Hagner, Donald A., 'Paul's Christology and Jewish Monotheism', in Marguerite Shuster and Richard A. Muller (eds.), *Perspectives on Christology: Essays in Honor of Paul K. Jewett*, Grand Rapids: Zondervan, 1991, pp. 19–38.

Halperin, David J., *The Merkabah in Rabbinic Literature* (American Oriental Series, 62), New Haven: American Oriental Society, 1980.

Hamerton-Kelly, R. G., *Pre-Existence, Wisdom, and the Son of Man. A Study in the Idea of Pre-Existence in the New Testament* (SNTSMS, 21), Cambridge: Cambridge University Press, 1973.

Hanson, Anthony Tyrell, *Jesus Christ in the Old Testament*, London: SPCK, 1965.

The New Testament Interpretation of Scripture, London: SPCK, 1980.

The Prophetic Gospel. A Study of John and the Old Testament, Edinburgh: T&T Clark, 1991.

Hanson, R. P. C., *The Search for the Christian Doctrine of God: the Arian Controversy 318–381*, Edinburgh: T&T Clark, 1988.

Hare, Douglas R. A., *The Son of Man Tradition*, Minneapolis: Fortress Press, 1990.

Harner, Philip B., *The 'I Am' of the Fourth Gospel* (Facet Books – Biblical Series, 26), Philadelphia: Fortress Press, 1970.

Harrington, Daniel J., *John's Thought and Theology. An Introduction* (Good News Studies, 33), Wilmington, DE: Michael Glazier, 1990.

Harris, Elizabeth, *Prologue and Gospel. The Theology of the Fourth Evangelist* (JSNTS, 107), Sheffield: Sheffield Academic Press, 1994.

Harris, Murray J., *Jesus as God. The New Testament Use of Theos in Reference to Jesus*, Grand Rapids: Baker Book House, 1992.

Hartin, P. J., 'A Community in Crisis. The Christology of the Johannine Community as the Point at Issue', *Neotestamentica* 19 (1985), 37–49.

Hartman, Lars, 'Johannine Jesus-Belief and Monotheism', in L. Hartman and B. Olsson (eds.), *Aspects of the Johannine Literature* (Coniecteanea Biblica, NT Series, 18), Stockholm: Almqvist and Wiksell International, 1987, pp. 85–99.

Harvey, A. E., *Jesus on Trial. A Study in the Fourth Gospel*, London: SPCK, 1976.

Jesus and the Constraints of History. The Bampton Lectures, 1980, London: Duckworth, 1982.

'Christ as Agent', in L. D. Hurst and N. T. Wright (eds.), *The Glory of Christ in the New Testament*, Oxford: Clarendon Press, 1987, pp. 239–50.

Harvey, Graham, *The True Israel. Uses of the Names Jew, Hebrew and Israel in Ancient Jewish and Early Christian Literature* (AGAJU, 35), Leiden: E. J. Brill, 1996.

Hay, David M., *Glory at the Right Hand. Psalm 110 in Early Christianity*, Nashville: Abingdon Press, 1973.

Hayman, Peter, 'Monotheism – A Misused Word in Jewish Studies?', *JJS* 42 (1991), 1–15.

Hayward, C. T. R., 'The Holy Name of the God of Moses and the Prologue of St. John's Gospel', *NTS* 25/1 (1978), 16–32.

Hengel, Martin, *Judaism and Hellenism. Studies in their Encounter in Palestine during the Early Hellenistic Period*, London: SCM Press, 1974.

Between Jesus and Paul. Studies in the Earliest History of Christianity, London: SCM Press, 1983.

The Johannine Question, London: SCM Press/ Philadelphia: Trinity Press International, 1989.

The 'Hellenization' of Judaea in the First Century after Christ, London: SCM Press, 1989.

Studies in Early Christology, Edinburgh: T&T Clark, 1995.

Higgins, A. J. B., *Jesus and the Son of Man*, London: Lutterworth Press, 1964.

Hill, David, *The Gospel of Matthew* (New Century Bible Commentary), Grand Rapids: Eerdmans/ London: Marshall, Morgan and Scott, 1972.

Hofius, Otfried, 'Struktur und Gedankengang des Logos-Hymnus in Joh 1 1–18', *ZNW* 78 (1987), 1–25.

'»Der in des Vaters Schoß ist« Joh 1,18', *ZNW* 80 (1989), 163–171.

Hofrichter, Peter, 'Logoslehre und Gottesbild bei Apologeten, Modalisten und Gnostikern. Johanneische Christologie im Lichte ihrer frühesten Rezeption', in Hans-Josef Klauck (ed.), *Monotheismus und Christologie. Zur Gottesfrage im Hellenistischen Judentum und im Urchristentum* (Quaestiones Disputatae, 138), Freiberg: Herder, 1992, pp. 186–217.

Holmberg, Bengt, *Sociology and the New Testament. An Appraisal*, Minneapolis: Fortress Press, 1990.

Hooker, Morna D., 'Were There False Teachers in Colossae?', in Barnabas Lindars and Stephen S. Smalley (eds.), *Christ and Spirit in the New Testament. Studies in Honour of C. F. D. Moule*, Cambridge: Cambridge University Press, 1973, pp. 315–31.

From Adam to Christ. Essays on Paul, Cambridge: Cambridge University Press, 1990.

Howard, George, 'Phil 2:6–11 and the Human Christ', *CBQ* 40 (1978), 368–87.

Hurst, L. D., 'The Christology of Hebrews 1 and 2', in L. D. Hurst and N. T. Wright (eds.), *The Glory of Christ in the New Testament. Studies in Christology in Memory of G. B. Caird*, Oxford: Clarendon Press, 1987, pp. 151–64.

Hurtado, Larry W., *One God, One Lord. Early Christian Devotion and Ancient Jewish Monotheism*, London: SCM Press, 1988.

'What Do We Mean by "First-Century Jewish Monotheism"?', in Eugene M. Lovering, Jr. (ed.), *SBL 1993 Seminar Papers*, Atlanta: Scholars Press, 1993, pp. 348–68.

'Christ-Devotion in the First Two Centuries: Reflections and a Proposal', *Toronto Journal of Theology* 12/1 (1996), 17–33.

Isaac, E., '1 (Ethiopic Apocalypse of) ENOCH', in James H. Charlesworth (ed.), *The Old Testament Pseudepigrapha, vol. I*, New York: Doubleday, 1983, pp. 5–89.

Johnson, Luke T., 'The New Testament's Anti-Jewish Slander and the Conventions of Ancient Polemic', *JBL* 108 (1989), 419–41.

Johnson, Marshall D., 'Reflections on a Wisdom Approach to Matthew's Christology', *CBQ* 36 (1974), 44–64.

Kanagaraj, Jeyaseelan Joseph, *'Mysticism' in the Gospel of John: An Inquiry into its Background* (JSNTS, 158), Sheffield: Sheffield Academic Press, 1998.

Katz, Steven T., 'Issues in the Separation of Judaism and Christianity After 70 CE: A Reconsideration', *JBL* 103/1 (1984), 43–76.

Kimelman, Reuven, 'Birkat Ha-Minim and the Lack of Evidence for an Anti-Christian Jewish Prayer in Late Antiquity', in E. P. Sanders, A. I. Baumgarten and Alan Mendelson (eds.), *Jewish and Christian Self-Definition. Volume Two. Aspects of Judaism in the Graeco-Roman Period*, London: SCM Press, 1981, pp. 226–44.

Klausner, Joseph, *The Messianic Idea in Israel from Its Beginning to the Completion of the Mishnah*, London: George Allen and Unwin, 1956.

Koester, Craig R., *Symbolism in the Fourth Gospel. Meaning, Mystery, Community*, Minneapolis: Fortress Press, 1995.

Kooy, Vernon H., 'The Transfiguration Motif in the Gospel of John', in James I. Cook (ed.), *Saved by Hope. Essays in Honor of Richard C. Oudersluys*, Grand Rapids: Eerdmans, 1978, pp. 64–78.

Kovacs, Judith L., '"Now Shall the Ruler of this World be Driven Out": Jesus' Death as Cosmic Battle in John 12:20–36', *JBL* 114/2 (1995), 227–47.

Kreitzer, Larry J., *Jesus and God in Paul's Eschatology* (JSNTS, 19), Sheffield: Sheffield Academic Press, 1987.

'Eschatology', in Gerald F. Hawthorne, Ralph P. Martin and Daniel G. Reid (eds.), *Dictionary of Paul and His Letters*, Leicester: IVP, 1993, pp. 253–69.

Kysar, Robert, 'Christology and Controversy: The Contributions of the Prologue of the Gospel of John to New Testament Christology and their Historical Setting', *CTM* 5 (1978), 348–64.

'The Fourth Gospel. A Report on Recent Research', *ANRW* 2.25.3, Berlin: Walter de Gruyter, 1985, pp. 2389–480.

'Pursuing the Paradoxes of Johannine Thought: Conceptual Tensions in John 6. A Redaction-Critical Proposal', in Dennis E. Groh and Robert Jewett (eds.), *The Living Text: Essays in Honor of Ernest W. Saunders*, Lanham, MD: University Press of America, 1985, pp. 189–206.

Lamarche, Paul, 'The Prologue of John', in John Ashton (ed.), *The Interpretation of John* (IRT, 9), Philadelphia: Fortress Press/ London: SPCK, 1986, pp. 36–52.

Lang, Bernard, *Sacred Games: A History of Christian Worship*, New Haven and London: Yale University Press, 1997.

Lataire, Bianca, 'The Son on the Father's Lap. The Meaning of εἰς τὸν κόλπον in John 1:18', *SNTU* 22 (1997), 125–38.

Légasse, S., 'Le logion sur le Fils révélateur (Mt., XI, 27 par. Lc., X, 22): Essai d'analyse prérédactionnelle', in J. Coppens (ed.), *La Notion biblique de Dieu: Le Dieu de la Bible et le Dieu des philosophes* (BETL, 41), Leuven: Leuven University Press, 1976, pp. 245–74.

Leivestad, Ragnar, 'Exit the Apocalyptic Son of Man', *NTS* 18 (1972), 243–267.

Létourneau, Pierre, 'Le Quatrième Evangile et les Prédictions de la Passion dans les Evangiles Synoptiques', in Adelbert Denaux (ed.), *John and the Synoptics* (BETL, 101), Leuven: Leuven University Press, 1992, pp. 579–86.

Jésus, Fils de L'Homme et Fils de Dieu: Jean 2,23–3,36 et la double christologie johannique (Recherches Nouvelle Série 27), Montreal: Bellarmin/ Paris: Cerf, 1993.

Levinskaya, Irina, *The Book of Acts in Its First Century Setting. Volume V. The Book of Acts in Its Diaspora Setting*, Grand Rapids: Eerdmans/ Carlisle: Paternoster, 1996.

Levison, John R., *Portraits of Adam in Early Judaism. From Sirach to 2 Baruch* (JSPS, 1), Sheffield: JSOT/Sheffield Academic Press, 1988.

Lieu, Judith, *The Theology of the Johannine Epistles* (New Testament Theology), Cambridge: Cambridge University Press, 1991.

Lightfoot, R. H., *St. John's Gospel: A Commentary*, Oxford: Oxford University Press, 1956.

Lincoln, Andrew T., 'Trials, Plots and the Narrative of the Fourth Gospel', *JSNT* 56 (1994), 3–30.

Lindars, Barnabas, *The Gospel of John*, Grand Rapids: Eerdmans/ London: Marshall, Morgan and Scott, 1972.

'The Son of Man in the Johannine christology', in Barnabas Lindars and Stephen S. Smalley (eds.), *Christ and Spirit in the New Testament*, Cambridge: Cambridge University Press, 1973, pp. 43–60.

'Traditions Behind the Fourth Gospel', in M. de Jonge (ed.), *L'Evangile de Jean. Sources, rédaction, théologie* (BETL, 44), Leuven: Leuven University Press, 1977, pp. 107–124.

Loader, William R. G., 'The Central Structure of Johannine Christology', *NTS* 30 (1984), 188–216.

'John 1:50–51 and the "Greater Things" of Johannine Christology', in

Cilliers Breytenbach and Henning Paulsen (eds.), *Anfänge der Christologie. Festschrift für Ferdinand Hahn zum 65. Geburtstag*, Göttingen: Vandenhoeck and Ruprecht, 1991, pp. 255–74.

The Christology of the Fourth Gospel. Structure and Issues (BET, 23; second edition), Frankfurt am Main: Peter Lang, 1992.

Lohse, E., 'ῥαββι', in Gerhard Friedrich, ed., *Theological Dictionary of the New Testament* (trans. and ed. Geoffrey W. Bromiley; 10 vols.; Grand Rapids: Eerdmans, 1964–76), VI, pp. 961–5.

Louth, Andrew, *The Origins of the Christian Mystical Tradition. From Plato to Denys*, Oxford: Clarendon Press, 1981.

Luz, Ulrich, *The Theology of the Gospel of Matthew* (New Testament Theology), Cambridge: Cambridge University Press, 1995.

MacGregor, G. H. C., *The Gospel of John* (Moffat New Testament Commentary), London: Hodder and Stoughton, 1928.

Maile, J. F., 'Heaven, Heavenlies, Paradise', in Gerald F. Hawthorne, Ralph P. Martin and Daniel G. Reid (eds.), *Dictionary of Paul and His Letters*, Leicester: IVP, 1993, pp. 381–3.

Malina, Bruce J., *The New Testament World. Insights from Cultural Anthropology*, Atlanta: John Knox Press, 1981.

Windows on the World of Jesus. Time Travel to Ancient Judea, Louisville: Westminster John Knox Press, 1993.

Manns, Frédéric, *John and Jamnia: How the Break Occurred Between Jews and Christians c. 80–100 A.D.*, Jerusalem: Franciscan Printing Press, 1988.

L'Evangile de Jean à la lumière du Judaisme (Studium Biblicum Franciscanum Analecta N.33), Jerusalem: Franciscan Printing Press, 1991.

Marcus, Joel, *The Way of the Lord. Christological Exegesis of the Old Testament in the Gospel of Mark*, Louisville: Westminster John Knox/ Edinburgh: T&T Clark, 1992.

Marsh, John, *The Gospel of St. John* (Pelican New Testament Commentaries), Harmondsworth: Penguin, 1968.

Marshall, I. Howard, 'The Development of Christology in the Early Church', *Tyndale Bulletin* 18 (1967), 77–93.

The Origins of New Testament Christology (updated edition), Leicester: Apollos/IVP, 1990.

Martin, Dale B., 'Social-Scientific Criticism', in Steven L. McKenzie and Stephen R. Haynes (eds.), *To Each Its Own Meaning. An Introduction to Biblical Criticisms and their Application*, Louisville: Westminster John Knox/ London: Geoffrey Chapman, 1993, pp. 103–19.

Martyn, J. Louis, 'Glimpses into the History of the Johannine Community', in M. de Jonge (ed.), *L'Evangile de Jean. Sources, rédaction, théologie* (BETL, 44), Leuven: Leuven University Press, 1977, pp. 149–75.

History and Theology in the Fourth Gospel (Second edition), Nashville: Abingdon Press, 1979.

'A Gentile Mission That Replaced an Earlier Jewish Mission?', in R. Alan Culpepper and C. Clifton Black (eds.), *Exploring the Gospel of John. In Honor of D. Moody Smith*, Louisville: Westminster John Knox, 1996, pp. 124–44.

Mastin, B. A., 'A Neglected Feature of the Christology of the Fourth Gospel', *NTS* 22 (1975), 32–51.

May, Gerhard, *Creatio ex Nihilo. The Doctrine of 'Creation out of Nothing' in Early Christian Thought*, Edinburgh: T&T Clark, 1994.

McEleney, Neil J., 'Orthodoxy in Judaism of the First Christian Century: Replies to David E. Aune and Lester L. Grabbe', *JSJ* 9/1 (1978), 83–8.

McGrath, James F., 'Johannine Christianity – Jewish Christianity?', *Koinonia Journal* 8/1 (1996), 1–20.

'Food for Thought: The Bread of Life Discourse (John 6:25–71) in Johannine Legitimation', *Theological Gathering* 2 (Winter 1997) [http://private.fuller.edu/~talarm/iss2/iss2a4.html].

'Uncontrived Messiah or Passover Plot? A Study of a Johannine Apologetic Motif', *IBS* 19 (1997), 2–16.

'Prologue as Legitimation: Christological Controversy and the Interpretation of John 1:1–18', *IBS* 19 (1997), 98–120.

'Going up and coming down in Johannine legitimation', *Neotestamentica* 31/1 (1997), 107–18.

'Change in Christology: New Testament Models and the Contemporary Task', *ITQ* 63/1 (1998), 39–50.

'A Rebellious Son? Hugo Odeberg and the Interpretation of John 5.18', *NTS* 44 (1998), 470–3.

'Christology on Two Fronts: A New Testament Model for Doing Christology in a Pluralistic Context', *Religion and Theology* 6/1 (1999), 65–82.

McNamara, Martin, *The New Testament and the Palestinian Targum to the Pentateuch* (Analecta Biblica, 27), Rome: Pontifical Biblical Institute, 1966.

Targum and Testament. Aramaic Paraphrases of the Hebrew Bible: A Light on the New Testament, Shannon: Irish University Press, 1972.

McReynolds, Paul R., 'John 1:18 in Textual Variation and Translation', in Eldon Jay Epp and Gordon D. Fee (eds.), *New Testament Criticism: Its Significance for Exegesis. Essays in Honour of Bruce M. Metzger*, Oxford: Clarendon Press, 1981, pp. 105–30.

Mealand, David L., 'The Christology of the Fourth Gospel', *SJT* 31 (1978), 449–67.

Meeks, Wayne A., *The Prophet-King. Moses Traditions and the Johannine Christology* (NovTSup, 14), Leiden: E. J. Brill, 1967.

'Moses as God and King', in Jacob Neusner (ed.), *Religions in Antiquity: Essays in Memory of E. R. Goodenough* (Numen Supplement, 14), Leiden: E. J. Brill, 1968, pp. 354–71.

'"Am I A Jew?" – Johannine Christianity and Judaism', in Jacob Neusner (ed.), *Christianity, Judaism and Other Greco-Roman Cults. Studies for Morton Smith at Sixty. Part One: New Testament* (SJLA, 12), Leiden: E. J. Brill, 1975, pp. 163–86.

'The Divine Agent and His Counterfeit in Philo and the Fourth Gospel', in Elizabeth Schüssler Fiorenza (ed.), *Aspects of Religious Propaganda in Judaism and Early Christianity*, Notre Dame: University of Notre Dame Press, 1976, pp. 43–67.

'Breaking Away: Three New Testament Pictures of Christianity's

Separation from the Jewish Communities', in Jacob Neusner and Ernest S. Frerichs (eds.), *'To See Ourselves as Others See Us'. Christians, Jews, 'Others' in Late Antiquity*, Chico, CA: Scholars Press, 1985, pp. 93–115.

'The Man from Heaven in Johannine Sectarianism', in John Ashton (ed.), *The Interpretation of John* (IRT, 9), Philadelphia: Fortress Press/ London: SPCK, 1986, pp. 141–73.

'Equal to God', in Robert T. Fortna and Beverly R. Gaventa (eds.), *The Conversation Continues. Studies in Paul and John in Honor of J. Louis Martyn*, Nashville: Abingdon Press, 1990, pp. 309–21.

Menken, Maarten J. J., 'The Christology of the Fourth Gospel: A Survey of Recent Research', in Martinus C. de Boer (ed.), *From Jesus to John. Essays on Jesus and New Testament Christology in Honour of Marinus de Jonge* (JSNTS, 84), Sheffield: Sheffield Academic Press, 1993, pp. 292–320.

Old Testament Quotations in the Fourth Gospel. Studies in Textual Form (Contributions to Biblical Exegesis and Theology, 15), Kampen: Kok Pharos, 1996.

'The Use of the Septuagint in Three Quotations in John. Jn 10,34; 12,38; 19,24', in Christopher M. Tuckett (ed.), *The Scriptures in the Gospels* (BETL, 131), Leuven: Leuven University Press, 1997, pp. 367–93.

Mercer, Calvin, 'Jesus the Apostle: "Sending" and the Theology of John', *JETS* 35/4 (December 1992), 457–62.

Metzger, Bruce M., 'The Punctuation of Rom. 9:5', in Barnabas Lindars and Stephen S. Smalley (eds.), *Christ and Spirit in the New Testament*, Cambridge: Cambridge University Press, 1973, pp. 95–112.

Meyer, Rudolf, 'κόλπος', *TDNT* III, pp. 824–6.

Michaels, J. Ramsey, *John* (New International Biblical Commentary), Peabody, MA: Hendrickson, 1984.

Milbank, John, *Theology and Social Theory. Beyond Secular Reason*, Oxford: Basil Blackwell, 1990.

Minear, Paul S., 'Diversity and Unity: A Johannine Case Study', in Ulrich Luz and Hans Weder (eds.), *Die Mitte des Neuen Testaments. Einheit und Vielfalt neutestamentlicher Theologie. Festschrift für Eduard Schweizer zum siebzigsten Geburtstag*, Göttingen: Vandenhoeck and Ruprecht, 1983, pp. 162–75.

'Logos Affiliations in Johannine Thought', in Robert F. Berkey and Sarah A. Edwards (eds.), *Christology in Dialogue*, Cleveland: The Pilgrim Press, 1993, pp. 142–56.

Mitchell, Margaret M., 'New Testament Envoys in the Context of Greco-Roman Diplomatic and Epistolary Conventions: The Example of Timothy and Titus', *JBL* 111/4 (1992), 641–62.

Moeller, Henry R., 'Wisdom Motifs in John's Gospel', *Bulletin of the Evangelical Theological Society* 6 (1963), 92–100.

Moloney, Francis J., 'The Fourth Gospel's Presentation of Jesus as "The Christ" and J. A. T. Robinson's Redating', *Downside Review* 95 (1977), 239–53.

The Johannine Son of Man (Biblioteca di Scienze Religiose, 14; second edition), Rome: LAS, 1978.

'Johannine Theology', in Raymond E. Brown, Joseph A. Fitzmyer and Roland E. Murphy (eds.), *New Jerome Biblical Commentary*, London: Geoffrey Chapman, 1989, pp. 1417–26.

Signs and Shadows: Reading John 5–12, Minneapolis: Fortress Press, 1996.

Moore, George Foot, *Judaism in the First Centuries of the Christian Era. The Age of the Tannaim. Volume I*, Cambridge, MA: Harvard University Press, 1927.

Morgan-Wynne, J. E., 'The Cross and the Revelation of Jesus as εγω ειμι in the Fourth Gospel', in E. A. Livingstone (ed.), *Studia Biblica 1978: II. Papers on the Gospels. Sixth International Congress on Biblical Studies. Oxford 3–7 April 1978* (JSNTS, 2), Sheffield: JSOT, 1980, pp. 219–26.

Morgen, Michèle, *Afin Que Le Monde Soit Sauvé* (Lectio Divina, 154), Paris: Cerf, 1993.

Moses, A. D. A., *Matthew's Transfiguration Story and Jewish-Christian Controversy* (JSNTS, 122), Sheffield: Sheffield Academic Press, 1996.

Moule, C. F. D., *The Origin of Christology*, Cambridge: Cambridge University Press, 1977.

Müller, Mogens, *Der Ausdruck 'Menschensohn' in den Evangelien* (Acta Theologica Danica, 17), Leiden: E. J. Brill, 1984.

'"Have You Faith in the Son of Man?"' (John 9.35)', *NTS* 37 (1991), 291–4.

Neirynck, Frans, 'John and the Synoptics: 1975–1990', in Adelbert Denaux (ed.), *John and the Synoptics* (BETL, 101), Leuven: Leuven University Press, 1992, pp. 3–62.

Neusner, Jacob, *Judaic Law from Jesus to the Mishnah. A Systematic Reply to Professor E. P. Sanders* (South Florida Studies in the History of Judaism 84), Atlanta: Scholars Press, 1993.

Neyrey, Jerome, 'The Jacob Allusions in John 1:51', *CBQ* 44 (1982), 586–605.

Christ is Community: The Christologies of the New Testament (Good News Studies, 13), Wilmington, DE: Michael Glazier, 1985.

'"My Lord and My God": The Divinity of Jesus in John's Gospel', *SBL Seminar Paper Series*, 25, Atlanta: Scholars Press, 1986, pp. 152–71.

An Ideology of Revolt. John's Christology in Social-Science Perspective, Philadelphia: Fortress Press, 1988.

'"I Said: You are Gods": Psalm 82:6 and John 10', *JBL* 108/4 (1989), 647–63.

Nicholson, Godfrey C., *Death as Departure: The Johannine Descent-Ascent Schema* (SBLDS, 63), Chico, CA: Scholars Press, 1983.

Nicol, W., *The Semeia in the Fourth Gospel. Tradition and Redaction* (NovTSup, 32), Leiden: E. J. Brill, 1972.

Nilsson, Martin P., 'The High God and the Mediator', *HTR* 56/2 (1963), 101–20.

Nineham, Dennis E., *Saint Mark* (Pelican Gospel Commentaries), Harmondsworth: Penguin, 1963.

O'Brien, Peter T., *Colossians, Philemon* (Word Biblical Commentary, 44), Dallas: Word, 1982.

Odeberg, Hugo, *The Fourth Gospel Interpreted in its Relation to Contemporaneous Religious Currents in Palestine and the Hellenistic-Oriental World*, Uppsala/Chicago: Argonaut Publishers, 1929.

Overman, J. Andrew, *Matthew's Gospel and Formative Judaism. The Social World of the Matthean Community*, Minneapolis: Fortress Press, 1990.

Pagels, Elaine, *The Gnostic Gospels*, London: Penguin, 1979.

Painter, John, 'Christology and the History of the Johannine Community in the Prologue of the Fourth Gospel', *NTS* 30 (1984), 460–74.

'The Enigmatic Johannine Son of Man', in F. Van Segbroeck, C. M. Tuckett, G. Van Belle and J. Verheyden (eds.), *The Four Gospels 1992. Festschrift Frans Neirynck. Volume 3* (BETL, 100), Leuven: Leuven University Press, 1992, pp. 1869–87.

The Quest for the Messiah. The History, Literature and Theology of the Johannine Community (second edition), Edinburgh: T&T Clark, 1993.

Pamment, Margaret, 'Is There Convincing Evidence of Samaritan Influence on the Fourth Gospel?', *ZNW* 73 (1982), 221–30.

'The Son of Man in the Fourth Gospel', *JTS* n.s. 36 (1985), 56–66.

Pancaro, Severino, *The Law in the Fourth Gospel. The Torah and the Gospel, Moses and Jesus, Judaism and Christianity according to John* (NovTSup, 42), Leiden: E. J. Brill, 1975.

Perkins, Pheme, 'The Gospel According to John', in Raymond E. Brown, Joseph A. Fitzmyer and Roland E. Murphy (eds.), *New Jerome Biblical Commentary*, London: Geoffrey Chapman, 1989, pp. 942–85.

Phillips, W. Gary, 'An Apologetic Study of John 10:34–36', *Bibliotheca Sacra* 146 (1989), 405–19.

Price, James L., 'Light from Qumran on Some Aspects of Johannine Theology', in James H. Charlesworth (ed.), *John and the Dead Sea Scrolls*, London: Geoffrey Chapman, 1972, pp. 9–37.

Pryor, John W., 'Jesus and Israel in the Fourth Gospel – John 1:11', *NovT* 32/3 (1990), 201–18.

'The Johannine Son of Man and the Descent-Ascent Motif', *JETS* 34/3 (1991), 341–51.

John: Evangelist of the Covenant People, Downers Grove, IL: IVP, 1992.

Rainbow, Paul A., 'Jewish Monotheism as the Matrix for New Testament Christology: A Review Article', *NovT* 33/1 (1991), 78–91.

Renner, George L., 'The Life-World of the Johannine Community: An Investigation of the Social Dynamics which Resulted in the Composition of the Fourth Gospel', PhD dissertation, Boston University Graduate School, 1982.

Rensberger, David, *Overcoming the World: Politics and Community in the Gospel of John*, London: SPCK, 1989 (first published as *Johannine Faith and Liberating Community*, Philadelphia: Westminster Press, 1988).

Rhea, Robert, *The Johannine Son of Man* (AThANT, 76), Theologischer Verlag Zürich, 1990.

Richter, Philip J., 'Recent Sociological Approaches to the Study of the New Testament', *Religion* 14 (1984), 77–90.

Riniker, Christian, 'Jean 6,1–21 et les Evangiles Synoptiques', in Jean-Daniel Kaestli, Jean-Michel Poffet and Jean Zumstein (eds.), *La*

Communauté Johannique et Son Histoire. La trajectoire de l'evangile de Jean aux deux premiers siècles (Le Monde de la Bible), Geneva: Labor et Fides, 1990, pp. 41–67.

Robinson, John A. T., 'The Destination and Purpose of St. John's Gospel', *NTS* 6 (1959–60), 117–31.

Twelve More New Testament Studies, London: SCM Press, 1984.

The Priority of John, London: SCM Press, 1985.

Roth, Wolfgang, 'Jesus as the Son of Man: The Scriptural Identity of a Johannine Image', in Dennis E. Groh and Robert Jewett (eds.), *The Living Text: Essays in Honor of Ernest W. Saunders*, Lanham, MD: University Press of America, 1985, pp. 11–26.

Rowland, Christopher, 'John 1.51, Jewish Apocalyptic and Targumic Tradition', *NTS* 30 (1984), 498–507.

Christian Origins. An Account of the Setting and Character of the Most Important Messianic Sect of Judaism, London: SPCK, 1985.

Ruckstuhl, E., 'Die Speisung des Volkes durch Jesus und die Seeüberfahrt der Jünger nach Joh 6,1–25 im Vergleich zu den Synoptischen Parallelen', in F. van Segbroeck, C. M. Tuckett, G. van Belle and J. Verheyden (eds.), *The Four Gospels 1992. Festschrift Frans Neirynck. Volume 3* (BETL, 100), Leuven: Leuven University Press, 1992, pp. 2001–19.

Sabbe, Maurits, *Studia Neotestamentica. Collected Essays* (BETL, 98), Leuven: Leuven University Press, 1991.

Sanders, E. P., *Paul and Palestinian Judaism*, London: SCM Press, 1977.

'Testament of Abraham', in James H. Charlesworth (ed.), *The Old Testament Pseudepigrapha. Volume I: Apocalyptic Literature and Testaments*, New York: Doubleday, 1983, pp. 871–902.

Jesus and Judaism, London: SCM Press, 1985.

Jewish Law from Jesus to the Mishnah. Five Studies, London: SCM Press/ Philadelphia: Trinity Press International, 1990.

Judaism: Practice and Belief 63 BCE-66 CE, London: SCM Press/ Philadelphia: Trinity Press International, 1992.

Sanders, J. N., *The Fourth Gospel in the Early Church. Its Origin and Influence on Christian Theology up to Irenaeus*, Cambridge: Cambridge University Press, 1943.

The Gospel According to Saint John, ed. B. A. Mastin (Black's New Testament Commentaries), London: A&C Black, 1968.

Sanders, Jack T., *Schismatics, Sectarians, Dissidents, Deviants. The First One Hundred Years of Jewish–Christian Relations*, London: SCM Press, 1993.

Schaberg, Jane, 'Daniel 7,12 and the New Testament Passion-Resurrection Predictions', *NTS* 31 (1985), 208–22.

Schelkle, Karl Hermann, 'Jesus – Lehrer und Prophet', in Paul Hoffmann, N. Brox and W. Pesch (eds.), *Orientierung an Jesus. Zur Theologie der Synoptiker. Für Josef Schmid*, Freiberg: Herder, 1973, pp. 300–8.

Schimanowski, Gottfried, *Weisheit und Messias. Die jüdischen Voraussetzungen der urchristlichen Präexistenzchristologie* (WUNT 2, 17), Tübingen: J. C. B. Mohr (Paul Siebeck), 1985.

Schnabel, Eckhard J., *Law and Wisdom from Ben Sira to Paul: A Tradition*

Historical Enquiry into the Relation of Law, Wisdom, and Ethics (WUNT 2, 16), Tübingen: J. C. B. Mohr (Paul Siebeck), 1985.

Schnackenburg, Rudolf, *The Gospel According to St. John. Volume I*, London: Burns and Oates, 1968.

The Gospel According to St. John. Volume II, London: Burns and Oates, 1980.

Das Johannesevangelium. IV. Teil. Ergänzende Auslegungen und Exkurse (HTKNT, 4.4), Freiburg: Herder, 1984.

'Synoptische und Johanneische Christologie. Ein Vergleich', in F. van Segbroeck, C. M. Tuckett, G. van Belle and J. Verheyden (eds.), *The Four Gospels 1992. Festschrift Frans Neirynck. Volume III* (BETL, 100), Leuven: Leuven University Press, 1992, pp. 1723–50.

Schnelle, Udo, *Antidocetic Christology in the Gospel of John. An Investigation of the Place of the Fourth Gospel in the Johannine School*, Minneapolis: Fortress Press, 1992.

Schnider, Franz, *Jesus der Prophet* (Orbis Biblicus et Orientalis, 2), Universitätsverlag Freiberg Schweiz/ Göttingen: Vandenhoeck & Ruprecht, 1973.

Schoonenberg, Piet, 'A sapiential reading of John's Prologue: some reflection on views of Reginald Fuller and James Dunn', *Theology Digest* 33/4 (1986), 403–21.

Schuchard, Bruce G., *Scripture Within Scripture. The Interrelationship of Form and Function in the Explicit Old Testament Citations in the Gospel of John* (SBLDS, 133), Atlanta: Scholars Press, 1992.

Scott, James M., '"For as Many as are of Works of the Law are under a Curse" (Galatians 3.10)', in C. A. Evans and J. A. Sanders (eds.), *Paul and the Scriptures of Israel* (JSNTS, 83), Sheffield: Sheffield Academic Press, 1993, pp. 187–221.

Scott, Martin, *Sophia and the Johannine Jesus* (JSNTS, 71), Sheffield: Sheffield Academic Press, 1992.

Scroggs, Robin, *The Last Adam: A Study in Pauline Anthropology*, Philadelphia: Fortress Press/ Oxford: Basil Blackwell, 1966.

Christology in Paul and John: The Reality and Revelation of God (Proclamation Commentaries), Philadelphia: Fortress Press, 1988.

Segal, Alan F., *Two Powers in Heaven. Early Rabbinic Reports about Christianity and Gnosticism* (SJLA, 25), Leiden: E. J. Brill, 1977.

'Ruler of this World: Attitudes about Mediator Figures and the Importance of Sociology for Self-Definition', in E. P. Sanders, A. I. Baumgarten and Alan Mendelson (eds.), *Jewish and Christian Self-Definition. Volume Two: Aspects of Judaism in the Graeco-Roman Period*, London: SCM Press, 1981, pp. 245–68.

Rebecca's Children. Judaism and Christianity in the Roman World, Cambridge, MA: Harvard University Press, 1986.

The Other Judaisms of Late Antiquity (Brown Judaic Studies, 127), Atlanta: Scholars Press, 1987.

Setzer, Claudia J., *Jewish Responses to Early Christians. History and Polemics, 30–150 C.E.*, Minneapolis, Fortress Press, 1994.

Sidebottom, E. M., *The Christ of the Fourth Gospel*, London: SPCK, 1961.

Smalley, Stephen S., 'The Johannine Son of Man Sayings', *NTS* 15 (1968–9), 278–301.

Smiga, George M., *Pain and Polemic. Anti-Judaism in the Gospels*, Mahwah, NJ: Paulist Press, 1992.

Smith, D. Moody, *Johannine Christianity. Essays on its Setting, Sources, and Theology*, Columbia: University of South Carolina Press, 1984.

The Theology of the Gospel of John, Cambridge: Cambridge University Press, 1995.

Smith, J. Z., 'The Prayer of Joseph', in Jacob Neusner (ed.), *Religions in Antiquity: Essays in Memory of E. R. Goodenough* (Numen Supplement 14), Leiden: E. J. Brill, 1968, pp. 253–94.

'Fences and Neighbours: Some Contours of Early Judaism', in William Scott Green (ed.), *Approaches to Ancient Judaism. Volume II* (Brown Judaic Studies, 9), Chico, CA: Scholars Press, 1980, pp. 1–25.

'Prayer of Joseph. A New Translation with Introduction', in James H. Charlesworth (ed.), *The Old Testament Pseudepigrapha. Vol. II*, Garden City, NY: Doubleday & Co., 1985, pp. 699–714.

Smith, Morton, 'The Origin and History of the Transfiguration Story', *USQR* 36 (1980), 39–44.

'Ascent to the Heavens and the Beginnings of Christianity', *Eranos* 50 (1981), 403–29.

'Two Ascended to Heaven – Jesus and the Author of 4Q491', in James H. Charlesworth (ed.), *Jesus and the Dead Sea Scrolls*, New York: Doubleday, 1992, pp. 290–301.

Stanton, Graham, 'The Origin and Purpose of Matthew's Gospel. Matthean Scholarship from 1945 to 1980', *ANRW* 2.25.3, Berlin: Walter de Gruyter, 1985, pp. 1889–951.

'Samaritan Incarnational Christology?', in Michael Goulder (ed.), *Incarnation and Myth: The Debate Continued*, London: SCM, 1979, pp. 243–6.

Steenburg, D., 'The Worship of Adam and Christ as the Image of God', *JSNT* 39 (1990), 95–109.

Stegner, William Richard, *Narrative Theology in Early Jewish Christianity*, Louisville: Westminster John Knox Press, 1989.

Stemberger, Günter, *Introduction to the Talmud and Midrash* (Second edition), Edinburgh: T&T Clark, 1996.

Stibbe, Mark W. G., *John as Storyteller. Narrative Criticism and the Fourth Gospel* (SNTSMS, 73), Cambridge: Cambridge University Press, 1992.

John (Readings: A New Biblical Commentary), Sheffield: Sheffield Academic Press, 1993.

Strachan, R. H., *The Fourth Gospel. Its Significance and Environment* (third edition), London: SCM Press, 1941.

Stuckenbruck, Loren T., 'An Angelic Refusal of Worship: The Tradition and Its Function in the Apocalypse of John', in Eugene Lovelace (ed.), *SBL 1994 Seminar Papers*, Atlanta: Scholars Press, 1994, pp. 679–96.

Angel Veneration and Christology: A Study in Early Judaism and in the Christology of the Apocalypse of John (WUNT 2, 70), Tübingen: J. C. B. Mohr (Paul Siebeck), 1995.

'"One Like a Son of Man as the Ancient of Days" in the Old Greek

Recension of Daniel 7,13: Scribal Error or Theological Translation?',
ZNW 86 (1995), 268–76.

Suggs, M. Jack, *Wisdom, Christology and Law in Matthew's Gospel*, Cambridge, MA: Harvard University Press, 1970.

Talbert, Charles H., *Reading John. A Literary and Theological Commentary on the Fourth Gospel and the Johannine Epistles*, London: SPCK, 1992.

'"And the Word Became Flesh": When?', in Abraham J. Malherbe and Wayne A. Meeks (eds.), *The Future of Christology. Essays in Honor of Leander E. Keck*, Minneapolis: Fortress Press, 1993, pp. 43–52.

Taylor, Miriam S., *Anti-Judaism and Early Christian Identity. A Critique of Scholarly Consensus* (Studia Post-Biblica, 46), Leiden: E. J. Brill, 1995.

Theobald, Michael, *Die Fleischwerdung des Logos. Studien zum Verhältnis des Johannesprologs zum Corpus des Evangeliums und zu 1 Joh* (Neutestamentliche Abhandlungen, 20), Münster: Aschendorffsche Verlagsbuchhandlung, 1988.

'Gott, Logos und Pneuma. "Trinitarische" Rede von Gott im Johannesevangelium', in Hans-Josef Klauck (ed.), *Monotheismus und Christologie. Zur Gottesfrage im Hellenistischen Judentum und im Urchristentum* (Quaestiones Disputatae, 138), Freiberg: Herder, 1992, pp. 41–87.

Thompson, Marianne Meye, *The Humanity of Jesus in the Fourth Gospel*, Philadelphia: Fortress Press, 1988.

'John, Gospel of', in Joel B. Green, Scot McKnight and I. Howard Marshall (eds.), *Dictionary of Jesus and the Gospels*, Leicester: IVP, 1992, pp. 368–83.

Trites, Allison A., 'The Transfiguration in the Theology of Luke: Some Redactional Links', in L. D. Hurst and N. T. Wright (eds.), *The Glory of Christ in the New Testament. Studies in Christology in Memory of G. B. Caird*, Oxford: Clarendon Press, 1987, pp. 71–81.

Turner, Max M. B., 'The Spirit of Christ and Christology', in Harold H. Rowdon (ed.), *Christ the Lord. Studies in Christology presented to Donald Guthrie*, Leicester: Inter-Varsity Press, 1982, pp. 168–190.

'The Spirit of Christ and "Divine" Christology', in Joel B. Green and Max Turner (eds.), *Jesus of Nazareth: Lord and Christ. Essays on the Historical Jesus and New Testament Christology*, Carlisle: Paternoster/ Grand Rapids: Eerdmans, 1994, pp. 413–36.

Twelftree, Graham H., 'Blasphemy', in Joel B. Green, Scot McKnight, and I. Howard Marshall (eds.), *Dictionary of Jesus and the Gospels*, Leicester: IVP, 1992, pp. 75–7.

VanderKam, James C., 'John 10 and the Feast of Dedication', in H. W. Attridge, J. J. Collins and T. H. Tobin (eds.), *Of Scribes and Scrolls: Studies on the Hebrew Bible, Intertestamental Judaism, and Christian Origins Presented to John Strugnell on the Occasion of His Sixtieth Birthday* (College Theology Society Resources in Religion, 5), Lanham, MD: University Press of America, 1990, pp. 203–14.

Vermes, Geza, 'He is the Bread. Targum Neofiti Exodus 16:15', in E. Earle Ellis and Max Wilcox (eds.), *Neotestamentica et Semitica. Studies in Honour of Matthew Black*, Edinburgh: T&T Clark, 1969, pp. 256–63.

Jesus the Jew. A Historian's Reading of the Gospels, London: Fontana/ Collins, 1973.

Vouga, François, 'Le quatrième évangile comme interprète de la tradition synoptique: Jean 6', in Adelbert Denaux (ed.), *John and the Synoptics* (BETL, 101), Leuven: Leuven University Press, 1992, pp. 261–79.

Walker, William O., Jr, 'John 1.43–51 and "The Son of Man" in the Fourth Gospel', *JSNT* 56 (1994), 31–42.

Watson, Francis, *Paul, Judaism and the Gentiles. A Sociological Approach* (SNTSMS, 56), Cambridge: Cambridge University Press, 1986.

'Is John's Christology Adoptionist?', in L. D. Hurst and N. T. Wright (eds.), *The Glory of Christ in the New Testament. Studies in Christology in Memory of G. B. Caird*, Oxford: Clarendon Press, 1987, pp. 113–24.

Wedderburn, A. J. M., 'Adam in Paul's Letter to the Romans', in E. A. Livingstone (ed.), *Studia Biblica 1978.III* (JSNTS, 3), Sheffield: Sheffield Academic Press, 1978, pp. 413–30.

Weder, Hans, 'L'asymétrie du salut. Réflections sur Jean 3,14–21 dans le cadre de la theologie johannique', in Jean-Daniel Kaestli, Jean-Michel Poffet and Jean Zumstein (eds.), *La Communauté Johannique et son Histoire. La trajectoire de l'évangile de Jean aux deux premiers siècles* (Le Monde de la Bible), Geneva: Labor et Fides, 1990, pp. 155–84.

Weiss, Herold, 'The Sabbath in the Fourth Gospel', *JBL* 110/2 (1991), 311–21.

Wengst, Klaus, *Bedrängte Gemeinde und verherrlichter Christus. Der historische Ort des Johannesevangeliums als Schlüssel zu einer Interpretation* (Biblisch-theologische studien, 5), Neukirchen-Vluyn: Neukirchener Verlag, 1981.

Whitacre, Rodney, *Johannine Polemic. The Role of Tradition and Theology* (SBLDS, 67), Chico, CA: Scholars Press, 1982.

Wiles, Maurice, *The Making of Christian Doctrine. A Study in the Principles of Early Christian Doctrinal Development*, Cambridge: Cambridge University Press, 1967.

'Person or Personification? A Patristic Debate about Logos', in L. D. Hurst and N. T. Wright (eds.), *The Glory of Christ in the New Testament*, Oxford: Clarendon Press, 1987, pp. 281–9.

Willett, Michael E., *Wisdom Christology in the Fourth Gospel*, San Francisco: Mellen Research University Press, 1992.

Wilson, R. McL., *The Gnostic Problem. A Study of the Relations between Hellenistic Judaism and the Gnostic Heresy*, London: A. R. Mowbray, 1958.

Witherington, Ben III, *The Christology of Jesus*, Minneapolis: Fortress Press, 1990.

Jesus the Sage, Minneapolis: Fortress Press/ Edinburgh: T&T Clark, 1994.

John's Wisdom. A Commentary on the Fourth Gospel, Louisville: Westminster John Knox, 1995.

Witkamp, L. Th., 'The Use of Traditions in John 5:1–18', *JSNT* 25 (1985), 19–47.

Wright, N. T., *The Climax of the Covenant. Christ and the Law in Pauline Theology*, Edinburgh: T&T Clark, 1991.

The New Testament and the People of God (Christian Origins and the Question of God: Volume I), London: SPCK, 1992.

Young, Frances, 'Christology and Creation: Towards an Hermeneutic of Patristic Christology', paper read at the conference *The Myriad Christ*, Catholic University of Leuven, 21 November 1997 (forthcoming in BETL).

Zwiep, Arie W., *The Ascension of the Messiah in Lukan Christology* (NovTSup, 87), Leiden: E. J. Brill, 1997.

INDEX OF BIBLICAL REFERENCES

INDEX OF AUTHORS

INDEX OF SUBJECTS